NEW CENTURY BIBLE
COMMENTARY

LIBRARY

RONALD E. CLEMENTS
(Old Testament)

MATTHEW BLACK
(New Testament)

Hosea

THE NEW CENTURY BIBLE COMMENTARIES

EXODUS (J. P. Hyatt)
LEVITICUS AND NUMBERS (N. H. Snaith)*
DEUTERONOMY (A. D. H. Mayes)
JOSHUA, JUDGES, RUTH (John Gray)
1 AND 2 KINGS, Volumes 1 and 2 (Gwilym H. Jones)
1 AND 2 CHRONICLES (H. G. Williamson)
EZRA, NEHEMIAH, AND ESTHER (D. J. Clines)
JOB (H. H. Rowley)
PSALMS, Volumes 1 and 2 (A. A. Anderson)
ECCLESIASTES (R. N. Whybray)
ISAIAH 1-39 (R. E. Clements)
ISAIAH 40-66 (R. N. Whybray)
JEREMIAH (Douglas Rawlinson Jones)
LAMENTATIONS (Iain W. Provan)
EZEKIEL (John W. Wevers)
HOSEA (G. I. Davies)
THE GOSPEL OF MATTHEW (David Hill)
THE GOSPEL OF MARK (Hugh Anderson)
THE GOSPEL OF LUKE (E. Earle Ellis)
THE GOSPEL OF JOHN (Barnabas Lindars)
THE ACTS OF THE APOSTLES (William Neil)
ROMANS, Second Edition (Matthew Black)
1 AND 2 CORINTHIANS (F. F. Bruce)
GALATIANS (Donald Guthrie)
EPHESIANS (C. Leslie Mitton)
PHILIPPIANS (Ralph P. Martin)
COLOSSIANS AND PHILEMON (Ralph P. Martin)
1 AND 2 THESSALONIANS (I. Howard Marshall)
PASTORAL EPISTLES (A. T. Hanson)
HEBREWS (R. McL. Wilson)
1 PETER (Ernest Best)
JAMES, JUDE, AND 2 PETER (E. M. Sidebottom)
JOHANNINE EPISTLES (K. Grayson)
THE BOOK OF REVELATION (G. R. Beasley-Murray)

Not yet available in paperback   *Other titles are in preparation*

NEW CENTURY BIBLE
COMMENTARY

Based on the Revised Standard Version

HOSEA

G. I. DAVIES

Marshall Pickering
An Imprint of HarperCollins*Publishers*

WILLIAM B. EERDMANS PUBLISHING COMPANY, GRAND RAPIDS

First published 1992 in Great Britain by Marshall Pickering
and in the United States by Wm. B. Eerdmans Publishing Co.,
255 Jefferson Ave., S.E., Grand Rapids, Michigan 49503.

Marshall Pickering is an imprint of
HarperCollins*Religious*,
part of HarperCollins*Publishers*
77-85 Fulham Palace Road, London W6 8JB

Printed in the United States of America

A catalogue record for this book is
available from the British Library

Marshall Pickering ISBN 0-551-02445-3

Eerdmans ISBN 0-8028-0656-2

CONTENTS

PREFACE

In writing this volume I have followed the general approach of
the series, both in format and in the level at which it is written.
I have, however, taken the view that the difficult problems of
textual criticism and translation which abound in Hosea should
not be passed over but should be clarified in terms that will be
as intelligible as possible to the non-specialist. Here as much
as anywhere in the Old Testament the general reader is likely
to be perplexed by the varied renderings in different modern
translations, and I have tried to explain what lies behind these
differences and what I believe to be the most likely solution
in each case. I have made a special point of explaining and
discussing the renderings of the New English Bible, which often
depart considerably from those of previous translations, as a
result of the adoption (following scholars such as G. R. Driver
and D. Winton Thomas) of new interpretations of Hebrew words
that are based on comparisons with other Semitic languages such
as Arabic. The Revised English Bible, which appeared when
this commentary was practically finished, has eliminated some
of these renderings, but it has retained others and has even
contributed one new one of its own (see the note on 13:1). Some
important new studies of Hosea have appeared even closer to the
submission of my manuscript (P. G. Borbone, *Il Libro del Profeta
Osea. Edizione critica del testo ebraico* (Turin, 1990); D. R. Daniels,
Hosea and Salvation History (BZAW 191, Berlin and New York,
1990). The New Revised Standard Version also appeared too late
for its renderings to be considered in the commentary. I hope to
discuss these works in future publications on Hosea. Through the
kindness of Robert Murray in sending me two draft chapters of
his forthcoming book (*The Cosmic Covenant*) it was possible for me
in the comments on 2:18 to take some account of his interesting
suggestions about an alternative covenant tradition.

In the fifteen years during which this commentary has been in
the making I have learned much from many colleagues, near and
far, as well as from several generations of students at Nottingham,
at Cambridge and (very early on in my work) at St George's

College, Jerusalem. I have, however, to acknowledge a particular debt to three scholars. The first is Professor Ronald Clements who, ever since he began to supervise my doctoral dissertation on a very different topic, has been a most generous teacher and friend and has shared with me, in many a conversation, the fruits of his reading and his own developing ideas about Old Testament prophecy and biblical scholarship in general. I am grateful to him for entrusting me with this volume of the New Century Bible Commentary at an early stage of my career and for being so patient when it took much longer to complete than either of us would have hoped. Secondly, it has been an unusually fortunate coincidence (though such things are more likely to happen in Cambridge than in most other places) for me that Andrew Macintosh, the Dean of St John's College, has also been working on a major commentary on Hosea for the past few years. The fact that the formats and emphases of our commentaries necessarily differ, because of the different series to which they belong, has served only to enhance the value of the numerous discussions which we have had. I am, finally, deeply aware of how much I, like all other recent commentators on the Minor Prophets, owe to Professor Hans Walter Wolff of Heidelberg. It was a great privilege for me to spend a semester in Heidelberg at the very beginning of my work on Hosea, and my thanks are due to the staff of the Ökumenisches Studentenheim, to the Deutsche Akademische Austauschdienst and to Professor Wolff himself for making my stay so pleasant and useful. His commentaries on the Minor Prophets remain, in my view, unequalled for their combination of literary, exegetical and theological insight. I also benefited greatly during my visit from the very stimulating sessions of his advanced seminar which I attended and from his readiness to discuss problems of interpretation with me. I hope that he will recognize in this commentary some indications of my debt to him. I should also like to record my gratitude to my son Peter, who during his school holidays successfully transferred a large part of the first draft from typescript to magnetic disc and so greatly facilitated its correction and modification.

G. I. DAVIES
January 1991

ABBREVIATIONS

BIBLICAL

OLD TESTAMENT (OT)

Gen.	Jg.	1 Chr.	Ps.	Lam.	Ob.	Hag.
Exod.	Ru.	2 Chr.	Prov.	Ezek.	Jon.	Zech.
Lev.	1 Sam.	Ezr.	Ec.	Dan.	Mic.	Mal.
Num.	2 Sam.	Neh.	Ca.	Hos.	Nah.	
Dt.	1 Kg.	Est.	Isa.	Jl	Hab.	
Jos.	2 Kg.	Job	Jer.	Am.	Zeph.	

APOCRYPHA (Apoc.)

1 Esd.	Tob.	Ad.Est.	Sir.	S3 Ch.	Bel	1 Mac.
2 Esd.	Jdt.	Wis.	Bar.	Sus.	Man.	2 Mac.
			E.Jer.			

NEW TESTAMENT (NT)

Mt.	Ac.	Gal.	1 Th.	Tit.	1 Pet.	3Jn
Mk	Rom.	Eph.	2 Th.	Phm.	2 Pet.	Jude
Lk.	1 C.	Phil.	1 Tim.	Heb.	1 Jn	Rev.
Jn	2 C.	Col.	2 Tim.	Jas	2 Jn	

DEAD SEA SCROLLS (DSS)

1QH Hymns of Thanksgiving (Hodayoth)
1QM The War Scroll
1QS The Community Rule (Manual of Discipline)
CD The Damascus Document (Zadokite Fragments)

(On the fragmentary MSS containing passages of Hosea see below, p. 38.)

GENERAL

AB	The Anchor Bible, Garden City, NY
AJ	Antiquities of the Jews (Flavius Josephus)
AnBib	Analecta Biblica, Rome
ANEP	*The Ancient Near East in Pictures Relating to the Old Testament*, ed. J. B. Pritchard, Princeton, 1969²
ANET	*Ancient Near Eastern Texts Relating to the Old Testament*, ed. J. B. Pritchard, Princeton, 1969³
AOAT	Alter Orient und Altes Testament, Kevelaer and Neukirchen
AOTS	*Archaeology and Old Testament Study*, ed. D. Winton Thomas, Oxford, 1967.
ATD	Das Alte Testament Deutsch, Göttingen
Aq.	Aquila
AV	The Authorized (King James) Version
B.	Babylonian Talmud
BA	*Biblical Archaeologist*
BASOR	*Bulletin of the American Schools of Oriental Research*
BAT	Die Botschaft des Alten Testaments, Stuttgart
BBB	Bonner Biblische Beiträge, Bonn
BDB	*Hebrew and English Lexicon of the Old Testament*, ed. F. Brown, S. R. Driver and C. A. Briggs, Oxford, 1907
BET	Beiträge zur evangelischen Theologie, Munich
BHS	*Biblia Hebraica Stuttgartensia*, ed. K. Elliger and W. Rudolph, Stuttgart, 1977
BHT	Beiträge zur historischen Theologie, Tübingen
BH³	*Biblia Hebraica*, ed. A. Alt and O. Eissfeldt, Stuttgart, 1937³
Bib	*Biblica*
Bib et Or	Biblica et Orientalia, Rome
BiOr	*Bibliotheca Orientalis*
BJRL	*Bulletin of the John Rylands Library*
BKAT	Biblischer Kommentar, Altes Testament, Neukirchen
BRL	*Biblisches Reallexikon*, ed. K. Galling, Tübingen, 1977²
BWANT	Beiträge zur Wissenschaft vom Alten und Neuen Testament, Stuttgart

BZ	*Biblische Zeitschrift*
BZAW	Beihefte zur Zeitschrift für die Alttestamentliche Wissenschaft, Berlin and New York
CAH	*The Cambridge Ancient History*, 3rd ed. (vols. I–II), 2nd ed. (vol. III/1), Cambridge, 1970–82
CAT	Commentaire de l'ancien testament, Neuchâtel
CBC	Cambridge Bible Commentary on the New English Bible, Cambridge
CHB	*The Cambridge History of the Bible*, ed. P. R. Ackroyd et al., Cambridge, 1963–70
CML	J. C. L. Gibson, *Canaanite Myths and Legends*, Edinburgh, 1978²
DBS	*Dictionnaire de la Bible*, Supplément, Paris, 1928–
DJD	*Discoveries in the Judaean Desert*, Oxford, 1955–
DOTT	*Documents from Old Testament Times*, ed. D. Winton Thomas, Edinburgh and London, 1958
DSSE	G. Vermes, *The Dead Sea Scrolls in English*, Harmondsworth, 1975²
EAEHL	*Encyclopaedia of Archaeological Excavations in the Holy Land*, ed. M. Avi-Yonah and E. Stern. London, 1975–8
EHS	Europäische Hochschulschriften, Frankfurt and Berne
ESI	*Excavations and Surveys in Israel*
ET	English Translation
EVV.	The English Versions
EvTh	*Evangelische Theologie*
ExpT	*Expository Times*
FS	Festschrift
GK	*Gesenius' Hebrew Grammar*, ed. E. Kautzsch, revised by A. E. Cowley, Oxford, 1910²
GS	H. W. Wolff, *Gesammelte Schriften zum Alten Testament*, Munich, 1973²
HAL	*Hebräisches und Aramäisches Lexicon*, ed. W. Baumgartner and J. J. Stamm, Leiden, 1967–
HAT	Handbuch zum Alten Testament, Tübingen
Heb.	Hebrew
HKAT	Handkommentar zum Alten Testament, Göttingen
HSM	Harvard Semitic Monographs, Missoula

HTOT	L. H. Brockington, *The Hebrew Text of the Old Testament: The Readings Adopted by the Translators of the New English Bible*, London, 1973
HUCA	*Hebrew Union College Annual*
IB	The Interpreter's Bible, New York
ICC	International Critical Commentary, Edinburgh
IDB	*The Interpreter's Dictionary of the Bible*, ed. G. A. Buttrick, Nashville, 1962
IDBS	*The Interpreter's Dictionary of the Bible*, Supplementary Volume, ed. K. R. Crim. Nashville, 1976
IJH	*Israelite and Judaean History*, ed. J. H. Hayes and J. M. Miller, London, 1977
Int	*Interpretation*
IR	*Inscriptions Reveal. Documents from the time of the Bible, the Mishna and the Talmud*, ed. R. Hestrin et al., Jerusalem, 1973²
JB	The Jerusalem Bible
JE	*The Jewish Encyclopaedia*, New York and London, 1901–06
JJS	*Journal of Jewish Studies*
JQR	*Jewish Quarterly Review*
JSOT	*Journal for the Study of the Old Testament*
JSOTSS	Journal for the Study of the Old Testament Supplement Series, Sheffield
JSJ	*Journal for the Study of Judaism*
JSS	*Journal of Semitic Studies*
JTS	*Journal of Theological Studies*
KAT	Kommentar zum Alten Testament, Leipzig and Gütersloh
KB	*Lexicon in Veteris Testamenti Libros*, ed. L. Koehler and W. Baumgartner, Leiden, 1953
KHAT	Kurzer Hand-Commentar zum Alten Testament, Tübingen
KS	A. Alt, *Kleine Schriften zur Geschichte des Volkes Israel*, Munich, 1953, 1959
LXX	Septuagint
M.	Mishnah
mg.	margin
MS(S)	manuscript(s)

MT	Masoretic Text
NCB	The New Century Bible
NEB	The New English Bible
NF	Neue Folge
NJPS	*The Prophets. A New Translation of the Holy Scriptures according to the Masoretic Text* (Jewish Publication Society), Philadelphia, 1978
NS	New Series
OBO	Orbis Biblicus et Orientalis, Freiburg and Göttingen
Or	*Orientalia*
OTS	*Oudtestamentische Studiën*, Leiden
OTL	Old Testament Library, London and Philadelphia
PL	*Patrologia Latina*, ed. J. P. Migne
POTT	*Peoples of Old Testament Times*, ed. D. J. Wiseman, Oxford, 1973
REB	The Revised English Bible
RQ	*Revue de Qumran*
RSR	*Revue des Sciences Religieuses*
RSV	The Revised Standard Version
RV	The Revised Version
SAT	Die Schriften des Alten Testaments, Göttingen
SBLDS	Society of Biblical Literature Dissertation Series, Chico and Atlanta
SBLMS	Society of Biblical Literature Monograph Series, Missoula
ScrHier	*Scripta Hierosolymitana*
SOTSMS	Society for Old Testament Study Monograph Series, Cambridge
Symm.	Symmachus
Syr.	The Syriac Version (Peshitta)
T.	Tosefta
Targ.	Targum
TDOT	*Theological Dictionary of the Old Testament*, ed. G. J. Botterweck and H. Ringgren, Grand Rapids, 1974– (ET of *TWAT*)
TGI	K. Galling, *Textbuch zur Geschichte Israels*, Tübingen, 1979³
Th.	Theodotion
ThZ	*Theologische Zeitschrift*

TIP	K. A. Kitchen, *The Third Intermediate Period In Egypt (1100–650 B.C.)*, Warminster, 1986²
THAT	*Theologisches Handwörterbuch zum Alten Testament*, ed. E. Jenni and C. Westermann, Munich and Zurich, 1971, 1976
TWAT	*Theologisches Wörterbuch zum Alten Testament*, ed. G. J. Botterweck, H. Ringgren and H.-J. Fabry, Stuttgart, 1973–
UF	*Ugarit-Forschungen*
UT	C. H. Gordon, *Ugaritic Textbook* (Analecta Orientalia 38), Rome, 1965
Vss.	The (Ancient) Versions
VT	*Vetus Testamentum*
VTSuppl	Supplements to Vetus Testamentum, Leiden
Vulg.	The Vulgate
WMANT	Wissenschaftliche Monographien zum Alten und Neuen Testament, Neukirchen
Y.	Jerusalem Talmud
ZAW	*Zeitschrift für die Alttestamentliche Wissenschaft*
ZTK	*Zeitschrift für Theologie und Kirche*

SELECT BIBLIOGRAPHY

COMMENTARIES (*cited by author's name only*)

Ackroyd, P. R., "Hosea", in *Peake's Commentary*, revised ed., ed. M. Black and H. H. Rowley, London and Edinburgh, 1962, 603–13.

Andersen, F. I. and Freedman, D. N., *Hosea* (AB), 1980.

Frey, H., *Das Buch des Werbens Gottes um seine Kirche. Der Prophet Hosea* (BAT), 1957.

Gressmann, H., *Die älteste Geschichtsschreibung und Prophetie Israels* (*von Samuel bis Amos und Hosea*) (SAT), 1921².

Harper, W. R., *Amos and Hosea* (ICC), 1905.

Jacob, E., Keller, C.-A., and Amsler, S., *Osée, Joel, Amos, Abdias, Jonas* (CAT), 1965.

Jeremias, J., *Der Prophet Hosea* (ATD, revised ed.), 1983.

McKeating, H., *Amos, Hosea and Micah* (CBC), 1971.

Marti, K., *Das Dodekapropheton* (KHAT), 1904.

Mauchline, J., "Hosea: Introduction and Exegesis" (IB), 1956.

Mays, J. L., *Hosea* (OTL), 1969.

Nowack, W., *Die Kleinen Propheten* (HKAT), 1905².

Robinson, T. H., and Horst, F., *Die Zwölf Kleinen Propheten* (HAT), 1964³.

Rudolph, W., *Hosea* (KAT), 1966.

Sellin, E., *Das Zwölfprophetenbuch* (KAT), 1922, 1929²/³.

Ward, J. M., *Hosea: A Theological Commentary*, New York, 1966.

Weiser, A., *Die Propheten Hosea, Joel, Amos, Obadja, Jona, Micha* (ATD), 1974⁶.

Wellhausen, J., *Die Kleinen Propheten*, Berlin, 1898³, repr. 1963.

Wolff, H. W., *Hosea* (Hermeneia), Philadelphia, 1974 (ET of *Hosea* (BKAT), 1965²).

OTHER WORKS (*cited by Author's name and short title only*)

Balz-Cochois, H., *Gomer. Der Höhenkult Israels im Selbstverständnis der Volksfrömmigkeit. Untersuchungen zu Hosea 4,1–5,7* (EHS XXIII/191), 1982.

Barr, J., *Comparative Philology and the Text of the Old Testament*, Oxford, 1968.

Bitter, S., *Die Ehe des Propheten Hosea. Eine Auslegungs geschichtliche Untersuchung*, Göttingen, 1975.

Blommerde, A. C. M., *Northwest Semitic Grammar and Job* (Biblica et Orientalia, 22), Rome, 1969.

Borbone, P. G., *Il Libro del Profeta Osea. Edizione critica del testo ebraico*, Turin, 1990.

Brueggemann, W., *Tradition for Crisis*, Atlanta, 1968.

Buss, M. J., *The Prophetic Word of Hosea: A Morphological Study* (BZAW 111), 1969.

Cathcart, K. J., and Gordon, R. P., *The Targum of the Minor Prophets* (The Aramaic Bible, 14), Wilmington, 1989.

Clements, R. E., "Understanding the Book of Hosea", *Review and Expositor* 72 (1975), 405–23.

Clines, D. J. A., "Hosea 2: Structure and Interpretation", in *Studia Biblica 1978. I. Papers on Old Testament Themes* (JSOTSS, 11), 1979, 83–103.

Daniels, D. R., *Hosea and Salvation History* (BZAW 191), 1990.

de Vaux, R., *Ancient Israel*, London, 1965² (ET of *Les institutions de l'ancien testament*, Paris, 1958, 1960).

Emmerson, G. I., *Hosea. An Israelite Prophet in Judaean Perspective* (JSOTSS, 28), 1984.

Fohrer, G., "Umkehr und Erlösung beim Propheten Hosea", in *Studien zur alttestamentlichen Prophetie 1949–1965* (BZAW 99), 1967, 222–41 (= *ThZ* 11 (1955), 161–85).

Geller, M. J., "The Elephantine Papyri and Hosea 2, 3", *JSJ* 8 (1977), 139–48.

Gelston, A., *The Peshitta of the Twelve Prophets*, Oxford, 1987.

Habel, N. C., *Yahweh versus Baal*, New York, 1964.

Hahn, J., *Das "Goldene Kalb". Die Jahwe-Verehrung bei Stierbildern in der Geschichte Israels* (EHS XXIII/154), 1981.

Hunter, A. V., *Seek the Lord! A Study of the Meaning and Function of the Exhortations in Amos, Hosea, Isaiah and Zephaniah*, Baltimore, 1982.

Jenks, A. W., *The Elohist and North Israelite Traditions* (SBLMS, 22), 1977.

Jeremias, J., "Hosea 4–7. Beobachtungen zur Komposition des Buches Hosea", in *Textgemäss* (FS E. Würthwein), ed. A. H. J. Gunneweg and O. Kaiser, Göttingen, 1979, 47–58.

Jeremias, J., "Zur Eschatologie des Hoseabuches", in *Die Botschaft und die Boten* (FS H. W. Wolff), ed. J. Jeremias and L. Perlitt, Neukirchen, 1981, 217–34.

Jeremias, J., "'Ich bin ein Löwe für Efraim . . .' (Hos 5, 14). Aktualität und Allgemeingültigkeit im prophetischen Reden von Gott am Beispiel von Hos 5, 8–14", in *"Ich will euer Gott werden". Beispiele biblischen Redens von Gott*, ed. H. Merklein and E. Zenger, Stuttgart, 1981, 75–95.

Kinet, D., *Ba'al und Jahwe. Ein Beitrag zur Theologie des Hoseabuches* (EHS XXIII/87), 1977.

King, P. J., *Amos, Hosea, Micah – An Archaeological Commentary*, Philadelphia, 1988.

Kuhnigk, W., *Nordwestsemitische Studien zum Hoseabuch* (Biblica et Orientalia, 27), Rome, 1974.

Lindblom, J. *Prophecy in Ancient Israel*, Oxford, 1962.

Muraoka, T., "Some observations on the LXX Book of Hosea", in *Studies in the Bible and the Hebrew Language* (FS M. Wallenstein), ed. C. Rabin et al., Jerusalem, 1979, 180–87 (Heb.).

Muraoka, T., "Hosea IV in the LXX Version", *Annual of the Japanese Biblical Institute* 9 (1983), 24–64.

Muraoka, T., "Hosea V in the LXX Version", *Abr Nahrain* 24 (1986), 120–38.

Neef, H.-D., *Die Heilstraditionen Israels in der Verkündigung des Propheten Hosea* (BZAW 169), 1987.

Nyberg, H. S., *Studien zum Hoseabuche*, Uppsala, 1935.

Renaud, B., "Genèse et Unité Redactionelle de Os 2", *RSR* 54 (1980), 1–20.

Rowley, H. H., "The Marriage of Hosea", *BJRL* 39 (1956–7), 200–33 (reprinted in his *Men of God*, Edinburgh and London, 1963, 66–97).

Sakenfeld, K. D., *The Meaning of Ḥesed in the Hebrew Bible* (HSM, 17), 1978.

Sakenfeld, K. D., *Faithfulness in Action: Loyalty in Biblical Perspective*, Philadelphia, 1985.

Schreiner, J., "Hoseas Ehe, ein Zeichen des Gerichts", *BZ NF* 21 (1977), 163–83.

Snaith, N. H., *Mercy and Sacrifice*, London, 1953.

Tadmor, H., "The Historical Background of Hosea's Prophecies", in *Yehezkel Kaufmann Jubilee Volume*, ed. M. Haran, Jerusalem, 1960, pp. 84–8 (Heb.).

Utzschneider, H., *Hosea: Prophet vor dem Ende* (OBO, 31), 1980.

Vollmer, J., *Geschichtliche Rückblicke und Motive in der Prophetie des Amos, Hosea und Jesaja* (BZAW 119), 1971.

von Rad, G., *Old Testament Theology*, Edinburgh, 1962, 1965 (ET of *Theologie des Alten Testaments*, Munich, 1957, 1960).

Wacker, M.-T., "God as Mother?: On the Meaning of a Biblical God-Symbol for Feminist Theology", *Concilium* 206 (1989), 103–11.

Watson, W. G. E., *Classical Hebrew Poetry: A Guide to its Techniques* (JSOTSS, 26), 1984.

Wolff, H. W., *Anthropology of the Old Testament*, Philadelphia, 1974 (ET of *Anthropologie des Alten Testaments*, Munich, 1973).

Wünsche, A., *Der Prophet Hosea übersetzt und erklärt mit Benutzung der Targumim, der jüdischen Ausleger Rashi, Aben Ezra und David Kimchi*, Leipzig, 1868.

Yee, G. A., *Composition and Tradition in the Book of Hosea. A Redaction-Critical Investigation* (SBLDS, 102), 1987.

INTRODUCTION

The Book of the Twelve

The twelve Minor Prophets (Hosea to Malachi) were already a distinct literary unit before the collection of the Hebrew Scriptures in *codices* (books) or larger scrolls led to some fixing of the arrangement of the biblical books. Ben Sira, or Ecclesiasticus, writing early in the 2nd century BC, already refers to them (49:10) as "the twelve prophets", alongside Isaiah, Jeremiah and Ezekiel. They were reckoned as a single "book" in both systems of counting the total number of books (twenty-four or twenty-two), which go back at least to the 1st century AD (2 Esd. 14:45; Josephus, *Against Apion* 1:38–42; see further *CHB*, vol. I, pp. 135–42). Modern discoveries of manuscripts in the Judaean wilderness have shown the antiquity of the custom of writing the twelve books on a single scroll. A Hebrew manuscript from Wadi Muraba' at from the first half of the 2nd century AD, although damaged at both beginning and end, probably once contained all twelve books. The same may well be true of a less extensively preserved Greek manuscript from Nahal Hever from the 1st century BC or the 1st century AD (for these MSS, see *DJD* II, pp. 181–205, and *DJD* VIII). Together the twelve books, as we know them, are almost as long as one of the "Major" prophetic books, Isaiah, Jeremiah and Ezekiel. There is some reason to think that the number twelve was deliberately sought after, as chapters 9–11 and 12–14 of Zechariah, which are generally agreed to have nothing to do with the prophet Zechariah himself, are headed by the same title – "An Oracle" (Heb. *massa'*) – as the book – of Malachi and were probably, like it, originally anonymous collections of oracles that existed separately prior to the assembly of the Book of the Twelve (cf. G. Fohrer, *Introduction to the OT*, London, 1970, p. 465). Chapters 6 and 7 of Micah may also once have been a separate "book".

The date and circumstances in which the Book of the Twelve was put together are unknown. However, the date must lie between the production of the latest of the once independent books (Zechariah 12–14, around 300 BC?) and the early 2nd

century BC, when Ben Sira wrote. As with the Psalms, the final
collection may have been preceded by earlier ones containing
only a few of the books. Some editorial changes may have been
made after the books were joined together, but there is no sign of a
systematic attempt to correlate them with one another. The order
of the books seems to be based mainly on what was taken to be
their chronological sequence. This is clearest in the second half of
the collection, which consists of three books (Nahum, Habakkuk
and Zephaniah) deriving from the 7th and early 6th centuries BC
followed by three from the post-exilic period (Haggai, Zechariah
and Malachi). (It is, incidentally, striking that there is no
complete book in this collection which originated in the exiled
community in Babylonia, although numerous sections of all three
of the Major prophets have such an origin.) Equally, four of the
first six books may owe their position to the fact that they could
be readily associated with the 8th century BC: Hosea, Amos
and Micah by virtue of their titles, and Jonah by comparison
with 2 Kg. 14:25 (even though the book is in fact probably a
post-exilic fiction). The position of Joel and Obadiah, however,
can scarcely be due to chronological considerations, as the latter
plainly refers to the fall of Jerusalem to the Babylonians in 587–6
BC (cf. vv. 10–14), and the former contains no explicit indication
of its date at all (though there are good reasons for regarding it as
post-exilic). In these cases subject-matter seems to have played
the decisive role. H. W. Wolff has pointed out that each of these
books is in a different way a commentary on the book of Amos,
which lies between them and displays both at its beginning and at
its end precise correspondences of content with the neighbouring
books (cf. Am. 1:2 with Jl 3:16, and Am. 9:12 with Ob. 18–21:
H. W. Wolff, *Joel and Amos* (Hermeneia), Philadelphia, 1977,
p. 3, *Obadiah and Jonah*, Minneapolis, 1986, p. 17). In the
Greek tradition the order of the first six books is commonly
somewhat different (for example, in Codex Vaticanus), with the
three clearly dated books (Hosea, Amos and Micah) preceding
the three undated books (Joel, Obadiah, Jonah).

The position of Hosea at the head of the whole collection is
not fully explained by reference to the title alone. Since Amos
is connected with Jeroboam (II) alone, while Hosea's ministry
is said to extend into the reigns of Judaean kings who certainly

ruled after his death, it might have been expected that Amos would take first place. The fact that it did not do so is sometimes attributed to an intention on the part of the collectors to arrange the major books in this section in a descending order of length (cf. A. Weiser, *Introduction to the OT*, London, 1961, p. 232). But early references to the collection suggest that either of two other factors may have been more influential. Ben Sira (49:10) praises the Twelve for having "comforted Jacob", which suggests that Hosea, of whom this would be particularly true, might have been placed first for theological reasons. Alternatively, it is clear from a later tradition, preserved in the Talmud, that the words of Hos. 1:2 were taken by the rabbis to imply that Hosea was the first of all the writing prophets (B. Baba Bathra 14b–15a), and the fact that his book did not come before Isaiah, Jeremiah and Ezekiel was attributed to its association (i.e. in the Book of the Twelve, which could not be broken up) with the later prophets Haggai, Zechariah and Malachi. In many Greek sources the Minor Prophets actually come before the Major, so that there Hosea does come first. Such an interpretation of Hos. 1:2 may also have played a part in the original ordering of the Twelve.

Hosea and His Circumstances

Like most of the other prophets, Hosea is known to us only from the evidence contained in his book. The various later traditions about him (on which see briefly Harper, p. 202) contain nothing of historical value. Nor is the heading to the book (1:1–2a) as informative as some others. His name (more accurately Hoshea) means "salvation", from the verb *hôšîaʿ*, which he uses in 13:4, 10 and 14:4 (cf. the redactional addition in 1:7), and which is presumably a shortening of the theophorous name Hoshaiah. The name (in both forms) occurs several times elsewhere, both in the Old Testament and in Hebrew inscriptions. The prophet is distinguished from his namesakes, who include the last king of the northern kingdom, Hoshea the son of Elah, by the patronymic "son of Beeri", a name meaning "my well". Beeri is not a gentilic, as some have thought, and so it cannot be used to link Hosea with a particular region. The absence of any indication of origin (contrast, e.g., Am. 1:1) may imply that a prophet came from the chief city of his kingdom (cf. B. Megillah 15a), in Hosea's case Samaria, the capital of the northern kingdom. His knowledge of political intrigue (e.g. 7:3–7), his interest in foreign policy (7:8–9, 11–13; 8:9–10; 10:4; 12:1) and the frequent references to Samaria itself (7:1; 8:5–6; 10:5, 7; 13:16) would support this view. The geographical references generally and the fact that references to "Ephraim" far outweigh those to "Judah" (some of which are in any case redactional) leave no doubt that he was active in the northern kingdom, and in the absence of indications to the contrary we should assume that he was a native of it. The religious traditions on which he depends (see below) are also those which were most characteristic of the north: no weight should be attached to the mention of David in 3:5, as this is an editorial addition (see the notes). Whether Hosea's sayings reflect the use of a northern dialect of Hebrew has been and continues to be a subject of discussion (cf. Harper, pp. clxxiii, 202 (with refs.); Nyberg, passim; Rudolph, pp. 20–21; Kuhnigk, passim; E. Y. Kutscher, *A History of the Hebrew language*, Jerusalem, 1982, pp. 31, 70; S. Morag, *Tarbiz* 43 (1984), 489–511). There are peculiarities in his vocabulary and style, some of which could be dialectal (especially where Aramaic or Phoenician influence is likely), but in the absence of a larger body of north Israelite text for comparison it is generally not possible to distinguish such items from those which are due to other factors such as individual preference, textual corruption and rare (especially poetic) forms.

The superscription places Hosea's activity in the last generation of the independent life of the northern kingdom, and allows the possibility that it continued after the fall of Samaria in 722 BC. To be more precise is difficult in view of the problems of Old Testament chronology in the monarchy period (for discussion see *IJH*, pp. 678–83; H. Tadmor, in J. A. Soggin, *History of Israel*, London, 1984, pp. 368–83). The reference to Jeroboam and the implications of 1:4 indicate that Hosea began his preaching not later than 745 BC (to follow the lowest chronology for

Jeroboam's reign), and a date several years earlier is perfectly possible. The list of Judaean kings, and especially the mention of Hezekiah (725–697 or 715–687), implies that Hosea's activity continued at least until the last years before the fall of Samaria. Older commentators (e.g. Harper) and some more recent ones (Tadmor, in M. Haran (ed.), *Yehezkel Kaufmann Jubilee Volume*, Jerusalem, 1960, pp. 84–8; Andersen and Freedman) have confined Hosea's preaching to the earlier part of this period (before c. 735), but it is generally agreed now that 5:8–15 reflects the events of the Syro-Ephraimite War (see the introduction to that section) and that the references to diplomatic relations with Egypt fit best with events in the 720s. On the detailed historical background to Hosea's sayings see the next section. The theory that Hosea himself lived in the 9th century and was the author only of ch. 1–3, put forward by Y. Kaufmann (*The Religion of Israel*, abridged Eng. ed., London, 1961, pp. 369–71) and supported by H. L. Ginsberg (*Encyclopaedia Judaica* 8:1014–16) was based on *a priori* views of Israelite religion and not on defensible arguments (cf. B. Uffenheimer, *Immanuel* 3 (1973/74), 9–21).

Some details of Hosea's personal circumstances are given in ch. 1 and 3, but they are selected and presented in such a way that their theological meaning is plainer than their biographical basis. Reconstructions of the history of "Hosea's Marriage" have often hindered more than they have helped the understanding of his message, particularly in ch. 4–14. For a discussion of various theories see the Excursus on pp. 105–9. Apart from this all that we know of him is that on one occasion, not surprisingly, his preaching at one of the major shrines brought him hostility and abuse (see the introduction to 9:1–9).

The Historical Context and Development of Hosea's Message

The reign of Jeroboam II (c. 787–747) is represented in the Bible as a period of national revival and expansion for Israel

(2 Kg. 14:23–29). The losses of territory in Transjordan suffered under his predecessors were restored, and a new era of confidence and prosperity was born (cf. Am. 3:15; 5:11; 6:1, 4–6, 13). At this time Israel was the beneficiary of Assyrian power, for the Assyrians under Adad–nirari III had checked the advances of the Aramaeans (Syrians) of Damascus, and the resulting weakness of the latter provided the space into which Israel could grow both militarily and economically. No doubt other factors were involved which are as yet imperfectly understood. Archaeological excavations at a number of sites in northern Palestine provide some "scenery" against which to view the preaching of Hosea (and Amos). At the major sites, such as Samaria and Megiddo, the great palaces, fortifications and administrative buildings constructed a century earlier seem to have remained in existence, even if a little worn with age. The ivories found in the ruins of Samaria no doubt decorated the furniture in the royal palace throughout the period. At Hazor the prosperity of the age is reflected in well-built houses with some luxury items, though earthquake damage is a reminder of the constant threat to house and home. More houses of wealthy citizens have been excavated at Tell el-Far'ah (North), probably the site of Tirzah, which had once briefly been the royal capital (1 Kg. 15:33; 16:8). In another part of the site smaller, more crowded houses belonging to the poorer citizens were found, providing some indication of the growing rift between rich and poor. Some light on the use of writing and royal bureaucracy may be obtained from inscribed potsherds found at Samaria (the "Samaria ostraca"). These contain names of people and places and references to quantities of wine and oil which were brought to the palace, either as tax in kind or as contributions from the royal domains – it is not clear which (*DOTT*, pp. 204–8). For the religious importance of these inscriptions see below, p. 30, and for further information about archaeological evidence see King, *Archaeological Commentary*.

Within a year of Jeroboam's death two kings had been murdered and a period of internal division and uncertainty had been ushered in. It was to last until the fall of Samaria in 722 (2 Kg. 15:8–16). After the two short reigns Menahem, from the old capital of Tirzah, seized the throne. He was quickly faced with the need to come to terms with a renewed attempt by the Assyrians, under their new king Tiglath-pileser III (Pul), to establish their hegemony in the Levant. Menahem paid heavy tribute (financed by a special tax on the leading families) in exchange for Assyrian help in confirming his position as king (2 Kg. 15:19–20). The tribute is mentioned in Tiglath-pileser's inscriptions along with payments made by neighbouring states c. 737–736 B.C. (*ANET*, p. 283; L. D. Levine, *BASOR* 206 (1972), 40–42). Menahem was succeeded by his son Pekahiah, but after two years he became the victim of a conspiracy based in Transjordan and led by one Pekah, who assumed the throne (2 Kg. 15:22–25). Pekah had been an aide to the king (Heb. *šālîš*: cf. 2 Kg. 9:25) and the otherwise unintelligible figure of "twenty" years for his reign (2 Kg. 15:27) may indicate that initially he ruled over a semi-independent kingdom in Transjordan. In any case it is likely that his conspiracy was designed to change the submissive policy of his predecessors towards Assyria. The details of his reign have to be pieced together from 2 Kg. 15–16, Isa. 7–9 and Tiglath-pileser's fragmentary annals, but the main outlines at least seem to be clear. He allied himself with Rezin (more correctly Rezon) of Damascus, and together they marched in force to Jerusalem, intending either to persuade the Judaean king Ahaz to join them in an anti-Assyrian coalition or to replace him with another of like mind to themselves. This probably took place in 735 or 734. Fearing for his position, Ahaz, apparently against the advice of the prophet Isaiah, appealed for help to Assyria, pledging his loyalty with a gift (2 Kg. 16:5–8; Isa. 7). We know from the Assyrian eponym lists that in 734 Tiglath-pileser campaigned in Philistia, and this may have been sufficient to lift the siege of Jerusalem. Two years later he attacked and defeated Damascus, but apparently he had already (in 733?) attacked the northern kingdom of Israel and deported large numbers of the population (2 Kg. 15:29; 16:9; *ANET*, pp. 283–4). Pekah was killed, and a new king, Hoshea, was installed, who paid tribute to Assyria (2 Kg. 15:30; *ANET*, loc. cit.; R. Borger and H. Tadmor, *ZAW* 94 (1982), 244–51). But he ruled over only a remnant of the kingdom, as Galilee and Transjordan became, like the territory of Damascus, provinces of the Assyrian empire. In 727 Tiglath-pileser died and was succeeded by Shalmaneser

V (727–722/721). Hoshea may have first attempted to resist the
demands of the new king, but when confronted once again by an
Assyrian force he submitted and paid tribute. His submission
was, however, only temporary and, following negotiations with
an Egyptian king who was probably Osorkon IV of Tanis
(Kitchen, *TIP*, p. 551), he rebelled. But it was to no avail: an
Assyrian force besieged and captured Samaria, Hoshea himself
having been an early prisoner (2 Kg. 17:1–9; 18:9–12). Many of
the remaining population were deported to Mesopotamia and
beyond (though scarcely all of them, as 2 Kg. implies), and
aliens were brought in to take their place (2 Kg. 17:24–34, 41;
cf. *ANET*, pp. 284–85, where the number is given as 27,290).
Some of the exiles were apparently enlisted in the Assyrian army
as expert charioteers (S. Dalley, *Iraq* 47 (1985), 31–48). Two
texts of Shalmaneser's successor, Sargon II, suggest that in 720
there was a short-lived rebellion against him in which "Samaria"
and several neighbouring peoples participated: this seems not to
be referred to in the Old Testament. Archaeological evidence
from Samaria, Megiddo and Hazor confirms the destruction of
the Israelite cities and their reconstruction as Assyrian towns or
fortresses.

Against this background the development of Hosea's message
can be readily understood. To the confident but increasingly
pagan nation of Jeroboam's time he spoke of religious corruption and imminent disaster (1:2–6, 8–9; 2:2–5, 8–13; 4:1–19;
12:2–10). As suggested in the commentary, 2:2–3 may represent
Hosea's earliest preaching (cf. 12:6), which called for national
repentance as a means of avoiding the threatened disaster.
At this stage exile seems not yet to be in view, and natural
catastrophes are the expected form of Yahweh's judgment (2:3,
9, 12; 4:3; 12:9). The passages which refer to the murder and
replacement of kings (7:1–7; 8:4) must be later, and there is
little doubt that 5:8–15 relates to events of the years 734–32.
At this time of acute distress Hosea seems to have wanted
above all to convince his hearers that the troubles through
which they were passing were the result of Yahweh's judgment
and therefore could not be resolved by diplomatic negotiations
or acts of religious devotion (cf. 7:8–16; 8:1–3, 11–14; 9:1–9).
5:15 and possibly 6:1–3 and 14:1–3 point to a renewed call to

repentance at this time, coupled with the idea that a time of
trouble might bring Israel to her senses (2:6–7, 14–15). Later
oracles reflect the negotiations with Egypt and the renewed
confidence which followed Tiglath-pileser's death (7:11; 10:3–6,
13–15) and the removal of objects of false trust (3:1–5). A feature
of this period is the reflections on the traditions of Israel's origin,
and several "historical retrospects" explain how there is no basis
for confidence in them (9:10–17; 10:1–2, 9–13; 13:1–11). Hosea
here undoubtedly refers to and challenges the contemporary
cultic responses to the situation, and Ps. 80 probably gives
a very good idea of the form which these took. Increasingly
Hosea's message of judgment found its grounding in Israel's
failure to respond to Yahweh's loving call to repentance (5:4;
7:1–2 (10?); 13:13 – cf. 11:1–7). In one late passage, probably
from this period, we see the prophet breaking through to the
insight that Yahweh's love for his people is so great that, even
in the face of her obstinacy, he cannot and will not give her
up utterly (11:1–9). It is possible to understand how, in the
light of this, he might subsequently have spoken of an eventual
restoration of the people, which would include an ingathering
of the exiles (11:11) and a renewal of the fertility of the land
(2:21–3; 14:5–8), but also a moral and religious change, in
which the "healing" would be done by Yahweh himself (2:16,
19–20; 14:4). But such hopes seem to have emerged only at the
very end of his ministry, probably after Samaria had fallen to
the Assyrians. Not all the oracles, of course, can be dated even
approximately, and polemic against the religion of the shrines,
for example, seems to have been a constant theme of the prophet
throughout his ministry.

Hosea's Relation to
the Religious Traditions of the Northern Kingdom

To understand Hosea, it is necessary to know something of the
religious behaviour and attitudes which he attacked, but also

the tradition in which he stood. To a large extent these were interwoven, though a polarization had already occurred in the northern kingdom in the 9th century under Ahab. Then, under royal leadership, the worship of Baal and Asherah had flourished as never before (1 Kg. 16:32–33; 18:19). Over against it, there had arisen a prophetic movement headed by Elijah which stood for loyalty to Yahweh alone and which eventually, in partnership with the even more extreme followers of Jehonadab the son of Rechab and the army commander Jehu, succeeded in overthrowing the dynasty and its religious officials (2 Kg. 9–10). The religious problem as Hosea perceived it was more complex and more radical, though there are signs, especially in ch. 2, that he at first saw it very much in the same terms as Elijah.

There is no doubt that aspects of Canaanite religion had remained, unaffected by the prophetic reforms of the 9th century. 2 Kings acknowledges that the Asherah cult-symbol was still in Samaria during the reign of Jehu's son Jehoahaz (13:6). In the Samaria ostraca (see above) several of the persons mentioned have names alluding to Baal (e.g. Baalzamar), indicating the reverence paid to that god in their families. The scenes on the Samaria ivories and some personal seals show the currency of mythological motifs among the upper classes, and the recent discoveries at Kuntillet Ajerud, which in part at least seem to relate to inhabitants of the northern kingdom, indicate devotion to Baal, Asherah and the Egyptian god Bes as well as to Yahweh (see King, pp. 104–7). That there was a public cult of Baal in Israel in Hosea's time is indicated only by the prophet's own words (see especially 2:13; 2:17 is probably redactional), but this is perfectly credible. 4:13–14 and 7:14 also clearly refer to practices of Canaanite origin at hill-top shrines, which probably included the worship of Asherah as well as Baal (see the notes on 4:18–19). Nevertheless, much of Hosea's criticism is reserved for aspects of the worship of Yahweh which he believed were alien to it, and it is interesting to observe that one of these is the designation of Yahweh as "My Baal" (2:16). Since Heb. ba^{c}al was a common word meaning "lord" or "husband" its use could have been defended as a proper expression of devotion and reverence towards Yahweh. Hosea, however, saw it as a corrupting influence, a sign of implicit acceptance of the religion of another people, and it is likely that his polemics against sacrifice, "pillars" and the calf-images had a similar inspiration. In his view those who paid attention to such things were deserting Yahweh for Baal just as much as those who actually addressed their worship to the Canaanite god.

The rationale for such worship – which certainly left a deep mark, though not an entirely negative one, on Israel's liturgy – has become much clearer since the discovery of the Ugaritic texts from 1929 onwards. It was not a religion which was exclusively concerned with fertility, as a Ugaritic prayer to Baal and the Zakur stele show (cf. *IDBS*, p. 930; *ANET*, pp. 655–56), but the classic myths do focus on Baal as the god of cosmic order, rain and life and on his opposition to powers of chaos and death. Sacrifices and self-mutilation (cf. Hos. 7:14 and the note) were evidently thought to strengthen his hands in the conflict with evil forces, and mourning over his death played an important part in the ritual which looked for a revival of his power in the autumn rains. See further the Excursus on Baal on p. 91–94 and, e.g., A. H. W. Curtis, *Ugarit (Ras Shamra)*, Cambridge, 1985, ch. 4–5.

Over against such thinking Hosea upheld a theology which saw Yahweh as Israel's god "from the land of Egypt" (12:9; 13:4). Long ago he had found Israel, brought her out of Egypt, cared for her and given her the land with its fruits (9:10; 11:1–4; 12:13; 13:4–5; 2:8). She stood in a covenant relationship with him (6:7; 8:1), like a wife with her husband (2:7), and this should have involved observance of his law (4:6; 8:2, 12). Where did Hosea find such a theology? In his commentary H. W. Wolff presented the view that Hosea derived it from the same prophetic and Levitical circles who, some generations later, produced the book of Deuteronomy. It has always been a problem with this view that it has to conjecture the existence of a group whose social position remained largely undefined. A similar problem arises with the older attempts to see Hosea as having built upon the viewpoint of the Elohist (E) source or stratum of the Pentateuch, as despite more recent studies its profile and origin remain unclear (but see H. W. Wolff, *EvTh* 29 (1969), 59–72 = *Int* 26 (1972), 158–73; A. W. Jenks, *The Elohist*, esp.

pp. 112–17). In fact it is likely that this underlying theology was preserved in the formularies of the very shrines of which Hosea is in other respects so critical. The evidence for this lies chiefly in two psalms, 80 and 81, which there are strong reasons for regarding as north Israelite in origin and designed for use in public worship at one of the major national shrines. Both of them are distinguished by the use of "Joseph" as a name for the people (Ps. 80:1; 81:5 – for its use as a name for the northern kingdom cf. Ps. 78:67; Ezek. 37:19; Am. 5:15) and by an absence of the themes which are characteristic of Jerusalem psalms. In addition Ps. 80 asks for Yahweh's help specifically for the tribes of "Ephraim, Benjamin and Manasseh" (v. 2). This probably fixes the date of this psalm as the period between 733 and 722, when only the territory of those tribes remained under north Israelite rule: in other words it is actually contemporary with the later part of Hosea's activity. A detailed comparison of these psalms with Hosea is not possible here, but the following points are of particular significance:

(1) Both psalms, like Hosea, affirm that Israel is Yahweh's "people" (80:4; 81:8, 11, 13).

(2) Both, equally, trace this relationship back to the Exodus from Egypt (80:8; 81:5–7, 10) and speak of Yahweh's continuing care for Israel in her history (80:1, 9–11, 15; 81:7).

(3) Both expect Yahweh to help his people in time of war (80:3–7, 12; 81:14–15) and to provide them with the fruits of the harvest (81:10, 16; cf. 80:1).

(4) Both refer to the people's loyalty to Yahweh, but they differ over whether this is the response to his help (80:18) or its precondition (81:11–13).

(5) In addition Ps. 80 makes reference to Yahweh's special relationship to the king (v. 17).

(6) Ps. 81, on the other hand, speaks of the ritual and religious obligations imposed on Israel at the time of the Exodus (vv. 4–5, 8–9).

(7) Ps. 81 consists largely of a prophetic oracle which, to judge from the context, was designed to teach the worshippers their obligations to their God (cf. Ps. 50:7–23; 95:8–11).

This "Exodus-covenant" tradition is specifically associated with the shrines of Bethel and Dan (I Kg. 12:28). It is also very probable that the tradition of an appearance of God to Jacob, to which Hosea refers in 12:4–5, was kept alive at the Bethel shrine (on the importance of this to Hosea see G. I. Emmerson, pp. 128–31, who also emphasizes Hosea's positive attitude to the northern shrines generally).

It thus appears that the view of such scholars as G. von Rad (*OT Theology*, Edinburgh, 1962–65, vol. 1, p. 66) and R. E. Clements (*Prophecy and Covenant*, London, 1965, pp. 86–102) that the classical prophets "have their roots in the basic sacral traditions of the early period" is correct as far as Hosea is concerned (cf. Weiser, passim; Brueggemann; Neef; Daniels). But, as these scholars themselves emphasized, Hosea was far from being a mere expositor of the existing cultic traditions. Just as his prophetic predecessors had not been afraid to denounce evil and threaten disaster of a limited kind (cf. 6:5), so he called in question any complacent interpretation of the traditions, only in a yet more radical way. For him the very apparatus of the shrines (images, sacrifice, priesthood) had fallen under the judgment of the God who demanded only "knowledge of God" – that is, recognition of himself, his actions and his demands (4:6; 6:6), which are summed up in the word "loyalty" (Heb. *ḥesed*; see the commentary on 2:19). And so the nation, deprived of the protection which it thought to find in its worship, was exposed to the full consequences of its departure from observance of Yahweh's demands for justice in society (4:1–2; 10:12; 12:6), reverence for life (1:4; 6:8–9; 7:7; 13:14) and avoidance of foreign alliances (5:13; 7:8, 11; 8:9; 10:4). No old prophecy (1:4), no covenant (1:9), no king (13:10) could save it when the only real Saviour (13:4) appeared no longer as the Shepherd (Ps. 80:1) but as a wild animal (5:14; 13:7–8). The "No" of Hosea to all that was most precious to Israel could not be more emphatic. And yet, it seems, that same unsettling ability to think new thoughts on the basis of received tradition which is characteristic of written prophecy enabled him also to speak of a new beginning beyond the "end", for which he uses the language of the traditions once again: Exodus (11:11), wilderness (2:14–15), covenant (2:16, 23 – cf. 2:19–20), answered prayer (2:21; 14:8), creation (2:22; 14:5–7). But he does not speak of images or sacrifice (unless in 14:2) or priesthood.

The Book: Its Character, Compilation, Redaction and Text

Apart from two short narrative sections (1:2–9; 3:1–5) and the introduction and conclusion (1:1; 14:9), the book consists entirely of prophetic oracles. Features of poetic composition, such as parallelism, lines of regular length and the tendency to avoid certain "prosaic" particles, are evident in most of them, and older commentaries (e.g. Harper; cf. Buss, pp. 40–46) attempted a quite precise delineation of their poetic form, while recognizing that the regularity of psalmic and proverbial poetry was not generally to be found in prophecy. More recently there has been a tendency to stress that prophetic poetry and rhetorical prose form a continuous spectrum, so that it is neither possible nor useful to draw a rigid line between the two (cf. Wolff, p. xxiv; Andersen and Freedman, pp. 60–66; and more generally J. L. Kugel, *The Idea of Biblical Poetry: Parallelism and its History*, New Haven and London, 1981). In some passages, e.g. 2:2–13, where there are parallelism and rhythm but also many "prosaic" particles (Andersen and Freedman, p. 62), the indicators appear to contradict one another. However, in one very important respect Hosea's oracles have a strongly poetic character: he has an exceptional predilection for the most varied and striking imagery, both as allegory (ch. 2 passim) and as simile or metaphor (e.g. 4:16; 5:1).

Like other prophets, Hosea commonly uses the first-person singular pronoun "I" to refer to God, presenting himself as the messenger or mouthpiece of God, and much of his discourse falls into the categories of accusation and announcement of judgment. But the classic pattern of prophetic judgment-speech (on which see C. Westermann, *Basic Forms of Prophetic Speech*, Philadelphia and London, 1967, pp. 129–98) is much rarer in Hosea than in other prophets, as he prefers to weave an oracle out of a succession of elements from both categories, along with other speech-forms such as complaints, disputations, admonitions, instruction and didactic presentations of history. Although more closely tied to tradition in some of the content of what he says, Hosea displays far more freedom in his handling of the traditional genres of prophecy than (for example) Amos or Isaiah do. Even in such matters as the use of divine speech and prophetic speech (the latter being the type where the prophet speaks in his own person, as in 9:8, 13–14) and the choice between direct address to the people and third-person speech about them Hosea shifts backwards and forwards within a single oracle, to the confusion of ancient translators and modern form-critics alike!

The sub-division of the book into separate sections is much more difficult in Hosea than in other books, partly because of the general absence of introductory and concluding formulae, such as "Thus says the Lord", and partly because even within sections that have a generally similar theme there are often frequent shifts of subject or mood. This led T. H. Robinson to divide the book into a very large number of textual units, many of them very short. Reacting to this and seeking to retain form-critical rigour, H. W. Wolff proposed that the book consisted of a series of "kerygmatic units", each deriving from a single appearance of the prophet but comprising a sequence of his utterances, which in many cases responded to objections raised by his audience that could be reconstructed. For example, ch. 4 comprised one such unit and 5:8–7:16 another. Although this produced a vivid picture of the prophet in debate with his audience, it sometimes at least involved unconvincing claims about the historical contemporaneity of different sub-sections. In his recent commentary J. Jeremias has retained many of Wolff's divisions of the text but has treated the "units" as redactional compositions from a later period rather than extracts from a single prophetic debate. Some of his arguments for redactional composition are, however, questionable (see further below). It is perhaps best to see the main sections as collections of material with a similar theme or historical background, without insisting either on rigorous form-critical uniformity in the original sayings or on such a close connection in time between them as Wolff does (cf. J. Lindblom, *Prophecy in Ancient Israel*, Oxford, 1962, pp. 242–45; Buss, ch. 3, part 1).

It appears that three major parts should be distinguished

within the book: two are of a mixed character (4:1–11:11 and 11:12–14:8), while the third (1:2–3:5) contains only material using sexual imagery (especially "harlotry") and other oracles that are directly dependent on it. All three collections contain material from the full extent of Hosea's ministry. It is clear that 1:2–3:5 was assembled according to a thematic principle, but it is not clear why the remaining material was assembled in two largely parallel collections. It is noteworthy that, in common with other prophetic collections, all three parts of the book culminate in prophecies of salvation. The placing of 1:2–3:5 at the beginning of the book was no doubt intended to highlight Hosea's use of sexual imagery to portray religious apostasy: it has certainly had an enormous influence on later perceptions of the prophet, from Jeremiah to the present day.

Echoes of Hosea's imagery and teaching are not difficult to find in the rest of the Old Testament, particularly in the prophecies of Jeremiah, Ezekiel and Deutero-Isaiah and in the book of Deuteronomy. Already in this there is evidence that his sayings were valued, studied and reapplied in later times, particularly in Judah. Further evidence can be found in redactional additions to the book of Hosea itself. While many oracles were presumably clear enough in their meaning not to need clarification (or alternatively too specific to permit reinterpretation), in other cases additions or alterations were required to make plain what "the word of the Lord that came to Hosea" meant for later generations. Very few such changes seem to have been made before the collections were brought to Judah: these could include the insertion of 2:17, 7:10 and 10:12, and the modification of 10:9–11, 13–15 to refer to a judgment that was now past. A first Judaean phase of redaction seems to be represented by passages which draw a distinction between Israel and Judah and assert that Judah will be preserved from undergoing a similar fate to Israel. 1:7 and 11:12 have such a character, and in their positive affirmations bear some resemblance to hopeful passages in Isaiah 1–39 which are now commonly dated to the reign of Josiah (R. E. Clements, *Isaiah and the Deliverance of Jerusalem*, JSOTSS 13, Sheffield, 1980), though they differ in that they make no specific reference to the Zion tradition. Possibly they derive from an earlier situation, such as the time when Jerusalem was threatened by Sennacherib in the reign of Hezekiah. Then there are a number of passages where Hosea's accusations or threats against Israel are said also to apply to Judah (4:15; 5:5c; 6:4, 11; 8:14; 10:11; 12:2). Very probably 4:5b ("the prophet also shall stumble with you by night") belongs here too, as its form and vocabulary are very like 5:5 and the conjunction of prophet and priest in judgment-sayings is common in the book of Jeremiah. The addition to 5:5 at least seems to have been made after the fall of Jerusalem to the Babylonians, as the Hebrew verb is in the past tense ("Judah also has stumbled"): this may be the setting of the other passages in this group, though some could well be earlier. In either case they would have enabled Hosea's prophecies to be read, like those of other prophets, as an explanation of the catastrophe of 587–6 BC. The longer heading (1:1) also seems to belong to this stage of editing.

The view taken in the commentary is that by no means all the hopeful passages in the book are secondary additions to the collection of Hosea's sayings: several of them can with good reason be ascribed to the later years of Hosea's own ministry. But there are others, mostly short, which seem to be more closely related to the teaching of those prophets who sought, in various ways, to kindle hope of a better future in the Jews of the Babylonian and Persian periods. They speak of the reunion of the two kingdoms under a common leader, in one passage explicitly of a new David; of a return of the exiles and their growth into a great nation, living in peace and safety in their land; and above all of a renewal of the covenant and the experience of Yahweh's compassion (1:10–2:1; 2:18; 3:5 ("and David their king"; "in the latter days"); 11:10, 12b). Parallel passages suggest a similar date for 12:5, which draws attention to the exhortation in 12:6. Finally the book came into a situation, probably in post-exilic times, in which it was valued for its embodiment of general principles of right and wrong, reward and punishment, and the epilogue (14:9) was added to guide and encourage future reflection on it.

The Hebrew text of Hosea is notoriously difficult to understand: a comparison of even a few verses in different modern translations will quickly reveal the extent of the problems. While a few modern scholars (e.g. Nyberg, Kuhnigk, Andersen and Freedman) have insisted that sense can and should be made of the text as it stands, their interpretations are often awkward or based on considerable speculation about Hebrew usage and the extent to which it can be illuminated by recourse to other Semitic languages such as Arabic and Ugaritic. Most commentators have recognized that a lot of the difficulties are due to scribal error – that is, mistakes made in the copying of the text, which must be corrected before the original meaning can be recovered. For a few passages additional evidence in Hebrew is available in the form of fragmentary biblical manuscripts from Cave 4 at Qumran or quotations in the sectarian writings from Qumran and the Damascus Document. The manuscripts published so far which contain parts of Hosea are the following:

4QXII^d	(L. A. Sinclair, *BASOR* 239 (1980), 61–65)	1:7–2:5
4QpHos^a	(*DJD* V, pp. 31–32)	2:8–14
4QpHos^b	(*DJD* V, pp. 32–36)	5:13–15; 6:4–10; 8:6–7, 13–14
4QpIsa^c	(*DJD* V, pp. 24–5)	6:9
4QXII?	(M. Testuz, *Semitica* 5 (1955), 37–38)	13:15; 14:1–6

There are quotations from 2:17 in the Qumran War Scroll and from 3:4, 4:16 and 5:10–11 in the Damascus Document. Unfortunately these fragments make little contribution to the solution of textual difficulties in the Masoretic Text, as for the most part they contain passages where the meaning is clear. More help is to be had from the ancient translations, especially from the Septuagint, which was based on a Hebrew *Vorlage* which, while sharing many of the errors of the Masoretic Text, also often differed from its readings (for details see Harper, pp. clxxiv–clxxviii; Borbone, passim; and the cautionary note in the recent studies of Muraoka). An important study of the Peshitta translation has recently appeared (A. Gelston, *The Peshitta*: see especially ch. 5), in which likely variations from the Masoretic Text in its *Vorlage* are listed. The Targum of Jonathan (now available in the translation by K. J. Cathcart and R. P. Gordon) and the Vulgate (cf. B. Kedar–Kopfstein, *JQR* 65 (1974), 73–97) have less to offer the textual critic, but they are of considerable interest, along with Jerome's commentary (*PL* 25:815–946), for the early history of the interpretation of the book.

An Analysis of the Book's Contents

A. CHAPTERS 1–3: FAITHLESS ISRAEL – JUDGMENT AND RENEWAL

1:1	Title
1:2–2:1	Hosea's children and their names (Heb. 1:2–2:3)
2:2–15	Yahweh and his faithless wife (Heb. 2:4–17)
2:16–20	Promises of a renewed relationship (Heb. 2:18–22)
2:21–23	The reversal of the children's names (Heb. 2:23–25)
3:1–5	The disciplining of the beloved

B. CHAPTERS 4–11: A HISTORY OF DOOM RELUCTANTLY IMPOSED

4:1–19	The effects of priestly negligence: a people without knowledge of God
5:1–7	Judgment on the leaders of a faithless people
5:8–6:3	Oracles from the Syro-Ephraimite war
6:4–10	Yahweh's unmet demands
6:11–7:7	Condemnation of a *coup d'état*
7:8–16	Foreign policy: a source of weakness, not strength
8:1–14	A catalogue of Israel's sins
9:1–9	The coming end of festal worship
9:10–17	A sinful history begets a barren future
10:1–8	Doom for king and "high place"
10:9–15	Two oracles of coming war
11:1–11	Divine love – slighted but not extinguished

C. CHAPTERS 12–14: DEATH AND NEW LIFE FOR GUILTY ISRAEL

11:12–12:14	Deceivers rejected and prophets vindicated (Heb. 12:1–15)
13:1–16	Death is unavoidable for guilty Israel (Heb. 13:1–14:1)
14:1–8	Two sayings on renewal (Heb. 14:2–9)
14:9	Conclusion (Heb. 14:10)

COMMENTARY

A. CHAPTERS 1–3:
Faithless Israel – Judgment and Renewal

TITLE

I:I

The book of Hosea begins, like several other prophetic books, with an emphatic declaration of the divine origin of what follows and an indication of the historical period in which Hosea was active as a prophet. The closest parallels are found in the books of Micah and Zephaniah, and these three books may have formed a preliminary collection of prophetic writings at some stage. Although Hosea was a northern prophet and the other two were southerners, it is clear from the priority given to the kings of Judah in 1:1 that Hosea was being presented to a Judaean readership by the authors of this title. Both the historical references and the formula **the word of the Lord . . . came** are strongly reminiscent of the books of Kings and it is plausible to associate these headings with the Deuteronomistic editors of those books, whose interest in the presentation of collections of prophetic sayings is particularly clear in the book of Jeremiah (cf., e.g., E. W. Nicholson, *Preaching to the Exiles*, Oxford, 1970). The presence of such a title, dating from over a century after the time of Hosea's own prophetic activity, prepares us to expect that in the body of the book too additions to Hosea's sayings may have been made to underline their relevance to the exilic generation, and a number of such additions can in fact be identified (see the notes on, e.g., 3:5, 4:5, 5:5).

It is likely that v. 2a contains an earlier title to the book, which is to be translated, "(This is) the beginning of the Lord's speaking through Hosea" (cf. NEB). A similar older title can be detected in Am. 1:1.

1:1. The word of the LORD: A "word from the LORD" was originally a specific message received by an individual, usually for transmission to others. As such the expression was at home in prophetic circles, where the introductory messenger formula, "Thus says (or said) the Lord" was also frequently employed (cf.

2 Sam. 7: 4–5). Comparable expressions were used in prophetic utterances elsewhere in the ancient Near East (cf. R. R. Wilson, *Prophecy and Society*, Philadelphia, 1980, p. 116). The plural could then be used to refer to a collection of such utterances (e.g. Jer. 25:13) or to prophetic utterances in general (Am. 8:11; Zech. 7:12), but the usage is less common than might be expected. Instead the singular was employed in a collective sense (e.g. 1 Sam. 3:1; Isa. 40:8) to refer to divine speech in general. From this it is but a short step to the idiom in which it appears as part of the titles of prophetic books, with reference to the often very diverse collections of oracles and other material contained in them (cf. P. K. D. Neumann, *VT* 23 (1973), 192–93: compare 4:1 below). There is then inevitably an implication that the books each convey a message with a degree of unity and consistency. But this should not be taken to mean that there is but one **word of the LORD** which presents itself under different manifestations (von Rad, *OT Theology*, vol. 2, pp. 80–98), for in each case it is defined and specified as **the word of the LORD that came** to a particular prophet.

that came (Heb. *hāyāh*, more often "was" or "became"): It is the normal idiom for the reception of Yahweh's word by a prophet, both in the headings to prophetic books (Jer. 1:2; Ezek. 1:3; Jl 1:1; Jon. 1:1; Mic. 1:1; Zeph. 1:1; Hag. 1:1; Zech. 1:1) and in prophetic narrative elsewhere (1 Sam. 15:10 etc.). The meaning "came" is not restricted to such contexts and there is nothing intrinsically mysterious about it (cf., e.g., Gen. 7:10; 17:16). The idea that *hāyāh* somehow conveys the notion, "became effective" is mistaken (cf. J. Barr, *The Semantics of Biblical Language*, Oxford, 1961, pp. 58–72): in fact where it was desired to emphasize the power of the divine word, some other construction tended to be preferred, such as "Yahweh sent his word" (Isa. 9:7; 55:11; Ps. 107:20; 147:15) or "Yahweh's word(s) came forth" (Heb. *yāṣā*': Isa. 45:23; 48:3; 51:4; 55:11). It remains to be clarified why this impersonal form of expression was preferred to the simple "that Yahweh spoke" which is used in Dt. 18:21–22 (cf. v. 2 here) Perhaps, while guarding the divine origin and authority of the prophets' words, the tradents hesitated to assimilate their mode of reception too clearly to direct address; and also they thereby laid greater emphasis on the existence of the **word** itself as a *traditum* than on the process by which it was received. The conception of the divine word described by Neumann, *VT* 23 (1973), 171–217, is thus present *in nuce* already in this kind of formula. The messenger formula employed by many prophets would then apparently represent a bolder claim to having had an "audience" with Yahweh (cf. Jer. 23:18–22).

to Hosea the son of Beeri: On the names see the Introduction, pp. 23–4. Hosea is mentioned by name only here and in v. 2.

in the days of Uzziah ...: On the period represented by these reigns and the probable duration of Hosea's ministry, see the Introduction, pp. 24–25. The precedence of the kings of Judah, in the title of a book chiefly addressed to the northern kingdom, is remarkable, as is the failure to mention the successors of **Jeroboam**, through whose reigns Hosea certainly continued to prophesy. The former peculiarity is very likely evidence that the book in its present form was edited in Judah: the sequence of kings makes Hosea a contemporary of the better-known Isaiah (Isa. 1:1; cf. also Mic. 1:1). There are several other passages where Judaean redactional work can be posited, though not all references to Judah in the book are secondary. The reference to **Jeroboam** alone may indicate that the original heading of the book was of the type which noted only the time when the prophet's activity began (cf. Jer. 1:2 (amplified, perhaps secondarily, in v. 3); Ezek. 1:1–3; and perhaps Isa. 6:1) V. 2a indeed may well be the remnant of just such an introduction (so Wolff, p. 4).

HOSEA'S CHILDREN AND THEIR NAMES

1:2–2:1 (Heb. 2:3)

The first main section of the book is concerned with events in Hosea's life and their significance for Israel's relationship to Yahweh. The only other passage of this kind in the book is ch. 3. It is possible to distinguish a narrative (1:2–9) and a group of short prophetic sayings which are attached to it by their shared focus on the names of Hosea's children (1:10–2:1). The difficulty of defining the end of the section is reflected in the different chapter divisions of the Hebrew and English texts. In the Heb. the break between ch. 1 and ch. 2 coincides with the change from judgment to hope after 1:9, and ch. 2 begins as it ends with reinterpretations of the names of Hosea's children (cf. vv. 22–23 in the English numbering). But the change of tone is no less abrupt between 2:1 and 2:2, and the symbolism of the children's names has been left behind in 2:2ff., where it is clear, particularly from the later part of the passage, that it is now Yahweh who is speaking about Israel, and not Hosea about his wife and children. The English chapter division, which breaks up the hopeful reinterpretation of the children's names, is perhaps due to the fact that both 2:1 and 2:2 are couched in the plural imperative form, but the two verses really have nothing in common as far as their content is concerned, and the case for a strong break after 2:1 is compelling.

The narrative relates four events in the life of the prophet with the minimum of circumstantial detail. This sequence of events must, in view of the reference to **the house of Jehu** (v. 4), have begun when Jeroboam II (or less likely his son Zechariah, who ruled for only six months) was still on the throne (cf. 1:1) and will have spread over a period of five to six years (see the note on v. 8), for which we are given no other information. This very selective account has clearly been deliberately put together to highlight the message symbolized by Hosea's family life, and it reflects the classic form of the prophetic judgment-speech, with accusation (v. 2) followed by the announcement of judgment (vv. 4–6, 9). The "memoir" in Isaiah 6–8 is somewhat similar, but even in its original form that passage included a greater diversity of material, both narrative and oracular. Hosea's actions belong more generally within the category of prophetic symbolic actions (on which see Lindblom, *Prophecy in Ancient Israel*, pp. 165–73; von Rad, *OT Theology*, vol. 2, pp. 95–98), and the pattern of their description is similar to other examples, e.g. Ezek. 4–5. The two essential elements are the divine command (e.g. v. 4, "Call his name Jezreel") and the explanation of the symbolism ("for yet a little while, and I will punish . . ."). The execution of the command is often passed over (although it is certainly to be assumed), because the narrator is concentrating on the meaning conveyed by the divine word, not on the action itself or the prophet's obedience (contrast the style of the priestly narrator in Exodus). This literary-theological feature has perhaps contributed to traditional attempts to evade what is seen as the moral offensiveness of the story by supposing that it is dealing only with episodes in the prophet's visionary experience, not real events in the external world (see the Excursus on "Hosea's Marriage"). Against this is the fact that what must have seemed the most offensive action, namely the "taking" of a "woman of harlotry", which led to her subsequent conception of children, is explicitly related, in v. 3.

The narrative has not come down to us in its original form. The clearest addition is v. 7, which represents a pro-Judaean standpoint (see the detailed notes on the verse), but it is not easy to specify the circumstances in which it was added. Most would agree that it is of pre-exilic origin (after 587 it was obvious that Judah could no longer rely on such deliverance), and there are clear affinities with passages in the book of Isaiah (e.g. 7:1–7; 9:1–7; 37:33–35). But the latter represent a tradition which had its roots in the Jerusalem temple tradition and probably resurfaced in the "Assyrian redaction" (H. Barth) in the reign of Josiah, and Hos. 1:7 could in principle belong to any stage in this development: before 701 (Wolff, as a possibility), after the deliverance of Jerusalem in 701 (Weiser, Rudolph, Mays) or in the reign of Josiah (Clements, *Isaiah and the Deliverance of Jerusalem*, p. 60). In any case it bears witness to the possession of Hosea's sayings in a circle to whom the Jerusalem temple theology was dear and among whom the prophet's denunciation of the northern kingdom was seen as well-deserved. 3:5 may have been supplemented by the same circle.

V. 5, which adds a second, less specific interpretation of the name Jezreel, is also probably an addition to the narrative. But in this case there is no reason why it should not be from Hosea himself; it may originally have been either an independent saying or part of an alternative version of the memoir.

It is much more difficult to be sure whether v. 2 has been transmitted in its original form. Until quite recently the majority even of critical commentators have treated the verse as an integral part of the narrative, though their acceptance of it has often been qualified and perhaps implicitly justified by the view that the expressions **a wife of harlotry** and **children of harlotry** were proleptic and the result of the prophet's looking back on a marriage which had turned out to be ruined by his wife's unfaithfulness and then realizing that Yahweh had foreseen this and indeed planned it. Already on this view the verse, while originating with Hosea, does not correspond to his actual experience at the time in the way that the naming of his children presumably does. Rudolph, whose view has recently gained in popularity (cf. Schreiner, Jeremias), has raised the telling objection to this that there is no word in the narrative of any unfaithfulness on Gomer's part subsequent to her marriage to Hosea. A different explanation of the expressions **a wife of harlotry** and **children of harlotry** is therefore required. Rejecting suggestions that Gomer was already known to be a prostitute or a participant in sexual rites at a sanctuary, Rudolph finds the explanation in the occurrences of the word **harlotry** ($z^e n\hat{u}n\hat{\imath}m$) in 2:2 and 2:4. The compiler of ch. 1–3, he supposes, mistakenly thought that the wife and children referred to there were Gomer and her children and therefore modified 1:2 accordingly. Originally it will have read something like: "Yahweh said to Hosea, 'Take a wife for yourself, so that she may bear you children.'" Schreiner has argued in addition that the form and vocabulary of the final clause of v. 2 are against its being original. This view is in many ways attractive and it does not depend on acceptance of Rudolph's much less likely interpretation of ch. 3 (see the notes there). But it does not wholly explain why the compiler modified ch. 1 in the way that he is supposed to have done (at the very least the addition of "but she played the harlot" in v. 3 might have been expected) and, if the view proposed here in the notes on v. 2 is accepted, it is not necessary. If Hosea's relationship with Gomer was an extra-marital liaison with a common prostitute, the text makes good sense as it is, without the need either to reckon with secondary elements in v. 2 or to import the notion that Gomer was an unfaithful wife. Of course, on this view the liaison represents Israel's relations not with Yahweh but with Baal, but these are just as much in view, both in 1:2 and in 2:5.

1:10–2:1 is not a single oracle. The change from indirect address to direct address after 1:11 points to 2:1 being a separate saying. Moreover, the differing usage of the expression

the people of Israel in 1:10 and 1:11 is against these two verses
having an original association. As is argued in the detailed notes,
these three short sayings are unlikely to be from Hosea, although
they each draw their inspiration from 1:2–9 and from other verses
in his book. They probably originated in the Babylonian exile,
among the Judaean community which had for some time held the
sayings of Hosea in high regard (see on 1:7); and it may be that
these "oracular commentaries" were pronounced by prophets
at occasions when the Hosea collection was read publicly in
a liturgical setting, as has been supposed for some redactional
additions to the books of Amos and Micah.

This remarkable chapter has given rise to a prolific history of
interpretations, much of it more ingenious than soundly based
in the text. For surveys see, on the pre-modern periods, S. Bitter,
Die Ehe des Propheten Hosea, Göttingen, 1975, and, on the modern
discussion, H. H. Rowley, "The Marriage of Hosea", *BJRL* 39
(1956–7), 200–33 (= *Men of God*, London, 1963, pp. 66–97),
and Rudolph, pp. 39–49. Early Jewish interpretation produced
both a literal and an allegorical reading of the narrative. The
former, amplified by haggadic midrash, appears in B. Pesaḥim
87a-b and seems to represent an Amoraic discussion; the latter
appears in the Targum, which views Gomer as nothing but a
symbol for wayward Israel. See further the Excursus on "Hosea's
Marriage". In the New Testament (Rom. 9:25–7; 1 Pet. 2:10) it
is the hopeful sayings at the end of the chapter which are cited,
with elements drawn from the similar verse 2:23, but they are
given a bold new interpretation which sees them as evidence for
God's purpose to bring the Gentiles ("not my people") into the
enjoyment of his fullest blessing (for details see commentaries on
Romans and 1 Peter). This way of understanding the passage is
also attributed to two rabbis in B. Pesaḥim 87b, and it exemplifies
a pattern of prophetic interpretation which is already evident in
the books of Isaiah and Jonah (cf. my study, "The Destiny of the
Nations in the Book of Isaiah", in J. Vermeylen (ed.), *The Book
of Isaiah*, BETL 81, Leuven, 1989, pp. 93–120, esp. p. 118; and
VT 27 (1977), 105–11).

1:2. When the LORD first spoke through Hosea . . .: While
the translation of the Heb. as a temporal clause, indicating

that the beginning of Hosea's prophetic ministry was a divine command to beget children (v. 2b), is now widely accepted (cf. JB, NIV, NJPS) and can be justified syntactically (cf. *GK* §130d), the four words can also be read separately as a kind of title: "(This is) the beginning of the Lord's speaking through Hosea" (cf. NEB, Wolff, Rudolph, Mays), i.e. the beginning of the book which contains his oracles (compare Mk 1:1 and 1QM 1:1 (*DSSE*, p. 124)). The titular understanding of the words is probably reflected in the placing of a Masoretic "open section" after them. Alternatively, as Wolff suggests, it may be the superscription for 1:2–9, a "first period" of the prophet's ministry. On the possibility that 3:1 contains an explicit reference back to this (Rudolph, p. 86), see the notes there. In early times these words were thought to imply that Hosea was the first of the canonical prophets (Jerome, *PL* 822A; cf. N. H. Snaith, *Mercy and Sacrifice*, p. 10). For **through Hosea** NJPS has "to Hosea" (so also Rudolph): there is early precedent for this in some LXX manuscripts and Syr., and Heb. *b^e* (lit. "in") can have either meaning. But **to** later in the verse is a different preposition (*'el*). For an explanation of the occurrences of *dibber b^e* in the OT see N. G. Cohen, *ZAW* 99 (1987), 219–32; but her proposal that it indicates an enthusiastic visionary experience at the time of a prophet's "commissioning" by Yahweh is unlikely to be correct.

Go, take to yourself a wife of harlotry: "a woman of harlotry", i.e. a prostitute: Heb. *'iššāh*, while used for "wife" (e.g. Gen. 2:24–25), basically means simply "woman". It is normally assumed that **take** is here used technically of taking in marriage, as, e.g., in Gen. 4:19, but it need not mean this, and the following instruction to **have children of harlotry** makes better sense if Hosea was to have sexual relations with a prostitute outside marriage. For other instances where **take** seems to include extra-marital relations see Lev. 20:14, 17, 21. In that case Hosea would stand in this symbolic prophetic action not for Yahweh but for Baal. **wife of harlotry** (*'ešet z^{e}nûnîm*) is a unique phrase in the OT, the normal expression for "prostitute" being (*'iššāh*) *zōnāh*. But its structure is of a very common kind (*GK* §128s-v) and the abstract *z^{e}nunim* is more common in Hosea than in any other OT book (in addition to the very next phrase, see 2:2, 4; 4:12; 5:4). It may have been chosen to lay greater

emphasis on the woman's character than on her profession, or
to match more closely the form of the following phrase. NIV's
"an adulterous wife" is imprecise, as are NEB's "wanton" and
REB's "unchaste".

It has been held that the phrase refers not to a common prostitute but to a woman who, like all Israelite brides at this time,
would have been forced to engage in an act of cultic prostitution
(Wolff) or to a cult-prostitute from the temple staff (Mays). It
has also been held that the specification **of harlotry**, together
with its interpretation later in the verse, derives from a redactor
who mistakenly thought that 2:2–5 referred to Hosea's own
family (Rudolph, Jeremias). On these views see the Excursus
on "Hosea's Marriage" and Balz-Cochois, *Gomer*, pp. 60–65.

and have children of harlotry: There is no separate word
in the Heb. for **have**, the verb **take** (*qaḥ*) being zeugmatically
used in slightly different senses with its two objects: here it
comes close to instances where it means "procure", or "get"
(e.g. Exod. 5:11). **children of harlotry** are mentioned again
in 2:4: the word for **children** is different there (*bᵉnê*, usually
"sons", instead of *yaldê*). This may reflect the distinction between
a reference to Hosea's own children (who included a daughter)
and one to Israel as a whole. On the usual understanding of
this chapter Hosea's children are called **children of harlotry**
because, it is supposed, two of them at any rate were fathered by
someone other than Hosea (see the note on v. 6). But the text of
ch. 1 makes no reference in this connection to any unfaithfulness
to Hosea on Gomer's part, and it must be presumed that Hosea
was their father. In that case it is his union with Gomer which
is described as **harlotry**, which most naturally means that it was
an extra-marital liaison with a prostitute, though the possibility
may exist that it is so called because of a bridal rite of the kind
envisaged by Wolff.

**for the land commits great harlotry by forsaking the
LORD:** An explanation of Yahweh's command in this form
follows each of the symbolic names to be given to Hosea's
children (cf. vv. 4, 6, 9), though the use of a symbolic action
by the prophet to represent a present state of affairs appears
to be unique, and indeed contrary to what is now understood
to be the function of other such actions, viz. in some sense to

"create history" (von Rad, *OT Theology*, vol. 2, p. 97). But the symbolic action in 3:1 is not essentially different (Balz-Cochois, *Gomer*, p. 179). Analogies may also be found, on the one hand, in cultic symbolism and, on the other, in the use of allegories to expose the heinousness of Israel's sins (cf. Hos. 2:2ff.; Isa. 5:1–7; Ezek. 16 and 23). **harlotry** as a metaphor for religious apostasy appears to go back to the religious conflicts of the 9th century (2 Kg. 9:22 - cf. Exod. 34:15–16). To attribute the sin of **harlotry** to **the land** (sc. of Israel) is unusual, though the terms in which judgment is threatened in 2:3 perhaps imply that the woman there also represents **the land**. Commentators have seen here, and elsewhere in Hosea, a deliberate echo and parody of the mythology of the fertility cult, according to which Baal would have sexually impregnated the earth (**the land**) so as to produce its fruits. This sacred marriage, enacted in rituals of cultic prostitution, is then supposed to be represented by Hosea as nothing other than **harlotry** (cf. Wolff, pp. 15–16). But, although Canaanite mythology displays some general parallels with more widely attested beliefs about the impregnation of the earth-mother, this specific idea is not attested in the surviving texts, and it is therefore an insecure basis for exegesis. More probably **the land** here stands, as it does in some other passages (Lev. 19:29; Dt. 24:4; Ezek. 14:13), for its inhabitants. The accusation against them is twofold: they give their love away promiscuously in return for payment (**harlotry**: cf. 2:5, 12), and in so doing they **forsake** their true husband, Yahweh (**the LORD**). Later in the book **harlotry** is an image for misplaced foreign alliances (8:9–10) as well as religious apostasy (9:1), and it is possible that the former are included in Hosea's criticism here. The final phrase of the verse certainly takes it for granted that Israel is "married" to Yahweh, as does the diatribe in 2:2–13. The verb **commits . . . harlotry** is in the imperfect, expressing repeated action (*GK* §107f-g): to render it by a future (NJPS; cf. LXX, Vulg.) is artificial and contrary to the prophets' normal concern with existing corruption (cf. also 2:5).

1:3. and took: NJPS and NIV, "married", make explicit the understanding of Hosea's relationship with Gomer which is normally assumed. But the phrase "as his wife" (*le'iššāh*), which would make the idiom unambiguous, is not in the Heb., and so the possibility remains that the relationship was an extra-marital one, as suggested above in the note on v. 2.

Gomer the daughter of Diblaim: The name **Gomer** is found elsewhere in the OT only as the name of a people in Asia Minor (Gen. 10:2–3 etc.), but it occurs as a personal name in one of the Samaria ostraca (no. 50). It is probably a typical shortening of a name meaning "(name of a god) has successfully completed (sc. the birth of the child)", cf. Gemariah (Jer. 29:3). Commentators assume that the omitted name of the god here too was Yahweh, but that need not be the case, as many north Israelite names at this time were compounded with Baal (cf. *ANET*, p. 321 (Samaria ostraca 1 and 2)). **Diblaim** (not attested elsewhere) should represent Gomer's father's name (for it to be her home town would be exceptional, and the closest parallel so far is *bt ủgrt*, "daughter of Ugarit", in a Ugaritic list of names), but the ending is unusual for a personal name: Ephraim is usually thought to have been originally a place-name (cf. *IDB*, vol.2, 119), which leaves only Cushan-rishathaim, Appaim and Shaharaim (Jg. 3:8; 1 Chr. 2:30; 8:8), all probably special cases. Some believe that it is not a name at all, but the dual form of a word that means "fruit-cake". **daughter of** will then have a qualitative sense, as in 1 Sam. 1:16 (where "base woman" is literally "daughter of Belial": cf. *GK* §128s): hence NEB "a worthless woman". Addiction to the fertility cult could be implied (cf. 3:1 and Mays) or "cheapness", but in either case the expression would be most unusual. It is better to attribute the dual ending to a misunderstanding of the consonantal text *dblym*, which can plausibly be identified as a theophorous name, perhaps Dabal-yam (Rudolph). The first element, still of uncertain meaning, occurs in two non-biblical names of the same form, while the second will be the god Yam, "Sea", well known as a Canaanite deity from the Ugaritic texts (cf. *CML*, pp. 7–8, 37–45; cf. Ps. 74:13) and occasionally found in personal names (Abijam, "Yam is my father" (1 Kg. 14:31 etc.): see also H. B. Huffmon, *Amorite Personal Names in the Mari Texts*, Baltimore, 1965, p. 210, and Taanach letter 2:2, in W. F. Albright, *BASOR* 94 (1964), 20). In Ugaritic there are two names in which *ym* occurs as the first element (cf. *UT*, p. 411): compare perhaps Jemuel in Gen. 46:10 and Exod. 6:15 (*HAL*, p. 396).

and bore him a son: It is clear from this that Hosea himself was the father of the first child. The absence of **him** in the similar statements in vv. 6 and 8 need not mean, as has sometimes been thought, that the second and third children had another father. Had Gomer been unfaithful to Hosea, it is likely that this would have been explicitly stated, in view of its symbolic potential.

1:4. Call his name: The choice of an appropriate and meaningful name for a child was a regular action in Israel and is highlighted in traditional narrative (*IDB*, vol.3, 504–05; e.g. Gen. 29:32). But for God to determine the name, as here, is peculiar to prophetic narratives (Isa. 7:14; 8:3; cf. Mt. 1:21).

Jezreel: The name means "El (God) sows" (or "sowed" or "will sow"), and is of an ancient type once commonly used for personal names (cf. "Israel"). But in the OT it occurs (apart from this section of Hosea: cf. 2:22) only as a place-name (in 1 Chr. 4:3 it represents the place in Judah mentioned in Jos. 15:56 and 1 Sam. 25:43 etc.), chiefly with reference to the city of Issachar (Jos. 19:18), which gave its name to **the valley of Jezreel** (v. 5), the wide plain which separates the hills of Galilee from Mount Carmel and Mount Gilboa. The name survives at Zer'in, twenty-five miles south-east of Haifa. It came early into Israelite hands (2 Sam 2:9), and under Ahab it contained a royal palace (1 Kg. 21:1, cf. 2 Kg. 8:29). It was the scene of the murder of Naboth and later of bloodshed associated with the revolt of **Jehu** against the Omride dynasty c. 842 (1 Kg. 21:2–16; 2 Kg. 9:16–37; 10:1–11). Excavations were recently begun at the site and early reports speak of buildings, walls and wine-presses from the monarchy period (*ESI* 7–8 (1988–89), 189–95).

the house of Jehu or "the dynasty of Jehu": **Jehu** was an army commander who had, with the support of the prophet Elisha and other religious conservatives, overthrown the dynasty of Omri in a bloody *coup d'état* which left none of the royal house alive and culminated in a massacre of Baal-worshippers under the guise of a religious festival (2 Kg. 9–10). Jeroboam (v. 1) was the penultimate ruler of the Jehu dynasty, and his successor Zechariah was murdered after a reign of only six months around 746, in the first of a series of *coups* (2 Kg. 16:10: see also the Introduction, p. 26–7). This oracle, unless it is a *vaticinium ex eventu*, must precede the fall of the dynasty. The best manuscripts of LXX here read "the house of Judah": this is very probably the original Greek reading, and will be an example of a relatively late reinterpretation of the text as applying specifically to Judah. Compare the substitution of "Jerusalem" for "Israel" in LXX at Am. 1:1.

for the blood of Jezreel: Since it is **the house of Jehu** which is to be punished, the reference here can only be to the massacres which accompanied their rise to power. It is striking how differently Hosea judges them from Elisha on the one hand and the Deuteronomistic historian on the other, despite the fact that he was every bit as opposed as they were to the Baal-worship encouraged by the Omride dynasty. For Hosea murder is a sin (cf. 4:2; 7:7), and the end does not justify the means. It is clear from this charge that from the beginning of his activity Hosea is concerned with more than religious apostasy, however much the latter theme predominates in ch. 2 in particular.

I will put an end to the kingdom of the house of Israel: This most likely does not refer, in the first instance, to the destruction of the whole people (although kingdom (*mamlākût*) can have a territorial sense), but reasserts, in typical poetic parallelism, the doom that is coming upon the royal house. For **put an end to** "remove" may be better, as also in Ps. 89:44, Isa. 17:3 (where a related word for "kingdom" is used in the same sense as here) and Ezek. 23:48. The end of royal rule and independence in **Israel** (i.e. the northern kingdom) did not in fact coincide with the fall of **the house of Jehu**, as a succession of short-lived dynasties followed it until the final capture of Samaria in 722.

1:5. And on that day: The transitional formula (cf. 2:18, 23; Isa. 7:18–25; 11:10–11) links on a once separate saying which gives an alternative interpretation of the name **Jezreel** as the place not only of the crime but also of the punishment (Rudolph). There is no reason to doubt its Hosean authorship.

I will break the bow of Israel: The **bow** (for which see also 1:7 and 2:18) was, because of its long range, a fearsome weapon, and this may explain its literary use as a symbol of military strength (O. Keel, *ZDPV* 93 (1977), 141–77; on the technology see Y. Yadin, *The Art of Warfare in Biblical Lands*, London, 1963, pp. 62–64, 80–83, 295–96, and *BRL*, pp. 49–50). But, being made of wood, it could easily be disabled by being "broken", and this served often to describe military defeat (e.g. 1 Sam. 2:4; Ps. 46:9 and Jer. 49:35 (where Yahweh is again the subject of the verb "break")). Some Egyptian reliefs show the Pharaoh with his feet on bows belonging to his enemies, symbolizing their defeat (Keel, p. 167). On other similar texts see R. Bach, in H. W. Wolff (ed.), *Probleme Biblischer Theologie* (FS G. von Rad), Munich, 1971, pp. 11–26, though he probably underestimates the direct contribution of the "holy war" tradition to this motif.

in the valley of Jezreel: The great plain (see the note on **Jezreel** in v. 4) was a frequent scene of battles (cf. G. A. Smith, *The Historical Geography of the Holy Land*, 25th ed., London, 1931, ch. 19): here no doubt a confrontation between Assyria and the rump-state of Israel after 733 is meant. As often the punishment is expected to fit the crime (cf. P. D. Miller, *Sin and Judgment in the Prophets* (SBLMS 27), Chico, 1982, though strangely he does not refer to this very clear example).

1:6. Not pitied: Heb. *lō'ruḥāmāh* (cf. NEB, NJPS, NIV), which is strictly a verbal form: "She is not pitied". As Wolff pointed out, the "she" is scarcely the child; perhaps **the land** (cf. v. 2), which is feminine in Hebrew was meant. The verb expresses the natural love of parents for their children, which makes allowance for their weakness (Ps. 103:13; Isa. 49:15; see also the note on **finds mercy** in 14:3): it is related both to the word translated **mercy** in 2:19 and to the Islamic title for God – *'al-raḥmān*, "the Compassionate".

for I will no more have pity on the house of Israel: Probably it is still the northern kingdom of Israel that is specifically in mind here: certainly that is how the redactor who composed v. 7 understood Hosea's words. **no more** implies that in the past Yahweh has been ready to **have pity** on his people; and presumably therefore that Hosea was aware of traditional statements to this effect. An overly psychological approach to Hosea, which was also too preoccupied with the contrasts with his close contemporary Amos, credited Hosea with the "discovery" of the love of God, perhaps through his own marital experience. But the implications of this verse are totally against such a view, and there is evidence elsewhere of a pre-prophetic belief in Yahweh's love for his people (Exod. 33:19; 34:6 – cf. 2 Kg. 13:23 and Ps. 78:38). Hosea, in fact, begins by denying the love of God which tradition had previously assumed would save Israel from disaster.

to forgive them at all: So modern EVV, Harper, Jeremias and others. For **forgive** (Heb. *nāsā'*, lit. "take (away)"), cf. 14:2: it is normal, but not essential, for a word for "sin" to follow when it is used in this sense. An alternative translation, already found in Syr. and AV, and favoured by Snaith, *Mercy and Sacrifice*, p. 37, Rudolph and Mays, is "but I will surely carry them away" (cf. the use of *nāsā'* in 5:14). For discussion of the philological arguments, and other less likely suggestions, see Harper and Rudolph.

1:7. But I will have pity on the house of Judah: The destinies of the **house of Israel**, the northern kingdom (v. 6), and **the house of Judah**, the southern kingdom, are sharply contrasted, as the word order of the Heb. emphasizes. Such a contrast is no part of Hosea's teaching (cf. 5:14; 6:4–6): it is most closely paralleled in Ps. 78 (see vv. 65–68), a southern psalm with a strong attachment to Jerusalem. On the likely redactional origin of this verse see the introduction to this section; but there is no justification for relegating it, as NEB did, to a footnote, as it is present in all the textual traditions.

and I will deliver them by the LORD their God: deliver commonly refers to victory in war (cf. Dt. 20:4). The idea that Yahweh alone can **deliver** is Hosean (13:4): it is Israel's folly to suppose that her king or Assyria could fulfil this role (13:10; 14:3 – cf. 5:13). The emphatic promise of divine help (**by the LORD their God**) is also prepared for in a genuine saying of Hosea, 12:7, although there the reference is, characteristically, to an overcoming of inward resistance, and the expression is grammatically smoother: the transition from first- to third-person reference to God here is, to say the least, awkward. The sense here is given by the contrast with the second half of the verse: Yahweh will **deliver** the house of Judah without any need for a battle. Compare, in the narrative tradition, the victories over the Amorites (Jos. 24:12), the Midianites (Jg. 7) and the Assyrians (2 Kg. 19:32–36). In prophecy Isa. 7:1–7 is a close parallel, as well as other passages in Isaiah attributed to the "Josianic Redaction", the basis for which probably lies in Jerusalem psalms such as 46 and 48 (cf. also 44:1–7).

not . . . by bow, nor by sword: The **bow** (cf. v. 5) and the

sword are mentioned again, together with **war** (see the next note), in 2:18. The pairing of them is traditional (Gen. 48:22; 2 Sam. 1:22 etc.) and reflects the alternatives of long-range and hand-to-hand combat. Swords from the Israelite period found in Palestine are mainly of bronze and rarely over 40 cm. in length (see further *BRL*, pp. 57–62).

nor by war: In 2:18 and Ps. 76:3 **war** is short for "(other) weapons of war", and this has been thought to be the meaning here (NEB – cf. G. R. Driver, *JQR* 37 (1946–47), 85). But the more general meaning fits just as well.

nor by horses, nor by horsemen: These two items, which do not occur in 2:18, are found together in several passages (1 Kg. 20:20; Isa. 31:1; Ezek. 23:6, 12; 26:7; 38:4): the series of occurrences in Ezekiel, particularly those in ch. 23 with its echoes of Hos. 1–3, may indicate the redactor's general background. The reference is probably to chariotry rather than ridden cavalry (LXX inserts "nor by chariots" to make this explicit), although by Hosea's time the latter was increasingly common (cf. S. Dalley, *Iraq* 47 (1985), 37–38, 47–48). For **horsemen** (Heb. *pārāšîm*) Jeremias has "teams" (*Gespanne*) (sc. of chariot-horses), following Mowinckel, *VT* 12 (1962), 289–95; but, however convincing that meaning may be for some passages, it does not fit here.

1:8. When she had weaned: In antiquity the period of nursing lasted longer than is normal today: three years according to the Instruction of Ani (*ANET*, p. 420) and 2 Macc. 7:27 (cf. also 1 Sam. 1:24 with 2:11). The lapse of time (presumably longer than that between the births of the first two children) has been seen as evidence of God's patience (Wolff) or of a period in which Hosea urged the people to repent (Rudolph), but there is no hint of this in the text: it may be only a circumstantial detail to which no particular significance is attached.

and bore a son: In the absence of any indication to the contrary, it is again (cf. the note on v. 6) to be assumed that Hosea was the child's father.

1:9. And the LORD said: The Heb. has "And he said" (cf. NJPS). Yahweh is clearly meant, but the increasingly abbreviated narrative is worthy of note.

Call his name Not my people: Heb. *lō' 'ammî* (cf. NEB, NJPS, NIV).

for you are not my people: That Israel was the **people** of
Yahweh was a very ancient conviction (Jg. 5:11, 13), which was
the basis both for their prayers (Ps. 80:4) and for their obligation
to obey Yahweh (Ps. 81:8–9, 13). This relationship might be
strained by disobedience and failure (Ps. 81:11–12), but it was
grounded in the historical events of the Exodus and the settlement in Canaan (Ps. 80:8–11; 81:6–7, 10) and it was assumed
on all sides to be irrevocable. At some stage prior to Hosea – how
much prior is not at all clear (cf. E. W. Nicholson, *God and
His People*, Oxford, 1986, ch. 9) – this belief was enshrined in
the affirmation that Yahweh had made a covenant with Israel
(Exod. 24:3–8; 34:10–27: see also the notes below on 6:6 and
8:2). Against this background the radical character of Hosea's
teaching (comparable at least to what Amos expressed in a
different way in 5:1–2 and 8:2) is clear: from now on Israel
(including Hosea himself: cf. **you**, not "they") no longer merits
the status conferred by this relationship. No explanation of this
is given here, but v. 2 has already pointed to Israel's infidelity,
and 2:2–13 will elaborate its character in more detail.

and I am not your God: So also NEB ("I will not be . . ."),
JB, NIV, following an emendation (*ʾᵉlohêkem* for *ʾehyeh lākem*)
proposed by Wellhausen, which was anticipated in some secondary LXX witnesses. This reading makes Hosea's words a
negation of the "covenant-making formula" (for this term see
R. Smend, *Das Bundesformel*, Zurich, 1963, p. 6), whose classic
form appears in somewhat later passages (Dt. 26:17–18; Jer.
11:3–5: cf. Hos. 2:25). Unfortunately 4QXII^d has a lacuna
at this point, but the major Vss. support MT and it should
be retained, with Wolff and other recent commentators. The
meaning is then "and I will not be on your side" (for this
sense of *lākem* cf. Gen. 31:42; Ps. 56:9; 124:1–2): Israel is to
forfeit the divine protection on which she has relied (Rudolph).
The avoidance of the correlative expression **your God** may be
deliberate; while Israel loses her uniqueness, Yahweh does not
lose his. W. Robertson Smith's identification of MT's *ʾehyeh* (**I
am**, lit. "I will be") as an allusion to Exod. 3:14, where the
same form is used as a name for God expressing his commitment
to Israel (*The Prophets of Israel*, London, 1882, p. 388; similarly
Mays ("And I am not I AM for you"), Buber, Wolff) is ingenious

and may have been intended by the LXX translator. The Exodus passage has commonly been attributed to a north Israelite writer (the "Elohist") living shortly before Hosea, so the prophet could have had it in mind.

1:10–2:1. In the Heb. the chapter division comes before these verses, presumably because their character contrasts so sharply with what has preceded. To a large extent, however, they take up the themes of 1:4–9 and they are best regarded as a later commentary (or rather, in view of the repetition, a series of short commentaries) on that passage. (The relocation of them after 3:5 (JB) or after 2:23 (Wolff, Harper) is without any justification.) 2:21–23 give a further commentary on 1:4–9, again with the reversal of the judgment embodied in the names of Hosea's children. But unlike that passage, these verses are probably not from Hosea himself, as their language and thought are much closer to the situation and thinking of the Babylonian exile.

1:10. the people of Israel: Unlike **the house of Israel** (vv. 4, 6), this expression (literally "the children of Israel") normally refers to both kingdoms seen as a unity (v. 11 is exceptional). The promise of an increase in numbers **like the sand of the sea which** cannot **be numbered** recalls the language of the promise to Jacob in Gen. 32:12 (cf. 22:17; 28:14), and this also suggests an "all-Israel" reference. This should mean that the saying **You are not my people** is now understood to refer to Judah as well as Israel, i.e. that this verse belongs to a different stage of redaction from 1:7, which can also be recognized in 5:5 and 12:2, in which Judah is seen to be destined for the same fate as the northern kingdom. Beyond this common fate, the redactor affirms, lies the fulfilment of the ancient promise to the patriarchs (cf. Dt. 4:30–31; Mic. 7:19–20). 4QXII[d] may have included additional words derived from Genesis ("and like the stars of heaven" (22:17)?) here, as MT does not fill all the space available.

in the place where it was said . . . : So also JB, NIV, whereas NEB and NJPS follow the non-local interpretation of *bimᵉqôm*, "instead of", adopted already by Kimchi and more recently by Wolff and others (cf. *HAL*, p. 592). No real parallel to the latter use exists in biblical Hebrew. Targ., followed by Rashi and Ibn Ezra, identified **the place** as the land of exile, and this fits in well with one interpretation of **they shall go up from the land**

in v. 11. But Canaan (or possibly specifically Jezreel (cf. v. 5), as Mays suggests) is on the whole more likely, so that a return from exile is presupposed.

it shall be said to them, "Sons of the living God.": The name is not simply a return to the traditional status of Israel as the **people** of Yahweh after a time of estrangement: the closer relationship of father and son is now made the definitive model (cf. 11:1–4; Exod. 4:22–3) and Yahweh's continuing guidance of history and faithfulness are affirmed in the title **the living God**. Cf. Ringgren in *TDOT*, vol.4, 338–40 for a review of all occurrences of this title for God: he concludes that it expresses the idea of "intervening actively" and being "obviously present". It seems possible to trace its use from old "holy war" traditions (Jos. 3:10; 1 Sam. 17:26; Ps. 18:46), through the language of worship in the Jerusalem cult (Ps. 42:2; 84:2), to a later polemical usage, where it contrasts the true God with powerless idols (Dt. 5:26; Jer. 10:10; Dan. 6:20, 26). In a book which is much concerned with the conflict between true and false religion it is tempting to associate the title with this latter group of occurrences in particular. See further H.-J. Kraus, *EvTh* 27 (1967), 184–90.

1:11. And the people of Judah and the people of Israel shall be gathered together: Here the theme of the reunion of the divided peoples of north and south is explicit. **gathered together** is more likely to refer to an assembly (as, e.g., in 1 Sam. 7:6) than to the ingathering of exiles. Recent commentators have tended to see this programme of reconciliation and (see below) united leadership as deriving from Hosea himself in the years after the two Israelite kingdoms had been at war with each other in the Syro-Ephraimite conflict (cf. 5:8ff. and the notes there). If that is so, it is surprising that there is no trace of the idea in Hosea's later prophecies of salvation in ch. 11 and 14. In fact the priority given to **the people of Judah** makes it improbable that this verse is from Hosea himself: like the title in v. 1 it is more likely to have a Judaean origin. There are a number of prophetic passages which speak of a reunion of the two peoples (Isa. 11:12–13; Jer. 3:11–18; 31:27–34; Ezek. 37:15–23 (cf. 48 passim), and all of them probably come from the 6th century BC. A slightly earlier date may be possible, since already in Deuteronomy's "all Israel" orientation and in the policies of

Josiah a similar aim is discernible. On the other hand, the
Chronicler's account of Hezekiah's mission to the northern tribes
(2 Chr. 30:1–12) is probably unhistorical: cf. L. K. Handy, *ZAW*
100 (1988), 111–15.

and they shall appoint for themselves one head: head
(Heb. *rō'š*) is a word for "leader" that could be used of a chief
(Jg. 11:8 – cf. Num. 14:4) or a king (1 Sam. 15:17). But the
avoidance of "king" (Heb. *melek*) is probably a deliberate way of
excluding the kind of monarchic institution which had developed
in both kingdoms and had been so severely criticized by Hosea
(cf. 13:10–11), while recognizing that a common centralized
leadership is desirable. The emphasis on popular appointment,
as in the stories of the beginning of dynasties (1 Sam. 11:15; 2
Sam. 2:4; 1 Kg. 12:20), is notable and scarcely fits the mere
recognition of an existing monarch, such as Josiah, for example.
The exact sense of these words is obscure and many suggestions
have been made about their meaning.

and they shall go up from the land: Traditionally **the land**
was taken to refer to the exile in Babylon (so Targ.), and this
interpretation has also attracted critical support (Wellhausen,
Harper and Jeremias). A variation on it is Robinson's view that
the whole "earth" is meant, which the Heb. *'ereṣ* allows. For **go
up** with reference to the return from exile cf. Ezra 7:7. Others
believe that Canaan is meant (cf. 1:2; 2:18; 4:1) and that the
reference is to expansion beyond the old borders (so JB). The
possible military overtones of the previous statements would
support this, but it connects poorly with what follows. Probably
no specific **land** is meant, and the expression is best understood
as a metaphorical one in which Israel is compared to a plant or
a tree, which "grows up from the ground" (so Reuss, Vriezen,
Rudolph, REB: for the image cf. 14:5–6 and Ps. 80:9–11 and
for this use of *'ālāh* (**go up**) cf. 10:8 and, in a metaphor, Isa.
53:2). This leads well into the reference to **Jezreel** (see the note
below) and is more likely than a reference to resurrection (W. L.
Holladay, *VT* 19 (1969), 123–24; Kuhnigk), although the latter
is used as a picture of Israel's renewal in Ezek. 37:12–13. The
view that *'ālāh* can mean "become master of" (Wolff, Mays,
NEB, comparing Exod. 1:10) is certainly to be rejected (cf. K.
Rupprecht, *ZAW* 82 (1970), 442–47).

for great shall be the day of Jezreel: On the location and history of **Jezreel** see the note on v. 4. The name of Hosea's first son is, however, probably introduced here for the sake of its etymology, "God sows/has sown", which would be clear to any Hebrew speaker. The connection is explicitly made in 2:22–23, a passage on which the present verse is likely to be dependent.

2:1. Say to your brother ... and to your sister: RSV's rendering implies that **Say** is addressed to Jezreel, who is told to rename his brother and sister, in the light of the promised restoration of Israel. But **Say** is in the Heb. a plural imperative (*'imrû*), and cannot be addressed to an individual, and likewise **your** has a clear plural reference. Moreover, the singular forms **brother** and **sister** are adopted from LXX and Syr. (so also JB), whereas MT and Targ. read the words as plurals: cf. NEB "your brothers ... your sisters". The difference between the alternative readings is only in their vocalization, which was not fully represented in early times. MT's reading is certainly to be preferred: if Jezreel is not the subject of **Say**, then a direct reference to Hosea's other children as the addressees is excluded. Rather, their names are treated as having been transferred to the people, in line with the interpretations given in 1:6 and 1:9, and as about to be changed to designations which reflect the renewal of God's relationship with them. The subject of the plural imperative **Say** has been differently identified: some (e.g. Targ.) think of special representatives of God (e.g. prophets) who are commissioned to bring this message of restoration to the rest of the community; others (e.g. Wolff) think that it is northern Israel which is to bring this good news to Judah (an unlikely scenario, surely) or vice versa (Rudolph, Jeremias). Given the lack of any specific indication, the most likely view is that it is the community as a whole which is to declare the titles which have been once again conferred upon it (Mays). For "brothers" and "sisters" in the sense of "each other" cf. Lev. 25:46, Neh. 5:8: the reference to both sexes dignifies the status of the women members of the community as well as underlining the allusion to the original story of Hosea's children.

It is notable that in this verse, which is probably a separate saying from the two that precede it, only the names of the second and third of Hosea's children are taken up and reversed.

The reason may be that these names expressed the loss of the people's status, without which there could be no continuation of their religion, whereas the latter was able to integrate what was signified by the name Jezreel in its original interpretation (i.e. accusation and judgment) into its traditions and beliefs (cf. the Deuteronomistic History). This did not of course prevent a new significance being given to Jezreel as well by other prophetic voices (cf. 1:11 and 2:22–23).

YAHWEH'S MARRIAGE: ORACLES OF JUDGMENT AND RENEWAL

2:2–23 (Heb. 2:4–25)

The boundaries of this section are determined more by literary genre than by harmony of subject-matter. The transition from narrative (with associated sayings) in 1:2–2:1 to this long series of prophetic sayings is very clear, as is the reversion to narrative in 3:1. But while 2:2–20 have a certain unity based on their use of the marriage motif (though even these verses, as will appear, are likely to have been composed in a number of stages), vv. 21–23 are related to chs. 1 and 14 rather than the earlier part of ch. 2, and make only a passing allusion to the marriage motif. This section is also marked off by its introductory formula in v. 21, but the latter appears again in v. 16 and is a first indication that vv. 2–20 are themselves not an original unity. It is common also to place a division after v. 13, where **says the Lord** can be ascribed the same concluding function as it has in 11:11 and in other prophetic books, and to contrast 2–13 as oracles of judgment with 14–23 as oracles of salvation (Rudolph, Jeremias). But this overlooks the close links between 6–7 and 14–15 and the very mixed character of 2–13, which is by no means a straightforward oracle of judgment. Moreover, **Therefore** at the beginning of v. 14 makes a strong link with the preceding verses.

Further examination of the chapter must therefore proceed from the recognition of these three sub-sections: 2–15, 16–20, 21–23.

(a) **2: 2–15.** It is clear in the later verses of this section that the **I** who speaks is Yahweh and that the unfaithful wife stands for

Israel. It has sometimes been held that in vv. 2–5 (or 2–7) it is
Hosea who is addressing his own children about the behaviour
of their mother Gomer (so Rowley, *Men of God*, p. 70, following
R. Gordis, *HUCA* 25 (1954), p. 22). The distinction between
mother and children is supposed to require this. In the detailed
commentary an explanation for this distinction is offered which is
compatible with Yahweh being the speaker from the beginning.
There is certainly no indication after v. 5 or v. 7 that the speaker
and addressee have changed. Further, if our argument in the
notes on ch. 1 is correct, Hosea never married Gomer and
therefore she could not have been described as if she were
his wife. The passage, like many in Hosea, alternates between
accusations of infidelity (vv. 2a, 4b–5, 8, 13b) and other types of
saying, but the diversity of the latter is extraordinary. First there
is a call to repentance, cast in the form of a "proposal to reach a
settlement of the dispute" (Wolff), vv. 2b, 3, 4a. The other three
non-accusatory sections all begin with **Therefore**, and indicate
how Yahweh intends to respond to Israel's unfaithfulness, but
they differ considerably in their contents. According to vv. 6–7
he will block off the way to Israel's **lovers** (the false gods), which
will bring her to her senses so that she returns to him. Vv. 9–13a
speak of the devastation of the crops, the end of cultic worship
and "punishment". Finally, in vv. 14–15, Yahweh promises a new,
loving approach to Israel, through which, apparently following
the devastation already spoken of, she will once more gain
possession of the land of Canaan and as a result respond
positively (**answer**) to Yahweh. It is inconceivable that these
four sections originated at one and the same time. In addition
vv. 6–7, which is very closely related to 14–15 (see the first
note on v. 14), awkwardly interrupts the connection of thought
between v. 5 and v. 8. Some commentators and versions therefore
transpose 6–7 to follow v. 13 (Weiser; Rudolph, pp. 68–69; JB),
but this does not produce a smooth sequence of thought, nor
has a convincing explanation of these verses' removal to their
present position been proposed. The measures which Yahweh
takes show an increasing severity (in the first three cases) and
reflect the growing seriousness of Israel's position. As a completed
text the four sections correspond plausibly to a retrospective view
of Yahweh's dealings with faithless Israel; first warning, then

corrective measures, then punishment, and finally renewal. This must correspond to four stages in the growth of the passage, which in all probability can be correlated with the development of Hosea's message as it is evident elsewhere in the book, a development in which the prophet bore witness to Yahweh's word in a rapidly changing political situation. But in view of the awkwardness of vv. 6–7 in their present position, it is unlikely that the four sections originated in the order in which they now appear. We may suppose that the original oracle consisted of vv. 2–3 only, and that it represents a rare example of Hosea's earliest preaching, prior to the unqualified rejection of Israel in 1:6 and 1:9. When this message was rejected (for this theme cf. 4:16; 5:4; 11:5), it was extended by the addition of announcements of judgment (4a, 9–13a), which include (in vv. 9b–10) the fulfilment of the threat made in v. 3, and an elaboration of the accusation of infidelity (4b–5, 8, 13b). The parallels between this section and 9:1–9 (and also 4:1–5:7) deserve note. Into it were later inserted 6–7, which reflect a corrective view of punishment that seems to have been held by Hosea around the time of the first Assyrian conquest of Israel c. 733 (cf. 5:15). Hosea's subsequent reversion to a proclamation of unconditional judgment (cf. ch. 7) seems not to have left any mark on this passage, but the hope of a new beginning, a new Exodus, as Yahweh's ultimate response to Israel's infidelity (vv. 14–15), fits in well with the final stage in Hosea's preaching as reflected especially in 11:8–9, 11 and 14:4. At this time (and especially in the hands of Hosea's disciples) the call to repentance in 2–3 gained a new prominence as an essential part of the prophetic message to the remnants of Israel. There is thus no need to attribute the theological and literary development of this passage to anyone but Hosea, and its inclusion in the introductory collection of his sayings in ch. 1–3 reflects its unique character as a text that he added to throughout his long ministry.

The portrayal of Yahweh's relationship to Israel as a marriage may owe something to mythological ideas about a sacral marriage between a deity and the earth (Wolff, p. 35). If so, Hosea uses the image to attack paganism on its own ground: Yahweh is Israel's true husband, and he, not Baal, gives her the fruit of the land. But it is not certain that these particular

ideas were current in Hosea's time (cf. the brief comment above
on 1:2), and the image should probably be credited to Hosea's
remarkably creative use of language in the formulation of his
message.

(b) **2: 16–20.** The divine I is maintained in this section and
reinforced by **says the Lord** in the introductory formula. But
in the Heb. Israel is referred to by a variety of pronouns: "you"
(fem. sing) in v. 16, "her" in v. 17, "them" in v. 18, and "you"
(fem. sing) again in vv. 19–20. The feminine forms appear in the
verses whose content is most closely related to vv. 2–15. Such
variation is occasionally found within that passage, where it does
not necessarily indicate secondary matter (see the notes on vv. 6
and 8). Here it is more disturbing, and from the LXX to RSV,
JB and REB translations have smoothed out the unevenness by
emendation. But to do this obscures what may be important
evidence about the passage's composition. It should first be
borne in mind that these verses, like the end of the previous
section, speak of the restoration of Israel, largely in terms of the
marriage-image (vv. 16, 17 (cf. **her**), 19–20). Further, the use of
on that day in 1:5 to introduce a further exegetical reflection on
the preceding verse should lead us to expect a similar relationship
here. In fact v. 16 can very plausibly be seen as an elaboration of
she shall answer as in the days of her youth in v. 15, and vv.
19–20 express in different terms the same essential truths as vv.
14–15 do as a whole. The possibility certainly exists (is this why
"says the Lord" is added to the introductory formula?) that both
these sayings are from Hosea himself in his late period. But in
view of the change to direct address (**you**), they are unlikely to
have been originally attached to vv. 14–15. Their position, if not
their composition, must be due to a redactor, who saw them as
an interpretation of those verses. It may well have been he who
composed v. 17, echoing the third-person form of the passage
on which he was commenting, to express what v. 16 does not
explicitly say – that is, that in her new relationship with Yahweh
Israel would abandon altogether the worship of Baal, which had
been the cause of her earlier punishment (v. 13). V. 18 appears to
be more loosely attached to the context, since it makes no direct
reference to the marriage-image, and the repeated **on that day**

looks like a further connecting link. In the detailed notes we
have drawn attention to some ways in which the language and
theology of v. 18 seem to be typical of sixth-century literature. It
seems likely that it was added by someone who was familiar with
the salvation-oracles of Ezekiel (which are themselves indebted
in various ways to passages in Hosea) and who was trying to
supply what he saw to be a missing element in the older book's
account of the blessings to come (Jeremias, pp. 49–50). Similar
additions were made in exilic times to the books of Amos, Micah
and Isaiah (see also the notes below on 3:5 and 11:10).

(c) **2: 21–23.** Taken first of all by themselves, without what
is probably a secondary introductory formula, these verses
comprise a promise of salvation which falls into two parts, which
speak respectively of the restoration of the fertility of the land
(21–22) and the re-establishment of Israel as Yahweh's people
in the land (23). Both these themes are paralleled elsewhere in
the book of Hosea (1:10–2:1; 6:1–3; 11:11; 14:4–8) as well as
in other prophetic books, but unlike most of vv. 16–20, they
do not have an immediate connection with the main theme of
ch. 2. They are not so much drawn out of it as brought into
harmony with it by a systematizing process which seeks to make
a comprehensive presentation of Hosea's message of salvation.
Probably, therefore, their appearance here is to be attributed
to a redactor who was seeking to combine together ch. 1 and
ch. 2; he may already have had before him the whole collection
of Hosean material in the book. The two sections of the oracle are
neatly joined together by the etymological link between **Jezreel** in
v. 22 and **I will sow him** (Heb. "her") in v. 23 (see the detailed
notes), but it is no longer clear whether this is a "catchword" link
joining two originally independent, probably Hosean, sayings or
a deliberate exegetical move which extended vv. 21–22 so as to
include a reversal of the names of Hosea's other two children. The
original "her" of the Heb. makes best sense if at least the first line
of v. 23 was written specifically for its present context to cement
the link with vv. 2–20. In any event, it is likely that vv. 21–22
(apart from the introductory formula) represent an originally
independent saying which has a particularly close connection
with 6:3 and 14:8. The redactor who placed these verses here

no doubt saw vv. 21–22 as elaborating the promise of v. 15 that
the conditions described in vv. 9 (cf. **grain**, **wine** there) and 12
would be reversed, while v. 23 reconciles the promise of a renewed
relationship between Yahweh and Israel (vv. 14, 19–20) with the
judgment-bearing names given to Hosea's children in ch. 1.

The chapter thus bears witness to a process of reinterpretation
and systematization of Hosea's message which began already
during his own lifetime. To a small degree that message also
seems to have been integrated with that of later prophecy (v.
18), but unlike the surrounding chapters (cf. 1:7 and 3:5) there
are no overt allusions to Judaean themes. The view that all or
most of the oracles of salvation in this chapter are secondary
and late in origin (e.g. Harper and recently Jeremias and Yee)
imposes, without good reason, a strait-jacket on Hosea's thinking
and does not do justice to the close connections between his words
of judgment and salvation, both here and in ch. 11. On literary
aspects of the chapter as a whole see, e.g., D. J. A. Clines, *Studia
Biblica 1978*, vol. 1 (JSOTSS 11), Sheffield, 1979, pp. 83–103, and
B. Renaud, *RSR* 54 (1980), 1–20.

Early post-biblical interpretation is reflected in some adapta-
tions of the language to city life in LXX (Wolff: see the notes on
v. 5), in the Qumran commentary's identification of the **lovers**
with the Gentiles rather than with other gods (4QpHos[a]: Vermes,
DSSE, p. 230) and in Paul's application of v. 23 to the election of
the Gentiles (Rom. 9:25).

2:2.Plead ... plead: Heb. *rîbû* does not mean "plead with" or
"entreat": the meaning here, as the parallel **accuse** in 4:4 makes
clear, is "rebuke" (NIV, JPS).

With your mother: **your mother** is not Gomer but the whole
people (in practice the population of the northern kingdom must
originally have been in mind), who are not always sharply
distinguished from the land in which they live (cf. 1:2). The
identity of the "you" whom Yahweh commands to rebuke the
nation is less clear, but it is probably not all "the individual
members of Israel" (Mays): a more specific audience is likely
to be in mind. Targ., as in v. 1, thinks of prophets, but it is, in
the absence of any clear indication, more likely that Hosea was

calling on some lay members of the community to join him in denouncing the rampant paganism of his day.

for she is not my wife, and I am not her husband: These words have often been understood as a formula employed in divorce proceedings (Robinson, Wolff; M. J. Geller, *JSJ* 8 (1977), 139–48). Such evidence as there is, however, is against this view. Even in post-exilic times different formulae were normally used (cf. Rudolph, p. 65; Jeremias, p. 41). As a declaration by Yahweh a divorce-formula would in any case contradict his subsequent attempt to prevent a final break-up of the marriage. The words should be taken as an accusation (which is expected after *rîbû*: see the note above), stating the *de facto* abandonment of the marriage relationship by the wife, i.e. Israel: for the two-part formula in a marriage-contract at Elephantine see *ANET*, p. 222 (Cowley no. 15:4). The emphasis falls on the pronouns **my** and **I**: she has in effect become another's **wife** (lit. woman), and he is now her **husband** (lit. man). Cf. v. 7: **my first husband**. NEB curiously turns the clause into a question: "Is she not my wife . . . ?"

that she put away . . . : The purpose of the rebuke is here not condemnation, but reformation and (v. 3) avoidance of the due consequences of unfaithfulness. Here at any rate it is correct to speak of "a proposal to achieve reconciliation" (Wolff).

harlotry . . . adultery: The words are plural in the Heb., as is common with abstracts, probably to express an intense, enduring quality (cf. *GK* §124e). The **face** and **breasts** are then mentioned for their erotic functions (cf. NEB, "those wanton looks"). But they were also places where jewellery was worn (cf. Ezek. 16:12; Ca. 1:13), and it is possible that it is the removal of these aids to seduction that is demanded (abstract for concrete: cf. W. G. E. Watson, *Classical Hebrew Poetry* (JSOTSS 26), Sheffield, 1984, p. 314).

2:3. lest I strip her naked . . . : The call to self-reformation is followed by a warning of the impending consequences of Israel's wrongdoing which only it can avert. Stripping a woman naked for adultery is mentioned again in vv. 9–10 as well as in some other prophetic passages (Jer. 13:22, 26–27; Ezek. 16:37–39; 23:29; Nah. 3:4–5), and it was apparently a punishment which the wronged husband himself could inflict, prior to or instead of the death penalty imposed by law (Lev. 20:10; Dt. 22:22):

cf. R. Gordis, *HUCA* 25 (1954), 20–22, and H. McKeating, *JSOT* 11 (1979), 61–62. It may symbolize the renunciation of the husband's responsibility to clothe his wife as well as to feed her (cf. Exod. 21:10, and the similar provision in *ANET*, p. 160, para. 27). Such a sanction is known from legal texts elsewhere in the ancient Near East, where it sometimes at least was part of the procedure for divorce. The alleged parallel to the custom in the curses of the Sefire treaty-text (Mays, p. 38: cf. D. B. Hillers, *Treaty-Curses and the OT Prophets* (Bib et Or 16), Rome, 1964, p. 58ff.) is very dubious. The meaning here probably includes both the repudiation of Israel by Yahweh and her abandonment to the mockery of other nations (for shaming as a Hosean theme cf. 4:19; 10:6): deprivation of the products of the land (as in v. 9) may also be implied, but this is more clearly in mind in the second half of the verse.

and make her like a wilderness ... and slay her with thirst: In the thought of the prophet the object of Yahweh's wrath, symbolized by the faithless wife, is alternately the land and, once again, the people. The fruitful land will become a desert, that no longer bears crops (4:3; 8:7; 9:2); and there will be a devastating drought (13:15).

2:4. Upon her children also: The Heb. lacks **also**. The **children** stand for the population, to whose doom the prophet now returns, no doubt with his own symbolically named children particularly in mind (cf. especially 1:6). It is not easy to specify the force of the distinction between mother and **children**, unless real **children** are meant, as in 9:12–16 and 10:14. It seems to reflect an awareness of the fact that the behaviour and the destiny of individuals is very largely shaped by the community to which they belong, while they nevertheless possess a consciousness of their own and (v. 2) even the ability and indeed the duty to challenge what passes for normative custom in society. The same dual perception is expressed in other ways, for example in the alternation in Deuteronomy between second-person singular ("thou") and second-person plural ("you") pronouns to refer to Israel.

children of harlotry: As in 1:2 (see the note) the phrase indicates the nature of the parents' relationship (cf. v. 5) rather than, as Wolff thinks, the character of the **children**. In Hosea's eyes Israelite society was institutionally unfaithful to Yahweh, and each new generation was branded with the same mark from birth. Hosea denotes the same uncontrollable tendency towards apostasy elsewhere by speaking of a **spirit of harlotry** which leads the people astray (4:12; 5:4).

2:5. I will go after my lovers, who gave me my bread and my water: lovers is no doubt a euphemism, perhaps drawn from contemporary speech, for a prostitute's "clients". As the following description makes clear, they symbolize the fertility divinities, to whose activity the crops, the rain and the growth of the flocks were attributed in the current ideology. They will have included Baal, Asherah, Ashtart and perhaps the deity Sheger, now known from the Balaam text from Tell Deir 'Alla (J. Hoftijzer, *Aramaic Texts from Deir Alla*, Leiden, 1976). Although Hosea normally refers only to Baal, a reference to a goddess has been detected in 4:18–19 (see the notes there).

my drink: So also JB, NJPS, NIV. Since **water** has already been mentioned, the reference is presumably to wine (cf. vv. 8–9). NEB, "my perfumes", apparently reads *nišqî*, as originally proposed by Sellin (cf. 1 Kg. 10:25), although *HTOT*, p. 245, notes no divergence from MT's *šiqûyāy*. The latter word is well attested (Ps. 102:9; Prov. 3:8) and there is no good reason to change it.

my wool and my flax: As Wolff notes (p. 30), LXX substitutes manufactured products, "garments and linen cloth", for the raw materials. This is an interesting example of the adaptation of the texts for a city community (see also the note on v. 15). NIV and JPS, "linen" instead of **flax**, show the same tendency.

2:6–7. Therefore ... : As often in prophecy (though rarely in Hosea) Heb. *lākēn* introduces Yahweh's response to the sins of the people. It is no longer a mere appeal for reform, as in v. 2, but nor is it yet, as in vv. 9ff., comprehensive punishment: it is diversion, by a blocking-off of the way that leads to **her lovers**, which is intended to lead to a return to Yahweh. The same policy is encountered in 3:3–5. Just how Yahweh would bar the way to the other gods is not specified here: perhaps Hosea expected some specific disaster to befall the sanctuaries (cf. 8:5; 10:2), or perhaps a failure in the crops would have been seen in such terms (Mays). Similar imagery is used of God afflicting men in

Job 19:8 and Lam. 3:7–9, but the point made there is somewhat different.

I will hedge up: Heb. adds "behold" (cf. RV).

her way: MT reads *dark^{e}kā*, "your way" (cf. Targ., Vulg.). But the similar-sounding reading implied by LXX and Syr. (*darkāh*) is generally followed, because it maintains the third-person reference to Israel which is characteristic of the passage. Even so, MT may be right, as several other passages in Hosea have an isolated line with a direct address to the people (cf. 8:5 and the passages referred to there).

and I will build a wall against her: Literally MT means "and I will wall up her wall", but the possessive suffix sometimes expresses a relation that is yet to be established (cf. *GK* §135m). Using as an object a word which is etymologically related to the verb is a frequent Heb. idiom (*GK* §117r). NEB, "and obstruct her path with a wall", reads *dargāh*, "her path", for *g^{e}dērāh*, "her wall", citing LXX's rendering in support (*HTOT*, p. 245). It presumably assumes the existence of a word *dereg* in Hebrew, which does not occur elsewhere, on the basis of similar words in Akkadian and Arabic which mean "path". But this is highly speculative and there is no justification, even in LXX, for departing from MT. The lemma of 4QpHos^a actually omits these words altogether (cf. *DJD* V, p. 31), but the commentator was not obliged to comment on every phrase.

but shall not find them: Kuhnigk (p. 16) renders "shall not reach them", comparing the use of *mẓ'* in Ugaritic (cf. also *HAL*, p. 586). But after **seek**, **find** (the normal meaning of *māṣā'* in Hebrew) is undoubtedly correct. The first half of v. 7 is omitted in the lemma of 4QpHos^a (compare the previous note), and in this case it is possible that the commentator was either using a shorter, defective form of the text or accidentally passed over a section: the last two words of the Heb. of v. 6 (**cannot find . . .**) are identical to the Heb. of **shall not find them** (*lō' timṣā'*), and omission in such cases is quite frequent (homoeoteleuton).

JB places vv. 6–7 after v. 13, thus bringing together the verses in which Yahweh says that he will take action to bring about Israel's repentance. This "tidying up" of the text is favoured by several commentators (e.g. Weiser, Rudolph), but it is both unjustified and unnecessary (see the introduction to this section).

2:8. And she did not know: Heb. w^e (**And**) often means "but", and this fits the sequence of thought here better. **she** is represented by an emphatic pronoun in the Heb., the force of which is well brought out by JB's addition of "not she". For **know** JB (cf. NIV) has "acknowledge", which corresponds to the frequent use of Heb. *yāda*^{c} for an appropriate response to what is perceived as well as the perception itself (cf. *TDOT*, vol. 5, p. 462, and the note below on 2:20) and provides a more solid basis for the judgment pronounced in v. 9.

the grain, the wine and the oil: These are the classic products of the land (cf. D. Baly, *The Geography of Palestine*, London, 1957, pp. 97–98) and they are frequently mentioned together in the Bible, especially in Deuteronomy (7:13; 11:14; 12:17; 14:23; 18:4; 28:51). But the combination is a much older one, as a Ugaritic example shows (CTA 16:3:13–16: *CML*, p. 98). **wine** (Heb. *tîrôš*) is the word for new, but not unfermented, wine (see the note on 4:11).

silver and gold: These metals are not native to Canaan (cf. Dt. 8:9) and the reference must be to their acquisition by trade, for which see, in relation to an earlier period, 1 Kg. 9:28; 10:14–15, 22, and the ostracon from Tell Qasileh recording "gold of Ophir for Beth-horon" (*IR*, no. 42). Probably the precious metals were obtained in exchange for agricultural products, and so indirectly they were **lavished** upon Israel by Yahweh's blessing on the land. LXX and 4QpHos^a (*DJD* V, p. 31) seem to have known slightly different Heb. texts here, but the variations are not significant.

which they used for Baal: For this use of *'āśāh* (**used**) Exod. 38:24 and 2 Chr. 24:7 offer possible parallels. The Heb. might also mean "which they offered to Baal" (cf. Exod. 10:25; Lev. 14:30; 2 Kg. 17:32) or, less likely, "of which they have made Baals" (Vss., JB, Wolff, Mays). The use of the plural form **they** instead of **she** is exceptional and is often seen as evidence that these words are a later addition (Wellhausen, Wolff etc.) or that the text should be emended to read "and made gold (and) not Baal" (H. J. van Dijk, *Ezekiel's Prophecy on Tyre (Ez 26:1–28:19). A New Approach* (Bib et Or 20), Rome, 1968, p. 66; cf. Rudolph). But they contain nothing alien to Hosea, and the prophet may have temporarily abandoned allegory to make his accusation

more concrete. **Baal** was originally a word which meant "lord"
(CTA 6.6.57: *CML*, p. 81), "owner" (e.g. Exod. 21:28–29) or
"husband" (e.g. Exod. 21:3), but it had become already in the
Late Bronze Age a title for various gods, particularly the West
Semitic storm god Hadad (cf. also the use of "Bel" as a title for
Marduk). In one Ugaritic text Hadad is given the fuller title "lord
(Baal) of the earth" (CTA 3.1.3–4: *CML*, p. 46), and elsewhere
he is sometimes described as "lord (Baal) of Zaphon", his sacred
mountain. In the OT he is normally referred to simply as "the
lord" (*habba'al*), but see the note on v. 13 on the combinations
which sometimes occur. The Ugaritic texts have added greatly
to our knowledge of the mythology concerning Baal of which the
OT gives few details: see the Excursus on pp. 91–94.

2:9. Therefore: This time the consequence of Israel's wrongdoing (v. 8) is, as it so often is in prophecy, a punishment which
has a special appropriateness (cf. P. D. Miller, *Sin and Judgment*,
passim): the people who did not recognize the true source of their
material goods are not worthy to retain them.

my grain . . . my wine . . . : The echo of the repeated **my** of
v. 5, with a subtle change of reference from Israel to Yahweh,
is no doubt deliberate. The loss of food, clothing and oil (cf. v.
12) appears among the curses of an Assyrian treaty with Tyre
(*ANET*, p. 534) as a deprivation of the essentials for life, but
a much older legal text indicates that they were also what any
husband was expected to provide for his wife (*ANET*, p. 160
(para. 27)).

in its time . . . in its season: Presumably harvest-time is
meant, and the prophet explicitly contradicts the expectation
associated with this **time** (Ps. 104:27; 145:15).

which were to cover her nakedness: For the abbreviated
underlying Heb. construction see *GK* §114k and 155e. LXX and
4QpHos[a] (*DJD* V, p. 32) read "so as not cover . . .", adding a
letter and producing an easier construction. But MT probably
has the original reading.

2:10. Now I will uncover her lewdness: Neither **lewdness**
nor "shame" (JB, NJPS, REB, *HAL*: the last in the sense of
pudenda) exactly captures the meaning of biblical Heb. *nablût*.
There is no compelling reason to separate it from the word-group
which centres on the adjective *nābāl* (on this see W. M. W. Roth,

VT 10 (1960), 394–409; *THAT*, vol. 2, 26–31). It is applied not only to sexual crimes (Gen. 34:6; Dt. 22:21) but to senseless, unruly behaviour of any kind (cf. Jos. 7:15; 1 Sam. 25:25; Jer. 17:11). It carries an overtone of contempt and is readily applied to those outside the community (Ps. 74:18; Job 30:8): "mindless, disgraceful behaviour" comes close to what is meant. Yahweh will demonstrate just how despicable Israel is in the presence of those whom she has sought to attract.

2:11. And I will put an end to all her mirth . . . : Hosea's view of Israel's regular worship is that it is self-indulgent and is disowned by Yahweh (cf. 6:6; 9:1–6); consequently, far from offering protection from disaster, it is itself destined to be brought to an end. This is very close to Amos' teaching (cf. 4:5; 5:5, 21–3), but for Hosea the infection of the cult by devotion to Baal is an additional reason for its unacceptability (v. 13; cf. 9:1). **mirth** has no special cultic connotations, and so serves well to express the distortion of a true attitude to worship. The occasions of worship are mentioned in an increasing order of frequency. **feasts** (*ḥaggîm*) are the annual pilgrimage festivals (cf. NEB, NIV), such as the feast of Tabernacles and the Feast of Unleavened Bread (cf. on 9:5). **new moons** and **sabbaths** are mentioned several times in pre-exilic texts (cf. 2 Kg. 4:23; Am. 8:5), from which it is clear that they were days not only of rest but also of worship, presumably at the local shrines. These passages firmly contradict the theory that the sabbath was an institution derived from Babylonian religion at the time of the exile; nor is there any basis for the view that in pre-exilic times "sabbath" meant "full moon" (on this cf. R. de Vaux, *Ancient Israel*, 2nd ed., London, 1965, pp. 476–78 (cf. NEB mg.)). The repeated **her** contrasts with the frequent assertion that days of worship are "for" (that is, belong to,) Yahweh (Exod. 12:11, 14; 20:10; Lev. 23:3–4): no more emphatic way could be found for expressing Yahweh's repudiation of the whole cultic system.

and all her appointed feasts: The *waw* (**and**) is explanatory (*GK* §154a, note) and is best left untranslated (NJPS, NIV).

2:12. JB and NEB remove this whole verse to before v. 11, following a suggestion popular some decades ago (cf. Nowack, Harper), to create a supposedly more logical sequence of thought.

This is not necessary and the theory does not explain why the imagined transposition of verses took place.

my hire: The unusual form of **hire** (Heb. *'etnāh*: cf. the note on **hired** in 8:8–9) may be a dialectal variation. Its choice here could be dictated by the possibility of a word-play with **fig trees** (Heb. *tᵉ'ēnāh*): so Jeremias.

2:13. And I will punish her: For the idea of punishment cf. 1:4; 4:9; 8:13; 9:7, 9 and the notes on these passages.

the feast days: Literally "the days", not either of the technical words used in v. 11.

the Baals: So also in v. 17 and 11:2, whereas in 2:8 and 13:1 the singular is used (cf. also the notes on 2:16 and 9:10). The god Baal (on whom see the note on v. 8) was worshipped in the Levant under a great many names, some of which survive also in the form of place-names, referring to the location of a shrine (compare St Mary's, St John's). Hosea himself refers to Baal–Peor (9:10: see the note): for others in the OT see *IDB*, vol. 1, 331–32. In Phoenicia the worship of Baal–Shamem ("the lord of heaven") and Baal–Melqart ("Baal the king of the city") was widespread. It is easy to see how in the eyes of its opponents, such as prophets (1 Kg. 18:18; Jer. 2:23; 9:13) and the OT historians (e.g. Jg. 2:11; 2 Chr. 17:3), this religion would seem to envisage a plurality of **Baals**, and indeed some of its adherents may have so regarded it. But, as with other comparable examples, to which must now be added Yahwism itself (cf. J. A. Emerton, *ZAW* 94 (1982), 2–20, with reference to the texts from Kuntillet Ajerud), the names will in fact have represented a multiplicity of manifestations of one and the same god (cf. Mays, p. 43). It is less likely that **Baals** is a general term for all gods other than Yahweh (Wolff).

when she burned incense: As in 11:2 (see the note) the Heb. is *qtr*, which is rendered more generally "make offerings" in 4:13. The verb can refer to any kind of cultic action that produces smoke, and JB and NEB see a reference to "burnt offerings" here. The verb is in the Hiphil form, which makes a specific reference to incense more likely here (but not inevitable: cf. *BDB*, p. 883) than in 4:13 and 11:2, where the Piel is used. But given Hosea's preoccupation with sacrifice generally as a futile act of worship, it would be surprising if his criticism here did not include a reference to it. "made smoke for them" is suitably unspecific.

On incense and its uses see K. Nielsen, *Incense in Ancient Israel* (VTSuppl 38), Leiden, 1986.

and decked herself with her ring and jewelry: Elsewhere in the OT such adornment is generally mentioned without specific reference to participation in worship (Gen. 35:4 is exceptional), although no doubt men as well as women did "dress up" for the big festivals. It is best seen here as part of the symbolic depiction of Israel as a flirtatious woman (compare the next line, which need not have in mind a cultic procession following an image of the god (Wolff)). Archaeological evidence illustrates the many forms that were current: cf. *BRL*, pp. 282–89; A. Wilkinson, *Ancient Egyptian Jewellery*, London, 1971.

and forgot me: me is emphatically placed before the verb, as NIV excellently renders: "but me she forgot". Forgetting Yahweh or his law (4:6; 8:14; 13:6) implies not just a lapse of memory but culpable neglect (compare the note on 7:2 and *THAT* vol. 2, 898–904). It became a common charge in later preaching (see the passages cited in the note on 13:6).

says the LORD: This common prophetic formula (*ne'um yahweh*) occurs only four times in Hosea, twice at the end of a passage (2:13; 11:11) and twice at the beginning of a saying after the words "in that day" (2:16, 21: see the note on 2:16). Its primary function is to assert the divine origin of the text in which it occurs (on its origin in early prophecy see F. Baumgärtel, *ZAW* 73 (1961), 277–90), but it can also assist in the sub-division of prophetic material (see the introduction to this section).

2:14. Therefore, behold, I will allure her: The verse begins with the same two particles as v. 6, so that there is connection of form as well as of content between them. **behold** (*hinnēh*) is used in Hosea, apart from these two verses, only in 9:6, where the idiom is different. Here it is used to draw attention to Yahweh's unexpected action, just as rhetorical questions are used in 11:8. The connection indicated by **Therefore** is probably once again with the statement of Israel's guilt (v. 13): but now the divine response is no longer stern corrective measures (vv. 6–7), nor outright punishment (vv. 9–13), but a tender word of love leading to a fresh beginning. **allure** (*pittāh*) is a word that means "make compliant", with a variety of nuances: persuasion (Prov. 25:15), deceit (2 Sam. 3:25; Ezek. 14:9), enticement (Prov. 1:10; 1 Kg.

22:20–22) and, in a sexual context, seduction (Exod. 22:15). In the context the last of these comes readily to mind, but it is qualified by the fact that according to the imagery Yahweh is Israel's true husband, and by the following statement that he will **speak tenderly to her**. There is a curious parallel in Jg. 19:2–3, where (in MT) a Levite's concubine turns to prostitution and deserts him, and he seeks to win her back with tender words of persuasion.

and bring her into the wilderness: It is clear from the next verse that the prophet's thought here is typological: Yahweh intends to begin again with Israel in the same way as he had done in the past. Several passages later in the book speak of judgment in terms of a return to Egypt (7:16; 8:13; 9:3; 11:5) and one looks beyond this to a new Exodus (11:11). It is doubtful whether that particular pattern can be presupposed here, so that to **bring her into the wilderness** (or, as it may be translated, to "lead her in the wilderness" (cf. Jer. 2:6)) would already refer to a deliverance from the trials to come. More likely **the wilderness** itself here represents judgment, and perhaps exile, but in such a way that its potential as a place of purification is already in mind, since so many positive traditions about Israel's past were associated with it (2:15; 13:5). Such removal is well suited to be the first stage of the "allurement" which Yahweh intends.

and speak tenderly to her: The second stage comprises a new word from Yahweh. The Heb. is literally "and speak upon her heart", an idiom which can stand for "comfort" (Isa. 40:2: so NEB here). But it is also used in a sexual context (Gen. 34:3; Jg. 19:3) of a lover's winsome words, and this seems particularly appropriate here.

2:15. And there I will give her her vineyards: This sounds like the miracle of "grapes in the desert" (Weiser: see the note on 9:10). But Heb. has "from there" (NJPS), making **the wilderness** the place of the giving but not of **her vineyards**, presumably those in the land of Canaan, which had been laid waste in punishment (v. 12). This corresponds typologically to the original "promise of the land" given in the wilderness (Exod. 3:7–8, 17): cf. Vollmer, *Geschichtliche Rückblicke*, p. 87.

and make the Valley of Achor a door of hope: Hosea is fond of using place-names to recall episodes in his people's

history (compare Jezreel in 1:4, Baal-peor in 9:10 and Gibeah
in 10:9, among many examples), and here he will certainly have
had in mind the story related in Joshua 7, which explains why
"to this day" **the Valley of Achor** ("the valley of trouble") is
so called. This same place, which lay on the way into Canaan,
Yahweh says he will **make** into **a door of hope** (*petaḥ tiqwāh*).
In other words, the new entry into the land will surpass the
earlier one by being free from disobedience and the "trouble"
which it brought: instead the people will have **hope**, even in
this inhospitable place (cf. Isa. 65:10). The related verb occurs
in 12:6: see the note on **wait** there. The words are quoted in the
War Scroll (1QM) 11:9 (Vermes, *DSSE*, p. 138). NJPS reads
"a plowland of hope", but this meaning of *petaḥ* is not attested
elsewhere. The precise location of **the Valley of Achor** has been
a matter of dispute. The Joshua narrative implies that it was near
where the Israelites had their "base camp", which is elsewhere
placed at Gilgal near Jericho (Jos. 4:19; 5:10; 9:6; 10:6 etc.):
on the location of Gilgal see the note on 4:15. The boundary
descriptions of Judah and Benjamin (Joshua 15:5-8; 18:16-19)
confirm this, but the detailed information which they provide
has been variously interpreted (cf. F. M. Abel, *Géographie de la
Palestine*, Paris, 1933-38, vol. 1, pp. 406-07; Wolff, pp. 42-43;
Z. Kallai, *Historical Geography of the Bible*, Jerusalem, 1986,
pp. 118-21, with bibliography). Most scholars now favour
el-Buqeiah, near Khirbet Mird, a shallow valley about ten
miles south of Jericho, but Wolff notes several difficulties in this
and prefers Wadi Nuweime, three miles north-west of Jericho
and much closer to the likely site of Gilgal: so recently H.-D.
Neef, *ZDPV* 100 (1984), 91-107. Much depends on the weight
given to the different pieces of evidence, and it is arguable that
neither Jos. 7 nor the present passage is so concerned to preserve
precise geographical detail as Jos. 15:5-8, and that the latter
passage favours neither of these alternatives but, perhaps, the
lower part of Wadi Qilt.

    and there she shall answer: It is typical of Hosea to look for
a response to Yahweh's new act of mercy: cf. 2:16, 20, 23; 3:5.
NIV (cf. Vulg., Saadya, Ibn Ezra, Kimchi etc.) renders "she will
sing", deriving Heb. *'ānᵉtāh* from *'ānāh* IV, which is used in Exod.
15:21 and Num. 21:17 of Israel's response to Yahweh's help. But

note the recurrence of the "answer" motif in 2:21–22. Less likely suggestions are that *'ānᵉtāh* includes the idea of "follow" (cf. Wolff, p. 43; L. Delekat, *VT* 14 (1964), 41–42), and that it means "love" (A. Deem, *JSS* 23 (1978), 25–30, working back from the use of *ᶜānāh* III Piel for "rape").

as in the days of her youth ... : That is, before she was corrupted by temptations to apostasy after the settlement in the land of Canaan (9:10, 15). The picture of the wilderness period as a "golden age", when Israel lived in close harmony with Yahweh, is also found in Jeremiah, who speaks of her "devotion" (2:2: Heb. *ḥesed*, on which see the note below on 2:19). But it is an idealized picture, to judge from the "murmuring" tradition in the Pentateuch (cf. C. Barth, VTSuppl 15 (1966), 14–23; G. W. Coats, *Rebellion in the Wilderness*, Nashville, 1968).

... when she came out of the land of Egypt: Other direct references to the Exodus tradition occur in 11:1; 12:9, 13; 13:4, and elsewhere the motifs of a "return to Egypt" (7:16; 8:13; 9:3; 11:5) and a "new Exodus" (11:11) occur. The prominence of this tradition in Hosea corresponds to its central place in north Israelite Yahwism (cf. 1 Kg. 12:28; Pss. 80, 81: von Rad, *OT Theology*, vol. 1, p. 73; Clements, *Prophecy and Covenant*, pp. 46–49; Neef, *Heilstraditionen*).

2:16. And in that day, says the LORD: For earlier occurrences of these formulae see 1:5 and 2:13; they recur together in v. 21 below. The exegetical intention associated with **And in that day** in 1:5 is present here too: the implications of **she shall answer as in the days of her youth** for Baal-worship are spelt out in this and the next verse. For **says the LORD** in the introduction to an oracle see, e.g., Isa. 1:24; Am. 3:13: NEB's transposition of these words, in a different rendering, to the end of v. 17 is quite unjustified.

you will call me "My husband" ... : The change to direct address suggests, like the introductory formulae, that an originally separate saying has been tacked on here to provide a particular interpretation of the preceding promise. This and the following verses alternate between second- and third-person references to Israel in the Heb.: for the details and possible significance of this see the introduction to this section. There is no reason, with JB and NEB, to prefer the harmonizing "she" of Vss. **husband** is Heb. *îš*, as in vv. 2 and 7, literally "man"; it is the word normally used by a wife addressing her husband (Gen. 29:32, 34; 30:15, 20 etc.). On **Baal** see the note above on v. 8. It too could be used as a word for "husband", but it belongs to the language of description and legislation (e.g. Prov. 12:4; Exod. 21:22) and probably carried with it the connotations of ownership and lordship noted above. Wolff therefore sees the primary reference here as being to the introduction of a new, more intimate, conception of the relation between Yahweh and Israel (p. 49): the same idea is reflected in NIV's rendering of *ba'alî* as "my master". Whether or not this is correct, it is certain that the introduction of the word *ba'al* into the language of Israelite worship, which is presupposed here, facilitated the acceptance of the Baal cult together with its associated practices. What is then peculiar about this verse in contrast to the rest of Hosea, and to the OT more generally, is that it implies that Yahweh was worshipped *as* Baal. This is a different matter from the usual prophetic charge that Baal was worshipped instead of or alongside Yahweh; in other words this verse envisages a syncretistic cult in which the two gods were identified. It is doubtful whether most of the occurrences of the name Baal in theophoric personal names, such as those in the eighth-century Samaria ostraca, should be seen as further evidence of such syncretism than as evidence of straightforward polytheism (Wolff, loc. cit.). But the Asherah cult (cf. 2 Kg. 13:6 and King, pp. 97–107) and the later association of Yahweh with Anat at Elephantine (cf. *DOTT*, p. 257) certainly seem to suggest syncretism, and so may the name Baaliah in 1 Chr. 12:5. Isa. 54:5 seems to revert to the "dangerous" language which is condemned here, as "husband" there represents a form of the root *b'l* (but see the commentaries).

2:17. the names of the Baals: See the note on v. 13: here there is no doubt that the worship of Baal as a god distinct from Yahweh is meant.

I will remove ... from her mouth: The reversion to the third person (**her**) is best explained if one supposes that the compiler of Hosea's sayings, having joined a separate saying of Hosea to vv. 2–15, now interpreted it to refer to Yahweh's initiative (cf. vv. 14–15, 19–20) in ending Baal worship (v. 13).

A wider application of this saying to the worship of all pagan deities is found in Zech. 13:2: cf. also Exod. 23:13.

they shall be mentioned by name: Or "they shall be remembered" (Heb. *zkr*). But **by name** strongly suggests that the Niphal is here used as the passive of the Hiphil (cf. *GK* §51b) in its frequent meaning of "mention, declare", especially in a cultic setting (cf. Exod. 23:13; Ps. 71:16; Isa. 12:4; 26:13; see also *THAT*, vol. I, 513). The reference is then specifically to the cessation of hymns and prayers addressed to **the Baals**. The **name** of a god was always prominent at the beginning of such utterances (cf. H. Gunkel and J. Begrich, *Einleitung in die Psalmen*, Göttingen, 1933, pp. 40–41, 121–3).

2:18. for you . . . you: In both places Heb. reads "(for) them" (cf. NJPS, NIV), maintaining the third-person reference to Israel but in the masculine plural form instead of the feminine singular used in v. 17. The verse is thus formally isolated from those which precede and follow it. A logical link with the preceding context is achieved by **on that day**, but the content is only loosely related to it and it is more likely that the redactor wanted to present these eschatological hopes (see below) as the prelude to the marriage of Israel to Yahweh and her consequent social renewal, of which Hosea had spoken in vv. 19–20. Compare the eschatological "timetabling" in the additions in 11:10, and the notes there.

I will make a covenant: Literally "I will cut (*kārat*) a covenant", as in 10:4 and frequently elsewhere. On the probable origin of this expression and the concept of covenant generally see M. Weinfeld, *TDOT*, vol. 2, 253–79, and E. W. Nicholson, *God and His People*. To **make a covenant** "for" (*l^e*) a people is an idiom distinct from making a covenant "with" (*'et* or *'im*) them: it "implies the imposition of terms upon the vassal or the subordinated (*sic*)" (Weinfeld, p. 256: cf. 2 Kg. 11:4), a notion which came increasingly to dominate the understanding of Israel's covenant with Yahweh in later times (cf. the LXX rendering by *diathēkē*). In prophecy the closest parallel is Ezek. 34:25, where the emphasis, as here, is on the blessings of **safety** which Yahweh undertakes to give to his people (cf. Isa. 61:8; Ezek. 16:60; 37:26).

with the beasts of the field, the birds of the air and the

creeping things of the ground: For the terminology cf. in part 4:3, and most exactly Gen. 8:19 (P) and Ezek. 38:20. The covenant to be imposed on Israel is one which establishes unity between her and the animal creation, an idea which has some affinity with the Noah covenant in Gen. 9:8–17 (P) but which is more closely paralleled in later passages in Isa. (11:6–9; 65:17–25) and in Ezek. 34:25, 28. The origin of this form of covenant theology may well lie in creation-based motifs of the pre-exilic cult with a wider Near Eastern background (so B. F. Batto, *CBQ* 49 (1987), 187–211, and R. Murray, *The Month*, Aug/Sept 1988, pp. 800–03: see also his *The Cosmic Covenant*, London, forthcoming), but its presence in Lev. 26:5–9 should not be overlooked. As a prophetic eschatological idea it seems mainly to belong to the 6th century, but the language of Hos. 2:21–23 is probably already pointing towards it (see the notes below). Within Hosea, the contrast with the activity of **the beasts of the field** in v. 12 is notable and no doubt intentional.

I will abolish: Literally "I will break" (*šbr*), as in 1:5, where see the note. Here **the bow** and **the sword** of Israel's foes are probably foremost in mind, so that she can now **lie down in safety** (cf. Isa. 2:4; 9:5; Mic. 4:3–4; Ezek. 34:27–28: behind these passages lies the tradition represented by Ps. 46:8–11). But it follows that **on that day** she herself will no longer have any need of the weapons of war.

war: See the note on 1:7.

2:19. And I will betroth you to me for ever: Israel is again referred to as **you**, which suggests a close link with v. 16, as does the content. **betroth** (Heb. *'ēraś*) is a term which has no precise modern equivalent. It does not refer to engagement, i.e. a promise to marry, for the "betrothed" maiden is already the "wife" of her husband (cf. Dt. 22:24). It stands for the legally binding agreement which preceded the wedding and the beginning of family life (cf. Dt. 20:7; 28:30). Some details of the procedure can be gleaned from the (admittedly irregular) instance of David and Michal (2 Sam. 3:14; 1 Sam. 18:20–27) and from extra-biblical documents (e.g. *ANET* pp. 222–23, CTA 24:16–37 (*CML*, pp. 128–29)): the bridegroom negotiates with his prospective father-in-law, and they agree the bride-price and other terms of the marriage contract. The expression **for ever**

occurs in later Jewish marriage contracts (cf. above: also *ANET* p. 548), where it refers to the lifetime of the couple. Naturally it here takes on the connotation of eternity, which is elsewhere associated with Yahweh's covenant promises (e.g. Gen. 9:16; 17:7 (P); 2 Sam. 23:5; Isa. 55:3; Jer. 32:40). See further *THAT*, vol. I, pp. 240–42, and H. W. Wolff, *Anthropology of the OT*, London, 1974, pp. 166–69. The fact that the prophet uses the language of betrothal of Yahweh's imminent action, rather than speaking of the recovery of a faithless wife, lends particular emphasis to the newness of what is to come. It is only at the most superficial level a contradiction of Hosea's habit of speaking of Israel as having already been Yahweh's "wife" (2:2 etc.): in fact, in a characteristically typological way of thinking, this saying presents Yahweh as entering once again into an intimate relationship with Israel, but with expectations which so far surpass previous history that the old order is no longer felt to be in force.

in righteousness ... betroth ... : in (Heb. *bᵉ*) is the technical expression for the payment of the bride-price (*beth pretii*: cf. 2 Sam. 3:14); in English the preposition "with" (JB, NJPS) may bring this out more clearly. Most modern commentators have thought that such an allusion is intended here: the qualities which follow are in some sense to be "given" by Yahweh in the establishment of the marriage. The imagery is not exact (no "father" of Israel to whom the bride-price is paid is envisaged), but it is not inappropriate, as the bride-price was commonly passed on by the father to the bride in the form of a dowry (cf. Gen. 31:15: alternatively the *beth pretii* might here refer to the gift made by the bridegroom to the bride, as in Gen. 24:22, 53 (Nowack)), and it is strongly suggested by the surrounding context. On this view the "giving" has been interpreted by the majority as meaning that these are the qualities which Yahweh himself displays in establishing and maintaining the new relationship: they are all qualities commonly ascribed to God in the OT, although it should be noted that in Hosea **steadfast love** is always (except possibly in 10:12) a human quality. Robinson and Wolff have pressed the notion of "gift" further and argue that these qualities are to be imparted by Yahweh to Israel, so that this passage (like 14:4) anticipates the promises of inward transformation of character found in Jer. 31:31–34 (verses probably based on this passage and others in Hosea), Ezek. 36:26–27 and, with particular reference to the king, in Isa. 11:2–5 (cf. Dt. 30:6–8 and Ps. 72:1–4). Again parallels can be found for all the words as denoting human qualities, though **mercy** is not so used in Hosea, and he does not give **righteousness** and **justice** the prominence accorded to them by Amos and Isaiah (cf. Hos. 4:1, 6:6 with Am. 5:7; Isa. 5:7). Alternatively b^e may simply indicate the character of Yahweh's action (as, e.g., in Isa. 42:6; Zech. 8:8), without any echo of marriage customs as such (Marti, Andersen and Freedman). To decide between the different possibilities is difficult, and some have suggested that both divine and human qualities may be in mind (Wellhausen, Jeremias) or that the character of the new relationship as a whole may be in view. If a choice has to be made, the fact that the verb **betroth** has Yahweh as its subject, added to the emphasis laid upon it by its threefold repetition, must favour the view that divine attributes are meant, and in this case a reference to the bride-price is less natural.

On the individual qualities see the notes below. The sequence of them is nowhere exactly paralleled, but in different ways Exod. 34:6–7 (and related passages), Ps. 36:5–6; 85:10–13; Isa. 30:18; Hos. 4:1 and Zech. 7:9 reflect a similar desire to build up a comprehensive theological (or ethical) statement.

righteousness ($ṣedeq$: cf. 10:12) and **justice** ($mišpāṭ$: cf. 12:6) are qualities which are valued especially in judges, human and divine, although both words (and the former particularly) also have a wider application. They refer as much to the acquittal of the innocent as to the punishment of the guilty, and consequently appeal could be made to God's **righteousness** or **justice** by those who believed themselves to be suffering unjustly (cf. Pss. 5:8; 119:149). More generally **righteousness** stands for the performance of one's obligations to another, and since Yahweh was expected to give aid to his people in a time of need, the word frequently approximates in meaning to "salvation" when it refers to him (see the notes on 10:12). Both words can thus have a place in hymnic passages (e.g. Ps. 85:10–11) and in prophecies of salvation (Isa. 30:18; 62:1–2 (RSV, "vindication")), to which they contribute the particular notion that things are now or are to be as they should be. Cf. Snaith, *Mercy and Sacrifice*, pp. 70–79. As qualities to be desired in human society these words are frequently paired together in classical prophecy (see above, and A. Heschel, *The Prophets*, Philadelphia, 1973, vol. I, pp. 195–220; H. W. Wolff, *Amos the Prophet*, New York, 1962, pp. 59–67). For the suggestion that they denote an underlying "order" in the world cf. H. H. Schmid, *Gerechtigkeit als Weltordnung* (BHT 40), Tübingen, 1968; *ZTK* 70 (1973), 1–19 (= B. W. Anderson (ed.), *Creation in the OT*, London, 1984, pp. 102–17), and the articles of K. Koch and G. Liedke in *THAT*, vol. 2, 507–30, 999–1009: such an abstraction is difficult to substantiate.

in steadfast love, and in mercy: Both these terms represent ideas which are frequent in Hosea, but they characteristically appear in different contexts, **steadfast love** (*ḥesed*) being elsewhere in Hosea predominantly (and possibly exclusively) a human quality (4:1; 6:4, 6; 10:12; 12:6), and **mercy** (*raḥᵃmîm*) (1:6–7; 2:1, 23; 14:3) an attribute of God. Elsewhere in the OT they appear together chiefly as attributes of God (e.g. Pss. 25:6; 103:4) and as human attributes only in Zech. 7:9 (Dan. 1:9 involves a late, untypical use of *ḥesed*). The precise sense of *ḥesed* has been much discussed: see the Excursus below. The most satisfactory definition would seem to be "an act or attitude of kindness and help which can be expected of the giver by virtue of his relationship, temporary or lasting, with the recipient", but it sometimes (as done by humans) approximates to "duty". **mercy** is among humans normally predicated of parents (of whom it is expected: cf. Ps. 103:13, where *riḥam* is rendered "pity" in RSV) and of conquerors and rulers (where it cannot be relied upon: cf. Am. 1:11, RSV "pity"). It thus represents the kindly treatment of the helpless by a superior. Only in Zech. 7:9 and Ps. 112:4 does it appear as a general human virtue. When used of God *riḥam* and its cognates express his fatherly love and warmth towards his people in general, and only in some places are they associated specifically with the forgiveness of sins (e.g. Isa. 55:7; Mic. 7:19). See further *THAT*, vol. 2, 761–68.

2:20. in faithfulness: Formally and in its substance this third statement about "betrothal" echoes the first (v. 19a), for **faithfulness** (Heb. *ᵉmûnāh*) implies reliability, doing what one has undertaken to do. It is ascribed to God and men with approximately equal frequency (cf. Ps. 89:1–2; Prov. 12:22). *'emet* has the same meaning in 4:1, where it is clearly a human quality. See on these terms *TDOT*, vol. I pp. 309–320, where it is suggested that generally *'emet* represents character, while *'emûnāh* describes conduct. Both words are rather rare in 8th-century prophecy and other pre-exilic literature.

and you shall know the LORD: Here at any rate the prophet speaks about a human response, either as the climax of a series of human qualities or as the response of Israel to Yahweh's action. It is a response about whose absence Hosea frequently complains (cf. 4:1, 6; 5:4; 6:6), and it is also mentioned in the exhortation in 6:3. The emphasis is certainly on practical rather than theoretical "knowledge", but Wolff has shown that for Hosea true knowledge of Yahweh was mediated through the traditions of *Heilsgeschichte* and law (*EvTh* 12 (1952–53), 533–54 = *GS* 182–205). To "know" Yahweh is here not a mystical experience but to recognize his action in nature and history (cf. Isa. 5:12–13) and to submit to his law (cf. 4:6). Cf. NIV "you will acknowledge the Lord", NJPS "you shall be devoted to the Lord". A different view, akin to an almost sexual intimacy and enjoyment of the beloved, may be implied in the prayer cited but repudiated in 8:2; but, despite the arguments of E. Baumann (*EvTh* 15 (1955), 416–25), this is far from Hosea's own understanding. The expression is one that has a restricted currency in the OT; it appears in Jeremiah's prophecy of a new covenant (31:34), in two narrative passages dealing with the Shiloh sanctuary (I Sam. 2:12; 3:7) and only rarely elsewhere.

2:21. And in that day, says the LORD: For these introductory formulae compare v. 16. They introduce a salvation-oracle (vv. 21–23) which has no direct connection with vv. 16–20, but develops themes from the earlier part of the chapter (esp. v. 8) and from ch. I. The Heb. has an additional "I will answer" between **And in that day** and **says the LORD**. RSV follows the shorter text of LXX and Syr. (cf. Robinson, Marti, JB), but the repetition is an effective literary device, and more use is made of it later in the oracle. MT should be followed, with most commentators and versions.

I will answer … : As often in the OT, to **answer** here

means more than a merely verbal reply: it refers to the action
carried out in response to a plea (e.g. 1 Kg. 18:37; Ps. 3:4).
Here the appeal of the people for renewed fertility in the form
of a community lament of the kind that is adopted in Jl 1:15–20
is presupposed: possibly Hos. 6:1–3 has such a purpose in
view along with the more general restoration of the land.
answer occurs again in a salvation-oracle in 14:8, but there
is no justification for introducing specifically fertility or sexual
nuances into the meaning of the word (as do A. Guillaume, *JTS*
N.S. 15 (1964), 57–58, and C. J. Labuschagne, *THAT*, vol. 2,
337). What is unusual is that (at least after the initial "I will
answer", not represented in RSV) the oracle speaks of Yahweh's
response as mediated through a "chain" in the natural world,
where the crops, **the earth** and **the heavens** are presumed, in a
poetic fancy, to have echoed in turn the plea of Israel (cf. Kimchi
in Wünsche, pp. 98–99). Targ. prosaically explains what is meant
in each case. This "natural chain" reflects an understanding of
the world which is more characteristic of wisdom literature, but
cf. 4:3 and Gen. 1:20–24 for examples of it elsewhere in the OT.
The divine initiative and control of nature which is emphasized
here is also to be presupposed in the other passages, but any
identification of Yahweh with the natural forces is excluded; see
further W. Zimmerli, *The Old Testament and the World*, London,
1976, ch. 2 and 3.

Commentators have noted similar "chains" in magical texts
(especially in a Neo–Babylonian incantation against toothache,
ANET, pp. 100–01), but these are more likely to be a distinct
application of the same basic way of thinking than inspiration
for the present oracle.

and they shall answer the earth: As Targ. saw, it must be
rain which **the heavens** bestow on **the earth**. The parallel with
the "speech" of heaven and earth in the Ugaritic Baal myth
(CTA 3C 21: *CML*, p. 49 – cf. Kuhnigk, p. 25) is therefore not
particularly close. One should rather note the contrasts between
this oracle and the whole presentation of drought and fertility in
the Ugaritic Baal-cycle (CTA 3–6): cf. D. Kinet, *Ba'al und Jahwe*,
pp. 212–17.

**2:22. and the earth shall answer the grain, the wine and
the oil:** Possibly here the thought is a little different, with **the**

grain, the wine and the oil being the substance of **the earth**'s response rather the recipient of it: cf. NJPS "the earth shall respond with new grain and wine and oil". The verb **answer** (Heb. *ᶜānāh*) can have as its object either the content of the reply or the person replied to, or both (cf. *BDB*, p. 722b). **the grain, the wine and the oil** were the staple products of Palestine: cf. on v. 8. For this material, agricultural aspect of future salvation cf. Ezek. 34:26–27, 29; Jl 3:18; Am. 9:13–14.

and they shall answer Jezreel: Jezreel has apparently here become a cipher for Israel, which has a similar sound in Heb. too, although the words are etymologically quite distinct. The shift may have been aided by a misunderstanding of 1:11, where **Jezreel** in fact still represents a place (see the note), and by the fact that both Hosea's other children were symbols for the people and their condition.

2:23. and I will sow him for myself in the land: I will sow draws directly on the etymology of **Jezreel**, which means "God sowed" (Heb. *zāraᶜ*). For **him** MT and all the ancient versions have "her" (*-hā* rather than *-hû*). Modern commentators and versions have thought that **him** would be more natural, since Hosea's child **Jezreel** was a boy (1:3–5). Wolff, who does not emend the text, assumes a lacuna between vv. 22 and 23, supposing that a reference to Jezreel's mother has fallen out by homoeoteleuton. Neither of these expedients is necessary or justified: with the shift in the meaning of **Jezreel** it was natural to use the feminine pronoun, which had represented Israel through most of ch. 2. With the etymological interpretation of the name a smooth transition is made to the renewal of the life of the people themselves: they will once more be established ("sown") as Yahweh's people (**for me**) in their **land**, with all the promise that sowing holds of future growth and fruitfulness (cf. 1:10–11; 14:5–7). The names of Hosea's other two children are also turned, by a "negation of the negation", into bearers of hope: Israel will once more enjoy Yahweh's compassion (**pity**, Heb. *rḥm*) and the privilege of being his people (see the notes on 1:6 and 1:9 for these traditional terms). And, typically for this book (cf. 2:15, 16, 20; 3:5; 14:2–3), she will make an appropriate response: **"Thou art my God."** This is the response that was previously criticized (8:2) or judged to be misplaced (14:3; cf. 2:5, 13): now it betokens the renewal of true devotion to Yahweh by the restored people, who enjoy again the rich produce of their land.

Excursus: Baal in the Ugaritic Texts

The Ugaritic texts found at Ras Shamra on the Syrian coast in 1929 are by far the most informative (though not the only) evidence outside the Bible for the nature of Baal. Their discovery has given a sharpness of profile to descriptions of Canaanite religion which was quite impossible before. Although it must not be assumed that the religion of Ugarit and the religion of Canaan itself were identical at every point, the texts have proved to coincide with OT references to Canaanite beliefs and practices at so many points that they probably give, in the main, a faithful picture of the religion against which Israel's prophets and reformers contended.

The texts are written in a North-West Semitic language that is related to Hebrew (itself from a linguistic point of view a Canaanite dialect) and for which an alphabetic form of the cuneiform script was used. The copies that survive were apparently written between 1400 and 1350 BC, but the stories that they tell no doubt have an earlier origin. The widespread use of a stock of standard formulaic expressions suggests an ultimately oral poetic background for them. The most directly relevant texts are a series of twelve which have been placed at the beginning of the now standard numbering system for the Ugaritic texts as a whole (CTA 1-12; KTU 1:1-12). They are not always easy to understand, and different interpretations of a number of points are current. Some of the texts are badly damaged, and their relationship to one another is in certain cases in dispute. Sometimes we seem to be dealing with parts of parallel versions of the same story or with parts of two similar stories.

In the first two texts (which seem to be alternative versions of the same story) the central issue is who is to be king among the gods, a theme which is frequent in ancient Near Eastern mythology. Although one of the other gods is already king (Baal in one version, Athtar in the other), the high god El is determined to replace him with his son Yam, the god of the sea. So El commands the divine craftsman Kothar wa-Khasis to build

Yam a palace. In the ensuing conflict with Yam Baal is close to defeat but, encouraged and re-armed by Kothar wa-Khasis, he conquers him and kills him. Passages in other texts refer more briefly to Baal's (or his sister Anat's) conquest of a dragon or serpent, who is once called Lotan (cf. Leviathan in the OT). These are not creation stories in the strict sense, but assert that Baal holds the mastery over the forces of chaos and evil (see below) which Yam and the monsters probably represent.

Texts 3 and 4 (which again could be parts of parallel versions of a single story) are the natural sequel, as they deal with the building of a palace, not for Yam but for Baal. At the beginning Baal is enjoying a great feast and his sister-consort Anat is fighting a battle against a human army. Baal calls her to desist and to come to him, with the promise that he will seek out the lightning, whose secret he alone (as the storm-god) knows. When she arrives she finds Baal complaining of his lack of a palace, and so she goes to El to plead for one on his behalf, but without success. Baal therefore commissions Kothar wa-Khasis to make a present out of precious metals for Athirat (Asherah in the Old Testament), El's consort, to win her support for his cause. The plan works, and Athirat and Anat secure El's approval for the building of Baal's palace. Kothar wa-Khasis is entrusted with the task, and a palace of silver and gold is completed. After a celebratory banquet for the gods Baal agrees to the suggestion (which he had earlier resisted) that his palace should have a window. This is said to correspond to a "rift" in the clouds, and through it Baal at once "utters his holy voice" (the thunder), which makes the earth and its inhabitants tremble. Full of confidence in his power, he invites Mot (the god of death) to devour any who challenge his now firmly established rule. The myth thus portrays how Baal entered upon his life-giving activity towards mankind and, given the symbolic correspondence between a god's earthly temple and his heavenly palace, how the effectiveness of this activity is bound up with Baal's shrine at Ugarit and the festivals celebrated there.

If the next two texts (which certainly tell a connected story) follow directly on the story of Baal's palace, the invitation to Mot receives an ironic twist. For it is Baal himself whom Mot summons to his domain, and Baal seems to have no option but to agree, although by intercourse with a cow he generates a male offspring whom he clothes in his own robe and apparently presents to Mot as a substitute for himself. When the news of Baal's (apparent) death is brought to the gods, they lacerate themselves in mourning for him, knowing that his death means ruin for humanity. A vain attempt to make Athtar king of the gods in Baal's place comes to nothing. Eventually Anat finds Mot, cuts him in two and so apparently releases Baal from his power. El dreams of restored fertility, but the fields are still dry, and he sends the sun-god to bring Baal back. Baal reappears, but so does Mot, and once again they argue and fight, until Mot finally recognizes that Baal is supreme. There can be no doubt that Mot here represents the forces of drought and sterility which appear to have overcome life and fertility in the dry Mediterranean summer, and even more so when the rains fail over a period of years. The myth reassured the people that such conditions were only temporary and probably provided the rationale for certain ritual practices.

The following texts, which are much shorter, seem to belong to the cycle of myths just described, but they contribute little additional information. The same applies to the more recently discovered text 101 (*Ugaritica V*, no. 3), which describes Baal on his sacred mountain of Zaphon and could be the beginning of a version of the palace story. Text 10 and the very short texts 11 and 96 recount episodes in Baal's love-affair with Anat, culminating in Anat's giving birth to one or more animals. Probably this was meant as a vivid demonstration and guarantee of Baal's life-giving potency. Text 12 is in some respects similar to the story of Baal and Mot, though the details are obscure. Baal is apparently trapped into having intercourse with some cow-like creatures which some scholars have identified as locusts, but they (or their offspring) get the better of him and make him ill, and this causes a drought for seven years. Blood-covered friends come and rescue him, however, and possibly a water rite is performed. The text may therefore be related to the effects of locust plagues and ritual counter-measures.

In some of the other narrative texts Baal appears as a helper to the heroes of the stories. Thus he intercedes with El for the childless Daniel (whose title "man of Rapiu" also points to a special dependence on Baal), and it is to Baal that Daniel prays after his child Aqhat has been killed. Again, in the Keret story Baal has a part to play in ensuring that the king fathers a child. Some recently published ritual texts also show that at Ugarit Baal was expected to come to the aid of a contemporary individual or the city. For example, in text 82 various physical ailments are traced to the influence of evil forces that are equated with monsters defeated by Baal and Anat in the myths, and Baal is called upon for help. Text 108 invites various gods to a great (sacrificial) banquet, but it is Baal, "the Healer, the Eternal King", who is the central figure, and it is presumably to him that the concluding prayer seeking blessing and protection for the city of Ugarit is addressed. Finally we may mention text 119, which lists offerings for "Baal of Ugarit" and other deities and then prescribes a form of prayer to Baal, to be followed by sacrifies, for use when the city is under enemy attack. It concludes: "Then Baal will hear your prayer: he will drive away the mighty man from your gate, the warrior from your walls." Thus, while Baal's activity was particularly associated with fertility and the natural cycle of the year, it was not limited to this: he was also regarded as the divine protector of the city.

The most recent English translation of the main religious texts is by J. C. de Moor, *An Anthology of Religious Texts from Ugarit*, Leiden, 1987, which includes all the texts referred to here. Gibson, *CML*, provides a translation of many of them, together with a transliteration of the Ugaritic originals, a glossary and a very helpful introduction to the texts. See also *ANET*, pp. 129–42; N. C. Habel, *Yahweh versus Baal* (New York, 1964); D. Kinet, *Baᶜal und Jahwe*; and, for more general aspects of the discoveries at Ugarit, A. H. W. Curtis, *Ugarit*, and *DBS* 9, cols. 1123–1466. The famous stele from Ugarit portraying Baal and the lightning (now in the Louvre) is illustrated, e.g., in *ANEP*, no. 490, and in Curtis, p. 89.

Excursus: *ḥesed*

The influential studies of N. Glueck (Ḥesed *in the Bible*, Cincinnati, 1967 (German ed., Giessen, 1927), and N. H. Snaith (*The Distinctive Ideas of the Old Testament*, London, 1944,

pp. 94–130) have made it a commonplace of OT theology that
ḥesed, generally rendered "(steadfast) love" in RSV, refers to
the fulfilment of the requirements of a covenant relationship
(although Glueck in fact only affirmed this for the theological
usage). 1 Sam. 20:8 is frequently quoted in this connection as a
clear example on the human level, and the association of *berît* and
ḥesed in passages such as Dt. 7:9 and 1 Kg. 8:23 has been held to
support this view. But recent work has shown that the existence
of a covenant is by no means essential for the occurrence of *ḥesed*
(E. Jacob, *Theology of the OT*, London, 1958, pp. 103–04 (some
passages); H. J. Stoebe, *VT* 2 (1952), 244–54, and *THAT*, vol. 1,
600–21; H. J. Zobel, *TDOT*, vol. 5, 44–64; K. D. Sakenfeld *The
Meaning of* Ḥesed, and *Faithfulness in Action*; S. Romarowski, *VT*
40 (1990), 89–103) and that the introduction of concepts like legal
obligation was a serious error. Cases such as Gen. 40:14 make
this particularly clear. Instead it has been suggested that *ḥesed* is
used quite generally to mean "kindness" (Stoebe, Romarowski)
and even "something beyond duty" (Gerleman, *VT* 28 (1978),
151–164: esp. p. 153, "(something that) über das Mass hinaus
geht, eine übliche Norm übersteigt"). This is to go too far, for the
use of *ḥesed* does seem to refer to action that could be expected of
an individual within a definite social context, whether this be the
family or hospitality towards a guest, or even a context created by
the generous initiative of one party towards the other (Zobel). In
some such cases a formal agreement (*berît*) or oath may be made,
but it is not essential to the performance of *ḥesed* and may as
easily be the consequence of an act of *ḥesed* (Gen. 21:23–24,
Jos. 2:12) as its motivation (1 Sam. 20:8 etc.). Sakenfeld has
suggested (pp. 38–40) that such measures were taken when the
death of the beneficiary was in view or where other circumstances
(especially hostility) may have made performance uncertain. In
the case of Yahweh's *ḥesed*, it would appear that the use of the
term does not of itself presuppose the explicit formulation of
the covenant (*berît*) concept, and certainly not the kind of
quasi-legal obligation envisaged by Glueck: it does, however,
assume the special relationship between Yahweh and Israel (or
the individual worshipper), which eventually came to be defined
as one of election or covenant, but which may have received
its original formulation simply in the designation of Israel as

Yahweh's people (Jg. 5:11, 13 etc.) and existed as a practical reality from the moment that Israel first began to worship Yahweh. The strictly "covenantal" interpretation of *ḥesed* is only valid in Deuteronomy and in passages dependent upon it. It has even been claimed (by A. Jepsen, *KuD* 7 (1961), 261–271, and Zobel) that the element of mutuality is lacking altogether in the theological uses of *ḥesed*, since *ḥesed* is never used certainly to refer to a human attitude towards God. There are passages which are difficult to accomodate to this view (especially Hos. 6:4 and Jer. 2:2 – also Neh. 13:14 etc.), and other passages do appear to make the manifestation of God's *ḥesed* dependent on a human response (cf. the passages in Dt. and Exod. 34:7 – cf. Exod. 20:6). Thus the view of Jepsen and Zobel cannot stand as a full account of the theological use of *ḥesed* in the OT. It may, nevertheless, be true of the sense in which the term *ḥesed* was originally given a theological use (by the Yahwist, according to Zobel). Sakenfeld, taking up a suggestion of some earlier scholars, has identified the situational superiority of the agent as a further characteristic of *ḥesed*. It is true that this often applies, but it can hardly be regarded as a defining characteristic if it is accepted that *ḥesed* could be done by men towards God, as is apparently the case in some passages (cf. above). It is possible, of course, to treat these cases as a special development in meaning (Sakenfeld, pp. 175–181), but the difficulties involved suggest that this theory should be abandoned (cf. also 2 Sam. 3:8; Gen. 21:23b; Ru. 3:10; I Sam. 20:15). Further, if the word "help", which implies exactly what Sakenfeld has in mind, is substituted for the more regular renderings, the result by no means always suits the context.

In Hosea, for whom it was clearly a central theme, *ḥesed* is generally a human attitude or disposition (10:12 and 2:19 are disputed), and it is likely that in certain passages at least it is something directed towards God as well as man (6:4 – also 6:6?). What is distinctive is that (a) it is talked about in quite general terms, i.e. as a quality of the life of the community as a whole rather than of particular individuals, and that (b) its presence or absence is a matter of vital concern to God (6:6) and the basis for his treatment of his people (4:1 – cf. 2:19). It seems most likely that it embraced for Hosea living up to one's responsibilities both to Yahweh and to fellow members of the community: sometimes one is foremost in his mind, sometimes the other (the same may be true of *da'at* *'elōhîm* and *'emet*): cf. Sakenfeld, *Meaning*, p. 181, n. 23.

THE DISCIPLINING OF THE BELOVED

3:1–5

Like chapter 1, this chapter reports an episode in Hosea's life and presents it as a symbol for Yahweh's attitude and intentions with regard to his people Israel. Chapter 1 is deliberately recalled (cf. **again** in v. 1), but there is a striking difference in the statements that are made about Yahweh's love: now it is something which continues even **though** Israel's affections are directed elsewhere (v. 1: contrast 1:6) and seeks by disciplinary measures to win her back to an undivided devotion to her God (vv. 4–5). The influence of the theology expressed above all in 2:14–15 is very apparent.

On the biographical level, the chapter has caused great difficulties to modern commentators, as they have endeavoured to discover the nature of Hosea's action in vv. 2–3 and its relation to what is described in ch. 1. On the assumption that 1:2 refers to Hosea's marriage to Gomer, scholars have regarded ch. 3 as an account either of the same event, or of a later reconciliation with Gomer after her (supposed) adultery, or of a liaison with a different woman altogether. For a discussion of these views see the Excursus on Hosea's Marriage. In fact it is by no means certain that Hosea married Gomer (see the notes on 1:2), and the interpretation of ch. 3 is best approached apart from any attempt to correlate it with ch. 1. The indefinite **a woman** in v. 1 strongly suggests that the episode concerns someone with whom Hosea had had no previous relations. There are two main theories about the action taken by Hosea, and particularly the payment made to secure this woman for himself: by some it is viewed as the precondition of her liberation from slavery, by others as the payment of a bride-price (see the notes on v. 2). The latter view appears to be the more probable.

It is commonly assumed, particularly by those who believe that Gomer is the woman referred to here, that this episode took place (like those described in ch. 1) in the early years of Hosea's

ministry, i.e. probably in the 740s. However, an examination of
the development of Hosea's message based on ch. 4–14 suggests
that the theology of Yahweh's loving discipline of his people only
emerged after the Assyrian invasions of the late 730s, and some
aspects of the message correspond most closely to oracles from
the 720s (see on v. 4). The writing-up of the chapter, and probably
the event itself, should probably therefore be placed quite late in
Hosea's ministry, a conclusion which gives great importance to
the work of the collector(s) who brought together the disparate
materials of ch. 1–3 and placed them at the beginning of the other
collections of Hosea's oracles.

Apart from two small but significant additions in v. 5 and a
possible scribal error at the end of v. 3 (see the detailed notes), the
chapter has probably come down to us in its original form. The
additions served, like others elsewhere in the book, to associate
Hosea's prophecy with the themes of Judaean salvation-prophecy
of a later period (compare the notes on 1:10–11 and 11:11).
Theories which envisage more extensive redactional activity lack
a secure foundation in the next. The view that the whole of v. 5
is secondary, which goes back to Marti, Harper and Robinson
and has been revived by Rudolph and Jeremias, places too much
weight on the lack of complete parallelism between sign and what
is signified in vv. 3–5. Already in vv. 1–2 such parallelism is not
complete. Moreover, Wolff has shown that the keyword **love** in
v. 1 requires a sequel that involves the full restoration of the
relationship between Yahweh and Israel (cf. also 2:15). The
proposal that the whole chapter is exilic in origin (so recently
Yee, pp. 57–64; see p. 332, n. 32, for earlier advocates of this
view) is based on parallels with the thought and language of
exilic writings and on the view that the chapter "is essentially
an interpretive commentary on the tradition found in Hos. 1–2"
(Yee, p. 62). But in neither case are the arguments conclusive.

3:1. And the LORD said to me, "Go again . . .": In contrast
to ch. 1, where Hosea is referred to in the third person, this
narrative is presented as Hosea's own account of his experience
(cf. **me** and **I** in vv. 2–3). The episode probably belongs to a
much later period in his life than ch. 1 (see the introduction
to the chapter). **"Go again"** implies that this is a separate

and in some sense a parallel event to that referred to in 1:2–3: those who see it as a different account of the same event have to regard **again** as an addition by a redactor who mistakenly (in their view) thought that a later episode in Hosea's life was recorded here. Rudolph, who is followed by Mays and NJPS ("The Lord said to me further, 'Go . . .'"), takes **again** (Heb. *ʿôd*) with **said** (cf. R. H. Pfeiffer, *Introduction to the OT*, 2nd ed., London, 1952, p. 567; Gordis, *HUCA* 25 (1954), 29; and a few 19th-century commentators in Harper, p. 216n.), supposing that the echo is of 1:2a, "When the Lord *first* spoke . . ." This rendering (which may, despite what Gordis and Rudolph say, run counter to the Masoretic accents) does not make any real difference to the meaning, because the normal rendering (as in RSV) is already open to the interpretation that the **woman** is not Gomer, and the inclusion of **again** anywhere excludes the view, mentioned above, that this is an account of the same event as 1:2–3.

love a woman who is beloved of a paramour: In 1:2 Hosea is told to **take** or "get" a woman, which may imply no more than the physical act of sexual intercourse (see the note there): here, by contrast, he is told to **love** one. The root *ʾhb* (**love**) occurs no less than four times in this verse and is clearly its keynote: as such it provides the context within which the disciplining of vv. 3–4 is to be understood (cf. Prov. 3:11–12). Rudolph's view that **love** is meant ironically, so that the passage originally carried only a message of doom, is unjustified and implausible. The indefinite **a woman who is beloved of a paramour** leaves open the possibility that this chapter relates not to Gomer but to some other woman (so Rudolph), though if it could be accepted that ch. 1 describes Hosea's marriage to Gomer, then this phrase could be taken as a deliberately allusive way of referring to her. NIV, "your wife", prejudges the question. For **paramour** (Heb. *rēaʿ*) JB has "her husband", following the interpretation of Targ., Rashi amd others (see Harper, p. 218), which claims support in the use of *rēaʿ* in Ca. 5:5 and Jer. 3:20. The absence of "her" in the Heb. is against this view. Weiser, Wolff and Jeremias follow LXX, Syr. and Vulg. in reading "loves" for **is beloved of** (changing the vocalization of MT), since this makes the parallel between the woman and Israel closer. The *difficilior lectio* of MT (cf. Aq., Symm.) is to be preferred, with RSV.

and is an adulteress: The woman is to be a married woman who has been unfaithful, so as to represent Israel in the terms already used in ch. 2. On the view of ch. 1 taken here, this would exclude Gomer from consideration (unless her marriage had gone unreported in the text).

as the LORD loves the people of Israel: This statement, like the use of the same verb *'āhēb* of Yahweh in 14:4, parallels the affirmation that Yahweh will in the future revive his compassion (*raḥᵃmîm*) for his people (2:19, 23: cf. 2:1). In this case too the background is Hosea's message of judgment that, because Israel has not responded to Yahweh's love (11:1-4), Yahweh has ceased to love them (9:15), but behind this there lies an older cultic tradition which affirmed Yahweh's love for his people (Ps. 47:5; cf. 78:68; 87:2).

they turn to other gods: Although the substance of this accusation corresponds to Hosea's message elsewhere (cf. 2:13; 11:2 and the notes there), the language is more typical of later literature (cf. Lev. 19:4, 31, 20:6, and esp. Dt. 31:18, 20), where **other gods** becomes a stereotyped expression (cf. Dt. 6:14 etc.). It is possible, therefore, that this phrase was added later to the verse to clarify the meaning of **love cakes of raisins**, which is formally more closely parallel to the description of the woman whom Hosea is told to **love** (Jeremias, p. 55). But she receives a twofold characterization (**beloved of a paramour** and **adulteress**), and perhaps **Israel** did too from the beginning.

and love cakes of raisins: While Hosea elsewhere denounces Israel's diversion of her love to other gods (4:18; 8:9), and the imagery would have suggested that here, his criticism also highlights the gross materialism of his contemporaries' religion (cf. 9:1 illustrated by 2:5 and 14). The **cakes of raisins** (*'ᵃšîšê ᶜᵃnābîm*) must here be those consumed on ritual occasions (as NEB and NIV emphasize by their glosses), as in 2 Sam. 6:19, but the non-cultic references to them in Ca. 2:5 and Isa. 16:7 show that they were a favourite dish. Presumably eating **cakes of raisins** played a prominent part in the Baal-worship which Hosea condemns, and so could be used in mocking condemnation of it. Jeremias (p. 54) prefers to associate it with the Astarte-cult, like the **cakes** (*kawwanim*) mentioned in Jer 7:18; 44:19.

3:2. I bought her: There has been much discussion about

which Heb. root underlies the form *wā'ekkᵉrehā*: for the details
see Rowley, *Men of God*, p. 68 n. 5. NEB, "I got her back",
and NJPS, "I hired her" (cf. LXX and Arabic *karā*), reflect this
discussion. But **bought** remains the only philologically plausible
meaning. After the indefinite "a woman" of v. 1, **her** is surprising:
it might imply that a particular woman was already in mind there
(presumably Gomer). But Rudolph renders "one", arguing that
the Heb. pronoun suffix here has an indefinite reference, as in
Isa. 46:7b and Lam. 3:34 (cf. also v. 36). Although the parallels
are not exact, this seems to be a possibility, which is important
for discussion of the relation between ch. 3 and ch. 1. But to
what does this "buying" refer? It has been thought to be the
payment of a bride-price (so recently M. J. Geller, *JSJ* 8 (1977),
144–47), the purchasing of a slave-girl or a cult-prostitute out
of her bondage (e.g. Harper, Wolff: for the rationale see the
note below on **a homer and a lethech of barley**), or the
cost of keeping a mistress (Rudolph). This last view is hard to
reconcile with **bought**. A decision between the other theories is
difficult, because the text gives too few details. Evidently what
was important was to record that the "loving" of the woman cost
Hosea something. Since the narrative presents Hosea's actions
as symbolic of Yahweh's dealings with Israel, it may be correct
to see in the mention of this a reflection of the "price" which,
according to one view, Yahweh undertakes to "pay" in 2:19–20,
when establishing his new relationship with Israel.

a homer and a lethech of barley: The **homer** (not to be
confused with the omer, a much smaller measure) was equal to
ten ephahs (Ezek. 45:11), a measure variously estimated, chiefly
on the basis of much earlier and much later data, as between
about fifteen and about forty litres (cf. *IDB*, vol. 4, 834–35; de
Vaux, *Ancient Israel*, pp. 201–03; *BRL*, p. 205). The **lethech**
appears only here in the OT, but it is possibly the same as the *lth*
in Ugaritic, despite the different final consonant. Later usage (cf.
Aq., Symm., Th., Vulg.) equates it with half a homer. According
to 2 Kg. 7:16–20 (cf. 1–2) two seahs (RSV "measures") of barley
were sold for a shekel, and on this basis it has been calculated
that the barley handed over by Hosea would have been worth
another **fifteen shekels**, making a total value of thirty shekels,
the cost of a slave (Exod. 21:32) and the valuation of a free

adult female (Lev. 27:4): cf. Wolff, Jeremias, G. J. Wenham, *ZAW* 90 (1978), 264–65. But the basis of the calculation is shaky (cf. Rudolph, p. 92), and nothing can be built upon it. LXX (which is followed By NEB and REB) has, in place of **and a lethech**, "and a skin of wine", which seems to represent an independent tradition rather than an attempt to make sense of the obscure word **lethech** in MT.

3:3. you must dwell as mine: Heb. *yāšab* (**dwell**) is more appropriately translated "remain, stay (in)" here and in the next verse (Wolff, Jeremias). For the sense "stay at home" cf. Dt. 21:13; 1 Sam. 1:23, and perhaps Lev. 12:4–5, and compare Syr. and Vulg.

for many days: A long period of confinement and discipline is envisaged but, as the interpretation in vv. 4–5 shows (**many days . . . afterward**), it is not a permanent situation. There is no justification in the text for holding that the period was at first regarded by Hosea as unmitigated punishment and only secondarily interpreted (by the addition of v. 5) as disciplinary (Rudolph, Jeremias).

so will I also be to you: The Heb. is difficult, and commentators have often sought to ease the problem by supplying a negated verb of motion. The most likely suggestion is to add *lō' 'ēlēk*, "I will not come", which could have been lost by homoeoteleuton: for the sexual sense cf. Am. 2:7. In any event, the meaning is clear: the woman is for a time not even to have sexual intercourse with the man to whom she now belongs. No explicit interpretation of this is provided in vv. 4 and 5, but the latter verse presupposes that Israel has been separated from Yahweh for a time (**return and seek**: cf. 5:15).

3:4. For: As in a divine command to perform a symbolic action (1:2, 4, 6, 9), so here in a prophetic narrative of the execution of one, **For** introduces the meaning of the symbol. This way of introducing the interpretation is most unusual, and the avoidance of both divine speech and direct address to Israel is paralleled only in secondary passages such as 1:10–11; 7:10 and 11:10. On the other hand, as the detailed notes will show, the content of the interpretation is largely drawn from Hosea's other oracles, and the overall pattern of a period of deprivation leading to repentance and restoration is closely paralleled in 2:6–7, 14–15;

5:15–6:3. One should then, perhaps, allow for the possibility that Hosea himself here departs from the normal way of presenting a symbolic action and indeed supplies thereby a rare instance of prophetic symbolism which has not been entirely processed through the usual categories of an explicit divine instruction followed by the prophet's obedient response. Here at least the implication seems to be that, while the initial impulse to the action was prompted by Yahweh (v. 1), the significance of certain detailed aspects of it was an insight of the prophet himself.

shall dwell many days: Better "shall remain many days" (see the note above on v. 3).

without king or prince: The removal of **king** and **princes** is announced in 7:16; 10:3, 7; 13:10–11, and their misdeeds are a common theme of Hosea's (1:4; 5:1; 7:5–7; 8:4). **princes** (*śārîm*) is the general name for the king's officials: they would include district governors (1 Kg. 20:14; 22:26; and compare the Yavneh-Yam inscription (*ANET*, p. 568)), generals (1 Kg. 1:25), and other leading men at court (1 Kg. 4:2). See for a full review of the evidence U. Rüterswörden, *Die Beamten der israelitischen Königszeit* (BWANT 117), Stuttgart, 1985. No blood relationship to the king is implied, or indeed normal. The ruling elite is mentioned, like the other items which follow, as a potential rival to Yahweh in that it was seen by the people as a basis for confidence (cf. 13:10). These words are quoted in the Damascus Document (20:16; *DSSE*, p. 107), where the whole of vv. 3–5 seems to be in mind.

without sacrifice: Hosea clearly anticipated the destruction of the sanctuaries at which **sacrifice** was offered (10:2, 8; 12:11) and deportation to a land far away where it would be impossible (9:3–6; cf. 2:11). Opinions differ over whether Hosea's opposition to sacrificial worship was absolute (see on 6:6) and whether he would have favoured its eventual restoration: it is, at any rate, not a subject which is ever touched on in his oracles of salvation (but see the note on 14:2).

or pillar: Heb. *maṣṣēbāh*, as in 10:1–2, where see the note. To Hosea their proliferation was clearly an abuse.

without ephod or teraphim: Neither of these objects is mentioned elsewhere by Hosea, but they probably represent particular types of the "idols" whose use he frequently condemns

(4:17; 8:4; 13:2). The **ephod** is in priestly texts and some other passages the name for a priestly garment (Exod. 25:7 etc.; I Sam. 2:18; 22:18), but elsewhere it is an object used for divination (I Sam. 23:6; 30:7) or even an image of a god (Jg. 8:27; 17:5 – in this passage it is again associated with **teraphim**). See further *IDB*, vol. 2, 118–19. **teraphim** were a phenomenon of Israelite religion from patriarchal times to after the exile. Their possession was much sought after (Gen 31:19, 34–35), perhaps for their protective power, and they were also used for divination (Ezek. 21:26; Zech. 10:2). They were apparently of human form (I Sam. 19:13–16), but it is unclear whether they represented household gods or, as Balz-Cochois suggests (*Gomer*, pp. 108–11), the spirits of dead ancestors. Their use is condemned in I Sam. 15:23 and 2 Kg. 23:24 as well as, by implication, in this passage. It is probable that it is to the use of **ephod and teraphim** that Hosea alludes in 4:12.

3:5. shall return and seek the LORD their God: This is very close to what is represented in symbolic form in 2:7 as the consequence of Yahweh's barring of the way to Israel's "lovers". Compare also 5:15; 6:1–3. The notion that discipline will bring about repentance (**return**) goes beyond Hosea's earlier statements that inability to **return** renders Israel subject to inescapable doom (5:4), and it seems from 5:15 (see the notes there) that this notion appears in Hosea's preaching at the time of the Assyrian intervention in 734–732. Subsequently ([7:10]; 11:5) Hosea seems to have despaired of this hope, and his ultimate message of restoration is one which looks for an inward renewal of Israel which is entirely an act of divine grace and love (2:14–15, 19–20; 11:8–9; 14:4–8). On **seek** see the note on **seek my face** in 5:15.

and David their king: This phrase presupposes a recognition of the divine appointment of David and his descendants as rulers over all twelve tribes of Israel (2 Sam. 7), a doctrine which was rejected by the northern kingdom after Solomon's death, with the encouragement of the prophet Ahijah (I Kg. 11:26–39; 12:16–20), and there is no evidence anywhere else in his book that Hosea held a view different from his countrymen. It is probable that these words, which interrupt the account of Israel's return to Yahweh, were added by one of the Judaean

redactors whose work is discernible in several other passages
(cf. the note on 1:1), to associate this collection of prophetic
sayings with the hopes current in Josiah's reign and in the exile
for a re-establishment of Judaean rule over the whole Israelite
people (cf. Jer. 30:9; Ezek. 34:24; 37:23–4; and also the present
form of Isa. 9, on which see R. E. Clements, *Isaiah 1–39* (NCB),
London, 1980, pp. 67, 104–05).

and they shall come in fear to the LORD: Wolff suggests
that this refers to "utter excitement", comparing Jer. 33:9 for this
use of *pāḥad* (cf. NJPS "they will thrill over the Lord"). The same
usage is found in Isa. 60:5, and the ensuing reference to Yahweh's
goodness (see below) suggests that thankful exhilaration may
indeed be meant.

and to his goodness: Heb. *ṭûb* may refer to Yahweh's gracious
nature (cf. Neh. 9:25; Pss. 25:7; 145:7; Isa. 63:7), or to his "good
gifts" (Jer. 31:12, 14; so JB, NEB, NIV, NJPS here). The former
involves a hendiadys, being equivalent to "to the Lord who is
good"; the latter associates the promise more closely with the
materialistic aspect of Hosea's other salvation oracles (cf. 2:15,
21–22; 14:5–8).

in the latter days: The phrase has the effect of distancing the
fulfilment of the hope from the time of the prophet himself (cf.
Gen. 49:1; Num. 24:14; Dt. 4:30; 31:39) and, often, of placing
it in the context of a final, eschatological reversal of present
distress (cf. Isa. 2:2 = Mic. 4:1; Jer. 23:20; 30:24; Ezek.
38:16; Dan. 10:14). This seems to read more into the "many
days" of v. 4 than Hosea is likely to have intended, and the
phrase was probably added by a redactor, perhaps in the exilic
period.

Excursus: Hosea's Marriage

Until comparatively modern times the dominant view was that
Hosea 1–3 were not about Hosea's real dealings with one or
more women, but about related visionary experiences or parables
which served only to convey a message about the spiritual
relationship between God and Israel or between God and the
Christian Church. This does not mean that interpretations based
on a literal reading of the text were unknown. For example, in a

Talmudic passage (B. Pesaḥim 87a–b) the command to marry a prostitute in 1:2 is understood as a divine ploy to soften Hosea's harsh message of judgment, since after the birth of his three children God commands him to divorce his wife, and his reluctance teaches him that God too has no intention of abandoning his people. Again theological discussion of Hosea's action, for example among Christian theologians in the 13th century, sometimes proceeded on the assumption that real events were involved. But a symbolic reading was more typical, as in the Targum, where the taking of Gomer and the birth of the children is no more than a symbol for preaching against sinful Israel, and ch. 3 is represented as entirely a speech of God to Hosea about his love for his wayward people (for details of the history of interpretation see S. Bitter, *Die Ehe des Propheten Hosea*, Göttingen, 1975). Such views have survived into modern times (so van Hoonacker, Toy and others noted by Rowley, *Men of God*, pp. 79–83, where objections to this approach are set out), but they are now held by only a minority of scholars. The modern discussion until about 1960 centred on the questions of whether the woman in ch. 3 was Gomer or not and, if she was, whether ch. 1 (in particular verses 2–3) and ch. 3 were different accounts of the same event or, as has been more commonly held, accounts of two different events in Hosea's relationship with his wife (on this debate see the survey by Rowley, *Men of God*, pp. 66–97). No final resolution of this problem has been achieved, although the view that Gomer is the woman referred to in ch. 3 and that ch. 1 and ch. 3 relate to different episodes appears to have predominated (so Rowley and, in addition to those mentioned in his survey, Weiser, Wolff, von Rad and Mays; since he wrote, the view that ch. 3 is not about Gomer has been maintained by Fohrer and Rudolph, to whom we must return, and the view that ch. 1 and ch. 3 are, at least in part, parallel accounts of the same events has been taken by Eissfeldt, Lindblom, Ackroyd and McKeating).

Recent discussions have focused on the interpretation of 1:2. Wolff, in his commentary, suggested that **a wife of harlotry** meant a bride who had, according to the prevalent custom, submitted to an act of cultic prostitution before her marriage (a view proposed earlier by L. Rost and G. Böstrom). Such a woman would have both exemplified and symbolized the apostasy of the people as a whole. Against this Rudolph was able to show that none of the evidence to which Wolff appeals, biblical and extra-biblical, is adequate to prove the existence of such a custom in Israel and that two passages in Deuteronomy (22:13–21, 23–29) are evidence against it, or at least against its being prevalent in Hosea's time (*ZAW* 75 (1963), 65–73; and in his commentary). Rudolph's own view is that the references to **harlotry** in 1:2 are not original, but derive from the compiler of ch. 1–3, who mistakenly deduced from 2:4ff. that Hosea's marital life and Yahweh's relationship with Israel ran parallel and so inserted the references to harlotry into 1:2 to make this clear. Rudolph raises several objections to the most probable of the reconstructions that have been previously proposed, viz. that Hosea, following what he took to be a divine impulse, married a common prostitute to symbolize Israel's apostasy, and that she was subsequently unfaithful to him (so Rowley): *(a)* such an action would have been self-defeating, as no one would have taken its alleged symbolic purpose seriously; *(b)* it does not succeed as a symbol, since it is assumed elsewhere that Israel was pure and faithful when Yahweh "married" her (cf. 9:10; 11:1); *(c)* this would be the only instance in the OT of a prophetic symbolic action representing an existing state of affairs rather than a future event; *(d)* the wording of the divine command is irregular, as there is nothing in the Heb. corresponding to **have**; *(e)* **children of harlotry** cannot mean "children born of a prostitute", but means "children with an inclination to immorality", and there was no reason to expect that the children would follow the character of their mother rather than that of their father; *(f)* in any case the character of the children, like that of their mother, plays no part in the following narrative – it is only their names which are significant. Gomer was therefore, according to Rudolph, not in fact a prostitute, but was a woman of respectable character. The story in ch. 3 has nothing to do with her, according to him: **again** in 3:1 is to be taken with **said**, not **go**, and **her** in 3:2 is better translated "one" in view of the indefinite expression **a woman who . . .** in the preceding verse. He sees Hosea's buying of a prostitute and his confinement of her in his house as an act of symbolic

punishment and no more: in his view the references to **love** in
3:1 are ironical, and the whole of v. 5 is a secondary addition.
Both ch. 1 and ch. 3 therefore originally conveyed a message of
judgment against Israel in symbolic terms.

A similar understanding of ch. 1–3 is adopted by R. E. Clements (*Review and Expositor* 72 (1975), 405–24), J. Schreiner (*BZ* NF
21 (1977), 163–83) and Jeremias (in his commentary), though the
last-named occupies an intermediate position between the views
of Rudolph and Rowley, since he thinks that ch. 3 refers to Gomer
after she had been unfaithful to Hosea. Yee attributes the whole of
ch. 3 to the imagination of an exilic redactor. Other recent writers
have either not discussed Rudolph's overall view of these chapters
(Mays, McKeating, Andersen and Freedman) or have rejected it
(A. Deissler, in J. Schreiner (ed.), *Wort, Lied und Gottespruch* (FS J.
Ziegler), vol. 2, Würzburg, 1972, pp. 129–36: in favour of Wolff's
view). By no means all of Rudolph's arguments are convincing,
and the attempt of Schreiner and Jeremias to argue from the
language of 1:2b that it is a Deuteronomistic addition fails to
attend closely enough to the precise idiom employed, which is
well within the range of Hosea's usage (cf. 4:12; 9:1). Yet some
problems remain for a view such as Rowley's. The marriage to
a prostitute would not accurately symbolize Yahweh's election of
Israel; the phrase **children of harlotry** has not been adequately
elucidated; the narrator's silence makes it unlikely that Gomer
was unfaithful to Hosea; and the wording of 3:1 is rather against
that chapter referring to Gomer.

These problems can all be overcome if the following sequence
of events is presumed (for details see the notes on ch. 1 and ch. 3).
Hosea did not marry Gomer, who was a prostitute: he became
one of her clients, symbolizing thereby the apostate relationship
of Israel to Baal. His three children are called **children of harlotry** because they were born of this extra-marital union. Later
in his life, probably in the aftermath of the Syro–Ephraimite
War, Hosea "bought" and probably married another woman of
immoral character, to symbolize Yahweh's love for his people
Israel, despite their evil character. But he initially refrained
from full sexual relations with her, to represent the period of
discipline that would be required before Israel was ready again
for an intimate relationship with Yahweh. On the theological

level there is thus a continuity in the symbolism, but on the biographical level there was, so far as we can tell, none. (For a fuller account and discussion of Rudolph's views see ch. 6 of my volume on Hosea in the Old Testament Guides series (Sheffield, 1992).)

B. CHAPTERS 4–11:
A History of Doom Reluctantly Imposed

THE EFFECTS OF PRIESTLY NEGLIGENCE:
A PEOPLE WITHOUT KNOWLEDGE OF GOD

4:1–19

A comparison of recent commentaries will show that there is considerable disagreement about how this chapter should be analysed, even though it is generally acknowledged that, with the possible exception of v. 15, we are dealing throughout with authentic sayings of Hosea. Form-critical study certainly confirms the existence of a series of units with different themes and addressees (Robinson; cf. Mays).

Vv. 1–3 are a short and compact judgment speech, in which the accusation is formulated first negatively (v. 1b) and then positively (v. 2), and followed by the sentence (v. 3), which is typically introduced by **therefore** (Heb. *'al kēn*: cf. Westermann, *Basic Forms of Prophetic Speech*, pp. 169–176). Instead of the messenger formula, "Thus says the LORD", which does not occur in Hosea, the unit is introduced by a summons to hear ("proclamation formula") which has parallels in the most varied settings (cf. Wolff, p. 97, and below on v. 1), and then by what may be called an "introduction of the plaintiff", as is found also in 12:2 and Mic. 6:2 (on this cf. Westermann, pp. 199–200). Probably the former of these is the work of the editor of ch. 4–11. But the latter is sufficient to suggest that it is Yahweh himself who is the speaker in vv. 1b–3, even though the decisive proof of first-person pronouns is lacking (cf. Mic. 6:3ff; Isa. 3:13–15). The expression **knowledge of God** is no objection to this, since it is a set formula, and can appear in divine speech (cf. 6:6).

Vv. 4–6 comprise, after a transition (perhaps in dialogue form) which serves to identify a specific addressee, what is formally a prophetic judgment speech against an individual, no doubt a leading priest. Yahweh is the speaker (cf. v. 6). Accusation and sentence alternate in this speech, and the appropriateness of the sentence is underlined in each case by the use of a word from the accusation (**destroy, reject, forget**).

Vv. 7–10 are not a formal unity, precisely because their purpose is to make the transition back to the sin and punishment of the whole people. The priests are accused of wilfully misleading the people and using their misguided devotion to provide sustenance for their swelling ranks (vv. 7–8). This enables Hosea to return to his original theme of the coming judgment on the people (vv. 9–10a) and the reason for it, which he now analyses even more radically in terms of his favourite image of the wife who deserts her true husband for a life of promiscuity (v. 10b).

Two proverbial sayings (vv. 11, 14b) applied specifically to Hosea's times bracket vv. 11–14 (Rudolph). It is not certain that either of them was originally part of this passage, as the first could equally well be an exasperated conclusion to the previous section (Robinson, Frey) and the second shows some signs of being a redactional comment. Between them stands a judgment saying of an unusual kind, in which the accusation is used not to justify an announcement of coming judgment, but to explain an existing situation of social decay.

The introduction to vv. 16–19 (v. 16) employs similes and a rhetorical question to justify Yahweh's attacks on his people. The charge of unresponsiveness (cf. below on **stubborn**) could have arisen from a failure of the people to heed a prophetic warning such as that which precedes in v. 15. At all events, the continuation in vv. 17–19 amplifies the charge by denouncing the people's commitment to a worship that is corrupted by idolatry, drunkenness and sex and by proclaiming its imminent collapse. There is nothing in these verses which compels us to regard them as formally a divine speech, and it may be mistaken to employ the categories of the divine lawsuit here (Wolff, pp. 72, 92). The emphasis falls rather on the emptiness and futility of the pagan practices.

There are more or less clear links between several of these units, which led Wolff to envisage only a twofold division within the chapter. He regards vv. 4–19 as a collection of sayings which are in their original sequence and all derive from a single appearance of the prophet, when he made a series of utterances on related topics. The sayings were, he holds, probably written down quite soon afterwards. As will become clear, Wolff believes that this was in most cases the first stage in the compilation of Hosea's sayings. Rudolph too shows an awareness of connections when he treats

vv. 1–10 as a prophetic speech comprising three strophes, but he sees the connection with 11–14 and 16–19 as looser and due to a later redactor. Of course, some of the continuity that has been observed could equally well be due to careful editorial activity as to an original association. But it does seem most improbable that v. 4 (however exactly 4a is to be translated) was the beginning of a series of sayings, as Wolff originally thought, and it is notable that in the second edition of his commentary and in the English translation (p. 74) he was ready to give greater weight to the connection with vv. 1–3 which he had already partly recognized in the first edition (p. 93: cf. Weiser, p. 44). It is not unlikely that Hosea would pass from a general condemnation of the people to a denunciation of the priesthood, especially in view of what he says in v. 6. Evidently Hosea made this proclamation in a public place, most likely a sanctuary, where a priest was present. While an exact date cannot be given, in the absence of allusions to particular events, the lack of reference to the Assyrians and the turmoil of the years that followed Jeroboam II's death justify the common assumption that the saying belongs to the closing years of Jeroboam's reign (rather than the older view (e.g. Harper, p. 249) that it follows Jeroboam's death). If vv. 1–6 thus seem likely to have been originally associated, it also seems difficult to separate vv. 7–10 from them. Only so can the **they** of v. 7 have a clear reference, as it seems it must, to the priests. Yet the change from direct address to a statement in the third person does imply a development in the situation which we may perhaps understand in terms of a withdrawal by Hosea to the company of a more sympathetic audience. There is, despite Rudolph's objections, no reason why vv. 11–14, 15 and 16–19 should not have been uttered before this same audience (the last perhaps – see the commentary on v. 16 – in the course of discussion), since they develop and concretize the theme of the people's **harlotry**, which has already been introduced in v. 10. But these sections are capable of standing on their own and the possibility that their position is due to a redactor cannot be discounted.

The only certainly redactional element in the chapter is the second clause of v. 5, which broadens the scope of the threat to fit later conditions, probably in the time of Jeremiah. But it is also quite likely that the introductory summons to hear in v. 1 was composed by a redactor as a heading to the collection that begins here, probably with a view to the public reading of it in a later period, when it had come to be accorded a quasi-canonical authority. The marked proverbial air of the end of v. 14 may indicate that it too derives from editorial activity, and it does share the theme of **understanding** (*byn*) with the later didactic conclusion to the book in 14:9. Many (e.g. Rudolph, pp. 112–14) suppose v. 15 to be an insertion from a Judaean editor, but the terms used are scarcely such as are likely to have originated in such a setting, and it should probably be regarded as an isolated saying of Hosea, which has been incorporated here because of the themes of harlotry and criticism of the cult which it shares with its neighbours.

A further topic of disagreement among commentators is the extent of the references to the sins of the priests in particular. They are clearly in view in vv. 4–6 and 7–8, but Rudolph, who transposes vv. 9 and 10, believes that the latter verse still refers to the priests, and Wolff (in part following other scholars) sees allusions to them even in vv. 12–14. In this commentary (see the detailed discussions) the view is taken that v. 9 marks a reversion to the sins of the people in general and that no further specific references to the priests are made until 5:1.

4:1–3. The language of this and the following section is clearly borrowed from a judicial setting, and the occurrence of accusations framed in similarly judicial terms in two psalms which were certainly intended for cultic use (50 and 81) indicates that the "prophetic lawsuit" may well have developed from a feature of temple worship which, if not regular, was at least familiar to Hosea's hearers. There is no need to invoke parallels with ancient Near Eastern diplomacy to back this up, and it certainly cannot be the basis for claims that a covenant modelled on a treaty-form was part of Israelite religion at an early date (cf. R. E. Clements, *Prophecy and Tradition*, Oxford, 1975, pp. 17–20).

4:1. Hear the word of the LORD, O people of Israel: The introductory formula has many close parallels in prophetic literature (especially in Jeremiah and Ezekiel, but cf. also Am. 7:16; Isa. 1:10; 28:14; 39:5). In two respects the language is untypical of Hosea: the expression **the word of the LORD** only occurs elsewhere in the editorial introduction to the book in 1:1, and Hosea nowhere else addresses his hearers as **the people of Israel**: the expression only appears in 1:10–11 (Heb. 2:1–2), which are not Hosean, and in 3:1, 4 and 5. Since elsewhere appeals to hear Yahweh's word have been placed at the beginning of prophetic books or major sections of them (Am. 3:1; Mic. 1:2; 6:1 – cf. Jl 1:2) to affirm that what follows is still a **word of the LORD** to **the people of Israel** in a later age, it seems likely that this introduction too, which stands at the beginning of the main collection of Hosea's sayings, should be ascribed to a redactor, who believed that the words of the prophet had a continuing validity (Wolff).

a controversy: The legal connotations of the Heb. word *rîb* here are better brought out by NEB's "charge against" and JB's "indicts". Cf. RSV's own rendering of *rîb* as "indictment" in 12:2.

kindness: On the Heb. word *ḥesed*, normally rendered "steadfast love" in RSV, see the Excursus on p 94–97. Here, as in 6:4–6, it is clearly a human, not a divine attribute. Probably a failure in Israel's behaviour towards Yahweh as well as one another is criticized here (cf. 6:4). Stoebe (*THAT*, vol. 1, p. 615) suggests that the order of the qualities is deliberately different from 2:21: "if no faithfulness is there, there should at least be *ḥesed* ('devotion of heart'); if this too is missing . . ." But when *ḥesed* is properly understood (see the Excursus), this seems less likely: *ḥesed* is the outworking of the commitment expressed by **faithfulness** (*ʾemet*).

knowledge of God: See the note on **you shall know the LORD** in 2:20. It is unlikely that the alternation of **LORD** and **God** (for the latter cf. 6:6) is of major significance in the phrase (against J. L. McKenzie, *JBL* 74 (1955), 22–27). The destruction of the people is ascribed exclusively to **lack of knowledge** in v. 6 below, and that lack is blamed on the priests' failure to teach knowledge.

4:2. swearing: The Heb. word (*ʾālāh*) strictly refers to a conditional curse or one pronounced on a person as yet unidentified, and as such could relate to the curses which were a common feature of ancient Near Eastern treaties (cf. 10:4) or to the imprecations used in judicial inquiries (1 Kg. 8:31–32). This speaks against the view of recent commentators (Wolff, Rudolph and Mays) that the prophet means abusive cursing such as that referred to in Exod. 21:17; 22:28 (Heb. 27); Lev. 19:14. Targ. reflects an early opinion that false swearing, i.e. lying on oath, is meant (as it does also in Exod. 20:7), and Wellhausen, followed, e.g., by Mauchline, suggested that the words **swearing** and **lying** should be taken together (as a hendiadys) in this sense. On this basis a reference to perjury (JB) is possible. But since the next three words in the verse are not to be taken in this way, it seems more likely that **swearing** and **lying** refer to distinct activities and that Hosea is attacking the customary institution itself, probably because it was the vehicle of false accusations: hence the close association with **lying** here. Possibly v. 15 also refers to this, but see the commentary there.

killing, stealing, and committing adultery: These three charges echo exactly the words used in the sixth, seventh and eighth commandments of the Decalogue (according to the English numeration). **stealing** and **committing adultery** are in the reverse order to that in the MT of Exod. 20:13–15 and Dt. 5:17–19, but it is clear from Lk. 18:20 and Rom. 13:9, as well as evidence from Egyptian Jewish sources, that the order of the short commandments was not rigidly fixed even as late as New Testament times (E. Nielsen, *The Ten Commandments in Recent Perspective*, London, 1968, p. 12, with n. 4). The difference in order is scarcely a significant argument against the view that Hosea knew and is here alluding to the demands of the Decalogue, which is held, e.g., by Weiser, Rudolph and W. Brueggemann, *Tradition for Crisis*, pp. 38–43. There may be some connection between the references to **swearing** and **lying** and the third and the ninth commandments as well, although neither in language nor in scope is there an exact correspondence in these cases. If the Decalogue had already been formulated (at least in its original form) in the time of Hosea, then it is probable that he refers to it here. But this is a matter that is sharply debated (see J. J. Stamm and M. E. Andrew, *The Ten Commandments in Recent Research*, London, 1968, pp. 22–69; A. D. H. Mayes, *Deuteronomy* (NCB), London, 1979, pp. 162–65), and it is doubtful if the present passage can be used, as it sometime is, to determine it. At most it could be said that the idea of a catalogue of common sins seems to be shared in both texts, so that their formulation should be placed in the same stream of tradition (cf. Buss, pp. 100–101).

they break all bounds: As a general expression for lawlessness (cf. NEB "licence") this would be a unique use of the verb. More likely is either the meaning "act violently" (BDB, Marti – cf. the related adjective *pārîṣ* in Ezek. 18:10 etc.) or the meaning "increase" (as in v. 10 below, and several other passages), with the preceding sins being taken as the subject (so Wolff, Rudolph and Mays): the Hebrew has no equivalent to **there is**. It is not necessary to emend to an infinitive absolute form like those that have preceded (BHS, *HTOT*, p. 245). LXX adds "in the land" after **bounds**, giving a pointed contrast between what is not present in the land (v. 1) and what is, and Wolff and Rudolph regard this as original. Metrical considerations, however, seem to be against this view.

murder: Literally "blood (shed)". It is taken by Wolff to refer to capital punishment, the penalty prescribed for at least most of the offences previously mentioned. But probably this is, as RSV takes it, a recapitulation of the worst crime: for Hosea's sensitivity to this cf. 1:4 and 6:9. Kuhnigk follows Dahood in supposing that the Heb. *dāmîm* could mean "idols", from the root *dmh*, thus introducing a reference to idolatry as in the similar passage in Jer. 7:9 (pp. 26–28). But, while idolatry is elsewhere a theme of Hosea's rebukes (cf. 8:4; 14:8), it is linguistically unlikely that it is implied here.

4:3. Although it is not explicitly stated here that Yahweh will send the drought, this is implied not only by v. 9 below but by the fact (cf. above) that Yahweh has already been identified as the speaker in v. 1b. There is no room here for the idea of an automatic response of the natural world to the sins of the people (Wolff).

mourns: G. R. Driver, in B. Schindler and A. Marmorstein (eds.), *Occident and Orient* (Gaster Volume), London, 1936, pp. 73–82, showed that Heb. *'ābal* sometimes means "dry up" and not "mourn" (cf. Akkadian *abālu*, and the association with *'umlal* = "languish" here and elsewhere), so NEB's "shall be dried up" is to be followed (cf. KB, HAL, Wolff). A future interpretation of the verbs is also to be preferred (Wolff, Mays; against Rudolph), since v. 3b can only refer to a quite extraordinary phenomenon that must be a subject of prophetic expectation (cf. Am. 7:4) rather than present experience.

the beasts of the field: LXX adds "and the creeping things of the ground" (cf. 2:18), but this is probably secondary, as it gives the oracle an inappropriately prosaic conclusion.

4:4–6. This rejection of the priest and his family should be compared with that pronounced against Eli in 1 Sam. 2:27–36 and, for a close verbal parallel, with Samuel's repudiation of Saul (1 Sam. 15:22–3). But unlike these instances, Hosea has nothing to say about a replacement for the discredited official. It should not be supposed (against Wolff, p. 74) that Hosea excuses the people by his attack on the priesthood: their **lack of knowledge** is not an ignorance that frees them from blame but, as v. 1 shows, a basis for Yahweh's suit against them. The responsibility of the leader does not eliminate that of the led (cf. Ezek. 33:7–9).

4:4. contend . . . accuse: These legal terms refer to a possible (or actual) counter-charge (rather than a possible human accuser of the people (NEB)). There is no need to read these verbs as passives (Wolff), especially as it is doubtful whether *'îš 'al* could mean "not just anyone". A particularly vivid sequence is obtained if the first two lines of the verse are regarded as the attempt of a priest to silence Hosea (cf. Am. 7:12ff.), which provoked the following denunciation: "But with you is my contention, O priest." For **Yet** (Heb. *'ak*) introducing an objection cf. 12:9. For opposition to Hosea's preaching cf. 9:7, and the note in the commentary on that verse.

for: Rather "but"; see the preceding comment.

contention: Heb. *rîb*, as in v. 1, indicating how Yahweh's judicial action concentrates upon the priesthood. For a similar passage from a later period see Mal. 2:1–9. These prophets believed that their direct commission by Yahweh gave them the right to criticize and even (see below) condemn the established religious authorities.

The Heb. text of this line is awkward ("your people are like the adversaries of the priest"), although the general sense is evident. The emendation adopted by RSV is the one most likely to be correct. Sellin, followed by G. R. Driver, *JTS* 39 (1938), 155, proposed to read *kōmer*, "idolatrous priest" (cf. 10:5), from which NEB's "false priest" derives. Possibly the obscure MT reading is due to a deliberate attempt to soften the attack on the official priesthood.

priest: The following denunciation only makes sense if it was part of the function of priests at the time to teach the law: on this aspect of their work see P. J. Budd, *VT* 23 (1973), 1–14, and A. Cody, *History of OT Priesthood* (AnBib 35), Rome, 1969, pp. 116–18.

4:5. by day: *hayyôm* in fact means "today" (cf. Vulg.), and the RSV translation here (already in LXX, and cf. NEB, JB) can only be justified by emending the text (Neh. 4:16, cited by Wolff, is not a clear case of *hayyôm* meaning "by day"). The case for this is weak, being based only on the parallel **by night**, which is part of an addition to the text (see below). The original text was therefore a threat of immediate judgement on the priest, which a redactor misunderstood and amplified by what seemed an appropriate threat against false prophets.

the prophet also shall stumble with you by night: The reference to **the prophet** is not taken up by Hosea either here or elsewhere, and this part of the verse is probably an extension of the original threat, introduced by a redactor in a situation of "prophetic conflict" (cf. J.L. Crenshaw, *Prophetic Conflict* (BZAW 124), Berlin and New York, 1971, and S. J. de Vries, *Prophet Against Prophet*, Grand Rapids, 1978). The striking similarity in form to the addition in 5:5 suggests that this took place in Judah (Wolff), and the coupling of priests and prophets in Jeremiah's oracles may indicate the background against which the addition was made (cf. Jer. 6:13; 8:10).

and I will destroy: Both NEB (cf. *HTOT*, p. 246) and JB are based on an emended text (cf. Wolff), but neither sense nor grammar require this, and MT, rendered by RSV, can be retained (cf. Rudolph and Mays).

your mother: For judgment on the priest's family we may compare Am. 7:17, though it is unusual to find a mother singled out for mention. Of the passages cited as parallels by Wolff none is closely similar: Jer. 13:18 and 22:26 are a special case involving the queen mother, Ps. 109:14 mentions a mother's sin in an exhaustive catalogue of the family of the psalmist's enemy and 1 Sam. 15:33 is concerned with the effect of the killing of Agag on his mother, not with the latter directly. It is worth considering whether there may not be some echo of the metaphor used by Hosea in 2:2ff., where the mother stands for the whole people (cf. Targ. here, 10:14f., and Isa. 50:1), or whether the priest's city is meant (cf. 2 Sam. 20:19). But the text is probably disturbed. Rudolph's proposal to read *'ummeykā* in the sense of "your clans" keeps close to MT, and the rarity of the word in Heb. is to some extent compensated for by the existence of cognates in other languages (Robertson Smith (*The Prophets of Israel*, p. 408) cited Arabic *'ummah* with the same meaning, and a cognate also seems to exist in the Mari texts (cf. A. Malamat, *Mari and the Early Israelite Experience* (Schweich Lectures), London, 1989, pp. 41–43)). A more regular way of expressing the same meaning is obtained if a slightly more extensive emendation is adopted, reading *bēt 'ābîkā* for *'immekā*. Either of these conjectures would fit well with the general context, which seems to be a prophetic repudiation of a particular leading priestly family, to which a close parallel exists in 1 Sam. 2:27–36.

4:6. My people: There is no connective in the Heb. between this and the preceding verse, but possibly the conjunction "because" (*kî*) has been lost by haplography in the consonantal text. Who is the speaker here? It is more likely to be Yahweh, in view of the **I**'s of v. 5 and the second half of this verse (Wolff, Rudolph), than Hosea himself, although psalms of lament do sometimes make an individual speak of the troubles of "my people" (cf. also Mic. 2:8–9; 3:2). It is even possible that these words are once again an interjection of the priest addressed in v. 4, proposing as an excuse the ignorance of his people. To this v. 6b (**because you have rejected knowledge . . .**) would then be Yahweh's answer (**you** is emphatic in the Heb.). If the usual punctuation is retained this line becomes a lament of Yahweh on behalf of his people (cf. v. 8, but note the change in v. 12).

law: Or "instruction": cf. NEB "teaching".

4:7–10. The beginning of this section still refers to the priesthood and its offences, but it employs the third person plural (*they*) to generalize from the confrontation reflected in vv. 4–6. As it proceeds, the announcement is widened still further to include the whole people once again (vv. 9–10).

4:7. I will change . . . : JB renders "they have bartered" (cf.

Targ., Syr., Wolff), seeing this as an accusation comparable to
Jer. 2:11 and Ps. 106:20. This meaning can be obtained by a small
change to MT (read *hēmîrû* for *'āmîr*). Kuhnigk (pp. 43–44), taking
up an idea of Nyberg (p. 28), supposes that it can be derived
from the consonants of MT, but he makes the questionable
assumption that biblical Hebrew employed an Aphel causative
theme alongside the Hiphil.

   their glory: If **I will change** is retained, **their glory** will
refer to the honour enjoyed by the priests, but if JB's rendering
of the Heb. is followed it will mean Yahweh himself (cf. Ps.
3:4 for this use of "**glory**", and the similar use of "pride" in
Am. 8:7). According to a late Rabbinic tradition (Midr. Tanch.
p. 83ª Wilna) this is one of the places where MT represents
a modification of the original text by scrupulous scribes: "my
glory" (*kᵉbôdî*) was changed into **their glory** (*kᵉbôdām*) to avoid a
possibly blasphemous statement. But here at least this is unlikely
(cf. C. McCarthy, *The Tiqqune Sopherim*, (OBO 36), Freiburg,
1981, pp. 98–101, and *IDBS*, pp. 263–64).

   shame: This either refers to a coming calamity or, on JB's
interpretation of the verse, to "a shameful thing" (abstract for
concrete), i.e. another god in Yahweh's place.

   4:8. the sin: The Heb. word can also be used for a "sin-
offering" (cf. on 8:11), but this is less likely to be the sense
here, in parallel to **their iniquity**.

   my people: Cf. the note on v. 6. Yahweh also speaks thus in
4:12; 6:11 and 11:7, as though 1:9 had not been said!

   they are greedy for: This rendering (cf. JB, NEB, Wolff)
requires the emendation of MT *napšsô*, to *napšām*, a reading
attested in some late MSS and possibly in the ancient versions.
But the singular suffix of MT is the *difficilior lectio* and may
refer back to **my people** (Nyberg, p. 29, and H. Junker, *BZ* 4
(1960) 167). The phrase may then be translated, "they direct its
desire towards . . .": the priests draw the people into the error
which they have themselves initiated. If the construction thus
envisaged is unusual (so Rudolph p. 98; cf. Wolff, p. 71), this
may be because the action in question is itself unnatural.

   4:9. And it shall be . . . : "So it shall be . . ." is equally
possible.

them . . . their: The Heb. pronouns are singular, and must therefore refer back to **my people** in v. 8. This means that the phrase translated **like people, like priest** must be taken to mean that the people will find themselves entangled in the punishment that has already been announced for the priests (vv. 5–6).

4:10. They shall eat . . . : Here the verbs are plural, but it is evident from the connection with v. 9 that, by a natural transition in grammar (cf. *GK* §145g), it is the people who are meant. There is no justification for regarding v. 9 as either an interpolation (Wolff) or misplaced (from after v. 10 – so Rudolph), and v. 10 as therefore, like v. 8, referring to the priests alone.

Comparable punishments are found in Am. 5:11; Mic. 6:14–15; Zeph. 1:13 and Dt. 28:30–31, 38–40, and also in ancient Near Eastern treaties (cf. Hillers, *Treaty-Curses*, pp. 28ff.). The parallel between Mic. 6:14a and Hos. 4:10a is especially close. It has been suggested that this motif may have been borrowed by the prophets from the ritual of a covenant renewal festival that was modelled on the treaty pattern (Mays), but it is also possible that both the prophets and the treaties derived it from everyday life. There is, in any case, doubt over whether Israel's covenant with Yahweh had been formulated in a treaty-like form in the 8th century BC, (cf. Clements, *Prophecy and Tradition*, pp. 15–17). That such ideas could emerge out of everyday experience is shown by Ecclesiastes 6:1–2, 7 and other passages.

they shall play the harlot: The Hiphil of *zānāh*, which is used here, in 4:18 (twice) and in 5:3, is elsewhere causative (Exod. 34:16; Lev. 19:29; 2 Chr. 21:11, 13 (twice)). It might therefore here mean "they shall make (their women) act as prostitutes", and the reference could be to fathers dedicating their daughters to serve as cult prostitutes (cf. v. 14 for a clear reference to these), a practice attested in Babylonia in the Code of Hammurabi, para. 181 (*ANET*, p. 174), and specifically prohibited in Lev. 19:29. In any case, the logic of the verse (see the next note) presupposes that what was done could normally be expected to lead to plentiful offspring, and indicates that some kind of fertility ritual is in view.

but not multiply: For this meaning of *pāraṣ* cf. Exod. 1:12 (and elsewhere). NEB has "but their lust will never be overtaxed" (cf. Vulg.). Although a sexual use of the root is found in later Hebrew and Syriac, that is a weak basis for departing from the normal interpretation.

the LORD: The object is unusually placed before the verb in the Heb. to emphasize the enormity of what the people have done. The third-person reference to Yahweh is surprising in divine speech (which is indicated by the **I** in v. 9), and possibly we should read *'ōtî*, "me", for *'et yhwh* with Weiser and BHS, supposing that the consonant *yodh* was misread by a scribe as an abbreviation for the divine name (see G. R. Driver, *Textus* I (1960), 112–31, for other possible examples of such misreading). On the other hand the occurrence of "your God" in v. 6, also in divine speech, gives support to MT: both there and here the fuller expression strengthens the accusation.

to cherish harlotry: MT (cf. Targ., Vulg.) makes **harlotry** the first of three subjects of **take away** in v. 11. RSV is based on a different division of the verses supported by LXX and Syr., which has the advantage of providing an object for **to cherish** (so also NEB, JB and most commentators). Mays thinks that the word **harlotry** is needed in both places, and that one occurrence of it was lost by haplography (p. 72 n.). This is scarcely necessary. The verb translated **cherish** can have a deity as its object (cf. Ps. 31:6, "those who pay regard to vain idols"; cf. also Jon. 2:8), and Kuhnigk thinks that **harlotry** is intended as a title for Baal, like **shame** in v. 7 (p. 47). Since the image of prostitution is used for the people's action rather than the god himself, this seems unlikely.

4:11–14. These verses contain a fresh divine accusation against the people (cf. vv. 1b–2). It focuses on the religious practices of the time, which are permeated by the **harlotry** of which Hosea has already spoken (v. 12 – cf. v. 10). Typically, however, Hosea breaks out of the formal structure of the accusation to indicate that the sexual promiscuity of the young women of his time is but a consequence of the men's apostasy and is therefore not subject to the expected divine punishment for such behaviour (for which see Lev. 18:20, 29 and H. McKeating, *JSOT* 11 (1979), 57–72).

4:11. Wine and new wine: Most probably **Wine** and **new wine** were originally alternative readings which were both included in the standard text. **new wine** (*tîrôš*) is not, in the

biblical period, unfermented grape juice (against Wolff, p. 83),
since the Ugaritic cognate *trt* in one passage clearly refers to
intoxicating liquor (*Ugaritica* V, no. 1, obv. 4; *CML*, p. 137), and
the ancient versions in the present verse lay special stress on the
idea of drunkenness. Normally when rendering *tîrôš* they employ
their regular words for wine: it was only in post-biblical Hebrew
that *tîrôš* came to be clearly differentiated from *yayin* ("wine"), as
in T. Ned. 4:3, Y. Ned. 7:40b. It has been suggested that *tîrôš*
was in origin nothing but an archaic equivalent for *yayin* (L.
Koehler, *ZAW* 46 (1928), 218–20), but the view that it was a
special word for the new vintage remains possible (Rudolph),
even though the versions seem to know nothing of this special
meaning. The following words (**take away the understanding**)
can therefore be seen as a reference to intoxication, but Wolff's
suggestion that it is the overpowering desire for the fruits of
the new harvest which drives the people on to idolatrous rites
fits Hosea's thought better (cf. 7:14, where **wine** is *tîrôš*). If,
as many think, the verse is a popular proverb, it may have
been given a fresh turn by Hosea. The NEB footnote suggests
"embolden" for **take away the understanding**, reading *yōqîaḥ*
for *yiqqaḥ* (*HTOT*, p. 246) and deriving it from a Heb. cognate
of the Arabic *waqiḥa* ("be without shame"), which is supposed to
occur also in Num. 16:1 (cf. *HAL*, p. 411, and Barr, *Comparative
Philology*, pp. 17–19). But there is no strong reason to prefer this
to the obvious rendering of the traditional text.

    understanding: Heb. *lēb*, which is normally translated "heart"
but commonly has in view the capacity to think and act
sensibly.

    4:12. My people: This phrase can be understood as a genitive
depending on **understanding** in the previous verse: ". . . the
understanding of my people" (so NEB, following LXX and
many commentators). On this view v. 11 certainly provides an
explanation for what follows. But MT's verse division, followed
by RSV and JB, is also quite satisfactory and v. 11 (perhaps a
proverbial saying) may then be taken closely either with v. 10,
or with v. 12. Here there is no question of Yahweh taking the
side of the people in a lament, as might be suggested for the use
of **my people** in vv. 6 and 8: they themselves are accused here
(cf. 11:7).

a thing of wood: The Heb. has a possessive suffix which RSV does not translate: JB "their block of wood" is more exact in this, and conveys Hosea's point that the people choose their own sources of oracles instead of turning to Yahweh (Rudolph). The reference is presumably to a wooden idol: cf. Ezek. 21:21 (Heb. 26), "he consults the teraphim". Alternatively *'ēṣ* might be taken in its meaning "tree" and thought to refer to a sacred tree where oracles were given: compare the oak of Moreh in Gen. 12:6 and "Diviners' Oak" in Jg. 9:37 – "the oaks in which you have delighted" in Isa. 1:29 may also refer to this practice. Wolff aptly comments that by using the plain word **wood** or "tree" Hosea demythologizes the Canaanite cultic objects (p. 84).

their staff: The word can mean a "branch" (Jer. 1:11) or a "stick" used by a traveller (Gen. 32:11). Already Jerome in his commentary (*PL* 25:850) saw here a reference to the practice of rhabdomancy (divination by means of sticks), which was common in the classical world, and modern commentators have been content to follow suit, even though evidence of such a custom is hard to find in the ancient Near East (cf. A. L. Oppenheim, *Ancient Mesopotamia*, Chicago, 1964, pp. 208f.). Ezek. 21:21, often quoted in this connection, mentions arrows, not sticks, in the Heb. and LXX's "rods" there no doubt represents an assimilation to the practice familiar in classical literature. The use of the singular **staff** here perhaps points rather to a small wooden idol (W. Robertson Smith, *Lectures on the Religion of the Semites*, 3rd. ed., London, 1927, pp. 196–97), so called to deprive it of any mystique (cf. above). Compare the notes on **ephod** and **teraphim** in 3:4. A diviner's "wand" (*BDB*, REB) seems less likely.

a spirit of harlotry: Cf. 5:4. In both these passages **spirit** stands for what would now be called the will, or a disposition to act in a particular way (cf. Wolff, *Anthropology*, p. 38). Hosea's point is that the people are irretrievably set on a particular pattern of life, unable to respond to Yahweh's appeals to return to him. There is no suggestion that the people are in the grip of a power exterior to themselves (against Wolff, here).

4:13. poplar: Also mentioned in Gen. 30:37, it is etymologically a "white" tree (*libneh*), and the word is used in modern Heb. for "birch". In view of the Arabic and Ethiopic cognates, and LXX on Gen. 30:37, it is more likely here to be *Styrax officinalis*, the storax-tree, than the **poplar** (cf. *IDB*, vol. 2, 294, Wolff, p. 86, and *HAL*, p. 492). The storax is a common small tree of Eastern Mediterranean countries. Rudolph, however, retains the meaning "(white) poplar", following LXX, Aq. and Vulg. (cf. NEB, JB).

their shade: Literally, "its shade", so that NEB's "under oak and poplar and the terebinth's pleasant shade" is a more exact translation.

This verse clearly speaks of hill-top rituals and sacred groves: cf. the expressions "on every high hill" and "under every luxuriant [rather than "green"] tree", which later became conventional (Jer. 2:20 etc.). The choice of such sites was probably governed by both religious and other considerations. See further H. Ringgren, *Israelite Religion*, London, 1966, pp. 157–58 for this kind of cult, with its obviously Canaanite background, although his remarks on "high places" (*bāmôt*) need correction in the light of recent studies (see below on 10:8). A hill-top shrine with a splendid image of a bull dating from the Judges period was recently found in the hills east of Samaria (cf. A. Mazar, *BASOR* 247 (1982), 27–42; King, *Commentary*, pp. 95–97).

your ... your: Hosea turns to address the people directly. **your brides** (*kallôtêhem*) can equally mean "your daughters-in-law" (so JB, NEB), so that Hosea's audience may have consisted of the older generation.

play the harlot ... commit adultery: It is possible to see the offence as straightforward sexual promiscuity and infidelity, and the point of Hosea's **Therefore** will then be that religious apostasy is to blame for the breakdown of traditional sexual morality (for which cf. v. 2): for the women simply copy the example of their menfolk (v. 14b). This is essentially how the passage is understood by Harper, Robinson, Weiser and Rudolph (p. 112). But Wolff (pp. 86–87; cf. p. 14), following L. Rost, in W. Baumgartner et al. (ed.), *Festschrift Alfred Bertholet*, Tübingen, 1950, pp. 451–60, and earlier scholars, sees here a reference to the bridal rites of cultic prostitution whose existence he detects behind several of Hosea's sayings (cf. on 1:2). The **Therefore** then relates this activity to the general acceptance of alien religious practices or, as Wolff thinks, to "the priests' 'spirit of whoredom'" (p. 87), for he thinks that the "they" of vv. 12b–13a are the priests (surely an unnatural interpretation). Wolff's theory involves several difficulties (cf. on 1:2), and one cannot legitimately go beyond saying that Hosea's words would have included a reference to cultic prostitution along with promiscuity outside the cult (Marti; Wellhausen and Nowack emphasize the cultic aspect unduly).

4:14. the men themselves: Literally an emphatic "they". The reversion to the third person is surprising and the attempts of NEB ("your men") and JB ("everyone else") to gloss over it are scarcely true to the Heb. Some commentators smooth the unevenness by emending **your** to "their" in vv. 13b–14a (Marti, Robinson), while others suppose that a different group is meant by "they" here, either the elders or, more often, the priests (Harper, Jacob, Wolff). This may, however, be another case of Hosea turning temporarily towards and then away from a particular group (cf. 5:3; 8:5).

cult prostitutes: These are only rarely mentioned in the OT: in Gen. 38:20–22 Tamar is so characterized in a story that seems to take such behaviour as a matter of course, while in Dt. 23:17 it is completely forbidden. The same verse also prohibits male **cult prostitutes**. The masculine form is also used in texts referring to cultic activities in Judah (1 Kg. 14:24; 15:12; 22:46; 2 Kg. 23:7). It is not usually observed that it may be used as a general term for **cult prostitutes** of both sexes. In 2 Kg. 23:7 they are linked with the worship of Asherah, a Canaanite goddess well known from the Ugaritic myths (see also above on v. 12). Sexual rites in the religion of the northern kingdom are probably also referred to in v. 10 above, and possibly also in Am. 2:7. Such practices were evidently quite widespread both in the Levant and in Mesopotamia: for the references see H. Ringgren, *Religions of the Ancient Near East*, London, 1973, pp. 25, 81, 167. It is not clear whether worshippers in general or only cult functionaries would take part in them, but it is difficult to restrict the present context to the latter, as Wolff does. Presumably these rites were thought of as ensuring, by sympathetic magic, the fertility of the people and their animals (cf. on v. 10), but it has to be recognized that very little is in fact known about them, and a recent study has questioned whether actual rites are involved at all, as distinct from ordinary prostitution from which a shrine profited financially (K. van der Toorn, *JBL* 108 (1989), 193–205).

a people without understanding shall come to ruin: Both in its general form and in its concern with **understanding** this saying exhibits a proverbial character (cf. v. 11, although the words for **understanding** are different). It is probably no coincidence that the verb **come to ruin** occurs elsewhere in the Bible only in Prov. 10:8, 10. For the sense cf. Prov. 11:14, and especially Isa. 27:11. Hosea uses the root *byn*, "understand", only here (13:2 is corrupt and 14:10 is redactional – see the commentary), which suggests that this concluding half-line of the saying may be a later gloss (so also Nowack). On the other hand, it provides a natural conclusion to a passage which has been much concerned with lack of knowledge (vv. 1 and 6) and understanding (v. 11). Either way, it is more likely to refer to the people as a whole (Wolff) than only to the young women (Ehrlich, Rudolph, citing the Talmudic use of the phrase).

4:15. It is very doubtful whether MT, which is followed by RSV (and JB) and retained by Rudolph and Mays, gives the true sense in the first half of the verse. Its meaning would be that, while the northern kingdom of Israel has fallen prey to apostasy, Judah can still, and should, keep herself free from any such guilt. A century after Hosea both Jeremiah (3:6ff.) and Ezekiel (ch. 23) were to draw attention to the way in which Judah had failed to learn the lesson of Israel's demise, and there are indeed verses elsewhere in Hosea (most of them probably from a redactor) which emphasize that Judah's parallel offence merits a parallel punishment to that imposed on the northern kingdom (5:5; 6:4; 8:14; 10:11; 12:2 (Heb. v. 3)). This verse envisages a situation in which Judah has not yet **become guilty** in this way, but may do so. It is not impossible to attribute such an idea to Hosea, at least in an early phase of his ministry (for the period around 734 see, however, 5:10, 14). Nevertheless it is expressed in a curious way, and Heb. *'im*, translated **Though** here, normally means "if", except in a hypothetical sentence, which this is not. The word is also textually uncertain, as LXX and Syr. read *'im*, ("with") in place of it. There are other divergences from MT in the ancient versions, but it is not clear whether these are due to variations in the Heb. texts on which they are based or to their own inaccuracy. A number of attempts have been made to reach a likely sense by emendation and fresh interpretations of particular words (e.g. Wolff, p. 72), but none of them is obviously correct. Many commentators regard either the word **Judah** (Wolff) or the whole verse (Rudolph, G. Warmuth, *Das Mahnwort* (BET 1), Frankfurt and Berne, 1976, pp. 41–44) as secondary in the context, but this cannot in itself solve the textual problem. NEB, ". . . they are a mother turned wanton. Bring no guilt offering, Israel; do not come to Gilgal, Judah . . .", revocalizes *'im zōneh* (**though, play the harlot**) as *'ēm zōnāh*, "a mother turned wanton", treating it as the end of the previous verse; assumes that a second-person form of the verb *'šm* (**become guilty**) should be read and that it could be a denominative of the noun *'āšām* = "guilt-offering" (for the latter cf. Nyberg, pp. 30–31, *HAL*, p. 92, and comments below on 5:15); and divides the verse differently, with some support from the versions (not all these changes are acknowledged in *HTOT*, p. 246). The resulting sense is smooth and generally apt, but the alterations to MT are rather drastic. Best of all, perhaps, is Emmerson's suggestion (*Hosea*, p. 80–83) that the words **let not Judah become guilty** are a later addition and that the rest of the verse, with *'im* (**Though**) translated in its usual sense of "If", warns Israel to keep away from the holy shrines until she has ceased to **play the harlot**, presumably because they will gain nothing by attending them as they are (cf. 4:10; 5:6, 15).

Enter not . . . nor go up: From passages elsewhere in Hosea it is clear that both **Gilgal** (12:11) and **Beth-aven** (10:5) were famous shrines, and so it will be worship at these shrines which is prohibited here. Amos likewise warned the people against attendance at well-known places of worship, including **Gilgal** (4:4–5; 5:5). In fact the wording here is so similar (though in no part identical) to Am. 5:5 that it is almost certain that this is a deliberate echo of Amos' words (see also below on **Beth-aven**). Another probable echo of Amos can be found in 8:14.

Gilgal is mentioned on a number of occasions in the OT, chiefly in connection with the Israelites' arrival in Canaan (Jos. 3–5, 10) and the beginning of the monarchy (1 Sam. 10–15), when it was already an important place of sacrifice.

It was located in the tribal territory of Benjamin, "on the east border of Jericho", according to Jos. 4:19, close to the Jordan, but its precise site is not certainly known. Most scholars now locate it near Khirbet el-Mefjir (Hisham's Palace), following J. Muilenberg's thorough study (*BASOR* 140 (1955), 11–27; cf. *IDB*, vol. 2, 398f.), but some difficulties remain with this identification (see J. A. Soggin, *Joshua*, London, 1972, p. 10, for more recent bibliography). It seems likely that the Gilgal shrine and its festivals played an important part in the early development of the OT traditions about the Israelite conquest and perhaps the Exodus as well (cf. G. von Rad, *The Problem of the Hexateuch and other essays*, Edinburgh, 1966, pp. 41–48; H. J. Kraus, *Worship in Israel*, Oxford, 1966, pp. 152–165; Soggin, *Joshua*, pp. 9–10 etc.; F. M. Cross, *Canaanite Myth and Hebrew Epic*, Cambridge (Mass.), 1973, pp. 103–105). But for Hosea it is only a place of sacrifice which is destined for ruin (12:11), because it has become the focus of all that is evil in Yahweh's eyes (9:15). It is only possible to speculate what this evil was, but presumably the Gilgal cult exhibited the tendencies which Hosea has already described earlier in this chapter. Possibly the "sculptured stones" (JB "idols", Heb. *pesîlîm*) of Gilgal (Jg. 3:19) earned his rebuke.

Beth-aven: As the reference to the "calves" of **Beth-aven** in 10:5 makes clear, this must be a derogatory name ("the house of evil") for the famous sanctuary of Bethel, "the house of God". The new name is in fact derived from the very similar saying in Am. 5:5, which concludes, "and Bethel shall come to naught" (*le'āwen*). A recent suggestion is that it was a deliberate distortion of "Beth-eben" ("the house of the stone"), which could have been an alternative name for the shrine in view of Gen. 28:18 and 35:14 (N. Naaman, *ZDPV* 103 (1987), 14). The invention of the name **Beth-aven** (for which see 5:8 as well as 10:5) is usually seen as an expression of Hosea's own disapproval of the Bethel sanctuary and all that it stood for. Emmerson, however, in line with her more positive estimate of Hosea's attitude to the shrine itself and her interpretation of the verse as a whole (see above), attributes it to a later Judaean point of view, which was critical of Bethel simply because it was a rival shrine to Jerusalem (*Hosea*, pp. 124–38). The location of Bethel at Beitin ten miles north of Jerusalem is generally accepted (but cf. J. Bimson, *Redating the*

Exodus and Conquest (JSOTSS 5), Sheffield, 1978, pp. 215–25 for recent discussion). Excavations have not so far identified the shrine, which probably lay outside the city, but a South Arabian seal from about the 9th century BC found there indicates trade with this incense-producing area (see *EAEHL*, vol. 1, 191–93 for details). Bethel had a long history behind it as a royal sanctuary (Am. 7:13) with an ancient tradition (cf. Gen. 28:11–22; 35:6–15; 1 Kg. 12:29–33; and Kraus, *Worship in Israel*, pp. 146–52). Hosea himself was later to refer to the story of Jacob's encounter with God there (12:4 (Heb. v. 5)). More recently, however, it had been the scene of a confrontation between the priest Amaziah and the prophet Amos, who had proclaimed its imminent doom (Am. 3:14; 5:5; 7:12–17).

   and swear not, "As the LORD lives": Oaths beginning with this formula (Heb. *ḥay yhwh*) are common in the OT, especially in the books of Samuel and Kings (e.g. 1 Sam. 14:39). Nowhere else in the OT is this practice as such called in question, and it was widely used by Hosea's prophetic predecessors in the 9th century (e.g. 1 Kg. 17:1; 22:14; 2 Kg. 2:2). In Jer. 12:16 and 44:26 it is identified as one of the marks of the chosen people. Commentators have therefore found it difficult to believe that Hosea can have meant to outlaw it altogether. There is also the fact that taken as it stands the prohibition seems to have little to do with the context, which is concerned with the cultic abuses of Hosea's times. Consequently it is widely held that a reference to Beersheba should be inserted (so Wellhausen, Nowack, Budde, Harper and Rudolph (p. 107): **swear not in Beersheba, "As the LORD lives"**); or that a reference to oaths at **Gilgal** and Bethel is implied by the context (Wolff, p. 90; cf. NEB); or even (Jacob, p. 43; cf. Mays) that Hosea thought the formula to have been corrupted by use in the fertility cult, which one might conjecture from words that greet the news of Baal's resurrection in the Ugaritic myth (CTA 6.3.20 = *CML*, p. 78). Nevertheless there is no support in the textual tradition for emendation, and it is not necessary to assume that Hosea meant more than what he said: that a practice was a "normal" aspect of contemporary religion did not protect it from his criticism, as the example of sacrifice shows, nor was he afraid to differ from earlier prophets (cf.

on 1:4). The objection that swearing is not in itself relevant
to the context loses force when passages like Dt. 6:13 and
Jer. 4:2 are compared: for the Israelite the connection was
closer than might seem the case now. As in the previous part
of the verse, there is an interesting connection with words of
Amos, this time with 8:14, where Amos pronounces doom on
"those who swear by Ashimah of Samaria and say 'As thy
god lives, O Dan' and 'As the way of Beersheba lives'". The
details are somewhat obscure, but it seems that Hosea has
turned rather specific criticisms of innovations in oath-taking
into an attack on a long-accepted formula. If Emmerson's
interpretation of the verse is followed (see above), there is of
course no problem, as the standard oath-formula would only be
prohibited for as long as Israel continued to **play the harlot**.

4:16–19. The opening appeal to reason in support of Yahweh's
judgment implies that Israel has brought her doom upon herself:
she can only be treated in a way appropriate to her character.
Hosea may well have been replying to an objection to his
message that was based on the traditional image of Yahweh
as the shepherd who cares for the flock Israel (cf. Ps. 80:1 (Heb.
v. 2)), an image which he himself was quite prepared to use of
Israel's early history (13:5–6). But typically he goes on to insist
that such a picture is conditional upon Israel's willingness to play
her appointed role in it, which she has not done.

4:16. stubborn: I.e. unresponsive, sc. to Yahweh's call to
return to him (cf. 5:4; 11:7); for this call in Hosea cf. 2:2–3
(Heb. 4–5); 10:12; 12:6; 14:1–3 (Heb. 2–4).

can the LORD ... : Cf. JB "How can Yahweh ..." NEB's
"Will the LORD ..." is an equally possible translation of the
Heb. imperfect here. The usual particle indicating a question is
not present in the Heb. but the context requires that the second
part of the verse be taken as a question.

4:17. Ephraim: A favourite designation of Hosea's for his
addressees (cf. 5:3 (twice), 5, 9, 11, 12, 13 (twice), 14 etc.). The
tribe of Ephraim occupied a large part of the central hill-country
which was the heartland of the northern kingdom of Israel, and
Shechem, its first capital, was in Ephraimite territory (1 Kg.
12:25 – cf. Jos. 21:21). From Gen. 48:14–20 and Jg. 8:1–2;
12:1 it appears that the Ephraimites traditionally laid claim

to a position of supremacy among the tribes, and this will help
to explain why Hosea uses the name of a single tribe as the
designation for the whole kingdom. In the later years of Hosea's
prophetic activity (see Introduction, pp. 27, 32), Tiglath-pileser
III's conquests reduced the nominally independent territory
of the northern kingdom to little more than the tribal territory of Ephraim, so that the expression then had added
point. But this will hardly explain the origin of the usage.

is joined to idols: Or "keeps company with idols" (cf. NEB).
The root is used several times to indicate partnership in an
enterprise (cf. Jg. 20:11; 2 Chr. 20:35–37), and aptly describes
the serious purpose of the worship which Hosea condemns. A
specifically sexual connotation (cf. JB "wedded") does not seem
to be implied.

let him alone: It is not clear who is addressed by the singular
imperative *hannaḥ* of MT. Wolff suggests a group of followers of
Hosea (p. 91); another possibility (cf. Marti), at least for the
redacted form of the text, might be Judah (cf. v.15). But most
modern commentators and versions have preferred to follow
the past tenses of LXX, Aq., Th. and Targ., reading either
wayyānaḥ, "and he rested" (BHS, Weiser; cf. JB), or *hinnîaḥ*, "he
has set up" (G. I. Emmerson, *VT* 24 (1974), 497; cf. NEB, "has
held", and Mays (p. 76 n.), "he has set (himself)"). Nyberg
ingeniously proposed to link *hannaḥ* with the following word
lô, **him**, and emend only the vowels to read *hinḥîlû*, which he
argued might mean "they have chosen" and was presupposed
in LXX (pp. 31–35). More drastic emendations are proposed by
Robinson and Rudolph, but they can probably be discounted.

4:18. A band of drunkards: RSV here follows a popular
emendation of MT's *sār sōb'ām* to *sōd sōbeʾîm*, which involves only
a small change to the Heb. consonants (so originally Houtsma,
followed by Wellhausen, Marti, Harper, Sellin[2], Robinson, Mays
and NEB). JB "*in* the company of drunkards" takes up an
additional suggestion (BH[3], Weiser, Deissler, *BHS*) to insert
the preposition *be*, "in", but this departs further from the text
transmitted by MT and the Vss. MT can be understood
to mean "(when) their drink has gone (i.e. finished)" (van
Gelderen, Wolff, Rudolph, Emmerson, van Leeuwen), indicating
a progression from imbibing to sexual rituals (see below): for

this meaning of *sûr* cf. Am. 6:7. MT is also retained by Nyberg, who translates it as an elliptical relative clause, "those whose drink is rebellious", meaning the idols (pp. 33f.), but this seems less likely.

they gave themselves to harlotry: See on **they shall play the harlot** in v. 10.

They love: Heb. *'āhᵉbû*. RSV assumes that the enigmatic *hēbû* which follows is due to dittography. Others have seen in it the remains of an emphatic form of the verb **love** (cf. Symm.), "they are infatuated with" (different possible forms are invoked by KB and Wolff on the one hand and by Nyberg (p. 36) and *HAL* (p. 170) on the other), and the requirements of the metre seem to favour this. The proposal of Ackroyd (p. 608) and Rudolph to read the difficult word as a form of *yāhab* is less natural.

shame more than their glory: A literal rendering of MT would be "her shields (*māginneyhā*) are shame". Like JB and NEB, RSV is based on the Heb. text implied by LXX, i.e. *miggᵉ'ônāh*, "from (or **more than**) her glory", assuming that the suffix -*āh*, "her", is a mistake for -*ām*, "their". The meaning is then similar to that implied by JB in v. 7 (see the commentary there). The assumption that the feminine suffix is an error is made in most recent treatments of the verse (cf. below on **them** in v. 19), and can claim the support of Targ. and many LXX manuscripts. However, it is possible that these ancient translations were only guided by the context in their rendering, and not by a different reading in the Heb. Nyberg (pp. 32–35) and Emmerson, *VT* 24 (1974), 492–97, cogently object that the more difficult feminine singular forms may and must be retained, the reference being to a goddess (most likely Asherah, one would think) who was the object of popular worship in Hosea's time (cf. on **cult prostitutes** in v. 14). The difficulty that no goddess has so far been mentioned in the context can be dealt with in one of two ways. Emmerson (pp. 496–97) supposes that a word has dropped out of MT at the end of v. 17, as suggested by LXX's *skandala*, "stumbling-blocks", and she notes that the verb there, *hinnîaḥ*, is once used of erecting idols in shrines (2 Kg. 17:29). She does not suggest what the missing word might be, but one might envisage the feminine form *makšēlāh*, "a stumbling-block", which in Zeph. 1:3 apparently refers to idols (cf. the use of *mikšôl* in Ezek. 14:3,

4, 7) and would make a good parallel to **idols** in v. 17 – a factor of which Sellin was already aware (2nd ed., p. 44), although his solution was different. But to rely on LXX at this point is perhaps precarious, especially as there is more to be said for Nyberg's view that it is precisely the present phrase, understood as an elliptical relative clause, which introduces the goddess to view. He translates: "(they make love to) her whose shields are a disgrace", supposing that the idol was decked with shields as emblems of some kind. This supposition is very speculative and hardly satisfactory, but if a more suitable meaning could be found for *māginneyhā* or something very like it Nyberg's general approach (which was anticipated by Symm) could be adopted. Some lexicographers have suggested that a root *mgn* may have existed in biblical Heb. meaning either "give as a present" or "be insolent" (*HAL*, pp. 517f., citing cognates in other Semitic languages and further possible occurrences in the OT: for "be insolent" see also G. R. Driver, *JTS* 34 (1933), 383–84, and J. J. Glück, *Die O.T. Werkgemeenskap in Suid-Afrika: Studies on the books of Hosea and Amos*, Potchefstroom, 1966, p. 57). One may on this basis propose that *māginneyhā* conceals a noun meaning "shameless ones" (Driver) or "insolence" (*KB*, Wolff, Glück, Emmerson) or "gifts" (C. Rabin, *ScrHier* 7 (1961), 389, Rudolph, *HAL*). Although Hosea's use of *mgn* in the sense "give" in 11:8 (see the comment on **hand you over**) might seem to indicate "gifts" here, it is the meaning "shameless ones" which fits the present context best (referring to her devotees, perhaps especially the male cult prostitutes (cf. 2 Kg. 23:7)), and there is no reason why Hosea should not have used the root *mgn* in both the senses which are now quite widely recognized. So the meaning may be: "they are infatuated with her whose shameless devotees are a disgrace".

4:19. them: So NEB, JB and most commentators. But MT reads "her", and this should be retained as a reference to the goddess or her statue (Emmerson – see the preceding note). To render the Heb. "her sign" (Nyberg) is theoretically possible but much less effective: it is the goddess herself, not just an emblem, whom the prophet foresees being confounded.

its wings: Or "her skirts".

altars: MT reads a unique form of the plural of *zebaḥ*, "sacrifice"; cf. NEB "their sacrifices". This form could be a dialectal variation (so Rudolph and Mays, after Nyberg, p. 35). RSV, like Wolff and JB, follows the reading implied by LXX, Syr., and Targ. (*mimmizbᵉḥôtām* instead of *mizzibḥôtām*).

JUDGMENT ON THE LEADERS OF A FAITHLESS PEOPLE

5:1–7

That the calls to hear in v. 1 mark the beginning of a new unit is universally agreed, and in recent years there has been similar agreement that an important division lies between vv. 7 and 8 (so already Harper), as against the older view (Nowack, Marti) that vv. 8–9 were the original continuation of v. 7. This change is no doubt largely due to the effect of Alt's convincing reconstruction of the historical background of 5:8–14 (see below, pp. 146–48). Commentators still, however, differ over whether vv. 1–7 should be seen as a unitary composition or as composed of two or three originally separate units. Even Wolff, who holds the former view, qualifies it by his theory that interruptions by Hosea's audience may have caused him to introduce new topics into his speech. It is pointed out by Rudolph (cf. Alt, Weiser and Mays) that vv. 1–2 deal with the leaders of the people, while what follows is concerned with the people as a whole, and that **I will chastise them all** (or "you" as Rudolph reads: cf. below) in v. 2 forms an apt conclusion. Further, the change from divine speech to prophetic speech and the introduction of a new accusation (**pride**) in v. 5 is thought to indicate that vv. 3–4 and 5–7 were originally separate. The three short units would have been brought together and joined to ch. 4 because of their common concern with cultic sins.

It is probably true that there is a change of emphasis between vv. 2 and 3 (see, however, the commentary on vv. 1–2), but it is scarcely one that justifies a division into separate units. It is entirely natural that an address to those who have misled the people and have been the real cause of their downfall should be developed by an account of the people's wrongdoing and its consequences. In all probability there is no new addressee in vv. 3ff. (see the commentary on **you have played the harlot**

in v. 3). The closing words of v. 2, as transmitted in the MT
and retained in RSV, JB and NEB, perhaps already refer to
the people as a whole as **them** (so Wellhausen). Still less can a
division between vv. 4 and 5 be justified. Form-critical analysis
does suggest a movement from divine speech to prophetic speech
("messenger speech" to "disputation" in Wolff's terminology),
but this occurs at the beginning of v. 4, which does not
correspond to any of the subdivisions of the passage that
have been proposed. It is probable that, here as elsewhere,
Hosea changes his style of address in the course of his speech,
as he takes on the role of an *advocatus Dei* and not simply that
of Yahweh's messenger or mouthpiece. The description of 5:1–7
as a "Levitical sermon" (Balz-Cochois, pp. 45–46; cf. Mays on
vv. 3–7) is hardly justified.

The themes of this passage are closely similar to those of ch.
4, with the exception that the royal family are charged along
with the priests with responsibility for the people's disloyalty
to Yahweh, which now appears irremediable (cf. 4:16). It may
be significant that whereas 4:1 (cf. 4) speaks of a **controversy**
between Yahweh and Israel, 5:1 uses the language of **judgment**
(cf. Wolff, p. 96). There is a stronger emphasis on accusation
in vv. 1–4 and on judgment in 5–7, but the two themes are
interwoven from beginning to end. Later editorial work can
most clearly be identified in v. 5[b], where the saying is applied to
the situation in Judah, perhaps after 587, but the widening of the
opening address to include the **house of Israel** in v. 1 (and the
change to a second-person form in v. 3?) may also be redactional
in origin (see the commentary on these verses). In addition,
marginal glosses or variants have apparently been incorporated
into the text itself in vv. 2[a] and 5. The close parallelism of wording
between v. 3[b] and 6:10 and between v. 5[a] and 7:10 does not justify
regarding these lines as later additions here, as Wellhausen and
others did in the first case and Robinson in the second.

The situation presupposed seems to be similar to that of ch.
4, but perhaps a little later. The conjunction of **priests** and the
house of the king is most likely to have occurred at a major
cultic festival, and such a setting would also be appropriate for
vv. 6–7.

5:1. O house of Israel!: Almost all recent commentators have thought that a reference to a particular leading group in Israel is required here between **priests** and **house of the king**, and consequently that either a word like "rulers" should be inserted or **house of Israel** should be seen as an abbreviated way of referring to such a group (for reviews of various suggestions see Wolff, p. 97, and Rudolph, p. 116). But since the ancient versions do not support emendation of MT, and there is no other instance of **house of Israel** having the restricted meaning suggested, there is a strong case for retaining MT, as RSV does (cf. JB, NEB), and understanding it in a straightforward sense as an address to the people as a whole. See, however, the end of the note below on **they have made deep the pit of Shittim**.

O house of the king!: Again (cf. 1:4) Hosea picks out the royal family for specific criticism, this time perhaps (see below) for a different reason.

For the judgment pertains to you: I.e. you are all threatened by Yahweh's imminent intervention. The word translated **judgment** (*mišpāṭ*) has a number of meanings, including "justice" (cf. 12:6), and Weiser, Robinson and Wolff therefore see an allusion here to the judicial responsibilities of the groups named earlier in the verse (cf. JB). Certainly both **priests** (Dt. 17:9) and royalty (Ps. 122:5) could act as judges in addition to the local elders (cf. de Vaux, *Ancient Israel*, pp. 150–55, and on the king, K. W. Whitelam, *The Just King* (JSOTSS 12), Sheffield, 1979). But this fits less easily with the following **for**, and the usual interpretation, adopted by RSV (cf. NEB), is probably correct.

5:2. They have made deep the pit of Shittim: Neither MT ("rebels have made deep the slaughter") nor the versions' renderings make much sense in the context. The reading adopted by RSV and REB, which requires only minor adjustments to MT, was first proposed by F. W. C. Umbreit in 1844 (so with a slight variation Wolff, Rudolph and Mays). JB accepts the emendation of *šaḥaṭāh* ("slaughter"?) to *šaḥat* ("pit"), but retains MT *sēṭîm* as an abstract noun, "deceitfulness" (cf. Ps. 101:3). NEB, "The rebels! they have shown base ingratitude", assumes that there is no error in MT, apparently giving to *šaḥaṭāh* a meaning loosely related to that of Syriac *šaḥēṭ* (= "corrupt" or "deprave") and other cognates (cf. G. R. Driver, *JTS* 34 (1933), 40, who actually suggested the meaning "lewdness" here). Whichever approach is adopted, **they have made deep** remains awkward after the direct address of v. 1 (though it is consistent with **them** at the end of v. 2). Some commentators therefore emend it to "you have . . .", though with only Vulg. as support, while Wolff, Rudolph and Mays treat it as equivalent to a passive in an elliptical relative clause: "a pit in Shittim that was dug deep" (Wolff). A further possibility arises from the fact that the same word occurs at the beginning of a line in 9:8–9, a passage which is in several respects similar to the present one. **they have made deep** may therefore have been originally a kind of cross-reference to that passage, such as can also be posited in Mic. 5:4. This device is also possibly used in the longer of the major Isaiah MSS from Qumran, 1QIs^a (cf. the list of passages in P. W. Skehan, VTSuppl 4 (1957), 152 n.). If that is so, the phrase should not be included in modern translations, but relegated to a footnote. It is even possible that the two preceding words, which RSV renders **the pit of Shittim**, have a similar origin, as they resemble very closely words in the Heb. of 9:8–9. In that event, the originality of **Give heed, O house of Israel** becomes more doubtful, as one argument that has been used against the suggestion that this whole line is secondary is the need for a threefold address to match the three clauses incorporating place-names (cf. Rudolph, p. 116).

at Mizpah . . . upon Tabor . . . Shittim: It is typical of Hosea to locate the sins which he criticizes by the use of place-names (cf. 1:4; 6:7–9 etc.). **Mizpah** (sometimes spelt "Mizpeh") is a common name in the OT. The most famous place thus named was Mizpah of Benjamin (Jos. 18:26) and it figures in tales of Israel's early history as a place of assembly and worship (Jg. 20:1; 21:5, 8; 1 Sam. 7:5ff.; 10:17ff.; cf. 1 Mac. 3:46). It was fortified by Asa of Judah c. 900 B.C. (2 Kg. 15:22) and served as the centre of Babylonian administration after the fall of Jerusalem in 587/6 (2 Kg. 25:23, 25; Jer. 40–41). Of its history in Hosea's time nothing is known. It is probably to be identified with Tell en-Nasbeh, 1.5 miles south of Ramallah (*IDB*, vol. 3, 407–408; Y. Aharoni, *The Land of the Bible*, 2nd ed., London, 1979, p. 439) or Nebi Samwil, 5 miles north-west of Jerusalem (J. Blenkinsopp, *Gibeon and Israel*, Cambridge, 1972, pp. 98–100, and many earlier scholars). Excavation at the former site indicated that it was a fortified town from the 11th century B.C. (cf. *EAEHL*, vol. 3, 912–18, *AOTS*, pp. 329–42). Another famous Mizpah was in Gilead in Transjordan, an area mentioned by Hosea in two places (6:8; 12:11): it was the place of the covenant between Jacob and Laban and the scene of Jephthah's tragic sacrifice of his daughter (Gen. 31:49; Jg. 11:34–40). Its identification is uncertain, and there is no certainty that it still existed in the monarchy period. In view of the word **upon, Tabor** is presumably the mountain (Jg. 4:6, 12, 14) and not one of the other places of that name (see *IDB*, vol. 4, 508–509). The mountain is an isolated dome lying between Nazareth and the Sea of Galilee. In the Israelite period it lay at the meeting-point of the tribal boundaries of Issachar, Naphtali and Zebulun (Jos. 19:12, 22, 34), and so formed a natural rallying-point before the battle with Sisera (Jg. 4). It is probably referred to in Dt. 33:19 as the cultic centre of Zebulun and Issachar, and this has led some scholars to investigate possible remnants of its liturgical traditions (cf. Kraus, *Worship in Israel*, pp. 165–172). The reading **Shittim** is obtained by an emendation (cf. above). The place is known only as one name for the final encampment of the Israelites east of the Jordan, at the end of their journey through the wilderness from Egypt (Num. 25:1; Jos. 2:1; 3:1 – cf. Num. 33:49), with which tradition associated an early outbreak of apostasy to Baal of Peor (Num. 25:2–5) that was well-known to Hosea (9:10). Early tradition located it in the Wadi Hesban (cf. my *The Way of the Wilderness*, Cambridge, 1979, pp. 36–37), but recent scholars have preferred the identification with Tell el-Hamman, further to the west (M. Noth, *Josua*, 2nd ed., Tubingen, 1953, pp. 29, 81; Aharoni, *The Land of the Bible*, 2nd ed., p. 429).

The metaphors from the hunt (on which cf. *IDB*, vol. 4, 687–88, and O. Keel, *The Symbolism of the Biblical World*, London, 1978, pp. 89–95, with figures 110–20) are used by Hosea in a similar way in 9:8, but it is not clear to what they refer. The analogies, for example, in the Psalms would suggest violence or cunning devices (cf. 1 Kg. 21:8–16; Hos. 6:9), but another possibility is that the introduction (or toleration) of the cultic practices described in ch. 4 is meant, as there is evidence of worship at all three of the places named, at least in an earlier period (Rudolph). It would not be surprising to find the kings

blamed for these as well as the priests, as the kings seem often to
have taken the initiative in cultic matters (e.g. 1 Kg. 12:26–33;
2 Kg. 9:18–28), and this was subsequently to become the major
criterion for their evaluation by the Deuteronomistic editors of
the books of Kings. The view of Alt (*KS*, vol. II, p. 187 n.) that
the three places named were administrative centres in the areas
lost to Tiglath-pileser III seems less likely, first because there is
no evidence that they had such a role, and second because it is
difficult to see why the priests should have been held to blame
for their loss.

I will chastise all of them: For **all of them** LXX has "you",
which implies only a slightly different Heb. text, and fits the
direct address of v. 1 much better. Either this or "all of you",
which is again very similar in Heb. is commonly read here
(cf. Wolff, Rudolph and Mays). On the other hand, the MT
reading, followed by RSV (and JB and NEB), may be defended
as a reference to the people as a whole, who are misled by their
leaders and suffer for it, thus providing a good transition to vv.
3ff. **Chastise** is a word that recurs several times in Hosea as a
description of divine activity (cf. 7:12, 15 ("trained"); 10:10). Its
real home is in family life (Dt. 21:18 (cf. 8:5)) and in the wisdom
literature (the root occurs over thirty times in Proverbs), where it
means "correct", whether by admonition alone or by punishment
(cf. Wolff, p. 99; *THAT*, vol. 1, 738–42). Here punishment is
certainly implied, but most probably punishment that is designed
to teach rather than simple retribution: it is characteristic of
Hosea that Yahweh sometimes presents his acts of judgment
as reformatory in intention (2:6–7, 14–15 (Heb. 8–9, 16–17);
3:4–5). Among the prophets it is only Hosea, Jeremiah (6:8 etc.)
and Zephaniah (3:2, 7) who speak of Yahweh's treatment of his
people explicitly in such terms, but the idea is also present in
passages like Am. 4:6–11; Isa. 9:13 (cf. also Lev. 26:18ff. and
Dt. 8:5).

5:3. I know Ephraim, and Israel is not hid from me:
I presumably refers to Yahweh, as it must in v. 2, not to
Hosea, as Mays and Balz-Cochois (pp. 41–42) suppose. NEB
translates somewhat differently: "I have cared for . . . I have
not neglected . . .", viewing this as a statement of Yahweh's
benefits to Israel in the past, as in 9:10; 11:1. The verb **know**

(*yāda'*) can have a stronger meaning than its English equivalent and "cared" is sometimes a justifiable translation, as in 13:5: cf. Nah. 1:7 and *THAT*, vol. 1, 691–92. But this seems unlikely here, as the parallel verb points clearly to the straightforward meaning **know** (to translate it as NEB does is to introduce an unparalleled nuance of meaning).

For now: *kî* (**For**) could be taken as an emphatic particle here, as in 6:9 (cf. JB). "But" (NEB) is also possible, but only likely if NEB's interpretation is followed for the previous words. "That" (Rudolph, Mays) is a common meaning of *kî*, but more difficult following **is not hid** than if **know** had immediately preceded. For **now** (*'attāh*) Wellhausen and Wolff, followed by JB, read an emphatic "you" (*'attāh*), but this is an unsupported conjecture and unnecessary: rather the possibility should be considered that Hosea uttered this saying as the rituals which he denounced were actually being performed.

you have played the harlot: See the commentary on 4:10. If the causative interpretation were adopted here, **Ephraim** could be the object ("you have caused Ephraim to act as a prostitute"): so Wolff. But the "you" here is singular, so it could not refer to the totality of those addressed in vv. 1–2, and Wolff's suggestion that an individual who had interrupted the prophet might be blamed in this way is very speculative. It is better with many commentators (e.g. Mays) to follow LXX in reading a third-person form, to avoid the sudden reversion to direct address in the middle of the verse: hence "Ephraim has played the harlot". NEB supposes that the original reading was *hiznāt*, a rare form of the third-person feminine singular (*HTOT*, p. 246); but although the people are sometimes referred to as a woman, the change of gender here would be surprising.

defiled: Or "unclean". This is a technical word which means "unfit for the worship of Yahweh" (cf. Lev. 7:20–21). It is normally used of a person who has either touched a corpse (Num. 9:6–7) or a carcass of certain types of animal (Lev. 5:2), or suffered from some kinds of skin disease (Lev. 13), or experienced various types of discharge from the body (Lev. 15). See further *IDB*, vol. 1, 641–48 and, for some interesting anthropological insights, M. Douglas, *Purity and Danger*, 2nd ed., London, 1969, ch. 3. The types of defilement referred to were readily removed by specified rituals. It might be thought that Hosea used the term here because prostitutes (cf. **played the harlot**) were excluded from the cult, but there is no clear evidence of this in the OT (note, however, Lev. 19:29 and Dt. 23:18). The prophet uses the idea of defilement in a transferred sense, and there is no suggestion that Israel as a nation could be purified by purely ritual means: only repentance (v. 4) can do that.

5:4. The verse takes up the theme of Israel's unresponsiveness to the prophetic call to **return** (cf. 4:16) and adds the insight that her sin is so disabling (**they know not the LORD**) that it actually leaves no possibility of repentance. This is to be understood not so much as a point of doctrine as in terms of the divine grief over a people, Yahweh's own people, who have got themselves into a situation from which there is apparently no escape. For the destructive effect (and the cause) of lack of knowledge cf. 4:6. Hosea's deeper analysis of Israel's situation is that they have by their devotion to Baal cut themselves off from an understanding of Yahweh's demands: "The narcotic of deception produced by the cult destroys their powers of orientation" (Wolff, p. 99). Thus they are no longer in a position to recognize that they have gone wrong. This phenomenon is also familiar to the authors of Proverbs, for whom it is the essence of folly (Prov. 13:19; 27:22). The people's claims to **know** Yahweh (8:2) are false. It will only be when Yahweh takes drastic action and withdraws from them (v. 6) that they can be expected to return to him and seek the knowledge of him which they lack (5:15–6:3; 2:14–20). Even this hope seems to have been disappointed (6:11–7:2; 11:7).

5:5. The pride of Israel: This might mean "the one in whom Israel takes pride", i.e. Yahweh, as in Am. 8:7 (so the older commentators), but then the expected citation of Israel's offence would be lacking. It is therefore better to see here a vivid metaphor: Israel's own attitude is witness against her (so Wolff, Rudolph). For the expression cf. Isa. 3:9.

testifies to his face: Literally "answers" **to his face**, but it is clear from Job 16:8 and 1 Sam. 12:3 that the expression is a technical one for an accusation in judicial proceedings. Cf. **judgment** in v. 1 and the note on **controversy** in 4:1 for Hosea's use of judicial language in his oracles. The opening words of the verse occur again in 7:10, but that is no reason for doubting their originality here, as Robinson did; if anything it is likely that they are an addition in 7:10 (see the commentary there).

Ephraim: MT has "and Israel and Ephraim", but "and Israel" is rightly regarded as an intrusive element in the text, as no distinction between the two terms seems to be recognized by Hosea. It may have originated as an alternative reading to "and Ephraim", with which it was mistakenly combined. RSV's omission of the second "and" is less justifiable, as it obscures the connection between accusation and threat in the prophet's language.

shall stumble: I.e., "fall". The fate of Israel/Ephraim exemplifies the truth of Prov. 16:18, whose very wording this verse echoes: "Pride goes before destruction, and a haughty spirit before a fall."

Judah also shall stumble with them: The introduction of Judah at this point is unexpected, and the form of this sentence is identical to **the prophet also shall stumble with you** in 4:5, which forms part of an addition to Hosea's words (see the commentary). It is therefore reasonable to ascribe this line also to the same redactor of Hosea's sayings, and his interest in the fate of Judah makes it probable that he was of Judaean origin. Instead of **Judah also shall stumble** it is preferable to translate "Judah also stumbled", i.e. the redactor was working at a time when Judah had already fallen, probably to the Babylonians in 587/6, and looking back on the way that Judah had followed exactly in her sister kingdom's footsteps – a point that was strongly made also by Ezekiel (ch. 23) and the Deuteronomistic historian (2 Kg. 21:3, 13): cf. also Mic. 1:5.

5:6. they shall go ... but they will not find him: This rendering of the Heb. imperfects implies that Hosea is threatening Israel with a future withdrawal of Yahweh, so that visits to the shrines, even with plenty of sacrificial animals (**flocks and herds**), will be futile. JB and NEB prefer to regard the verbs as frequentative presents, indicating an already existing state of affairs: Yahweh has already abandoned his people. A belief in the presence of Yahweh, in some sense, in his sanctuary was fundamental to the worship of the ancient Israelites (cf. R. E. Clements, *Old Testament Theology: A Fresh Approach*, London, 1978,

p. 40). The absence of their God brought terror and dismay to the
Canaanites (CTA 6.4. 28–29 = *CML*, p. 78; cf. CTA 5.6.22–24 =
CML, pp. 73–74, and I Kg. 18:27–28) and the Israelites (Ps 60:10;
89:46) alike. It is interesting that the wording here is precisely
the same as that used in 2:7 of Israel's unsuccessful quest for her
"lovers", i.e. Baal: to substitute Yahweh's name for Baal's in their
prayers is an inadequate reformation of national life, if it is not
accompanied by a recognition of Yahweh's religious and ethical
demands and their own failure to meet them (cf. 3:5; 5:15).

he has withdrawn from them: Cf. the similar statement in
v. 15 in the future; the verb here could be translated as a future
perfect, "he will have withdrawn from them". The Heb. verb
is found in this intransitive sense only here (though cf. Arabic
ḥalaṣa), and Kuhnigk (p. 67) therefore proposes to read *ḥōlᵉṣām*
("their deliverer") as the object of **they will not find** ("him" in
RSV has no equivalent in the Heb.). But the object is commonly
omitted in such phrases (cf. 2:7 and Am. 8:12), and the meaning
"deliver" is not attested for the Qal of *ḥālaṣ* either. For earlier
suggestions see Harper, Marti and *BH³*. The normal translation
(cf. JB, NEB), which is supported by the Versions, should be
retained (cf. *BDB*, *HAL*).

5:7. They have dealt faithlessly: In 6:7 this expression
amplifies the charge of breaking the covenant, and the latter
notion is probably presupposed here.

alien children: The word **alien** means someone who is outside
the family circle (cf. Dt. 25:5), and the reference here will be to
children conceived with the help not of Yahweh but of Baal: cf.
the expression **children of harlotry** in 2:4. By their apostasy the
people have forfeited the right to transmit to their descendants
the inheritance of the land and its fruits.

Now the new moon shall devour them: The word translated
new moon (*ḥōdeš*) could equally mean "a month", and it has
been taken to imply that within a month Israel and her **fields**
would be devastated (Rudolph). RSV gives a similar meaning,
that at the beginning of the next month judgment will fall. For the
image of devouring cf. 11:6. But here neither the expression nor
the idea is easy to parallel, and a number of attempts have been
made to secure a more natural sense by emendation (JB, NEB:
cf. Wolff, p. 95, and Rudolph, pp. 117f. for details). None of them,

however, is obviously correct. Kuhnigk's suggestion (pp. 69–70)
that *ḥōdeš* means "the Newcomer" (i.e. Baal, as the alien father
of the alien children just mentioned) deserves consideration in
the light of Dt. 32:17 and Jer. 3:24. But a reference to Baal is
only really credible if the verb is treated as frequentative present
rather than future in meaning, indicating the price that is being
paid for Baal's attention: he may bless the harvest but he takes
it back in the form of sacrifices. Another possibility is that the
subject of the verb is not *ḥōdeš* (or whatever is substituted for
it) but "he", i.e. Yahweh (for Yahweh himself as the Devourer
cf. 13:8), who responds directly to Israel's unfaithfulness to him
(cf. ch. 2 passim). *ḥōdeš* may then be an "adverbial accusative"
of time, i.e. "at the new moon festival" (for its importance in
the northern kingdom cf. 2:11; Ps. 81:3; Am. 8:5; 2 Kg. 4:23;
a reference to it was already seen here by Nyberg, p. 37, and
by Mauchline). A day of ritual celebration is to be turned into
a day of devastation.

ORACLES FROM THE SYRO-EPHRAIMITE WAR

5:8–6:3

(a) **5:8–14.** That 5:8 marks the beginning of a new section has
already been seen in the introduction to the preceding verses
(p. 135). There are, however, different views about the extent of
the section that begins here. Wolff argues strongly that the whole
of 5:8–7:16 is a "kerygmatic unit" comprising sayings that were
spoken on a single occasion during the year 733 (pp. 108–12),
and Jeremias also finds no decisive break until 7:16, although he
recognizes that several originally independent units have been
combined here by a collector, who composed 7:13–16 to bring this
section to an end. As we argue below (pp. 149–50, 164–66), such
an extensive composition, whether by Hosea or by a collector,
cannot be demonstrated, and it is necessary to consider smaller
units separately. Even the view that 5:8–6:6 belong together
in some sense (Mays, Jeremias) overlooks an important break
between 6:3 and 6:4. The question of the relationship of 5:15–6:3
to 5:8–14 will receive fuller discussion below (pp. 148–49).

5:8–14 stands out from what precedes and follows (and indeed
from most of the rest of the book) by the fact that here Hosea

himself has something to say about Judah as well as Israel. In place of the synonymous parallelism of Ephraim and Israel (5:3 (twice); 5:5; 6:10) there appears the complementary parallelism of Ephraim and Judah (5:9–10, 12, 13, 14), which is an example of what S. A. Geller has designated "list" parallelism (*Parallelism in Early Biblical Poetry* (HSM 20), Missoula, 1979, p. 35 etc.). Earlier commentators from Marti to Robinson regarded the references to Judah as redactional, like others in the book (so still Buss, p. 37), but they are more sustained and less obtrusive than elsewhere (contrast 5:5). And in addition, since A. Alt's essay of 1919 (*KS* II, pp. 163–87) a plausible reconstruction of the historical situation presupposed has been available, in the events of the so-called Syro-Ephraimite War and its aftermath (734–732). On the historical background see above all Donner, in *IJH*, pp. 425–32, and more briefly the Introduction to this commentary, p. 27. The precise occasion of these verses remains somewhat uncertain. Wolff, at one extreme, believes that the whole piece (and 5:15–7:16 as well) could have been uttered by Hosea on a single occasion after Tiglath-pileser III's defeat of Israel and the replacement of Pekah by Hoshea as king (pp. 110–12). Insofar as separate subsections can be distinguished, they represent for him only a series of speeches by Hosea in a debate with his audience. On the other hand, Alt (art. cit.) and Donner (cf. *Israel unter den Völkern* (VTSuppl 11), Leiden, 1964, pp. 47–51) ascribe vv. 8–9, 10, 11 and 12–14 to four distinct phases of the crisis. A middle position is taken by Rudolph (pp. 125–30), who dates vv. 8–9 soon after the withdrawal of the armies of Aram and Israel from Jerusalem (in this he agrees with Alt and Donner) but thinks that vv. 10–14 are probably a single unit from the time after the Assyrian victory (in partial agreement with Wolff). Other scholars agree in associating vv. 8–9 (Robinson) or 8–10 (Budde) with the Syro-Ephraimite War, but date the remaining verses to an earlier period altogether, under Menahem (see especially K. Budde, *JPOS* 14 (1934), 20–31). H. Tadmor believes that the whole passage, like most of Hosea's oracles, comes from this earlier period, which is essentially a return, at least as far as the chronology is concerned, to the view of the early critical commentators such as W. R. Harper (see *ScrHier* 8 (1961), 250).

The issues are complicated, involving problems of textual criticism, literary analysis and historical argument. As regards the first of these, there is no justification for departing from the MT either by substituting "Israel" for "Judah" in vv. 10, 12, 13 and 14 (see above) or by reading the participles in v. 11 as active rather than passive (see the notes on that verse). Consequently it is necessary to look for the context of these verses in a situation in which both Judah and Israel were involved in warfare (vv. 10–11: cf. v. 8) and had recourse to Assyrian help (v. 13). Given our present knowledge of the period, this was not the case prior to the Syro-Ephraimite War, and most of those who date the passage (or part of it) earlier have done so after accepting the emendations referred to above. The exception is Tadmor, but his view that Judah led an anti-Assyrian revolt in 738 has lost its main support with the revised dating of a crucial Assyrian text (N. Naaman, *BASOR* 214 (1974), 25–39).

A more exact placing of these verses requires consideration of their literary unity and especially of the way in which specific historical events are referred to in them. On a formal level it is possible (cf. Alt, Donner, Wolff (p. 108)) to identify distinct sub-units within the passage: alarm-cry and announcement of doom for Ephraim (8–9 (or 9a)); judgment-speech against the Judaean leaders ((9b–)10); lament over Ephraim's self-inflicted disaster (11); instruction about Yahweh's role in the contemporary history of Ephraim and Judah (12–14). But even if such a variation be thought unlikely in a single speech, it certainly does not require any great separation in time between the sub-units. On the other hand, it is scarcely possible to argue, as Wolff does (p. 109), that literary features such as metrical continuity point positively to the unity of the whole section, especially when there is a definite shift of mood between vv. 10 and 11. On the historical level it does seem that vv. 8–9 look forward to events (a Judaean expedition against the tribal area of Benjamin; and the desolation of the territory of the northern kingdom) which are presupposed as having happened in vv. 10–14, and that these two sections thus derive from sharply different situations. In one Hosea utters a warning about what is about to happen, while in the other, even if a note of announcement is not entirely lacking (vv. 13b–14), the emphasis falls on comment on what has already taken place. It seems best to locate these sections on either side of Tiglath-pileser III's invasion (most probably to be dated in 733) and the Judaean attack from the south, which must have occurred at about the same time. While v. 11 may well have led directly into the more general reflections of vv. 12ff., v. 10 seems most likely to be separate in origin. Its position is possibly due not to its being prior in time to vv. 11–14 but to a collector's wish to keep material about the Judaean attack together. Wolff's dating of the whole section after the Assyrian invasion runs into two main difficulties: the idea that a Judaean attack (v. 8) might still be undertaken after the Assyrians had ratified Hoshea's position in Israel is historically most improbable; and Wolff is forced into an unlikely interpretation of v. 10a as referring either to events a century earlier (1 Kg. 15:22) or to the very beginning of the Judaean campaign, when even Gibeah, only three miles north of Jerusalem, had not yet been reached (v. 8).

Of the sub-units which we have distinguished, v. 10 and vv. 11–14 certainly employ the divine **I**, and the same is probably true of vv. 8–9: the comparable alarm in 8:1 is in divine speech. The first sub-unit, by its very nature, was presumably uttered in a public setting: the setting of the other two is no longer evident, although they will, like Hosea's other oracles, have been delivered in the northern kingdom, and the **you** in v. 13 will refer more especially to its citizens. While Hosea is anxious to underline the parallel between Israel's and Judah's behaviour and destiny, he shows throughout a predominant interest in the northern kingdom. There is no reason to doubt Hosea's authorship of these verses, nor is there any sign of redactional additions or alterations (on the references to Judah see above). Rudolph's treatment of v. 9b as a gloss (p. 127) is quite unjustified, and the suggestion of Jeremias, in A. H. J. Gunneweg and O. Kaiser (eds.), *Textgemäss* (FS E. Würthwein), Göttingen, 1979, pp. 54, 57–58, that vv. 12–14 are too general to have come from Hosea himself would place a remarkable *a priori* limitation on the prophet's utterances. In more recent writings Jeremias seems to have abandoned this view (cf. his commentary, pp. 82–83).

(b) **5:15–63.** A number of commentators have doubted whether 5:15–6:3 can be the original continuation of v. 14 (Marti, Harper, Robinson), or at any rate have thought that

some time must have elapsed between them (Alt, Rudolph).
There is, it is true, at least a glimmer of hope in 5:15, which was
lacking in v. 14, and the image of Yahweh as a lion seems not to
be continued. Nevertheless, there are some strong considerations
in favour of a connection between this verse and vv. 8–14, chief
among them being the fact that the **they** of v. 15 is unexplained
if it is not seen as referring back to **Ephraim** and **Judah** in v.
14. Further, v. 15's use of the divine **I** gives it greater continuity
of style with what precedes than with what follows, as does the
fact that it looks forward to a divine incursion (like v. 14) rather
than back (like 6:1). This verse, then, is best regarded as the
conclusion of the unit which began in v. 12 (or v. 11). 6:1–3
are closely linked with 5:15 by the word **saying** in the RSV
rendering, which is based on the Vss. (except for Vulg.), but
this word is not represented in the Heb., and it is more likely
that it was secondarily added in the Vss. (or in Heb. texts
underlying them) than that it is an original part of the text
that was omitted in the MT (cf. JB, NEB). There are, it is
true, verbal echoes between 6:1–3 and 5:12–14, but these are
not such as to require that the two passages were originally
linked (see the detailed notes below). The same must be said
of the fact that 6:1–3 can be understood as a response to the
divine declaration in 5:15, as this very fact may have led to the
secondary association of two originally separate passages. 6:1–3
does not need any introduction such as is to be found in 5:15;
it is complete in itself. Some time would seem to have elapsed
between 5:15 and 6:1–3, in view of the fact that the former
looks forward to a future time of suffering while the latter
assumes that the suffering has already occurred (cf. **he has
torn . . . he has stricken** in 6:1). But the clear continuity of
theme makes it desirable to include 6:1–3 with 5:12–15. It is
possible that it was reflection on 5:12–15 that led the prophet
(or someone else) to compose the exhortation in 6:1–3. At the
least, it seems likely to have been a deliberate editorial decision
which placed these two passages side by side, so that from the
point of view of the structure of the book (if not from that of
the prophet's own ministry) they should be examined together.
It is generally believed that 6:4–6 constitute the direct response
of God (who is referred to as **I** there) to vv. 1–3. This view,

however, involves either a very forced interpretation of vv. 1–3 or an unwarrantably speculative reconstruction of events that intervened between v. 3 and v. 4 (cf. below) and it is best rejected (similarly Marti, Robinson, McKeating). 6:4, with its opening rhetorical questions, in fact has all the appearance of being the beginning of a new unit.

The form and function of 6:1–3 have occasioned much discussion, most of it controlled by the assumption that Yahweh's word in 6:4 about the fickleness of Israel's **love** is related to these preceding verses. It is not always easy to categorize the interpretations given by particular scholars, but they can be broadly assigned to one of the following types (they are arranged in the order in which they first appeared): (i) 6:1–3 are words that the prophet expects that the people will use (or prescribes for their use) and are in themselves an acceptable response to divine punishment (e.g. LXX, Keil, Sellin[1], Budde, McKeating); 6:4, if connected, refers to a failure to maintain this level of spirituality; (ii) 6:1–3 are an exhortation by the prophet in which he encourages his contemporaries to join him in turning back to Yahweh (F. Giesebrecht, *Beiträge zur Jesajakritik*, Göttingen, 1890, pp. 207–208; H. E. W. Fosbroke, *Divine Transcendence in the OT*, Evanston, 1950, p. 25); (iii) 6:1–3 are words that the prophet expects that the people will use, but they are (at least to some degree) an inadequate response to divine punishment (e.g. Wellhausen, Nowack, Harper, Alt, H. Schmidt, Sellin[2], Weiser); (iv) 6:1–3 are words actually used by the people, but they are (at least to some degree) an inadequate response to divine punishment (e.g. Robinson, Wolff, Mays); (v) 6:1–3 are words actually used by the people, and are in themselves an acceptable response to divine punishment (Rudolph). Advocates of (iii) and (iv) have pointed not only to 6:4 but also to features of vv. 1–3 themselves which seem to them to indicate a basically "Canaanite" outlook: the certainty of restoration, the fertility imagery and (according to some) an allusion to a belief in a dying and rising god in 6:2. None of these constitutes a decisive argument (see the detailed notes below), and it has properly been pointed out that these two types of interpretation are unable to do justice to the prominent place occupied in 6:1–3 by the ideas of **return** to Yahweh and knowledge of Yahweh, which correspond

to two very central demands of Hosea's message (cf. 5:15; 6:6).
It is quite unjustified to say that these terms are used here in
some lesser sense than that in which Hosea used them. Of the
remaining views, (i) is probably the least likely if **saying** is not
an original part of the text. This leaves a choice between (ii) and
(v), which is basically a matter of formal analysis.

In earlier commentaries 6:1–3 have been given such descriptions as "a confession of sin", "a song (or prayer) of repentance"
and even "a lament of the community", and not infrequently it
has been said that the verses reflect traditional motifs of cultic
songs (e.g. Gunkel-Begrich, *Einleitung in die Psalmen*, pp. 131–32).
These descriptions have identified one important feature of these
verses: that they are not the speech of God but the speech
of man (unlike what precedes and follows them). Even so, they
remain inadequate. It is characteristic of the genres mentioned
that God is addressed directly in the second person singular
and asked to forgive and deliver his people (cf. Gunkel-Begrich,
pp. 121–29). None of this happens here. On the contrary, the
prominent verbal forms are the first person plural cohortatives
Let us return . . . and **Let us know . . .** , which are lacking in
the genres mentioned. Close analogies of form are to be found
in what might be called the "summons to worship" (Pss. 95:2;
122:1; 132:7; Isa. 2:3 – cf. 1 Sam. 11:14), and it is possible that
Hosea may have been imitating this. But the closest parallel
of all comes in Lam. 3:40–41, where in the situation after the
fall of Jerusalem to the Babylonians the author issues a call to
repentance which is then followed by a passage modelled on
the "lament of the community". In other words, Hos. 6:1–3
is not itself a song of repentance but an exhortation designed
to call one forth, a variant form of the *Aufruf zur Volksklage* to
be added to that identified by Wolff in *ZAW* 76 (1964), 48–56
(= *GS*, pp. 392–401). In function (if not exactly in form) it
corresponds closely to Hos. 14:1–3, where a direct imperative is
used instead of the cohortative (cf. the imperatives in 10:12 and
12:6, and Brueggemann, *Tradition for Crisis*, pp. 80–86). While it
is perhaps conceivable that in 6:1–3 the people are summoning
one another (or the priests are summoning them) to repentance,
it is altogether more likely that they are the words which Hosea
himself used on occasion to do this. The use of the first person

plural cohortative is, of course, no objection to the utterance
being made by a single individual (cf., e.g., I Sam. 14:6).

There is no compelling reason for doubting the Hosean
authorship of these verses. The view that they come from a
much later period than Hosea's had some popularity at the
turn of the century (cf. Marti), but on the reading of the
passage suggested here it has little to commend it. There is,
of course, some similarity to the Deuteronomistic parenesis, but
the vivid imagery used is scarcely typical of the Deuteronomists.
It is only when we attempt to specify the occasion of this speech
that Hosean authorship becomes at all problematic. To what
does **he has torn ... he has stricken** refer? One might think
of the Assyrian conquests of 733, but 5:15 seems to look forward
to some further disaster, after which the people will return to
Yahweh, and 6:1–3 in its present position at least appears to
take up this expectation. As a separate unit, however, it could
have been spoken either after the invasion of 733 or after the
fall of Samaria in 722, as an appeal to the defeated remnants
of the northern kingdom. In the latter event the words should
perhaps be ascribed to a loyal disciple of the prophet who sought
to continue his master's work in the changed situation; some
significance might perhaps then be attached to his use of the
cohortative rather than the imperative which is used in similar
passages elsewhere in the book (cf. 10:12; 12:6; 14:1–3).

5:8. horn ... trumpet: The **horn** (*šôpār*) was made of
animal horn, and appears to have been the dominant wind
instrument in pre-exilic times, despite its very limited musical
range. The **trumpet**, made of metal, is only mentioned in
two, or possibly three, other pre-exilic passages (2 Kg. 11:14;
12:13 – cf. Ps. 98:6), but it is very common in the post-exilic
books of Chronicles (cf. *IDB*, vol. 3, 472–74, and Keel, *Symbolism*,
pp. 340–44, both of which give reproductions of ancient pictures
of these instruments). The **horn** was used in ritual ceremonies,
including the new moon festival (Ps. 81:4), in battle (e.g. Jg.
7:16–22 (where RSV mistakenly translates "trumpets"); Jer.
4:19, 21), to sound the alarm when danger approached (Am. 3:6)
and to rally the warriors together (Jg. 3:27; 6:34). It is the last
two uses which are relevant here. The other pre-exilic references

to **trumpets** are all in a context of worship or ceremonial.

Sound the alarm: The verb (*hērîaʿ*) can also mean "raise the battle cry" (so KB, Rudolph and NEB) or "shout in worship", but RSV's translation is preferable in the context.

Gibeah ... Ramah ... Beth-aven: Gibeah means simply "hill" in Heb., and not surprisingly it and related words occur as place-names quite frequently in the OT, notably in Jg. 19–21, an episode to which Hosea seems to refer in 9:9 and 10:9, and in 1 Sam. 9–14, where **Gibeah** is the name of Saul's home (10:26). The most important of the places called **Gibeah** is usually identified with Tell el-Ful, about three miles due north of Jerusalem, where excavations have been carried out (cf. *IDB*, vol. 2, 390–91, *IDBS*, 363–64, *EAEHL*, vol. 2, 444–46). Recently doubt has been cast on this theory by J. Maxwell Miller, *VT* 25 (1975), 145–166, and P. M. Arnold, *Gibeah: the Search for a Biblical City* (JSOTSS 79), Sheffield, 1990, who argue that **Gibeah** is simply a longer form of the name Geba, which often occurs in the same contexts, and that both names refer to the Arab village of Jebaʿ, three miles north-east of Tell el-Ful. It is true that the names Geba and **Gibeah** seem sometimes to have been interchanged, especially in 1 Sam. 10–14 (cf. A. Demsky, *BASOR* 212 (1975), 26–31), but on the other hand Isa. 10:29 is most naturally taken to mean that in the late 8th century B.C. **Gibeah** of Saul was distinct from Geba (Jebaᶜ). **Ramah**, literally "the height", is the name or part of the name of several towns in the OT (cf. *IDB*, vol. 4, 7–10): here probably Ramah of Benjamin is referred to (Jos. 18:25), a place linked with **Gibeah** in Jg. 19:13 and Isa. 10:29. Its name seems to have been preserved at er-Ram, on the watershed road 5 miles due north of Jerusalem, and as a border town between the two Israelite kingdoms its possession was a matter of frequent dispute (cf. 1 Kg. 15:17, 22). In 4:15 and 10:5 **Beth-aven** is clearly a derogatory name for the sanctuary at Bethel (see on 4:15) and it is commonly understood in that way here, with the alarm being carried further north to the border between **Benjamin** and Ephraim, which passed near Bethel (Jos. 18:13): so Wolff and Rudolph, and the recent studies of G. Schmitt, (with R. Cohen), *Drei Studien zur Archäologie und Topographie Israels* (TAVO Beihefte B44), Wiesbaden, 1980, pp. 33–34, J. Briend, in R. Aguirre and F. Garcia Lopez (eds.),

Escritos de Biblia y Oriente, Salamanca, 1981, pp. 65–70, and N. Naaman, *ZDPV* 103 (1987), 13–21. This is preferable to the view, based on passages elsewhere in the OT, that a different place of the same name, near the border with Judah, is meant (Aharoni, *Land of the Bible*, 2nd ed., p. 256; Kallai, *Historical Geography*, p. 128; Arnold, *Gibeah*, p. 114).

tremble, O Benjamin: The Heb. in fact reads "after [or "behind"] you, Benjamin", which has been interpreted as a warning or as a battle-cry (cf. Jg. 5:14 – so Rudolph; cf. NEB, "Benjamin, we are with you"). RSV presupposes an emendation of the text based on LXX and the context. Others (e.g. Wolff) adopt a slightly different emendation which gives the meaning "terrify Benjamin". The first two of the places mentioned earlier in the verse were in the tribal area of Benjamin, and presumably the reference is to a Judaean attack on them after the forces of Israel and Syria had withdrawn from Jerusalem.

5:9. Ephraim: I.e. the land of Ephraim, as the use of a feminine form for **shall become** indicates (cf. *GK* §122h).

the day of punishment: For the phrase cf. 2 Kg. 19:3. The idea of divine **punishment** (*tôkēḥāh*) was familiar to the psalmists: cf. Pss. 6:1; 38:1, where the related verb is used (RSV "rebuke"). The wise men of Israel saw God's punishments as essentially corrective and the expression of his love (Prov. 3:11–12), and it is possible that this was in Hosea's mind here too (so Wolff: see the note above on **chastise** in 5:2).

among the tribes of Israel . . .: Possibly this line should be read as the introduction to v. 10 (van Hoonacker).

I declare: Or "I have declared", referring to earlier sayings of Hosea (or other prophets (cf. 6:5), if the **I** refers to Yahweh) which threatened invasion (cf. Alt, *KS* II, pp. 169–170). The verb literally means "make known" (Hiphil of *yāda'*).

5:10. like those who remove the landmark: A **landmark** in the OT is a stone which marks the boundary between one man's land and that of his neighbour; the Heb. word *gᵉbûl* properly means "boundary". To move such a stone meant the appropriation of another's property and is prohibited in both legal and wisdom texts (Dt. 19:14; 27:17; Prov. 22:28; 23:10 – cf. Job 24:2); it was seen as a transgression of a divine order (Prov. 15:25; 23:11). Cf. *TDOT* vol. 2, 361–66. Some

commentators (e.g. Wellhausen, Robinson) have seen here a
reference to land-grabbing activities like those of Ahab (1 Kg. 21;
see also Mic. 2:2 and 2:9), while others have thought that serious
offences of some other kind are meant (Harper). The latter view
is at least ancient, as it is expounded in the Damascus Document,
of which fragments were found in the Qumran caves (CD 8:3ff.;
DSSE, p. 105); see also Philo, *de spec. leg.* 4:149f. But these views
do not explain the mention of **Judah** here, and the tendency of
those who advocated them to regard it as a redactor's alteration
of a supposed original "Israel" reveals their embarrassment. It
is more likely, therefore, that **The princes of Judah** are charged
with making inroads into territory that did not belong to them,
presumably at the expense of the northern kingdom of Israel (so
already Hitzig, and most recent commentators). On the historical
background see the introduction to this section.

my wrath: The Damascus Document manuscripts omit the
pronominal suffix **my**, but the MT reading is supported by LXX
and the other versions. The word for **wrath** is a strong one and
"fury" would be a better rendering.

like water: This phrase is omitted in the quotation in one
manuscript of the Damascus Document (which exhibits some
other divergences from the MT), but the metrical pattern of
vv. 10–11 and the consensus of the MT and versions favour
its retention in the text. The metaphor of Yahweh "pouring
out" his **wrath** became a common one, especially in Ezekiel
(cf. 14:19 etc.).

5:11. Ephraim is oppressed: So the Heb. and Syr., Targ.
and Vulg. LXX, however, implies an active form, "Ephraim has
oppressed (his adversary)", making this a renewed accusation of
the northern kingdom (cf. 12:7), and this reading was adopted by
Wellhausen and others, including JB and NEB (*HTOT*, p. 246).
But the second half of the verse presupposes a reference to the
sufferings of Ephraim, and the passive participle is to be preferred
(cf. *BHS*, Wolff, Rudolph).

crushed in judgment: A similar divergence between an active
and a passive reading also exists here (cf. JB, "he tramples on justice", NEB), but the passive is again preferable. The participles
oppressed and **crushed** appear to reflect a set formula, as they
reappear together in Dt. 28:33 (cf. Jer. 22:17, "oppression and

violence", and Am. 4:1, "oppress . . . crush", from the same Heb.
roots). The **judgment** is the divine activity which is discerned
in contemporary events: compare vv. 2, 5 and 9 for the judicial
language. *mišpāṭ* can also mean "justice" or "right order" (cf.
Wolff, *Joel and Amos*, p. 245) and is so understood here not only
by JB and NEB (see above) but also by Wolff. But his rendering
("justice is crushed": cf. Mays) requires a small emendation of
the Heb. (*rāṣûṣ* for *rᵉṣûṣ*), and this is best avoided. For the syntax
of MT cf. *GK* §128x.

was determined: The verb (cf. Jg. 1:27, 35) gives further
expression to Hosea's complaint about the stubbornness of the
people (cf. 4:16).

vanity: The word in the Heb., *ṣāw*, seems to mean "command"
or "precept" (cf. AV, RV), though it only occurs elsewhere in
Isa. 28:10, 13 and its meaning there is by no means certain
(cf. Clements, *Isaiah* 1–39, p. 228). This hardly gives good sense
(though Jacob defends it), and none of the versions renders the
word thus here. LXX, Syr. and Targ. all suggest "emptiness" or
"vanity", which has led to widespread acceptance (as by RSV
and JB) of the emendation to *šāw'*, "vanity", with the change of
one consonant and the addition of another (though the latter is
not essential: cf. Job 15:31). Others (e.g. *BH³*, KB, Rudolph,
Mays) have adopted Duhm's entirely conjectural emendation
to *ṣārô*, "his enemy", taking the reference to be to the northern
kingdom's alliance with Aram/Syria, its old enemy (cf. 2 Kg. 6–8
etc.), in the campaign against Judah mentioned in 2 Kg. 16:5. G.
R. Driver (*JBL* 55 (1936), 105–106; and in P. R. Ackroyd and
B. Lindars (eds.), *Words and Meanings* (FS D. Winton Thomas),
Cambridge, 1968, p. 55) and Wolff (p. 104) argue that *ṣāw* itself
might mean "emptiness", "worthlessness", the former pointing in
support to the Arabic *ṣawwun* ("empty") and the interpretation
of the passage in Damascus Document 4:19 (*DSSE*, p. 101).
Emendation is therefore perhaps unnecessary (cf. NEB).

5:12. Therefore I am like a moth: Therefore stands for the
conjunction *wa-*, which may mean no more than "And" or "But".
G. R. Driver suggested that here Heb. *'āš* means not "moth"
but "pus", comparing Arabic *ġaṯîtum* and some renderings of
Vss. (in H. H. Rowley (ed.), *Studies in OT Prophecy* (FS T. H.
Robinson), Edinburgh, 1950, pp. 66–67), and most subsequent

commentators and translators have followed him (not JB). It is claimed that "pus" is more appropriate to a human object (**Ephraim**) and to the continuation in the following verse (hence NEB's "festering sore"), while the moth is elsewhere the symbol of transience rather than destructiveness (cf. Ps. 39:11; Job 4:19). In fact Ps. 39:11 most probably speaks of the destructiveness of the moth (so Gunkel), as do Isa. 50:9, 51:8 and Job 13:28, and the other arguments do not allow for a possible brevity of expression (as the moth is to clothes, so Yahweh will be to Ephraim) and a change of image on Hosea's part. The traditional interpretation is probably correct.

like dry rot: The Heb. *rāqāb* refers in three of its four other occurrences to bone-rot, and this may equally well be the meaning here (so Rudolph and Wolff – cf. JB, NEB, "canker").

5:13. and sent: For the absence of an object in the Heb. cf., e.g., 2 Sam. 11:6. NEB's "he went in haste" is based on a small but unnecessary emendation (*HTOT*, p. 246).

the great king: Here and in 10:6 Hosea uses the Heb. form of a standard epithet of the Assyrian king, *šarru rabû*: cf. 2 Kg. 18:19, 28, though the Heb. is different there. The word for **great** here is peculiar (*yārēb*) and is often emended to the regular *rab* (e.g. *BHS*, Wolff), but G. R. Driver drew attention to the possibility, already noted by J. D. Michaelis, that *yārēb* may already have been in use as an alternative (Aramaic?) form in Hosea's time (*JTS* 36 (1935), 295: so Rudolph, *HAL*). Nyberg's view that this is a divine title (*Studien*, p. 38f.) is most unlikely and is now generally abandoned. Hosea is thinking of the political expedients employed by Judah and Israel, whether submission and paying tribute to Assyria or frenzied appeals for help like that made by Ahaz of Judah (2 Kg. 16:7), and perhaps also that made by Hoshea of Israel in the face of the Judaean counter-thrust referred to in vv. 8–10.

5:14. lion ... young lion: For the comparison see 11:10, 13:7 and Am. 1:2, 3:8. The words used here and in 13:7 (*šaḥal*, *kepîr*) are not the standard word for "lion" (*'aryēh*) and have been thought to refer to young lions in particular (so Koehler, *ZDPV* 62 (1939), 121ff.), but *IDB*, vol. 3, 136, denies any such limitation of the meaning. S. Mowinckel, in W. D. McHardy and D. Winton Thomas (eds.), *Hebrew and Semitic Studies presented to G. R. Driver*,

Oxford, 1963, pp. 95–103, argued that **lion** (*šḥal*) was originally
a word for a mythical monster, a meaning still discernible in
Job 28:8. An early commentary on this verse found among the
Qumran scrolls apparently took the verse to be a prediction of
Hasmonaean rule in the 2nd and 1st centuries BC (4QpHos[b]:
DJD V, p. 33, no. 167:2).

and none shall rescue: I.e. foreign alliances cannot divert
Yahweh's plans of judgment – a different point from that made
in Isa. 7 but close to several of the oracles against foreign nations
in that book (on which see G. R. Hamborg, *VT* 31 (1981),
145–159), and close also to Isa. 30:6–7. For the expression cf.
2:10, although the background there appears to be religious
rather than political.

5:15. I will return again to my place: As in v. 6, Hosea
speaks of Yahweh's withdrawal of his presence from the land,
such as was later vividly portrayed in Ezekiel's vision of the
departure of the divine glory from Jerusalem (Ezek. 11:22–23).
It is not completely certain what Hosea meant by **my place**.
Targ. glossed it "which is in heaven" and most commentators
have accepted this view (cf. Mic. 1:3). But 2:14 may mean that
Hosea thought of Yahweh's **place** as above all the wilderness
(McKeating). In any case Hosea is clearly more concerned with
the fact of Yahweh's withdrawal than he is with such questions.
On the consequences of such a withdrawal see the note on v. 6.

until they acknowledge their guilt: With the word **until** this
saying of Hosea goes beyond the unrelieved gloom of the message
of vv. 1–14. Yahweh's withdrawal is now seen to have both a
temporal limit and a positive purpose, a development in Hosea's
message which can also be seen in 2:6–7, 14–15 and 3:4–5. **they
acknowledge their guilt** represents a long-standing tradition
of interpretation (so already Targ.) which remains influential
(cf. JB, Weiser, Rudolph). But it cannot be right, as Hebrew
'āšam nowhere else bears this meaning. Its common meaning
is "become guilty", which is unlikely here, but it occasionally
means "suffer the consequences of guilt" (Ps. 34:22–23, where
RSV's "be condemned" is too weak; Isa. 24:6; Hos. 10:2; 13:16;
Zech. 11:5; cf. the use of the Hiphil in Ps. 5:10). This fits the
present context and Hosea's teaching as a whole well: Yahweh
awaits the time when his people will, while suffering for their

evil-doing, **seek** his **face** (so Buss, Mays). Alternatively, it is
possible with NEB, Wolff and many other scholars to follow LXX
(cf. Vulg.), which derives *ye'š^emû* not from *'āšam* but from *šāmēm*, "to
be desolated, appalled" (cf. **desolation** in v. 9) and to translate
the phrase as "until they are appalled" (NEB "in their horror").
The reference would probably be to their reaction to Yahweh's
judgment. This proposal involves a small change to the MT, but
this can be avoided if G. R. Driver's suggestion is accepted, that
there was a second verb *'āšam* in Heb., with the same meaning as
šāmēm (in Schindler and Marmorstein (eds.), *Occident and Orient*
(Gaster Volume), pp. 75–77; cf Kuhnigk, pp. 153–54). Nyberg's
view that Hosea was prescribing an atonement ritual (pp. 30–31)
is quite impossible in view of 6:6.

and seek my face: This idiom appears to be derived from
the royal court, where subjects or foreign emissaries would
endeavour to obtain an audience with the king (1 Kg. 10:24;
Prov. 29:26). It therefore carries with it overtones of submission.
Men **seek** the **face** of Yahweh in order to gain favours from him
and to pay him homage (2 Sam. 21:1; Pss. 24:6; 27:8; 105:4),
and one other passage (2 Chr. 7:14) sees this as part of the
appropriate procedure in a time of national **distress**. Like the
use of **seek** alone, the expression implies the earnest desire of
the worshipper to meet with God rather than any elusiveness
on the latter's part. It is probable, though difficult to prove,
that in religious use the phrase originally referred to a visit to
a sanctuary and to the associated rituals, as it was there that the
face (or "presence", as the word is often to be translated) of God
was believed to be in a special sense. Hosea himself seems to use
seek the LORD in this way in 5:6. Cf. *TDOT*, vol. 2, 236–39.
But here, like Amos (5:4), he will have had in mind something
quite different (see below on 6:1–3).

distress: Heb. *ṣar* normally refers to the external circumstances rather than an emotional state. The parallel with the previous line as it is most likely to be understood is thus very close.

they seek me: In parallel to **seek my face** Hosea uses a rarer
word whose use is apparently restricted to poetry (cf. Job 8:5;
Pss. 63:1; 78:34; Isa. 26:9).

saying: There is no equivalent to this word in MT (cf. JB,
NEB) and its inclusion follows the LXX text (cf. Targ., Syr.).

Most likely, however, it is a secondary addition there, designed to link this verse more closely with the following appeal. On the various suggestions that have been made about the connection between 5:15 and 6:1–3 see the introduction to this section.

6:1. Come, let us return to the LORD: Clearly this implies an end to the divine speech of the preceding verses. The identity of the speaker(s) of vv. 1–3 has been much discussed (see pp. 150–52 above). It seems most probable that, as a response to the divine declaration in 5:15, Hosea himself here exhorts the people to penitence. If so, it is noteworthy that he does this, not by using the imperative as in 14:2 (cf. 12:6), but by identifying himself as part of the nation which must **return** and speaking in the first person plural.

he has torn: The Heb. verb is the same as that translated "rend" in 5:14 and refers to a wild animal's mauling of its prey. As it is not found elsewhere in Hosea, it is commonly cited as an argument for an original connection between the sections in which these verses occur. Nevertheless it is to be noted that in 5:14 it is in the future tense (Heb. imperfect), whereas here the past is used (Heb. perfect), which suggests that whatever is referred to as "rending" has intervened between the occasions of the two sayings. Moreover, Hosea's comparison of Yahweh to a wild animal is not limited to these two verses (cf. 13:7).

that he may heal us: In prose the Heb. construction (simple *waw* plus imperfect) would certainly indicate purpose (cf. *GK* §165a), so that it would be proper to discuss whether healing is the purpose sought after by Israel in repenting or by Yahweh in afflicting her. But Heb. poetry is not so rigid in its use of this construction (cf. 4:6, 19; 6:3), and a simple future may be all that is intended, as in the next verse (cf. JB "but he will heal us"). The same idea that it is Yahweh who both smites and heals is expressed in Job 5:18, where it is preceded by a reference to Yahweh's chastening, a favourite theme of Hosea (cf. on 5:2). It is also found in some of the Psalms of Lament, where the psalmist identifies God as the cause of his suffering as well as calling on him for deliverance (e.g. Ps. 38:2; 39:10). The word **heal** is not necessarily evidence of an original link with the preceding section (v. 13), as this image too is found elsewhere in Hosea (7:1; 11:3; 14:5).

he has stricken: The natural meaning of MT (*yak*) is jussive, "let him strike", or less probably future, "he will strike" (cf. LXX, Vulg.), but Targ., Syr. and a quotation of the passage in Tertullian (*Adv. Marc.* 4:43) presuppose a past tense (probably *wayyak*, the *waw* having been omitted in MT by haplography), and this reading, which fits the context much better, is followed by all modern commentators and versions.

and he will bind us up: I.e. "he will bandage our wounds" (JB).

6:2. he will revive us . . . he will raise us up: A portrayal of national recovery as a resurrection (cf. Ezek. 37) is not in itself impossible and M. L. Barré has observed that 2 Kg. 13:20–21 (cf. Isa. 26:14, 19) provides evidence of the use of the key expressions to refer to a resurrection in a prophetic tradition from the northern kingdom that could well have been known to Hosea (*VT* 28 (1978), 131, 137). But in view of the imagery of the previous verse, it is most natural to understand these expressions too in terms of healing from physical sickness, for which parallels exist within the OT (cf. Exod. 21:19; 2 Kg. 20:7 etc.). Barré has shown that the temporal expressions **After two days** and **on the third day** (which are, of course, equivalent to one another semantically) resemble closely the language of Mesopotamian medical texts, in which (as elsewhere) "three days" is a vague expression for a short period of time (art. cit., pp. 139–140). What is more, **on the third day** occurs in Isaiah's "prognosis" for Hezekiah in 2 Kg. 20:5. Further close parallels to the wording here occur in a hymn to the Mesopotamian healing-goddess Gula (Barré, *Or* 50 (1981), 241–45). There is no reason to see either covenantal (J. Wijngaards, *VT* 17 (1967), 226–239) or cultic (Weiser) motifs in this verse, although Hosea may well not have been the first to employ the vocabulary of sickness and recovery as a metaphor for the state of the nation (cf. Ps. 80:18). Since W. W. Baudissin, *Adonis und Esmun*, Leipzig, 1911, and later H. G. May, *AJSL* 48 (1931–32), 73–98, many commentators have seen here echoes at least of the cult of a dying and rising god, but without any good reason: see the discussions of Wolff, pp. 117–18, and Rudolph, pp. 136–37. Among Christian writers Tertullian is the first to refer specifically to this verse as a prophecy of the resurrection of Jesus (*adv. Marc.* 4:43, *adv. Iud.* 13:23 – the texts are given in full by Wolff, *ad loc.*), but this understanding of it may well go back to the earliest Christian communities (I C. 15:4: cf. C. H. Dodd, *According to the Scriptures*, London, 1952, pp. 76–77, J. Dupont, *Biblica* 40 (1959), 742–761, and H. K. McArthur, *NTS* 18 (1971–72), 81–86, who also cites Rabbinic interpretations of the verse).

that we may live before him: This means in the first place that they will **live** under Yahweh's watch (cf. Vulg.) and protection (cf. Gen. 17:18), an idea found in other passages which speak of national restoration (Jer. 30:20; 31:36; Ps. 102:28). But there is also (cf. NEB "in his presence") an anticipation of what is clearly spoken of in the next verse, the return of Yahweh to his people.

6:3. Let us know, let us press on to know the LORD: This exhortation is parallel to the beginning of v. 1 and like it is followed by a reference to the consequences that are expected to follow if it is heeded. **to know the LORD** picks up the language of several of Hosea's accusations of the people (cf. 4:1, 6; 5:4) and makes an important contribution to the understanding of this expression by showing that it means something that is to be achieved by deliberate effort (see further the note on 2:22). The prophet begins to summon his hearers to **know** Yahweh, but before stating the grammatical object he corrects himself and calls them to **press on to know the LORD**, to make it their earnest concern (cf. NEB's "strive"), using an expression which is found elsewhere in injunctions to strive for justice (Dt. 16:20 – cf. Prov. 15:9; 21:21) and peace (Ps. 34:14). There may be a deliberate contrast with 2:7, where the Piel of the same verb (*rādap*) is used of Israel "pursuing" her lovers, i.e. the Baals (cf. also 12:1). There is no need to regard **Let us know** as a late addition, or perhaps a variant reading for the following words (Alt, Donner, Fohrer, JB). Nor is it probable that the first occurrence of the Heb. *yādaʿ* here has a meaning other than "know" (cf. NEB "Let us humble ourselves", following G. R. Driver in B. Gemser, *Sprüche Salomos*, 2nd ed., Tübingen, 1963, p. 111).

his going forth: Hosea here takes up a term from the descriptions of Yahweh's theophany in war (Jg. 5:4; Ps. 68:7 – cf. Ps. 108:11; Mic. 1:3, and J. Jeremias, *Theophanie*, Neukirchen, 1965, passim.) Possibly there is a deliberate play on words here, as the Heb. word is also used for the rising of the sun (Ps. 19:6).

is sure as the dawn: These words recur in 1 QH 4:6 (*DSSE*, p. 160), in what seems to be an allusion to this passage.

he will come to us: Again this is theophany-language: cf. Dt. 33:2, Hab. 3:3 and Ps. 68:17 (emended text). Yet it is striking that Hosea does not continue, as the other texts do, by speaking of the effects of Yahweh's coming on the world of nature or on Israel's enemies.

as the showers . . . : The point of this simile is different from **as the dawn** above, for **the showers** in Palestine are not at all **sure**, but they do bring prosperity and fertility to the land and consequently stand for what brings comfort and delight to men: cf. Prov. 16:15. They are essential to the ripening of the crop (Baly, *Geography*, pp. 47–52). In view of the association of Baal with the rains in Canaanite religion, it is a very daring comparison for Hosea to have used, but one that is entirely of a piece with his appropriation of marriage symbolism for Yahweh's relationship to Israel in ch. 2 (cf. also the language of fertility in 14:5–8).

ORACLES ABOUT POLITICAL LIFE

6:4–7:16

That 6:4 is the beginning of a new unit has already been argued for (pp. 149–50), against the common view that it expresses a (negative) judgment on 6:1–3. The question form and the direct address are a natural beginning to a speech and take nothing for granted (except a particular kind of situation, on which see the next paragraph). After 7:16 the direct address (to the prophet?) in 8:1 indicates a new beginning there. Within these limits subdivisions are commonly recognized, but generally at the wrong points. There cannot, as Wolff has seen (p. 109), be a break before 6:7, for there is then nothing for **they** to refer to (against almost all commentators). The change of person from second plural to third plural in 6:5 is rough (though not unusual in Hosea (cf. 2:16–17; 4:14; 5:13–14)), but there cannot be a real break here because of ᶜal kēn in 6:5 itself and ḥesed in 6:4 and 6:6. Therefore the first subsection of 6:4–7:16 must be regarded as

extending at least to 6:9. 6:10 might be a new beginning, but
more likely the piling up of proper names in 6:11–7:1 marks
the new start and 6:10 concludes the first unit. The reference
to **Samaria** in 7:1 links up well with the events at the court
in vv. 3–7, and (despite Rudolph, Mays etc.) 7:3 cannot be a
beginning of a new unit, for then **they** has no antecedent. It
is commonly agreed that 7:7 is an end and 7:8 a beginning:
the former concludes the denunciation of a *coup d'état*, while the
latter has the proper names appropriate to the start of a new
unit. Contrary to the view of several commentators, no further
divisions in the chapter are required, as Rudolph has seen. Once
v. 10 is removed (as a redactional element), the continuity of
vv. 9 and 11 is apparent (see the comment on v. 11); and **they**
in v. 12 requires **Ephraim** in v. 11 to be its antecedent (the
transition to plural verbs is already made in v. 11 in the Heb.).
For a similar reason v. 13 cannot be a new start: in any case *'ôy*
(unlike *hôy*) is not necessarily an introductory particle (cf. 9:12).
The artistic symmetry of 8–9, 11 deserves recognition: four 3 +
2 lines framed by a 2 + 2 line at each end. Three units are
therefore to be distinguished: 6:4–10; 6:11–7:7; 7:8–16. These
correspond closely to sections recognized by Wolff (pp. 108–109),
but it needs to be emphasized that nothing requires that they
have a common occasion, against Wolff. Even Jeremias' theory
(see the Introduction) that they constitute a redactional unity (or
rather part of a larger redactional unit extending from 5:8–7:16)
is not supported by conclusive arguments. Such views gain their
credibility from the ease with which widely accepted analyses of
these chapters can be refuted; but there are major breaks at two
points which are not to be overlooked.

Throughout the authentic verses divine speech is probably
maintained (*da⁽at 'elōhîm* in 6:6 does not indicate an exception,
in view of **I** referring to Yahweh earlier in the verse). The
non-appearance of the divine "I" in certain verses of course
proves nothing, though its absence from 7:8–9, 11 might justify
seeing those verses as a prophetic lament, to which 7:12–16 is
the divine answer. Direct address to the people is found only in
6:4 (apart from 6:11a, an addition). The *first unit* (6:4–10) reads
like a divine defence against criticisms, apparently set off by the
disaster brought on or at least threatened by prophetic words

in 6:5. It may well be a counter to claims that enthusiastic maintenance of the cult was sufficient to avert danger (cf. v. 6). Israel's short-lived *ḥesed*, seen in the recent outrages (vv. 7–10), is a sufficient justification for what has happened (or will happen). The *second unit* (6:11b–7:7) moves on to the attack: when Yahweh blesses the people they do not respond with righteousness but with evil, so much so that they even undertake an attempt on the king's life. When things go badly (v. 7b), they do not have recourse to Yahweh (but see below on the possibility that this part of the verse is a later addition). The *third unit* (7:8–16) concentrates first on Israel's foreign policy, complaining that it only weakens her (this, not Yahweh's neglect of her, is why things are going badly: vv. 8–9, 11). It then turns into an announcement of doom such as has not come since the end of ch. 5, in the course of which Yahweh protests at the misrepresentation, disloyalty and attempts to disown him which accompany the nation's *Realpolitik*, and probably also at the repudiation of the prophet's message, i.e. his own message, to them. This will bring Israel to an end, with no regrets being expressed by their erstwhile allies.

It is possible that the arrangement of these oracles was intended to add further instances of the failure of Israel's *ḥesed* to those in 6:4–10, but there is no sign of any extensive reworking of the units into a new rounded whole (except perhaps for the omission of introductory formulae, as elsewhere in Hosea). The editing is designed rather to embrace Judah within the range of the first unit (6:11a; also 6:4?); to supply an announcement of judgment that was felt to be lacking there (6:11a); and to bring out explicitly that the judgment announced by Hosea (and probably now brought to pass) was due to Israel's pride and failure to repent in the aftermath of a failed foreign policy (7:10). 7:7b may also be secondary: it has a finality (**all their kings have fallen**) which is not really intelligible until after 722, and perhaps (like 6:1–3?) it addresses the survivors of the final Assyrian attack.

The events referred to in 6:7–10 could well be connected with each other and one possibility is that they are associated with the accession of a king such as Pekah, who had Gileadite support (2 Kg. 15:25; cf. Alt, *KS* II, p. 186 n. 2). But **priests** are involved and some of the terms used favour the hypothesis of a purely religious conflict (so Wolff, p. 123). It is not certain whether the *first unit* presupposes an already past catastrophe such as occurred in 732: v. 5 may simply refer to the delivery of prophetic messages of doom, seen as having an inevitable (but still future) effect. The *second unit* seems to come from a time of prosperity in which various evils, including regicide, have occurred. It is unlikely that it refers to the murder of Zechariah (2 Kg. 15:10), in view of Hosea's threat against the house of Jehu in 1:4, though Hosea may perhaps have taken a different view of the matter after the house of Jeroboam was put down by a *coup*. Although the accession of Hoshea seems the most likely background to 7:3–7, any one of the later *coups* is possible if (as seems likely) 7:7[b] is an addition. The *third unit* presupposes dealings with both Assyria and Egypt. Negotiations with the latter are not known of until the 720s (2 Kg. 17:4; cf. Donner, *Israel unter den Völkern*, p. 80), though it is possible that they occurred in the course of the Syro-Ephraimite War (so Wolff, p. 111). The talk of "rebellion" (vv. 13–14) reflects the situation under Assyrian rule, when it would have had great contemporary relevance: when the rights and wrongs of rebellion against Assyria are on everyone's lips, the prophet addresses them about the much more serious matter of rebellion against Yahweh.

6:4. Yahweh challenges **Ephraim** and **Judah** themselves to declare what they have deserved by their rejection of him. Since the other reference to **Judah** in this unit (v.11a) is clearly secondary and the specific charges in vv. 7–9 relate to the northern kingdom alone, it is likely that **Judah** has been substituted for "Israel" by a redactor here, as in 12:2 (compare the parallelism of **Ephraim** and **Israel** in v. 10 and elsewhere). What Yahweh seeks above all is **love** (*ḥesed*, elsewhere (cf. v. 6) translated "steadfast love") or better, "loyalty" (NEB): see the note on this word in 2:19. Both the similes in this verse serve to show how short-lived Israel's **love** has been: the **morning cloud** is the early morning mist of some summer days in the Levant, which is quickly dispersed by the heat of the sun (Baly, *Geography*, p. 44). The same similes are used again in 13:3 as part of an announcement of judgment (but see the note on that verse, and compare also Mic. 5:7).

It is commonly thought that this verse (with vv. 5–6) contains the divine reaction to the previous three verses, or at any rate to a subsequent lapse from the resolve that is expressed in them (see the introduction to 5:8–6:3). This view has greatly affected estimates of these preceding verses, but it is not at all clear that it is correct. Indeed, when they are correctly understood as an exhortation rather than a song of penitence and as at any rate expressing Hosea's thoughts and probably also giving us words actually spoken by him, it is necessary to interpose not one but two episodes between them and v. 4 if a connection is to be affirmed, namely an initial positive response to Hosea's exhortation and then a relapse by the people into their old ways. Since there is no substantial connection of thought or wording between vv. 1–3 and v. 4, it is better to suppose that v. 4 (and vv. 5–6) originally had nothing at all to do with vv. 1–3. In this case Israel's short-lived **love** for Yahweh is best taken to mean her early devotion to him in the wilderness, prior to the settlement in Canaan (cf. 2:15; 9:10), so that these verses belong with the "historical retrospects" of later chapters (but note already 2:5, 8), on which see J. Vollmer, *Geschichtliche Rückblicke*, pp. 57–96.

6:5. I have hewn them by the prophets: It is in consequence of Israel's desertion of him that Yahweh has sent his **prophets**, whose words are "deadly weapons" (Wolff). The strong language is explained by the power that was believed to inhere in Yahweh's word spoken by a prophet: compare the words of Jer. 5:14 and 23:29, and more generally von Rad, *OT Theology*, vol. 2, pp. 80–95. The Heb. word for **hewn** (*ḥāṣabtî*) is, like its English counterpart, normally used of cutting stone (e.g. Isa. 5:2; 22:16), but a figurative use to refer to attacks on men is perfectly possible and perhaps even paralleled up to a point in Isa. 51:9 (though the text there is not completely certain). As Wolff and Mays have observed, in Ugaritic the Gt stem of *ḥṣb* is used several times of fighting (cf. CTA 3B.6, 20, 24, 30 = *CML*, pp. 47–48). There is therefore no need to suppose that there must be a reference here to the stone tablets "written by the finger of God" at Mount Sinai and then drastically emend the verse (Rudolph). By **the prophets** Hosea will mean men like Ahijah, Elijah, Micaiah ben Imlah, Elisha and probably especially Amos and himself.

I have slain them: NEB's "I have torn (you) to shreds" is an unjustified weakening of Hosea's words.

by the words of my mouth: The words of prophets are quite often described as Yahweh's own words (e.g. Jer. 23:22; Ezek. 3:4: see also the note on 1:1), and this reflects their use of both the divine "I" (as in this passage, for example) and the formulae "Thus says the Lord" and "says the Lord".

and my judgment goes forth as the light: MT's reading, "and thy judgments are (as) the light that goes forth" (cf. RV), is unintelligible (to whom is it addressed?) and RSV, with most modern commentators, follows the reading first proposed by J. A. Dathe in 1773 and implied by LXX, Targ. and Syr., from which the MT reading could have derived by a mistake in word division at a time when only the consonants were written (*wmšpty k'wr* being written instead of *wmšpty k'wr*). For other instances in the OT text, see E. Würthwein, *The Text of the Old Testament*, 2nd Eng. ed., London, 1980, pp. 107–108. The exact meaning of the words, however, remains a matter of disagreement. First there are those who believe that they are out of place here and actually belong in v. 3, either before (NEB) or after (Robinson, *BH³*, JB – cf. Marti) the words **his going forth is sure as the dawn**, to which they are a close parallel. This necessitates the reading "his judgment", which involves a further small change to MT besides that mentioned above. It would also be possible to argue that these words are a variant reading for **his going forth ...**, which was inserted first in the margin of a manuscript and then brought into the text by a later copyist who did not realize its correct position. On such "double readings" cf. Wurthwein, *The Text of the OT*, p. 108. But neither of these expedients should be adopted if a satisfactory meaning can be given to the words in the place which they occupy in the transmitted text. Much of the uncertainty about their meaning centres on the interpretation of **judgment** (Heb. *mišpāṭ*), which has already been seen to be a problem in earlier verses (cf. the notes on 5:1, 11). Traditionally (cf. Vss.) it has been understood to mean imminent judgment. The negative connotations were retained by Wellhausen (and Nowack), who thought that the manifestation of Yahweh's "justice" in the actions described in the first part of the verse was meant. Likewise Harper took **judgment** to mean

Yahweh's "verdict", whose execution lay before Israel, although
he also accepted the view (which has become very influential)
that **as the light** implies a favourable outcome. The impact
of this insight can be seen in Jacob's view that Hosea means
"the judgment which makes salvation come to pass". This
more positive understanding is typical of recent commentaries,
whether they take *mišpāṭ* to mean the "right order" which Yahweh
seeks to introduce by means of judgment (Weiser, Wolff) or see in
it the divine "demands" set out in v. 6 which offer the possibility
of a happy outcome if they are heeded (Alt, H. Schmidt, Budde,
Donner, Rudolph, Mays). While each of these interpretations
can be defended, they all suffer from a failure to take account
of the closely parallel expressions in Ps. 17:2 and especially 37:6
which refer to the vindication of the innocent man who has been
unjustly accused. Yahweh can confidently assert that his actions
will be vindicated in any investigation, because he has done no
more than deal appropriately with his people's failure to show
loyalty towards him. This is close to Wellhausen's understanding
of the sentence. Translate: "and my vindication shall go forth as
the light". The phrase **as the light** probably refers here to the
public recognition of Yahweh's right (cf. the commentaries on
Ps. 37:6). This passage (like Ps. 37:6) is one of those in which
it has been suggested that Hebrew *yāṣā'* means not "go forth"
but "shine", like Arabic *waḍu'a* (cf. G. R. Driver, *JTS* N. S. 20
(1969), 568): hence NEB "dawns".

6:6. For: The Hebrew *kî* can also mean "that", and it is
understood thus by those commentators who think that *mišpāṭ*
in v. 5 refers to the divine demands set out here.

I desire steadfast love . . . the knowledge of God: On these
two qualities, or activities, see the notes on 2:19–20. Both terms
are characteristic of Hosea's preaching (cf. vv. 3 and 4 of this
chapter). For **desire** (*ḥāpaṣtî*) it would be better to render "delight
in", "take pleasure in" (cf. *BDB*). In the Heb. **steadfast love**
stands before the verb, and so gains special emphasis: "steadfast
love is what I delight in, not . . ."

sacrifice: This is the general word *zebaḥ*, which normally refers
to the slaughter of an animal for consumption by the worshippers,
after appropriate parts have been removed for dedication to God
and the needs of the priests (cf. I Sam. 2:13–17; 9:12–13). By

contrast the **burnt offerings** (*'ōlôt*, the plural of *'ōlāh*) were burnt in their entirety on the altar, a more costly offering that could be presented on behalf of the whole community as well as by an individual (cf. 1 Kg. 18:30–38; 2 Kg. 16:15). This word only occurs here in Hosea.

There has been much discussion about the attitude to sacrificial worship reflected here and in similar passages in other prophetic books and the Psalter (cf. Isa. 1:11–15; 43:23; 66:3–4; Jer. 6:20; 7:21–23; Am. 4:4–5; 5:21–25; Mic. 6:6–8; Pss. 40:6; 50:8–13; 51:16). Very similar sentiments are also ascribed to Samuel (1 Sam. 15:22), and it is noteworthy how frequently the verb *ḥāpas* occurs in these passages, as though it almost became a technical term (Isa. 1:11; 66:3–4; Hos. 6:6; Pss. 40:6; 51:16; 1 Sam. 15:22). While they have often been understood as the expression of a total repudiation of all sacrifices and other rites, it has also been held that they are concerned only with sacrifices offered without the proper moral or religious attitude (e.g. H. H. Rowley, especially in *BJRL* 29 (1945–46), 326–345), or that the cult was criticized as an institution which had departed, for the most part, from its original purpose as a vehicle of the covenant faith (Clements, *Prophecy and Covenant*, pp. 93–102). It is probably a mistake to look for a single viewpoint in all these passages or, for that matter, in all the places in the book of Hosea which deal with sacrifice (2:11, 13; 3:4; 4:13, 14, 19; 5:6; 6:6; 8:11, 13; 9:4–5; 10:1–2, 8; 11:2; 12:11; 13:2). Certainly Hosea sometimes denounces sacrifices offered to Baal or in circumstances of which he disapproves (2:13; 4:13–14 (15?); 11:2; 13:2). But in 6.6, he seems, like Amos in 4:4–5 and 5:21–25 and perhaps in dependence upon him, to be saying something about sacrifice as such, irrespective of where or by whom it is offered. What exactly he is saying is another question and depends upon the interpretation that is given to **not** and **rather than**. While the *prima facie* meaning is that Yahweh has no use for sacrifice, it has been pointed out that "not X but Y" is in some biblical passages equivalent to "not so much X as Y" (Gen. 45:8; Jl 2:13; Mk 9:37; Jn 6:27; 7:16: cf. J. Lattey, *JTS* 42 (1941), 155, and Rowley, *art. cit.*, p. 340), and certainly Hebrew *min* can mean "more than" as well as **rather than**. On this basis some would hold that what Hosea means is that sacrifice, while acceptable, is not what Yahweh values most highly. Even such a "grading" of duties would of course represent a striking innovation on the part of the prophets. Yet 8:11, 13 seem to go further even than this and lend support to a stronger interpretation of 6:6 as a repudiation of all sacrifice (so Wolff, Rudolph, Mays: cf. R. Hentschke, *Die Stellung der vorexilischen Schriftpropheten zum Kultus* (BZAW 57), Berlin, 1957).

In the NT the first part of the verse is twice quoted in its Septuagintal form, "I desire mercy and not sacrifice", as justification for a departure from the strict Jewish religious practice of the day (Mt. 9:13; 12:7 (cf. Mk 12:33)).

6:7. But at Adam: MT reads "like Adam" or "like a man" (cf. Vss.), but the following **there** requires a reference to a place, and it is characteristic of Hosea to specify the places where evils were committed (cf. vv. 8–9, and 5:1). The small change from *keʾādām* to *beʾādām* proposed by Wellhausen is therefore adopted by most modern commentators and versions. **Adam** was in the Jordan valley (Jos. 3:16), perhaps at Tell ed-Damiye near the modern bridge, which is **on the way to Shechem** from **Gilead** (cf. vv. 8–9). NEB reads "at Admah" (cf. 11:8; Gen. 14:2), but this involves a further change to MT (cf. *HTOT*, p. 246) and is improbable, as the people of Admah, wherever it was, were not Israelites. A quite different translation of the verse is offered by Kuhnigk, following suggestions made originally by M. J. Dahood: "But see how they trod my covenant underfoot like the ground; look, they were unfaithful to me" (pp. 82–85). This makes emendation unnecessary, but it attributes new and controversial meanings to several of the Heb. words (like the older suggestion based on Arabic that *sam* here means not **there** but "then": Nyberg, p. 42).

the covenant: A **covenant** (Heb. *berît*) may be defined as a legal instrument which formalizes the relationship between two parties, either or both of whom undertake certain obligations. According to the situation the most appropriate translation may be "treaty", "covenant" or "bond". The theological uses of the term exhibit a similar diversity of meaning: in this passage it is clear that a **covenant** which imposed obligations on Israel in the form of law (cf. 8:1, 12) is presupposed (cf. on 4:2 for Hosea's possible knowledge of the Decalogue). There is no tension between this legal language and Hosea's frequent use of marriage as a metaphor for the relationship between Yahweh and Israel: marriage was itself based on a contract (*berît*; cf. Jer. 31:32; Ezek.16:8; Mal. 2:14; Prov. 2:17: examples from Elephantine are given in *ANET*, pp. 222–23, 548–49). The literature on the subject of covenant in the OT is immense: see especially E. Bickerman, in *Studies in Jewish and Christian History* I, Leiden, 1976, pp. 1–32; L. Perlitt, *Bundestheologie im alten Testament*, Neukirchen, 1969; D. R. Hillers, *Covenant: The History of a Biblical Idea*, Baltimore, 1969; E. Kutsch, *Verheissung und Gesetz* (BZAW 131), Berlin and New York, 1972, and in *THAT*, vol. 1, 339–352; D. J. McCarthy, *Old Testament Covenant*, Oxford, 1973; *Treaty and Covenant*, 2nd. ed., Rome, 1978; M. Weinfeld, *TDOT*, vol. 2, 253–279; Nicholson, *God and his People*.

Most probably the covenant referred to here is that between Yahweh and Israel (cf. 8:1), which was believed to have been established at Mount Sinai (Exod. 24:3–8; 34:10–27). According to some a breech of this **covenant** is ruled out by the association with a single event and place and the absence of the possessive adjective "my" with **covenant**, and either a covenant between the people and the ruling king or a treaty with another nation (cf. 10:4; 12:2) is meant (Fohrer, Rudolph; Perlitt, *Bundestheologie im alten Testament*, pp. 141–44; Kutsch, *Verheissung und Gesetz*, p. 59). Yet these alternatives are themselves problematic (so also J. Day, *VT* 36 (1986), 3–6), as there is no evidence that the people and the king regularly made a covenant with one another, and **Adam** on the river Jordan was inside Israelite territory and therefore an unlikely place for a breach of treaty with an ally to occur. Moreover, the following verses seem to speak of internal rather than external affairs, and Nicholson, *God and his People*, pp. 183–86, has pointed out the difference between the terminology used here and in 8:1 (**transgressed**) and the expression "to break (*hēpēr*) a **covenant**", which is normal where international treaties are involved. The absence of "my" is not a serious difficulty for the view taken here, as the second half of the verse makes it sufficiently clear which **covenant** is meant, the ideas of dealing **faithlessly** (cf. 5:7) and violation of **covenant** being practically synonymous (Andersen and Freedman).

On the events referred to in this and the subsequent verses

see the introduction to this section: the view of Sellin and Neef, *Heilstraditionen*, pp. 144–55, that v. 7 alludes to the story in Jg. 12:1–6, is less probable.

6:8. Gilead (cf. 12:11) is normally a name for the Israelite territories east of the river Jordan, or part of them, but it is not found as the name of a particular **city** elsewhere in the OT. It is sometimes so understood in Jg. 10:17, but the territorial meaning is also possible there. Possibly **Gilead** is here an abbreviation for one of the well-known cities of the region, such as Ramoth-gilead (Mays), a view that finds some support in what may be references to a town called **Gilead** in two Assyrian texts (cf. K. Galling, *TGI*, pp. 57–58). Alternatively the phrase **a city of evildoers** may be a colloquial one that is loosely applied to a whole area. NEB translates "a haunt of evildoers", giving to *qiryat* (**city**) a more general sense based on what is usually presumed to be its etymology (from *qārāh* = "meet", cf. *BDB*). On the history of **Gilead** cf. M. Ottosson, *Gilead. Tradition and History*, Lund, 1969: significant events of Hosea's times were the support which Gilead lent to Pekah's revolt (2 Kg. 15:25), which may indeed be what is referred to here (see above), and the region's capture by the Assyrians in 733 (2 Kg. 15:29).

evildoers (*pō'ªlê 'āwen*) probably refers to an act of violence, in view of the latter part of the verse, and not to cultic misdemeanours, although elsewhere in Hosea *'āwen* does have a cultic reference (4:15; 10:5, 8; 12:11 – cf. 1 Sam. 15:23; Isa. 1:13). For the more general use cf. Isa. 10:1; 29:20; 31:2; Mic. 3:2. The underlying idea seems to be one of "misused power" (cf. K. H. Bernhardt, *TDOT*, vol. 1, 140–47; R. Knierim, *THAT*, vol. 1, 81–84). The phrase *pō'ªlê 'āwen* is frequent in the lament psalms (e.g. Ps. 6:8), where it is translated "workers of evil": on its sense there see A. A. Anderson, *Psalms*, vol. 1, London, 1972, pp. 91, 230.

tracked with blood: Like a road leading up from a ford, **Gilead** as it were bears the footmarks of those who have shed blood, i.e. committed murder. For the belief that a murderer polluted the land cf. Num. 35:33; Ps. 106:38.

6:9. At several points the Heb. of this verse is difficult or uncertain (cf. Harper, pp. 287–91, and Rudolph, pp. 142–43, for details), but the general sense is clear enough, namely that the priests have acted outrageously, by plotting and committing murder like common brigands.

As robbers lie in wait for a man: RSV's interpretation (shared by NEB) assumes a Heb. construction that is attested but unusual (cf. *GK* §115k). Another possible translation is "As robbers lie in wait" (cf. JB, REB), taking *ʾîš* (**man**) not as the object but as in the construct state before *gᵉdûdîm* (cf. *GK* §124r). On **robbers** (*gᵉdûdîm*) see also on 7:1.

A fragmentary commentary on Isaiah from Qumran (4QpIsᶜ) cites these words in its explanation of Isa. 30:15–18, apparently seeing in them a reference to contemporary misdeeds of the priesthood (*DJD* V, pp. 24–25 (*DSSE*, p. 228) – cf. above on 5:14). The spelling of the first word in the quotation (*kyḥkh* for MT's *kḥky*) has some importance, as it helps to clarify the variant readings of MT and LXX and points behind them to an original *kḥkh*, i.e. *kᵉḥakkēh*.

are banded together: The sense sought by RSV can be obtained without emendation, if *ḥeber*, "a company", is construed with **the priests** as a nominal clause: "the priests are a company". Alternatively *ḥeber* may be taken with **the priests** in a genitive combination which forms the subject of the following verb (so JB). Hosea has already used a word from the same root as *ḥeber* in a bad sense in 4:17: Ephraim is joined to idols. Here the point is a different one, that the united front of **the priests** is merely a means to coordinate violence. For evidence outside the Bible for the use of *ḥeber* cf. *HAL*, p. 276, and CD 13:15, 14:16 (*DSSE*, p. 115).

they murder on the way to Shechem: The word-order of the Heb. is strange if this is the meaning, but perhaps possible (cf. D. N. Freedman, *Biblica* 53 (1972), 536). The Heb. word for **murder** is *rāṣaḥ*, as in the sixth commandment and in 4:2 above, but in the Piel instead of the Qal. It can be applied to unintentional killing as well as **murder** (cf. Dt. 4:42 etc. and Stamm and Andrew, *The Ten Commandments in Recent Research*, pp. 98–99), but that is hardly its meaning here. The use of the Piel may mean that **the priests** hired others to do the actual killing (cf. *GK* §52g and 2 Kg. 6:32) or that (as the imperfect tense of the verb certainly implies) a series of murders has been committed (cf. *GK* §52f). **Shechem** has an

important place in Israelite tradition from the patriarchal stories
on (cf. Gen. 12:6–7; 33:18–20; 34), and it is mentioned several
times in the Amarna letters of the 14th century B.C.. Important
religious ceremonies are located there (Dt. 27; Jos. 8:30–35; 24)
and according to Noth it was a central shrine of the Israelite
tribes in the time of the Judges (but his view is now generally
rejected: cf. A. D. H. Mayes, *Israel in the Period of the Judges*,
London, 1974, pp. 35–41). It was evidently still a major centre
in the early monarchy (1 Kg. 12:1, 25), but thereafter yielded its
position to Samaria, until it reappeared as a religious centre of
the Samaritan community in post-exilic times (cf. Sir. 50:26). Cf.
IDB, vol. 4, 313–14 and E. Nielsen, *Shechem. A Traditio-Historical
Investigation*, Copenhagen, 1955. It is identified with Tell Balatah,
1.5 miles east of the centre of the modern city of Nablus, where
large-scale excavations have been carried out under the direction
of E. Sellin and G. E. Wright (cf. Wright, *Shechem*, London, 1965,
and *EAEHL*, vol. 4, 1083–94), which exposed remains from many
periods, including the time of Hosea.

Wolff has argued that the mention of murder **on the way to
Shechem** has particular significance in the light of what he holds
to be Hosea's religious background (see the Introduction, p. 31).
He suggests that the Levites and prophetic groups from which
Hosea derived his ideals "could have had their chief residence in
the old amphictyonic centre of Shechem" (p. 122). **Shechem** was
a Levitical city (Jos. 21:21) and, unlike many other traditional
holy places, it is nowhere attacked by Hosea (or Amos). Hosea
refers to apparently violent opposition to prophecy in 9:7–9,
and one might connect this violence with the violence **on the
way to Shechem**. Possibly the phrase refers to pilgrims loyal
to Shechemite traditions (Kraus, *Worship in Israel*, p. 145). The
formulation of v. 5 also suggests that it was necessary for Hosea to
defend the prophetic message against criticism. It is not possible
to be certain which **way to Shechem** is meant. The watershed
road that ran from north to south between **Shechem** and Bethel
was famous (cf. Dt. 11:30; Jg. 21:19), but the phrase in the text
could refer to any number of routes which meet at **Shechem** (cf.
Wright, *Shechem*, pp. 2–3, 9–11). If vv. 7–10 are thought to allude
to a single episode or sequence of episodes, then the likelihood is
that the route from **Gilead** which crossed the Jordan near **Adam**

and continued to **Shechem** up the Wadi Fariᶜa is meant (there is a photograph in Baly, *Geography*, p. 181).

yea, they commit villainy: yea translates Heb. *kî*, which here serves to emphasize the following statement. Heb. *zimmāh* (**villainy**) has two clearly distinguished fields of meaning, "plans" (good or evil) and "outrage" (usually of a sexual nature). When used with *'āsāh* (**commit**) it always has the second meaning (cf. Jg. 20:6; Prov. 10:23; Ezek. 16:43; 22:9; 23:48). Here NEB's "outrageous" and JB's "appalling" reproduce the connotations of the word more accurately than **villainy**, connotations which can be identified with particular clarity in Lev. 18:17; 19:29; 20:14, where it is associated with ideas of uncleanness. Either the priests are additionally accused of sexual crimes or the point is that their violence is no less abominable than the practices listed in these laws, especially in those who are supposed to be the guardians of purity. For the pollution caused by **murder** see above on v. 8.

6:10. In the house of Israel: In Hosea this expression refers to the northern kingdom (cf. 1:4, 6; 12:1) rather than to the whole people of Israel, including Judah. This makes the following **there** awkward, as Ephraim is also a name for the northern kingdom (cf. on 4:17). The first part of the verse ought to specify where in particular Ephraim's harlotry is to be seen. Since Wellhausen a number of scholars have adopted the emendation to "Bethel", presupposing a tendency in later editors to replace the name of the famous sanctuary by a term of more general application as in Hos. 10:15 and Am. 5:6. On the other hand, considerable support can be found for the view that in these cases it is the reading house of Israel which is original (cf. Wolff and Rudolph on Hos. 10:15, and BH3 and Weiser on Am. 5:6), which weakens the argument for a change to "Bethel" here. A change does seem to be needed, however, and perhaps "my house" (*bêtî*) should be read, with MT being ascribed to a misunderstanding of the possessive suffix as an abbreviation for "Israel" (for textual corruption arising in such a way cf. G. R. Driver, *Textus* I (1960), 112–31, 4 (1964), 76–94, and *IDBS*, pp. 3–4). After the mention of the priests' crimes a reference to a sanctuary ("the house of Yahweh") as the locus of corruption would not be at all surprising (cf. also 9:8 and Jer. 23:11). Hosea uses the expression **the house of the Lord** to refer to a sanctuary (8:1; 9:4, 15: cf.

the notes on these verses). NEB, "at Israel's sanctuary", derives
a similar meaning from MT, but it is doubtful whether "house"
in combination with "Israel" was used in this way. Most likely
the sanctuary referred to would be that at Bethel, since it was
the chief sanctuary of the northern kingdom (cf. Am. 7:13 and
the comment on "Beth-aven" in 4:15).

I have seen a horrible thing: The **I** refers, as throughout
this section, to Yahweh himself. A word from the same root as
horrible (*ša'rûriyyāh*) is used of bad figs which are too rotten
to eat in Jer. 29:17, and the implication here is that Yahweh
feels a similar loathing for what he sees in his **house**. The other
three occurrences of the root (Jer. 5:30; 18:13; 23:14) apply to
sins which have a connection with the cult and the same is
probably the case here, whether or not one of the emendations
discussed above is adopted. The reference may be either to the
acts of violence committed or encouraged by the priests (cf. Jer.
23:14) or to the practices referred to in earlier chapters (e.g. 2:11,
13; 4:12–14 – cf. Jer. 5:30; 18:13). The following line, which is
closely similar to 5:3b, would seem to favour the latter alternative
(see the notes on **harlotry** in 1:2 and **defiled** in 5:3), but it is
also possible that Hosea is turning his favourite imagery to a
new purpose and asserting that the violent actions of the priests
are just as much **harlotry** and a source of defilement as the
apostasy which they encourage (see also the note on **villainy** in
v. 9). Because of the similarity to 5:3, Wolff regards 6:10b as an
explanation of **a horrible thing** added by a glossator (p. 106).

6:11. It is doubtful whether MT can bear the meaning
generally assumed by translators, as *gam* (**also**) is nowhere else
followed directly by a vocative (cf. the different order of words
in Zeph. 2:12). A more accurate translation would be "Judah
also [sc. 'is defiled']. He [or 'one'] has appointed a harvest for
you." The line is divided in this way in LXX (cf. Targ.). The
first two words are a redactional addition extending the force
of 6:10 to cover **Judah** as well (cf. 5:5 and 2 Kg. 17:19ff.),
while the remainder is a separate addition to Hosea's word
which supplied the threat of judgment which was felt to be
missing after the accusations of vv. 7–10, in language which
finds its closest parallels in Jer. 51:33, 39 (though cf. also Hos.
8:7; 10:12–13).

When I would restore the fortunes of my people: These words are closely parallel in meaning to the opening words of 7:1 and should be joined with them to form a single line of poetry. Apart from JB few modern interpreters retain the MT verse division (but cf. Robinson, Jacob). Most commentators connect this line with what follows, as in RSV, but Rudolph takes it with 6:11a, which he argues is a late Judaean gloss. His main argument is that **restore the fortunes** is an eschatological technical term that could not have been used by Hosea of a contemporary (or past) situation (such as is referred to in 7:1) and must mean the final salvation of Yahweh's people. Yet 6:11a is in its present position clearly speaking of judgment and not salvation, which compels Rudolph to take the desperate step of regarding the gloss as having been displaced from its original position (supposedly after 6:3). In fact his starting-point is mistaken, as the use of the expression in a fully eschatological sense is late and secondary (Jer. 48:41; 49:6, 39; Zeph. 3:20; Jl 3:1) and it occurs outside prophetic literature altogether (Dt. 30:3; Job 42:10; Ps. 14:7; 53:7; 85:2; 126:1, 5; Lam. 2:14). Essentially the same phrase is used of an already past event in an Aramaic text from Sefire in Syria of about 760 B.C. (J. C. L. Gibson, *Textbook of Syrian Semitic Inscriptions*, vol. 2, Oxford, 1975, 9.24). It comprises two cognate forms of the root *šwb*, "return, restore", not one from *šwb* and one from *šbh*, "be captive", as presupposed in Vss. and earlier English translations, e.g. RV. On the occurrences and interpretations of this phrase cf. R. Borger, *ZAW* 66 (1954), 315–16, and W. L. Holladay, *The root šûbh in the Old Testament*, Leiden, 1958, pp. 110–14. The occurrences in the Psalms, three of which are in congregational prayers (Pss. 85:2; 126:1, 5), show that the expression found its way into public worship, but the view that it referred to and indeed derived from a ritual which formed the climax of an annual festival (*Schicksalswende*: cf. S. Mowinckel, *The Psalms in Israel's Worship*, Oxford, 1962, I, pp. 146–48; A. Weiser, *The Psalms*, London, 1962, pp. 46–49) is not supported by the evidence. Rather, it means, as the parallel **heal** here shows, "the restoration of the people's wounded body" (Wolff, p. 123) by the removal of the cause of distress, whether famine or enemy oppression or whatever it might be. The RSV rendering is misleading in one respect (likewise, e.g., NEB), in that it treats the Heb. expression as stating only Yahweh's intention to **restore** his people's fortunes. While some support for this interpretation can be found in 2 Kg. 2:1 (cf. *GK* §114q), a straightforward past or present, such as Wolff's "Whenever I restored . . .", is equally possible.

7:1. when I would heal Israel: Here too there may be, and probably is, a reference to an actual turn for the better in Israel's fortunes, though we cannot be specific about its nature. Since this is Yahweh's doing, he could reasonably expect gratitude and obedience from Israel, but the reverse is the case: **the corruption of Ephraim is revealed. corruption** is Heb. *ʿāwôn*, a favourite word of Hosea which is better translated "iniquity" or "guilt" (cf. JB, NEB). The presence of such "guilt" is a cause of disaster (5:5; 14:1), for it is not dissipated by wealth (12:8) or time (13:12) but is remembered by Yahweh (8:13; 9:9) and punished (10:10), unless it is forgiven (14:2). The word is commonly said to be derived from a verb meaning "bend, twist" and so to characterize sin as a perversion or distortion of nature, but such a derivation is not borne out by the word's use and the underlying idea is probably one of "error, going astray" (cf. Arabic *ġawā(y)*, and S. R. Driver, *Notes on the Hebrew Text of the Books of Samuel*, 2nd ed., Oxford, 1913, pp. 170–71; against R. Knierim, *THAT*, vol. 2, 243–49). Evil is so deep-seated in Israel's nature that it forces itself to the surface (**is revealed**) even when it is most inexcusable.

the wicked deeds of Samaria: Samaria, the capital of the northern kingdom since the early 9th century BC (1 Kg. 16:24), is here mentioned for the first time in the book of Hosea (cf. 8:5, 6; 10:5, 7; 13:16). The site is a hill (cf. Am. 4:1) adjacent to the village of Sebastiye, which preserves the name (Sebaste) given to Samaria by Herod the Great, who rebuilt it (Josephus, *AJ* 15.292–93). Excavations have uncovered the finely constructed acropolis of the Israelite kings, with its palaces, towers and courtyards (*EAEHL*, vol. 4, 1032–50), and numerous inscribed ostraca have been found which indicate its importance as an administrative centre (cf. *DOTT*, pp. 205–208; *ANET*, p. 321; Gibson, *Textbook*, I, pp. 5–13; A. F. Rainey, *Tel Aviv* 6 (1979), 91–94). For Hosea it is a centre of Israel's guilt, partly because of its devotion to the calf-image (8:5, 6; 10:5) but also because

of its political intrigues (cf. vv. 3–7 below). For **wicked deeds**
Vss. have the singular "wickedness" (cf. v. 3), which is followed
by JB and NEB, and this is a better parallel to **corruption** (or
"iniquity", as above). There is no need to emend MT's *rāʿôt*, as
it may be a plural of intensity ("great wickedness": cf. *GK* §124e)
or perhaps a dialectal form of the singular (Kuhnigk, pp. 87–88),
but it remains possible that an original singular was changed to
the plural by a scribe with 10:10 (cf. Jer. 2:13) in mind.

   they deal falsely: The description of the capital's wickedness
begins in general terms, before going into detail about the
particular crimes of conspiracy and regicide (vv. 3–7). **they**
is probably indefinite in its reference (cf. 4:2 and *GK* §144f)
and means "people". Fraud is a common theme in Hosea (cf.
4:2; 7:3; 12:7). It may, like the offences which follow, be an
infringement of another's property. Hosea leaves no doubt that
these are **evil works** (v. 2).

   the thief breaks in: The Heb. strictly speaks not of breaking
but of entering (*yābô'*, from *bô'*, "to come, go in", which is used in
a comparison of locusts with a thief in Jl 2:9). NEB (cf. JB) adds
"into houses", claiming support from Targ. (*HTOT*, p. 247), but
Targ. is very free in its rendering of this part of the verse and
MT is quite satisfactory as it is.

   the bandits raid without: When words like **bandits** (Heb.
gedûd) and **raid** (Heb. *pāšaṭ*) are used, it is usually outsiders who
are being referred to (e.g. 2 Kg. 5:2; 13:20–21; 2 Chr. 22:1; and
especially 1 Sam. 30, where both words occur several times), but
the context implies that here men who have banded together
against their fellow-citizens are meant. In contrast to the thief,
they openly and violently make off with others' property. NEB's
different translation, "they strip people in the street" should
be rejected, as the Qal of *pst* is not used in this way and the
meaning **raid** fits the activity of **bandits** perfectly. Dahood's
emendation to *pešaṭ* = "and (bandits) roam" (Kuhnigk, p. 88)
is quite unnecessary and rests on the unfounded assumption that
pe could mean "and" in Heb. as it does in Ugaritic.

   7:2. Typically Hosea penetrates to the religious faults which
lie behind particular kinds of behaviour, in this case the failure
to reckon with the fact that Yahweh "remembers" sins (cf. 5:3;
8:13; 9:9), an expression which implies not only recollection but

an appropriate reaction, in this case judgment (cf. *TDOT*, vol. 4, 69–72; *THAT*, vol. I, 510; B. S. Childs, *Memory and Tradition in Israel*, London, 1962, pp. 17–34).

their deeds encompass them: Again, as in 5:4, **their deeds** are spoken of in an objective and quasi-personal manner, to emphasize their effects on Israel's present situation: they are like a besieging army which surrounds and threatens a city (2 Kg. 6:15), or like a floodstream (Ps. 88:17; Jon. 2:4, 6).

7:3. From here to v. 7 court intrigues are in view, probably a specific occasion during one of the *coups d'état* which took place in the years following the death of Jeroboam II. V. 7 seems to indicate that a succession of *coups* has occurred, which favours a reference to either Pekah's revolt c. 735 or Hoshea's c. 732. For further discussion of the historical background see the introductory remarks on 6:4–7:16. The Heb. text of these verses is corrupt in several places and difficult to interpret in others, and scholars have proposed a variety of solutions to the problems. See, in addition to the commentaries, G. R. Driver, *JTS* 39 (1938), 156–57, T. H. Gaster, *VT* 4 (1954), 78–79, S. M. Paul, *VT* 18 (1968), 114–20, and Kuhnigk, pp. 90–93. But it is clear enough that a group of conspirators take the opportunity afforded by a night of revelling at the royal court to kill the king and his advisers, and that Hosea, as fond as ever of a simile, compares them to a hot oven that is fanned into flame when the dough is ready. The incident was evidently of a similar type to that which ended Elah's reign in the 9th century (1 Kg. 16:9). In view of Hosea's apparent disapproval of the monarchy (cf. on 8:4) it may seem surprising that he should have regarded the removal of a king as something undesirable. But compare his statement on the revolution of Jehu in 1:4. Two factors may have been involved: 1. Murder was contrary to the will of Yahweh, whatever the circumstances (cf. the Decalogue). 2. Hosea seems to have shared the view expressed in 1 Sam. 8 that kingship was a divinely ordained institution, even if it was reluctantly granted (cf. 13:11). It was no man's right to strike down "the Lord's anointed": cf. the attitude ascribed to David in 1 Sam. 26:9–11 (cf. 24:6).

As the verse is translated in RSV, the meaning is that **the king** and his **princes**, or courtiers, are delighted by the evil

schemes of the mysterious **they**. But this is improbable, as
the schemes in question are those by which both king and
princes are to be brought down. Perhaps, the Heb. preposition
b^e should be translated "in" and not **By** (denoting manner and
not instrument), which is perfectly possible. The meaning then is
that they deceitfully "keep the king happy" (cf. JB) while plotting
his end (Rudolph suggests "make him merry", i.e. with wine (cf.
v. 5), but it is doubtful whether $\acute{s}\bar{a}m\bar{e}a\d{h}$ was used to mean "merry"
in the sense of "tipsy"). Alternatively $y^e\acute{s}amm^e\d{h}\hat{u}$ should be taken
in a different way, as in NEB, "they win over the king with their
wickedness . . ." or Driver's "they make sport of the king . . ."
(*JTS* 39 (1938), 156). Such meanings can scarcely be derived
from the standard meanings of $\acute{s}\bar{a}m\bar{e}a\d{h}$, "to rejoice", and in the
Piel, "to gladden". It is just possible that there was a second root
$\acute{s}m\d{h}$ (or $\check{s}m\d{h}$, which would be indistinguishable in an unpointed
text), meaning "attack", as such a meaning would fit well in
some other passages (Ps. 46:5; Isa. 66:5), but the interpretation
of JB is more likely.

    7:4. adulterers: Elsewhere in Hosea this word refers either
to adultery in the literal sense (4:1, 12–13) or to exchanging
Yahweh for Baal (2:2 – cf. 3:1), but neither of these uses is
entirely appropriate here. If MT is retained, the word is probably
used figuratively to describe the disloyalty and deceit of the
conspirators (cf. Jer. 9:2; 23:14). JB follows several commentators
in emending $m^e n\bar{a}\,{}^{\prime a}p\hat{\imath}m$ to ${}^{\prime a}n\bar{e}p\hat{\imath}m$ or ${}^{\prime}\bar{o}n^ep\hat{\imath}m$, "enraged", but the
development of the following simile (cf. also v. 6) requires a
reference here to the subtlety of the murderers, not merely to
their fury. Rudolph's "their heart holds their anger back" is
based on an unnecessarily extensive emendation.

    they are like a heated oven: All modern translators make a
small change to MT here, as first suggested by Oort, to remove
a grammatical difficulty: the consequence is that the **baker** is
treated as the subject of the following line. Wolff's rendering,
". . . an oven which burns without a baker", keeps closer to
MT, but it presupposes an awkward Heb. sentence and the
resulting sense is improbable. The kind of **oven** in question is well
known from archaeological excavations, ancient tomb-paintings
and analogies in modern times (cf. *IDB*, vol. 1, 340–41, 462;
vol. 4, 612–13, and references there). It was made of clay in a

truncated cone shape, with an aperture at the top and another, for attending to the fire, at the base. Its purpose was primarily the baking of bread, for which a variety of techniques seems to have been used.

whose baker ceases to stir the fire: Hosea is apparently thinking of a professional **baker**, such as were to be found at the royal court (1 Sam. 8:13 – cf. Gen. 40:1 etc.) and in large cities (Jer. 37:21). While archaeological evidence of ovens generally comes from domestic buildings, the remains of a bakery were found at Tell es-Sa'idiyeh in the Jordan valley (cf. *BA* 31 (1968), 51). The Heb. underlying **to stir the fire** may be construed either as a Hiphil participle (cf. *GK* §120b) or as a noun (cf. Jer. 15:8; Hos. 11:9): the sense is not greatly affected. **the fire** is not in the Heb., but is supplied to clarify the sense. Andersen and Freedman prefer "to be alert", which is closer to the normal meaning of the verb, but this makes the point of the line obscure. When the bread was baking, the **baker** would presumably from time to time **stir** the ashes to expose more hot embers, but at night (cf. v. 6), while the dough was rising (cf. G. Dalman, *Arbeit und Sitte in Palästina*, Gütersloh, 1935, vol. 4, p. 48), he would sleep and leave the oven unattended. It would soon cease to glow, but would remain hot to the touch. It is to the oven in this state that Hosea compares the misleading friendliness of the conspirators to the court.

7:5. On the day of our king: Possibly "their king" (NEB) should be read, with Targ., as **our** is rather incongruous in a divine speech (cf. v. 7: so Robinson, Wolff, Rudolph). The **day** of the **king** has been variously understood as his accession, its anniversary or his birthday (cf. NEB "festival day"). But in popular speech a person's **day** was normally the day of his death (cf. 1 Sam. 26:10 and *BDB*, s.v. *yôm*, 2. i), and this meaning fits the present context admirably. Several scholars emend the phrase more drastically (cf. JB, which omits **On the day of**), but this is unjustified.

became sick with the heat of wine: The intransitive use of the Hiphil of *ḥlh* (**became sick**) does not occur elsewhere, and it may be better to translate "they made (the princes) sick", i.e. the conspirators made the king's companions drunk, presumably to prevent any opposition to their plans (so JB, Mays). For

the heat of wine Andersen and Freedman suggest "poisoned wine", comparing Ps. 58:4 and 140:3 for *ḥēmāh* = "poison". Vss., presupposing a different vocalization of two words from MT, all translate "began to be enraged" (cf. NEB). This makes the line easier grammatically, especially at the end, but MT is defensible (*GK* §130a) and it is not clear why the "beginning" of the carousals should be picked out for mention.

he stretched out his hand with mockers: The subject, if MT is retained, is presumably the **king**, and the phrase is to be taken as an idiom for making common cause with someone. But *māšak* nowhere else means **stretched out**: its normal meanings are "draw, drag, continue". An Ugaritic text (CTA 15.1.1–2 = *CML*, p. 90) lends some support to MT, but the context is too broken for it to clarify the meaning. NEB's "joins in the orgies" and JB's "mixes" are only intelligent guesses. Other possibilities are to translate "its power (i.e. that of the wine) enchants the mockers", taking **hand** in its metaphorical sense of "power" (Wolff), or to adopt an ingenious emendation of Sellin and read "the rebels (cf. below) make him (i.e. the king) drunk" (Robinson, Rudolph). **mockers**, while in line with the use of the root in Proverbs, may be too weak a translation (cf. Isa. 29:20), and a connection with Arabic *lāṣa*, "turn aside, deceive", would permit the translation "renegades" (Rudolph) or even "deceivers", which fits the context excellently (cf. Targ. "liars").

7:6. For like an oven: *kî* (**For**) is here more probably emphatic: "yea, . . ." (cf. on 6:9).

their hearts burn: As the marginal note indicates, RSV (like NEB and JB) is based on the translation of LXX and Syr., which differ from MT and are commonly taken to be based on a more original Heb. text than it (*qādaḥ* or, less likely, *qād bô* (NEB: cf. *HTOT*, p. 247) instead of *qērᵉbû*, with the easy confusion of the letters *daleth* and *resh*). MT is vocalized as a Piel, which is mostly transitive, "they brought near", but this makes no sense in the context: RV's "they made ready" is hardly a legitimate rendering. But the Piel is occasionally intransitive (cf. Ezek. 9:1), like the Hiphil in Exod. 14:10, so that the rendering "they drew near" (Andersen and Freedman) is possible without alteration of the vowels. The following words may then be treated as a nominal

clause: "their hearts were like an oven". Yet there remains doubt
about MT, as it is hardly likely that Hosea himself would have
repeated the words "like/as an oven" three times in a short
passage, and it is the occurrence in this verse which seems most
obtrusive. If it is a gloss due to a copyist, then it is likely that
there was in the text before him some reference to burning,
which prompted his comment: in other words, that LXX and
Syr. (cf. above) give a more original reading than MT's "they
brought/drew near".

with intrigue: A better rendering of the Heb. word is "as
they lay in wait". The word is often emended (Wolff, Rudolph),
but without good reason. Possibly, however, for metrical reasons,
it should be taken with the following line, as Andersen and
Freedman suggest.

their anger: MT (cf. Aq., Symm., Th., Vulg.) "their baker" is
impossible in view of the following line: it is surprising to find that
Andersen and Freedman retain it. LXX "Ephraim" is also difficult. RSV and most modern scholars follow the reading implied
by Targ. and Syr., which involves only a different vocalization
of the same consonantal text (*'appᵉhem* (cf. *GK* §91c) instead of
'ōpēhem). The idea of **anger** "blazing" is a common one, and that
of its "sleeping" (cf. below), while unparalleled in the Bible, is not
unlikely, especially with a poet as fond of imagery as Hosea is.

smoulders: The Heb. *yāšēn* literally means "sleeping" or
"slept" (cf. NEB). Possibly RSV and JB, which gives the same
rendering, are simply adapting the metaphor to the context. But
they may be echoing a long-standing view that *yāšēn* is either a
mistake for *'āšan* (= "smoked") or "an obsolete orthography" for
the imperfect of this same verb, which is used with **anger** as its
subject in Dt. 29:10 (cf. the note by T. K. Cheyne in W. Robertson
Smith, *The Prophets of Israel*, 2nd ed., London, 1895, p. 413; *HAL*,
p. 427). In any case, the straightforward interpretation is quite
acceptable.

in the morning: The conspirators apparently waited until the
following morning before they struck. This may seem strange,
but the meagre information which Hosea's invective provides
inevitably leaves questions about the plot unanswered. It is,
however, noteworthy that in Jg. 16:1–2 the plot of the men of
Gaza to kill Samson involved waiting until daybreak.

7:7. their rulers: Heb. *šōpēṭ*, the word for "judge", which was also used more generally for the political leadership, including the king (e.g. Isa. 40:23; Mic. 5:1). Indeed it is possible that the more general use is the original one, and that the judicial use represents a specialization of the term to refer to one kind of leadership in the community. In any case, political and judicial authority were not sharply distinguished in ancient Israel (cf. on 5:2).

All their kings have fallen: fallen implies a violent death, which was a common fate for the rulers of the northern kingdom, where one dynasty followed another, especially in the last years of its existence (cf. 2 Kg. 15:10–30). Since it is implied that several assassinations have taken place, these words must either have in view the whole history of the northern kingdom or, more likely, they look back on all or most of the *coups* that took place in Hosea's own lifetime. They would fit best in the interval between the murder of Pekah in 733 and the Assyrian appointment of Hoshea to replace him, which is reported in the annals of Tiglath-pileser III (*ANET*, p. 284, *DOTT*, p. 55). It might be expected that in such a crisis the people would call upon their God for help, but they do not (cf. v. 10). Instead they direct their appeals for help to the great powers (v. 11, cf. 5:13). Alternatively the finality (**All**) may point to this line having been added by a redactor after 722.

7:8–12. Hosea here introduces a new topic for criticism, which has already been alluded to in 5:13: the intense preoccupation of his contemporaries with "foreign policy". This was, however, not unconnected with the plots against successive kings, for these frequently issued (and were no doubt designed to issue) in a change of foreign policy, particularly with respect to Assyria. Hosea does not take sides on the issue of policy, but exposes what is happening to Israel, whichever great power is approached for help.

7:8. Imagery drawn from baking continues to be used, and this is seen by Wolff as an argument for a close connection between vv. 7 and 8. Now the people as a whole (**Ephraim**) are accused of regarding themselves as simply ingredients to be **mixed** in with other **peoples** (for the culinary use of the verb cf. Lev. 2:4 etc.), quite forgetful of their distinctiveness (cf. Num. 23:9). The result is disastrous: varying the metaphor, Hosea compares them to **a cake not turned** – that is, one that is burnt on one side and uncooked on the other, of no savour to anyone. For **is** read "has become", with NEB.

7:9. Aliens devour his strength: Better, "have devoured". These **Aliens** (*zārîm*) are not immigrants (*gērîm*, "resident aliens"), but the foreign powers with which Israel enters into alliances. They are seen by her as a source of **strength**, but their real effect is to weaken the nation. The specific references may be to payments of tribute, already referred to under Menahem (2 Kg. 15:19–20) and certainly part of the agreement made by Hoshea with the Assyrians (cf. 2 Kg. 17:3), but the lopping off of large areas of Israelite territory by Tiglath-pileser III (2 Kg. 15:29) could also be described in these terms (cf. on 5:11).

grey hairs are sprinkled upon him: Grey hair is commonly a cause for pride (Prov. 16:31; 20:29), but here it represents the loss of youthful **strength. sprinkled** is not an exact translation of the Heb. *zāraq*, which means "throw" (cf. *BDB*), but none of the suggested alternatives is fully satisfactory. G. R. Driver derived the form from a second root *zāraq*, "be grey", comparing Arabic *zariqa* (*JTS* 33 (1932), 38), which is probably the basis for NEB's "turned white". An equivalent phrase is used in Akkadian of a mould forming on bread, which has prompted S. M. Paul to suggest that there is a return here to the cake-metaphor of v. 7 (*VT* 18 (1968), 119: so also Andersen and Freedman), but this is difficult after **Aliens devour his strength**.

and he knows not: The repetition of this phrase serves to emphasize the remarkable situation that it describes: Ephraim continues to act as if nothing has changed, either on the political or on the religious level.

7:10. The pride of Israel witnesses against him: These words occur also at 5:5, where the Heb. is identical despite the differences in the English translation. Either the prophet himself cites the words of an earlier oracle, which he sees as having a new application in the changed circumstances, or an editor has added them here because he thought that they (and no doubt their sequel in 5:5) were an apt comment on this passage. The latter view gives a more likely explanation of the appearance of this rather prosaic sentence in a context that is dominated by a succession of images, and is adopted by most commentators.

they do not return to the LORD their God: Israel's failure to repent is mentioned also in 5:4 and 11:5 and their refusal to **seek** Yahweh is implied in 5:15. The lack of an appropriate response to disaster is lamented also in v. 7. But while the thought is Hosea's the actual words may not be. Although it would not be a valid argument on its own (cf. on 4:10), the third-person reference to God in a divine speech (cf. v. 12) when coupled with the interruption of the succession of images favours the view that v. 10b is, like v. 10a, an editorial addition (so, e.g., Robinson, Donner, *Israel unter den Völkern*, p. 78): cf. I. Willi-Plein, *Vorformen der Schriftexegese innerhalb des AT* (BZAW 123), Berlin, 1971, pp. 159–60). By adding v. 10b the redactor takes the opportunity to bring out the heinousness of Israel's failure to repent, which for him, as for the Deuteronomistic editors of Kings (2 Kg. 17:13ff.), is above all else responsible for Israel's downfall (cf. Am. 4:6–11).

7:11. is like a dove: Better, "has become like a dove", with a stronger emphasis on the change in character. In this case the image describes Israel's behaviour itself, not its effects. The **silly** person is really the "simpleton" who appears frequently in Proverbs (e.g. 1:4) as one who has never learned about the realities of life and so is incapable of acting wisely. His lack of **sense** is a common theme (Prov. 7:7; 9:4, 16): see on **understanding** in 4:11. The **dove** (or "pigeon" (NEB): Heb. *yônāh* can mean either) is not elsewhere a symbol for such naivety (though cf. Mt. 10:16); its choice must have been designed to match Israel's flitting to and fro between the great powers of **Egypt** and **Assyria**, as policy alternated between willing submission to **Assyria** and attempts to reassert independence, usually with help from **Egypt**. Three times within a few years Israel went through this cycle, and each time the conclusion was the same: a devastating invasion by the Assyrian army (2 Kg. 16:29; 17:3–6).

calling to Egypt: They should be calling to Yahweh, it is implied (cf. v. 7).

7:12. Israel has acted like a bird, and so Yahweh, who now employs the first person singular again, will treat her like a bird (for the pattern of argument cf. 5:2, the note there and especially the pictures in Keel, *Symbolism*, pp. 92–93). The image of Yahweh as the hunter became a popular one with Ezekiel (cf. 12:13; 17:20; 32:3), who perhaps derived it from Hosea.

I will chastise them for their wicked deeds: For Yahweh's "chastisement" see the comment on 5:2. But RSV's rendering, with which JB in essence agrees, involves ignoring one word of MT and emending another. MT is certainly difficult, but can be made to yield a good parallel to the previous line without such extensive emendation: "I will take them captive as soon as I hear them flocking" (NEB; cf. Nyberg, pp. 56–57, and Rudolph, p. 151). The image indicates that Yahweh will take action to prevent the incessant appeals which Israel makes to her powerful neighbours, just as Hosea had earlier spoken of his "hedging up her way" to block her access to false gods (2:6–7). In neither case is the continuation of Israel's external history described in detail: as often, Hosea is more concerned to interpret, by means of imagery, what is happening in his time than simply to announce what tomorrow will bring.

7:13. Woe to them . . . : It is no light punishment that the prophet threatens, but **Woe** (*'ôy*, not *hôy*, which Hosea never uses; cf. 9:12 and Isa. 3:9, 11) and **destruction**, because the nation is not only **silly** (v. 11) but wayward and rebellious.

I would redeem . . . but they speak lies: The emphatic pronouns **I** (*'ānōkî*) and **they** (*hēmāh*) point to the contrast between Yahweh's readiness to restore a penitent people and Israel's defiance of him. Elsewhere there is a similar contrast between Yahweh's blessing and Israel's ingratitude (6:11–7:1; 7:15; 10:1–2; 11:1–5). For the syntax of **I would redeem them** cf. *GK* §107n: either this or "I (repeatedly) redeem them" (*GK* §107g: so Weiser) is preferable to the alternative rendering as a question (Harper, Wolff). The verb **redeem** (*pdh*: cf. 13:14) had from early times the general meaning "rescue" (cf. 2 Sam. 4:9 etc.) as well as a specific reference to the payment of a ransom (Exod. 21:8, 30; 34:19–20), and it is no longer clear that the former usage is derived from the latter (cf. J. J. Stamm, *THAT*, vol. 2, 389–406). In most places where it is used of Yahweh redeeming Israel the reference is to a deliverance from physical danger or oppression (e.g. Dt. 7:8; Ps. 44:26; Mic. 6:4): in the

OT the image of redemption is used in a spiritual sense only in Ps. 130:8. Here either impending liberation from Assyria or preservation from past military threats is probably meant.

but they speak lies against me: Or "about me" (JB, NEB). The meaning of this charge is not entirely clear. It is seen by some (e.g. Wellhausen, Jacob, Rudolph) as a new way of characterizing the quest for political alliances mentioned in the previous verses: such activity implies (the falsehood) that Yahweh himself cannot help. Others, pointing to the continuation in v. 14 and the overall context of 5:8–7:16, suppose that insincere or idolatrous worship is meant, specifically the (allegedly unacceptable) words of 6:1–3 (so Wolff, Mays; cf. M. A. Klopfenstein, *Die Lüge nach dem Alten Testament*, Zurich, 1964, pp. 228–30). Both these views equate this accusation too readily with those in neighbouring verses. Accusations such as this are found in the individual psalms of lament (cf. Pss. 4:2; 5:6, 9; 58:3; 62:4), as are charges that others "devise evil" (Pss. 43:1; 52:2, 4; 109:2; cf. v. 16). Yahweh speaks like the man who has been unjustly accused: in the context it is likely to be the claim that he is unable to afford protection to his people that is levelled against him by his "enemies".

7:14. In the Heb. this verse is connected to v. 13 by "and", so it continues Yahweh's accusation against his ungrateful people. Though they continue to use the language of the standard appeals to Yahweh in a time of trouble (cf. 8:2, where **cry** appears again), the appeal does not come **from the heart** – it does not express a genuine reliance on Yahweh for deliverance (cf. Isa. 29:13). This is evident from the fact that **They wail upon their beds**: the **beds** are probably the place of sexual rituals designed to ensure prosperity (cf. 4:14 and Isa. 57:7–8) – rituals which, like self-mutilation (see below), belonged to the worship of Baal rather than that of Yahweh and constituted rebellion against the God to whom their loyalty was due.

they gash themselves: The standard Heb. text (cf. *BH*[3], *BHS*) reads *yitgôrārû*, which AV and RV rendered "they assemble themselves". But the form *yitgôdādû*, **they gash themselves**, which is found in some Heb. manuscripts and is presupposed by LXX, is the better reading. Such cutting of the flesh was practised in Israel (Jer. 41:5 (cf. 16:6); Mic. 4:14), but it was prohibited in Deuteronomy (14:1), no doubt because of its

pagan associations (cf. 1 Kg. 18:28). Additional evidence of
the practice appears in the myths from Ugarit (CTA 5.6.19ff.,
6.1.3ff. = *CML*, pp. 73–74). It was in essence a mourning
custom and may here represent the idea that in summer or
in prolonged drought Baal died and only returned to life after
suitable mourning had taken place.

they rebel against me: RSV (cf. JB) is based on a small
change to the MT reading (*yāsōrû* for *yāsûrû*, "they turn away";
cf. NEB), which makes for an easier grammatical connection and
has support from Targ. and Syr.

7:15. Again (cf. v. 13) there is a contrast between what
Yahweh does and how his people respond, but in this case it
is emphasized by the placing of first-person pronominal forms
referring to Yahweh at the beginning of each half of the line:
wa'ᵃnî (**I**) . . . *wᵉ'ēlay* (**yet . . . against me**).

I trained: The verb *ysr* occurs several times in Hosea, but
elsewhere always in the sense "chastise" (cf. on 5:2). For the
meaning "train, educate" cf. Dt. 8:5, Prov. 31:1. G. R. Driver
suggested that a different root *ysr* was involved here, related to
Aramaic *'šr* Pael = "strengthen", and that the following word
ḥizzaqtî, **strengthened** (there is no "and" here in the Heb.), was
an explanatory gloss on this rare word. LXX may point to an
underlying Heb. shorter than MT. Driver's view is accepted by
HAL, Rudolph and, as far as the interpretation of *ysr* is concerned,
NEB ("I support them"), but the lack of correspondence between
the consonants of the Heb. and Aramaic words is a problem, and
trained is probably correct. The reference may be to military
training, seen as the work of Yahweh (so Kuhnigk, *Studien*,
pp. 98–100). There is, in any case, probably a deliberate
wordplay between this word and *yāsōrû* (*yāsûrû*) in v. 14, though
the words are not etymologically related.

yet they devise evil against me: This is another allegation
that is typical of the individual psalms of lament (cf. on v. 13).
The **lies** spoken about Yahweh are represented by Hosea as part
of a plan to get rid of him and, as the context shows, to replace
him by another god. It is noteworthy that, whereas vv. 8–9,
11–12 spoke of the ineptitude of Israel's foreign policy, these
verses present it as a personal affront to Yahweh and connect it
with the adoption of religious practices proper to Baal-worship.

7:16. They turn to Baal: Reading *labba'al* for MT's difficult *lō' 'āl*, with several commentators and JB. Renderings of the traditional text such as "but not to the Most High" (AV, cf. RV) and "(but) not upwards" (*BDB*, p. 752) are not convincing, and an explicit reference to Baal would fit the context well (cf. above). In recent years the idea that *'āl* is a divine title has been revived, because *'ly* occurs as a title of Baal in the Keret story (CTA 16.3.6, 8 = *CML*, p. 98) and several instances are claimed to exist in the OT itself (e.g. 1 Sam. 2.11; Ps. 7:11; 68:35– cf. NEB ad locc.). It is then possible to treat *lō' 'āl* as a compound name, "Not-Most-High", i.e. Baal, with a derogatory reference to his epithet (so Kuhnigk, p. 100), or to invert the consonants of *lō'*, "not", reading *'el*, "to", and translating "to the Most High", i.e. Baal (NEB, following Nyberg, pp. 57–61, and G. R. Driver, *JTS* 39 (1938), p. 157 n. 6). But doubt must remain, as elsewhere in the OT (except possibly in 11:7 – see the note there) "the Most High" is a title for Yahweh and would scarcely convey a clear reference to Baal here. For further discussion of this problem see the notes of Harper, Wolff and Rudolph.

they are like a treacherous bow: The simile is reminiscent of those in vv. 8 and 11 and itself recurs in Ps. 78:57, where it refers to Israel's apostasy in the time of the Judges. The same meaning fits well here, but the exact sense of the comparison is elusive: it is commonly taken to mean a **bow** that does not shoot straight and so misses the mark (the original sense of *ht'* = "sin"). The wording of Ps. 78:57 and 2 Sam. 1:22, however, may suggest that **treacherous** archers are meant, who do not stand firm in the heat of the battle (cf. B. Couroyer in *Estudios de Biblia y Oriente*, Salamanca, 1981, pp. 103–16: for **bow** = archers cf. Isa. 21:17). Heb. *r°miyyāh* can mean "slackness" rather than "treachery" (e.g. Prov. 10:4), and G. R. Driver suggested that a "slack" **bow** was meant here (*Alttestamentliche Studien* (FS F. Nötscher) (BBB 1), pp. 53–54); cf. NEB "Like a bow gone slack, they relapse into the worship of their high god". It is an attractive image, but a reference to "treachery" seems much more likely in the context.

the insolence of their tongue: This could be, as Wolff suggests, insults directed at Hosea himself by the **princes**, or courtiers (cf. 9:7): **insolence** (Heb. *za'am*) may be more properly

rendered "cursing" (cf. *HAL*, p. 265; *TDOT*, vol. 4, 107–108).
There is no need to invoke a supposed Arabic cognate *zagûmun*
= "stammerer" (G. R. Driver, *JTS* 39 (1938), p. 157; Rudolph).
NEB's "lies" is probably based on Targ., but attributes to the
word a meaning that it has nowhere else.

This shall be their derision: These words are commonly
regarded as a gloss, leaving **in the land of Egypt** to be construed
with **shall fall**: the **princes** shall meet their end in the foreign
land where they have gone to seek help. For **Egypt** as not only
a place of exile (8:13; 9:3; 11:5) but a deathbed cf. 9:6. But
it is equally possible that the words should be retained and
taken to mean that the death of the once-proud courtiers will
be a cause of **derision** in **Egypt**. Budde's suggestion, which
was taken up by Driver and Rudolph (cf. the preceding note),
that *la'ag* (**derision**) here has its other meaning of "stammering
(while using a foreign language)" (cf. Isa. 28:11; 33:19), is only
plausible if the line is regarded as a gloss (cf. NEB), and it is
unlikely that even a redactor would have seen a failure to speak
Egyptian properly as the cause of the **princes'** downfall.

A CATALOGUE OF ISRAEL'S SINS

8:1–14

Hosea 8 brings together a series of accusations against the
northern kingdom (and, in v. 14, also against Judah), in the
context of a warning of impending catastrophe (v. 1: cf. vv. 10
and 13, in which "now" (Heb. *'attāh*) emphasizes the imminence
of disaster). At first the accusations are in general terms (vv.
1–3), but they become specific from v. 4 on, where five particular
indictments can be distinguished: against unauthorized changes
in the leadership (4a), the making of images (4b–6), the conduct of
foreign relations by the leaders (8–9), sacrificial worship (11–13)
and trust in fortifications rather than in Yahweh (14). There is
thus a catalogue here of many of the sins for which Israel is
rebuked elsewhere in the book.

The three main sections of the chapter are each carefully constructed. The introduction (vv. 1–3) exhibits a chiastic pattern:
threat-explanation-response-explanation-threat (see the note on

v. 3). The second section (vv. 4–10) begins with an indictment of the royal court, which has no associated threat of judgment, so that the hearers remained in suspense as to its outcome. There follows the charge of image-making, which reaches its climax in the announcement of judgment in v. 6, and a pair of proverbial sayings which form a bridge to a section on the rulers' foreign policy, which concludes with the expected but delayed threat of judgment against them (v. 10b). The third main section (vv. 11–13) has a single theme, the preoccupation with sacrifice where obedience is required (cf. 6:6), and is held together by the mention of sin at the beginning and the end. It concludes with a solemn declaration of coming punishment, which also formed a coda to the chapter in its original form (cf. 9:9b). V. 14 is a later addition to this catalogue and its Hosean authorship is doubtful.

Except for the conclusion in v. 13 the style is divine speech throughout (cf. **my** in v. 1, **me** in vv. 2 and 4, **my** in v. 5, **I** in vv. 10 and 12 (cf. 14)). Israel is referred to in the third person (singular or plural), which is consistent with the chapter's being a report of words spoken by Yahweh to the prophet. A direct address to the people breaks in only in v. 5 (**your calf**), similar to those in 5:3, 13 and 6:4. Elements of the judgment-speech against the nation are mingled with lament-like sections (vv. 2, 5b and 8) and proverbial sayings (v. 7) in a way that is very typical of Hosea. Only in the secondary v. 14 is a "pure" judgment-speech found.

Additions to the original report can be recognized in vv. 4 (**for their own destruction**), 6 (**in Israel**), 7 (**if it were to yield, aliens would devour it**), and especially in the whole of v. 14, which comes too late after the formal conclusion of the passage: see the notes on these verses. In no case is it possible to be precise about the situation in which those additions were made, though v. 14 was presumably added in a Judaean setting. The occasion of the original composition is no more certain, but the reference to a single **calf** (vv. 5–6) and the situation presupposed in vv. 8–9 suggest a time after the accession of Hoshea. Some verses may be earlier than the main body of the chapter: e.g. vv. 1–3 may belong to the time of the Syro-Ephraimite War.

If **Samaria** in vv. 5–6 means the capital itself (see the notes), then the vocative in v. 5 may give an unusually clear indication of

the location of this saying, but the possibility cannot be excluded
that it is simply a rhetorical device.

8:1. Yahweh (cf. **my**) commands the raising of an alarm in
the face of an imminent enemy attack, which is the consequence
of Israel's sin. Most probably it is to Hosea himself that these
words are addressed, though they are too brief to be regarded
as his "call" (as supposed by Lindblom, *Prophecy*, pp. 185–86).

Set the trumpet to your lips: There is no word for **set** in
the Heb.: the abrupt style suits a situation of emergency. The
trumpet (Heb. *šōpār*, translated "horn" in the similar verse 5:8)
was used to sound an alarm (cf. Am. 3:6). Heb. *ḥēk* is strictly
"palate", but in poetry it can mean **lips** (Ca. 5:16; 7:10) or
"mouth" (Job 20:13; 31:30; 33:2): cf. Nyberg, pp. 61–62.

For a vulture is over the house of the LORD: Heb. *nešer*
can mean "eagle" as well as **vulture** (cf. G. Cansdale, *Animals
of Bible Lands*, Exeter, 1970, pp. 142–44), so that the idea that
Israel is already like a carcass may not be present. The MT in
fact reads "one like an eagle/vulture . . .", and RSV is based
on a small emendation first suggested by Wellhausen (*kî nešer*
for *kannešer*). The change is unnecessary, as is NEB's ommission
of the prefix altogether: cf. *BDB*, p. 453, for the use of *kᵉ. nešer*
is several times used of the swiftness of invaders (Dt. 28:49; Jer.
4:13; 48:40; 49:22; Lam. 4:19), and for **is over** it may be better
to render "comes against": the Heb., which is again very abrupt,
is capable of either interpretation. The simile fits well with the
reference to pursuit by the enemy in v. 3 and proposals to read
"like a watchman", by emendation of the Heb. (JB; cf. *BHS*),
or "like a herald", with a slight emendation and an appeal to
a supposed Arabic cognate (Tur-Sinai; cf. Barr, *Comparative
Philology*, pp. 26–28, G. I. Emmerson, *VT* 25 (1975), 704),
should be rejected. **the house of the LORD** is most naturally
taken as a reference to a temple or a sanctuary (cf. NEB), as
in 9:4 (cf. 9:8). This might mean the sanctuary at Bethel (cf. on
4:15) or a Yahweh-sanctuary in Samaria itself, the existence of
which has often been conjectured (cf. Alt. *KS*, III, pp. 294–95)
and is the more likely in view of the epigraphic evidence of the title
"Yahweh of Samaria" from Kuntillet Ajerud (cf. J. A. Emerton,
ZAW 94 (1982), 2–13. In either case the reason for mentioning

the danger to the sanctuary in particular could be either that Israel mistakenly confided in the rituals practised there as a safeguard against invasion or that the prophet was present at a cultic ceremony when he uttered these words. There is much to be said, however, for reading "Israel" instead of **the LORD** (Robinson, Ackroyd): confusion of the two names, which both begin with the same Heb. letter, occurs occasionally, perhaps through the use of an abbreviation (cf. the comment on **In the house of Israel** in 6:10). "The house of Israel" would be a welcome antecedent for **they** in the second part of the verse. Possibly **Israel** in v. 2, which is omitted by LXX and Syr. and is grammatically awkward, originally stood in the margin of a manuscript to indicate an alternative reading here. There is no good reason to suppose that **the house of the LORD** here means the whole land of Israel, as first suggested by Wellhausen and widely maintained at the present time (cf. Wolff, Rudolph, Mays; JB note). Of the other Hosean occurrences of the phrase or its equivalents (9:4, 8, 15; perhaps also 6:10) the only one (9:15) which even may bear this meaning seems to be a special case rather than a regular idiom (cf. Emmerson, *VT* 25 (1975), 708). The supposedly parallel expressions cited by commentators are in no case exactly analogous.

   they have broken my covenant: Cf. 6:7. Here there can be no doubt that the **covenant** between Israel and Yahweh is meant, and the following line makes explicit the association between this **covenant** and **law** (*tôrāh*) or "instruction" (NEB). It is by the contravention of Yahweh's declared will that the **covenant** has been **broken**: the verb (*'āberû*)would be more accurately rendered "transgressed" (as in 6:7) or "violated" (JB, REB). The **covenant** is here viewed in its regulative aspect, but there is no justification for limiting the meaning of *berît* here to "obligation" (so Kutsch, *Verheissung und Gesetz*, pp. 73–74). It is highly likely that Hosea's language was intended to recall the breach of the treaty with the Assyrians by Pekah which had had such devastating consequences for Israel (cf. the introduction to 6:4–7:16 (p. 165)), since *berît* means both "treaty" and **covenant** (cf. on 6:7).

   and transgressed my law: Better "and rebelled against (*pāše'û*) my law" (cf. JB, NEB). **law** is Heb. *tôrāh*, which can also mean "instruction" or "teaching" (cf. Prov. 1:8 etc.). References to Yahweh's "instruction" are found also in Isaiah (1:10; 5:24; 8:16, 20; 30:9), but in at least some of these passages the prophet's own words seem to be meant (cf. P. Jensen, *The Use of tôrâ in Isaiah*, Washington, 1973). Hosea seems to be thinking of something which is the responsibility of the priests (4:6), and he thus stands rather in the line of tradition represented by Dt. 33:10, according to which Yahweh's "instruction" was a comprehensive term for all the individual "ordinances" which were also "his" (cf. also the use for a "ruling" by a priest in a particular case, as in Dt. 17:11). The expression is likely to have stood in the first place for apodeictic series of commands like the Decalogue (cf. on 4:1–2). See further below on v. 12; also Lindblom, *Prophecy*, pp. 156–57, *THAT*, vol. 2, 1032–43, and B. Lindars, in Ackroyd and Lindars, *Words and Meanings*, pp. 117–36, especially pp. 120–22 and 132). It is clear from the parallelism of the verse that this "instruction" of Yahweh is not something which, in Hosea's mind at least, can be separated from his **covenant** with his people. Despite recently renewed doubts (on which see E. W. Nicholson, *Exodus and Sinai in History and Tradition*, Oxford, 1973, pp. 63–77) it is likely that the latter was already linked with Moses and Mount Sinai in Hosea's time (cf. Exod. 24:3–8).

The parallelism between **my covenant** and **my law** has led some scholars to question the Hosean authorship of v. 1b or even the whole of vv. 1–2 (Wellhausen, *Prolegomena to the History of Israel*, Edinburgh, 1885, p. 418; Marti; Harper; Fohrer, *TLZ* 91 (1966), 894 n. 59; and in greatest detail Perlitt, *Bundestheologie*, pp. 146–52). Certain aspects of the wording do find close parallels in Deuteronomistic literature, but in the light of 4:1–6 and 6:7 (as it has been interpreted above) it is entirely possible that Hosea himself held these ideas together, as has been the view of most recent commentators (cf. also J. Day, *VT* 36 (1986), 6–7).

8:2. In the dire situation evoked in v. 1 the people turn (or will turn) to prayer, using the traditional language of the Psalms (cf. Pss. 83:13 (and cf. Hos. 2:23); 36:10; 76:1 (contrast 79:6)). But their claims are false (cf. 1:9; 4:1) and, following the accusations of v. 1b, display an arrogance and a superficiality which Hosea has already condemned in 7:14.

To me they cry: The Heb. word order emphasizes **to me** by placing it first: Yahweh protests at the use of such familiar language in speaking to the very God whose **covenant** and **law** they have despised.

My God, we Israel know thee: The collocation of first person singular (**my**) and first person plural (**we**) is unlikely in a single utterance, so Hosea is probably quoting two quite separate phrases from the language of public prayer: **My God** and **we Israel know thee** (Wolff). NEB (*HTOT*, p. 247; cf. JB) gets round the difficulty by interchanging two Heb. words and altering a vowel in one of them: "We know thee, God of Israel" (cf. Kuhnigk, p. 102, and Andersen and Freedman, p. 490, for the suggestion that only the vowel change is necessary, MT being a "discontinuous construct chain" (cf. 6:9; 14:2)). But LXX and Syr. omit **Israel**, and it may have entered the text here as a misplaced variant reading from v. 1 (see above). To **know** Yahweh is both to have a right view of him and to enjoy a close relationship with him (see further the note on **you shall know the LORD** in 2:20).

8:3. Israel has spurned the good: From its climax in the people's unjustified and fruitless claims the saying returns, in a chiastic pattern, to the theme of an announcement of judgment which was set out more fully in v. 1. Except in late biblical Heb. (2 Chr. 11:14; 29:19) the verb **spurned** (Heb. *zānaḥ*) is used elsewhere only of Yahweh's repudiation of his people, their king or their altar (cf. v. 5). It expresses the act of a superior, which suggests again an attitude of self-assured arrogance, especially if **the good** is taken as "the Good One", i.e. Yahweh (so Kuhnigk, p. 104; Andersen and Freedman translate "the Good One rejects Israel", but the Heb. word order is against this). "Good" is an attribute of Yahweh elsewhere and expresses his faithfulness to bless his own (cf. Ps. 118:1; 136:1), but the abstract meaning is also possible here, in the sense of what is morally good and at the same time good for man (cf. Am. 5:14–15; Mic. 3:3, 6, 8). NEB has "Israel is utterly loathsome", deriving the verb from *zānaḥ* II = "stink", as in Isa. 19:6, and treating **good** as a way of expressing the superlative (as it is in Syriac but not, it would seem, in Hebrew): this is unlikely.

The following words indicate the fate that awaits Israel: **the**

enemy shall pursue him. The thought may be that Yahweh, who was imagined to be and was willing (on his terms) to be the people's friend and ally, had become his **enemy** (cf. 3:14). But since Yahweh is still probably the speaker, it is more likely that a human foe is meant (cf. 10:10b, 14). The form of the suffix **him** is unusual (cf. *GK* §60d), but it might be due to a northern dialectal variation (cf. 1 Sam. 18:1 Kethibh and J. C. L. Gibson, *Textbook of Syrian Semitic Inscriptions*, vol. 3, Oxford, 1982, p. 116). It should not be used as the basis for a radically different interpretation of the line (Kuhnigk).

8:4. The following verses cite specific examples of Israel's sinful behaviour: for the pattern of a general complaint followed by particular indictments cf. 4:1–2 and 6:4–10. The first (v. 4a) concerns the royal court, the establishment of **kings** and **princes** (for the association of these terms cf. 3:5; 7:3; 8:10; 13:10; on the meaning of **princes** see the comment on 3:5). Recent history would have provided ample illustrations of this charge, with the succession of *coup* and counter-*coup* during the period of Hosea's ministry. There is no evidence that a religious validation was claimed for any of these *coups*, and Hosea would probably have rejected any such claims that were made on their behalf (cf. on 1:4). It is interesting that Hosea presupposes that **kings** should have a divine appointment: this was the traditional view and the appointment was mediated by a prophet (1 Sam. 10:1–8; 16:12–13; 2 Sam. 7:8–16; 1 Kg. 11:30–39). The **princes** are presumably mentioned because the men of influence would change with the accession of a new king. The responsibility for these unauthorized political changes is laid on the people as a whole, a curious feature, but of a piece with the prophets' general tendency to treat the nation as a unity before God. It is possibly the case that Hosea's criticism was intended to apply to all the northern kings (though scarcely in support of Davidic claims: "to David" in 3:5 is a later addition) or even to the institution of kingship as such. But this particular verse need not be so interpreted and such views need to be based on evidence elsewhere in the book of Hosea (see the comments on 3:4, 9:15 and 13:10–11, and A. Gelston, *OTS* 19 (1974), 71–85).

They set up princes: The form of the Hiphil is not what one would normally expect and some manuscripts actually suggest a derivation from *sûr* (in the Hiphil, "remove") rather than from *šārar* (cf. Rashi, Ibn Ezra and Gelston, art. cit., p. 83). The translation "they remove them" (i.e. kings) would fit events like those described in 7:3–7, but MT, which is supported by all the Vss., should be preferred as the *difficilior lectio* (for the form cf. *GK* §67v). G. R. Driver (Nötscher Festschrift (BBB 1), p. 50) suggested interpreting both the verbs differently, to mean "take advice", on the basis of the use in cognate languages, but the obvious sense is sufficiently characteristic of Hosea to make such conjectures unnecessary, and NEB did not take them up (cf. also Barr, *Comparative Philology*, p. 165).

The second indictment (vv. 4ᵇ–6) is for the use of **silver and gold** to manufacture **idols**, in particular **The calf of Samaria**. 2:8 accuses Israel of using "silver and gold ... for Baal" (but see the comment there), and idolatry is a frequent theme in the later chapters of the book (10:5–6; 11:2; 13:2; 14:3, 8: cf. also 4:12, 17). These passages are among the earliest datable attacks on idolatry in Israel. The most famous instances of gold or silver images were the golden calves of Bethel and Dan (see on 10:5), and the fact that their manufacture was a royal initiative may explain the order of the indictments here (cf. 1 Kg. 12:28–30). See further *IDB*, vol. 2, 673–78 and *BRL*, pp. 99–119. The making of images was forbidden by the second commandment of the Decalogue (Exod. 20:4–6 – cf. 20:23; 34:17), and Hosea's polemic may be based on this (cf. the notes on 4:1–2). The final phrase of v. 4 is difficult, as it is not clear whether the subject is the people or their idols (cf. JB), and in any case the verb in MT is singular where a plural verb would be expected. Possibly it is a gloss (Mays, NEB: cf. *HTOT*, p. 247) or a cross-reference, which would explain the lack of grammatical concord; but the only other place where these two Heb. words occur together is Obadiah 9, and it is hard to see what the point of such a cross-reference might be.

8:5. I have spurned your calf, O Samaria: The **calf** is to be connected with the "golden calves" set up by Jeroboam I and will be either one of these (presumably that at Bethel: cf. on 10:5) or another one which stood in the capital city of Samaria itself (7:1), presumably in a shrine there (cf. above on v. 1). In the former case **Samaria** will either stand for the northern kingdom as a whole (as

in 1 Kg. 13:32) or indicate the close ties between the capital and
the great national shrines (cf. 10:5; Am. 7:13). The term **calf**, *ʿegel*
(which appears also in the story in Exod. 32 and its recapitulation
in Dt. 9:16ff.), has been thought to be a polemical substitute for
the supposedly more accurate "bull" (cf. the designation of the
image of Exod. 32 as a *šôr*, "ox", in Ps. 106:20), but *ʿegel* is best
rendered "young bull" (cf. Gen. 15:9) and could well be the
official name for the image (cf. J. Hahn, *Das "Goldene Kalb"*,
Frankfurt and Berne, 1981, pp. 12–19). The significance of these
images is variously explained. On the one hand, OT passages
clearly imply that the calf was seen as an image of the God of the
Exodus (Exod. 32:4; 1 Kg. 12:28), theriomorphism flourished in
the ancient Near East (especially in Egypt), and there is literary
evidence for gods being characterized as bulls (cf. "Bull El", *ṯr
ʾil*, in the Ugaritic texts, a variety of texts which equate Baal with
a bull, and perhaps the title "Mighty One of Jacob", which may
originally have meant "Bull of Jacob" (Gen. 49:24 etc.; cf. H.
Ringgren, *Israelite Religion*, p. 21)). On the other hand, the great
Semitic gods were normally portrayed in human form, and bulls
are better attested as pedestals on which statues of the gods (in
human form) were placed (cf. *ANEP*, pp. 163ff., 177ff.). This has
been taken to mean that the calves were not intended to represent
Yahweh visually but, like the ark in Jerusalem, to indicate the
place where his invisible presence was thought to be concentrated
(cf. R. E. Clements, *God and Temple*, Oxford, 1965, p. 77; Mays,
p. 118). This would have to imply that their significance was
misunderstood by some OT writers (including Hosea: see on v.
6), but it would help to explain why the calves were tolerated for
as long as they were. On this and other problems see the survey
of research in Hahn, *Das "Goldene Kalb"*.

The rendering **I have spurned** is based on a conjectural
emendation of MT, which reads "he spurned". The "he" is
anomalous in the context and some change is required. Another
possibility is the LXX reading "Spurn" (imperative), which is
preferred by Wolff. NEB again derives the verb from *zānaḥ* II
(cf. on v. 3) and translates (retaining MT): "Your calf-gods
stink . . ." On **Samaria** see the comment on 7:1. Here and in
v. 6 it may stand for the northern kingdom as a whole, as in 1
Kg. 13:32 (but see Wolff, p. 140).

The second half of v. 5 seems to interrupt the references to the calf-image (note the plural pronouns **them** and **they**), and it has probably been displaced from its original position after v. 4. A scribe may have accidentally omitted a line of text which was subsequently inserted in the wrong place (cf. Isa. 38:21–22).

How long will it be till they are pure in Israel?: The expression **How long** is characteristic of the prayers of lament in the Psalter (e.g. Pss. 4:2; 6:3). Here, as in 7:13 and 15, Yahweh himself takes up the language of complaint against his people. Hosea was not the first prophet so to use it (cf. 1 Kg. 14:18–21). **pure** is not a good translation of Heb. *niqqāyōn*, which is a judicial term: "innocent" (NEB) is what is required. **in Israel** follows the reading of LXX rather than MT, which has the unintelligible "for from Israel", but the expression remains awkward. JB's "the sons of Israel" introduces a phrase which Hosea generally avoids (cf. on 4:1), and H. Tur-Sinai's ingenious proposal (adopted by NEB) to redivide the consonants of MT to read *kî mî šôr 'ēl*, either "For who is the bull El?" or "For what sort of god is this bull?", is unconvincing (*Encyclopedia Miqra'it*, vol. 1, 31; *HTOT*, p. 247). Possibly a better solution is to regard "from Israel" of MT together with **for their own destruction** (literally "for its cutting off") in v. 4 (see the comment there) as a marginal gloss on **I have spurned your calf, O Samaria**, which was added by a scribe inspired by such verses as Mic. 5:12 and Nah. 1:14. The residual "for" would make a good transition from v. 5a to v. 6, which explains why the image is rejected.

8:6. A workman made it; it is not God: As a human artefact, the idol was subject to man's design and manipulation and was therefore not a superior being worthy of his worship. This theme is reflected many times in OT attacks on idolatry: cf. 13:2; 14:3; Dt. 4:28; 27:15; Ps. 115:4; 135:15; Isa. 2:8; 40:19–20; 44:9–20; 46:6; Jer. 1:16; 10:3–5; Mic. 5:13; Hab. 2:18; also Wis. 13:10–19; 15:7–17; E. Jer. The identification of a god with his or her image is common in religious texts from the ancient Near East (e.g. in the Nabonidus Chronicle, *DOTT*, p. 82, *TGI*, p. 81), but it was dependent upon rituals of initiation which indicate a complexity of belief to which the OT texts (understandably) do not do full justice (cf. S. Morenz, *Egyptian Religion*, London, 1973, pp. 150–56, A. L. Oppenheim, *Ancient Mesopotamia*, pp. 183–87).

The calf of Samaria shall be broken to pieces: The line begins with Heb. *kî*, which may have a deictic function (JB "Yea . . ."; cf. 5:3; 6:9). Alternatively it may be rendered "for": the coming destruction of the **calf** will prove that **it is not God**. The precise nature of the destruction is not clear: **broken to pieces** renders a single Heb. word, *šᵉbābîm*, whose meaning is uncertain, because it only occurs here. The rendering given is based on later Hebrew, Arabic and Targ., and (with the change of **broken** to "cut") is more likely than the alternative "shall go up in flames" (JB; cf. Albright, *BASOR* 84 (1941) 17, n. 26), which assumes that *šᵉbābîm* is either a mistake for or synonymous with *šᵉbîbîm*, the plural of a word found in Job 18:5, Sir. 8:10, 45:19 and also in biblical Aramaic. Both interpretations support the view that the silver and gold of v. 4 were only a covering for an image of wood (cf. Isa. 40:19–20). A manuscript from Qumran (4QpHosᵇ) has the variant reading *šwbbym hyh* which underlies the renderings of LXX ("was leading [them] astray"), Syr. and Aq. (cf. Quinta), but it is unlikely to be original (for the reading see J. Strugnell, *RQ* 7 (1969–70), 202).

8:7. The two sayings in this verse explain (**For**) the underlying principles which determine the consequences of Israel's evil actions as they are set out in vv. 1, 3 and 6, and they thus round off the first part of the chapter. The sayings were probably in popular use in Hosea's time. The first has, in various forms, enjoyed widespread currency (cf. Job 4:8; Prov. 22:8; 2 C. 9:6; Gal. 6:7–8) and affirms, with the help of a familiar analogy, the causal nexus that exists between a people's action and its consequences. Hosea's version of it also incorporates a play on words, for Heb. *rûaḥ*, **wind**, can mean "an empty, vain thing" (cf. 12:2; Ps. 78:39; Isa. 41:29) and so makes a natural connection with the **calf**, which is not what the people think it is. The second saying is variously interpreted, but the point seems to be that it is possible to tell in advance if the harvest is going to be bad by looking at the growth of the grain. Israel's failure is plain to see, her end is undeniable, and only a matter of time. Here too there is artistic subtlety, but of a different kind, in the form of a rhyme (which is rare in Heb. poetry) between **heads** (*ṣemaḥ*) and **meal** (*qemaḥ*): cf. 9:6.

The final line of the verse turns the metaphorical and general saying into a literal and specific one: Israel (despite all her involvement in a cult designed to ensure fertility) faces a disastrous harvest, and even if there is a harvest they will not benefit from it: **aliens** will **devour it**. This is reminiscent of the "futility curses" of Near Eastern treaties and passages like Am. 5:11 and Hos. 9:12, 16 (cf. on 4:10). Such a shift in the level of the saying is not likely to be the prophet's own work and the line is probably a later amplification based on the wider context (cf. vv. 3 and 8). On **aliens** see the comment on 7:9.

8:8–9. The next three verses resume the theme and the style of the criticism of Israel's foreign relations in 7:8–16 and comprise the third specific indictment that is laid against her in this chapter. In the background there is the assumption that in her distress Israel should have sought help from Yahweh (cf. 5:15–6:3; 7:7, 10, 14). There is a close link between the images which describe Israel's present situation and the second proverbial saying in v. 7, with its theme that present appearances reveal what is to come.

Israel is swallowed up: The image seems to be of a dish or a bowl of food which has been eaten clean, so that nothing remains except for the dish or **vessel** (cf. Jer. 51:34). Possibly there is the additional idea that the dish is damaged (cf. Jer. 22:28; 48:38). No doubt it is once again the consequences of Tiglath-pileser III's invasion in 733 BC which are in view. **Israel** no longer has any attraction or use for anyone **among the nations**. The only way that she can make friends (**lovers**), i.e. allies, is by paying for them, i.e. in the case of **Assyria** by paying the tribute demanded by the king. Hosea's contempt for the condition of his country emerges clearly in this ironical taunt.

a wild ass wandering alone: The **wild ass** or onager (*pere'*: cf. Cansdale, *Animals of Bible Lands*, pp. 94–95) can be an example of untamed and unrestricted freedom (Gen. 16:12; Job 39:5) or of the poor landless refugee (Job 24:5). Here it is probably closer to the latter, in view of the attribute **wandering alone** (*bôdēd*), which is used of a solitary bird in a picture of loneliness in Ps. 102:7 and of a straggler in an army in Isa. 14:32. It is therefore appropriate as a further image for forlorn **Ephraim** (Andersen and Freedman) rather than as a description of **Assyria** (JB) or as a contrast to **Ephraim**'s present behaviour (Wolff, Rudolph).

The assonance between *pere'* and **Ephraim** is no doubt deliberate and a further instance of the literary techniques employed in this chapter (cf. 9:16; 13:15; 14:8).

Ephraim has hired lovers: The verb **hired** (*tānāh*, Hiphil), which only occurs here and in v. 10, is usually taken to be related to *'etnāh*, "hire", in 2:12, which is a unique alternative form for the usual word *'etnān* (Hos. 9:1 etc.): cf. *BDB*, p. 1071. Instead of being pictured as a prostitute who is paid for her favours and so profits from her promiscuity, **Ephraim** here must pay a prostitute to satisfy his needs (or, as in Ezek. 16:33–34, is a prostitute who must, contrary to custom, pay her clients). For **Assyria** as a prostitute cf. Nah. 3:4. The sense is not greatly different if G. R. Driver's proposal is followed and the verb is connected with words in post-biblical Hebrew and Aramaic meaning "stipulation, contract", hence "make a bargain" (*JTS* 36 (1935), 296; cf. NEB). Rudolph (p. 159) prefers the meaning "seek eagerly", but this is pure conjecture. There is no justification for emending the text, as early critical commentators and Mays have wanted to do (cf. *BHS*). **lovers** is literally "loves", as in Prov. 5:19 (cf. 7:18): a case of abstract for concrete, as in Hos. 9:10.

8:10. Ephraim's quest for security in the sending of gifts will be to no avail, for the nations will be unable to protect her against the wrath of Yahweh, who is intent on bringing her political institutions to an end. For the temporary removal of **king and princes** cf. 3:4. The implication is that after a time of isolation from the nations Israel will be restored.

Though they hire allies: The Qal form of the verb is used here but RSV and JB assume that it has the same meaning as the Hiphil (cf. *BDB*, loc. cit.). G. R. Driver thought a Hiphil should be read here too (*JTS* 39 (1938), 158). It is better, however, to retain MT in the sense "earn hire" (Nyberg, Wolff), as Assyrian inscriptions show that in the later part of the 8th century Israelites were employed as mercenaries in the Assyrian army, and this could be what is referred to here, as S. Dalley suggested in the light of the clear evidence from after 722 (*Iraq* 47 (1985), 40: cf. 32–39). RSV's **allies** has no equivalent in the original (cf. RV): it is supplied by the translators to clarify the sense.

I will soon gather them up: Heb. *'attāh*, **soon**, more usually
means "now" (cf. v. 13), and there is no reason to depart from
this sense here (cf. JB, NEB). The verb **gather** is frequently used
in prophecy for the gathering in of Israel's exiles by Yahweh (cf.
2:2) and this has been the traditional interpretation here (LXX,
Targ.). But, as in some other passages (Ezek. 22:19–20; Jl 3:2;
Mic. 4:12; Zeph. 3:8), in the present case it probably means a
gathering for judgment (cf. 7:12; 9:6). For Hosea it is usually
judgment that is to come "now" and a reference to restoration would be strange before the description of punishment
in v. 12b, however exactly the latter is to be understood. The
expression has particular point after the reference to Israel's
wandering in v. 9.

**And they shall cease for a little while from anointing king
and princes:** The translation of this line is not at all certain.
MT reads "And they have begun a little thing because of [or
"from"] the burden of the king of (the) princes". RSV is an exact
translation of the LXX, which appears to be based on a Heb. text
which is divergent in several minor but significant ways (likewise
JB, NEB: cf. *BHS*). One problem is that it is doubtful whether
princes were anointed, and it is therefore perhaps better to retain
MT *maśśā'* as an Aramaizing infinitive of *nāśā'* meaning "setting
up, appointing" (cf. G. R. Driver, *JTS* 39 (1938), 158; NEB; *GK*
§45e; and the note on 13:6) than to emend to *mᵉšōaḥ*, **anointing**.
Driver also suggested that the meaning **cease** (attested by Th.,
Syr. and Vulg. as well as LXX) could be obtained from the
consonants of MT (rather than by supposing that a letter had
dropped out) if a verb *ḥālāh* = "cease" could be assumed to exist
in Heb. on the basis of cognates in Arabic and Akkadian (cf.
HTOT, p. 247). Wolff keeps very close to MT, emending only
the first word, and translates "so that they soon writhe under
the burden of the king of princes", i.e. the tribute imposed by
the Assyrian kings, who bore the title *šar šarrāni*, "king of kings"
(likewise Rudolph and Mays; cf. Gelston, *OTS* 19 (1974), 74).
This fits the context, but suffers from the fact that *melek śārîm* is
unlikely to be the Heb. equivalent of the Assyrian title.

8:11–13. The fourth area with which the prophet finds fault is
religious observance: the people show great enthusiasm for this,
constructing many altars and offering sacrifices upon them (cf.

10:1), but this is all unacceptable because they have no time for Yahweh's law. With this Hosea clearly aligns himself with Amos' sharp critique of contemporary worship (cf. Am. 4:4–5), but he adds an explicit reference to the neglect of divine law, as in 4:6 and 8:1.

8:11. altars for sinning . . . altars for sinning: The same phrase of two words is repeated in the Heb., but it is unlikely that it means the same both times. The first occurrence in MT should be translated "altars in his sin" (NEB): the **altars** built by a sinful people become the place for worship which is itself **sinning**. For such a characterization of sacrifice cf. 4:8. The pun is even more telling if in the first case we read not *laḥªṭō'* but *lᵉḥaṭṭē'*, "for sacrificing sin-offerings" (von Orelli, Nyberg, Rudolph, Kuhnigk): the **altars** intended for the removal of sin become the place where it is increased. The sin-offering (on which cf. de Vaux, *Ancient Israel*, pp. 418–20, 429–30) is only rarely mentioned in pre-exilic texts, but 2 Kg. 12:16 provides a clear reference to its existence in Judah in the 9th century BC. To judge from the regulations in Leviticus it was a remedy for ritual defilement, which was a far from trivial matter in Israelite society, and one can easily imagine that the **altars** came to have a place of honour in a town or village.

8:12. The theme of multiplication (cf. **multiplied** in v. 11) is continued as the accusation turns from commissions to omissions. The people have so little respect for Yahweh's laws that even if the written laws were to be multiplied many times they would still be ignored. The assumption must be that already in Hosea's time laws of a reputedly divine origin had been committed to writing. These laws need not have been very extensive and the Decalogue could be what was in Hosea's mind, both because of evidence elsewhere that he knew it or something very like it (4:2) and because it is in relation to the Decalogue alone that a tradition of divine writing of law is attached in the OT (Dt. 5:22). NEB's alternative rendering would imply that a very large amount of divinely authorized law was already in writing in Hosea's time. At any rate, this charge surely indicates that the sacrificial laws had not yet been written down, for otherwise Hosea's hearers would have been able to respond that their deference to Yahweh's law was evident in the very rituals which he condemned. Compare also the commentaries on Am. 5:25 and Jer. 7:22.

my laws: Or "instructions" (cf. on 8:1). Here, in contrast to 4:6 and 8:1, the plural **laws** is used, referring to the individual precepts, so that the theme of multiplication can be more effectively continued from v. 11. MT actually reads "my law", but both the context (**they would be regarded**) and the evidence of Vss. show this to be an error, due perhaps to *scriptio defectiva*.

as a strange thing: Or "as those of a stranger" (JB): for the syntax assumed cf. *GK* §141d.

8:13. They love sacrifice: they sacrifice flesh and eat it: On the text-critical problems of the first three words see Nyberg, pp. 65–67 and Rudolph, pp. 160–61. MT is obscure but can be rendered "Sacrifices of [i.e. "from"] my gifts they offer, (namely) flesh, and they eat it" (cf. BDB, RV). The main problem is to know whether the unique word *habhābay* is to be related to Heb. *yāhab*, "give", as above, or amended to a form of Heb. *'āhēb*, "love" (Nyberg, RSV, JB: for the form perhaps compare 4:18), or to some other verb (Rudolph). The second possibility is preferable in view of LXX and the similar expression in Am. 4:5: "for so you love to do, O people of Israel". In any case, the point of the line lies in the following words: **but the LORD has no delight in them.** However much pleasure, whether spiritual or sensual, they may gain from their sacrifices (most of which were normally eaten by the worshippers), they themselves are unacceptable to Yahweh. The effect is increased by the use of the verb *rāṣāh* (**has** (**no**) **delight in**), the technical priestly word (Lev. 1:4) for the acceptance of a sacrifice that has no blemish, which is used in a similar way in Am. 5:22. These words, together with the following line, are cited verbatim in Jer. 14:10, as though the later prophet saw Hosea's words as still having an application to the situation of his own day. The fact that Jeremiah's saying begins with "They *love* to wander . . ." may lend further support to the view taken above about *habhābay*.

he will remember their iniquity, and punish their sins: On **remember** see on 7:2 and on **iniquity** (*'āwôn*) see on **corruption** in 7:1. These words, which are a fine example of poetic parallelism, recur in 9:9, where they form the conclusion of a unit. NEB makes small changes to MT to avoid third-person references to Yahweh in a divine speech (*HTOT*, p, 247: cf. G. R. Driver, *JTS* 39 (1938), 158).

They shall return to Egypt: They here represents an independent pronoun, and is emphatic: the worshippers themselves will go into exile. Very similar words appear in 9:3 and 11:5, and the mention of **Egypt** as a place of exile is also found in 7:16, 9:6 and 11:11. Since Egypt was the land of bondage from which Yahweh had once called Israel to be his people (2:15; 11:1; 12:9, 13; 13:4), to **return** there was equivalent to a reversal of Yahweh's guidance of their history. This recurring theme of Hosea's message is to be seen in the light of the reversals in chapter 1, especially v. 9: "you are not my people and I am not your (God)". Some see this as a purely figurative expression for the imminent dissolution of Israel's relationship with Yahweh, and argue that Hosea envisaged only Assyria as a place of actual exile (cf. the parallelism in 9:3 (6?), 11:5, 11), but at least 7:16 and 9:6 require a literal interpretation, and the same is probably true of the other passages. That the OT historical books speak only of an exile to Assyria (2 Kg. 17:6, 23; 18:11) need not mean that Hosea did not expect some of his compatriots to be exiled to **Egypt**. What is interesting is that, whereas an exile to Assyria could be expected to follow on a defeat at the hands of that power (cf. B. Oded, *Mass Deportations and Deportees in the Neo-Assyrian Empire*, Wiesbaden, 1979), a return to **Egypt** was historically not to be anticipated but presumably suggested itself as a theologically appropriate place for Israel to undergo the impending judgment.

NEB follows LXX in adding at the end of the verse, "or in Assyria they shall eat unclean food" (*HTOT*, p. 249), but this reading is clearly due to harmonization with 9:3 and the shorter text of MT and the other Vss. is to be preferred.

8:14. For Israel has forgotten his Maker: For makes a logical connection with the preceding verses, which is unjustified, as the Heb. has the simple "And . . ." (likewise Vss.). The verse introduces a new, fifth, indictment against both Israel and Judah, that they have put their trust in **palaces** and fortifications instead of in Yahweh their **Maker**, and follows it with an announcement-of-judgment formula which bears a close resemblance to those in the foreign nations cycle of Am. 1:2–2:3.

The reference to Israel "forgetting" Yahweh is typical of Hosea (cf. 2:15; 13:6 (4:6)), and the folly of trust in military power appears again in 10:13–15, 11:6, 14:3 (1:7 is a later addition), but in other respects the verse looks like a later addition.

his Maker: Hosea does not elsewhere use this title for Yahweh: the closest that he comes to it is the implied reference to Yahweh as Father in 11:1 (cf. 1:10). By far the closest parallel is in the exilic passage Isa. 51:13, where the context is again the people's fear before a powerful enemy (see also Dt. 32:6, 15 (cf. 26:19); Isa. 17:7 (post-exilic according to Clements, *Isaiah 1–39*, p. 159); Prov. 14:31; 17:5; Job 4:17; 32:22). Yahweh's creation of Israel is a central tenet of Deutero-Isaiah's theology (cf. 43:1, 7, 15; 44:2, 21, 24; 54:5), and his preaching may lie close to the origin of this idea. Here too Yahweh as **Maker** should be relied on to care for his creature (cf. Pss. 95:6; 100:3), and it is lack of faith which lies behind the recourse to **palaces** and **fortified cities**.

palaces: Heb. *hêkāl*, at least in the singular, can also mean "temple", but the immediate context is clearly concerned with defence. **palaces** were often strongly fortified, as is particularly clear from the excavations at Hazor (Area B: *EAEHL*, vol. 2, p. 489) and the capital city of Samaria (*EAEHL*, vol. 4, pp. 1033, 1037–43).

fortified cities: There are frequent references to Judah's **fortified cities** in the OT historical books (e.g. 2 Kg. 18:13; 2 Chr. 11:5–12). They are also mentioned in Sennacherib's Annals (*ANET*, p. 288, *DOTT*, p. 67) and one, Lachish, is portrayed in reliefs from his palace at Nineveh (*ANEP*, nos. 371–73). Excavations at many sites have produced evidence of the thick walls and strongly defended gates that were built during the period of the monarchy: cf. King, *Commentary*, pp. 67–78. Particularly impressive is the city wall, seven metres thick, from around 700 BC found in Jerusalem by N. Avigad (illustrated in *EAEHL*, vol. 2, p. 586). In both kingdoms the building of such defences was a royal responsibility and it is against the policy of the kings that this verse is really directed.

and it shall devour his strongholds: MT actually reads "her" **strongholds**. The similar verses in Am. 1–2 indicate that "their" **strongholds** (i.e. those of the **cities**) is the meaning required here (Wolff, Rudolph). Either the feminine singular

pronoun suffix stands by an unusual idiom for the plural form
(*GK* §145m) or a scribe accidentally replaced -*hen*, "their", by -*hā*,
"her", because the latter form is so frequent with **strongholds**.
The **strongholds** (Heb. *'arm⁽ᵉ⁾nōt*) are not isolated forts (Heb.
m⁽ᵉ⁾ṣûdôt, 1 Sam. 22:4–5; 2 Sam. 5:17) but are always parts of a
fortified city, apparently buildings or parts of buildings (cf. 1
Kg. 16:18; 2 Kg. 15:25) of special strength, which would have
belonged to the richer citizens or the king.

THE COMING END OF FESTAL WORSHIP

9:1–9

The boundaries of this unit are clearly marked by its distinctive
subject-matter, the prophet's introductory challenge (v. 1) and
the change from prophetic diatribe to a divine oracle after v. 9.
It is, however, closely linked with the end of ch. 8 by phrases
in vv. 3 and 9 and may well, as Jeremias has suggested, form
the conclusion to one of the subsidiary collections in ch. 4–14
(cf. Marti). The opening words can plausibly be seen as an
interruption of a festival celebration, most likely the vintage
feast of Tabernacles in the autumn, which was celebrated in the
northern kingdom at Bethel (1 Kg. 12:33) or, as Hosea usually
calls it (see on 4:15), Beth-aven. Several allusions indicate that
the practice of worship is central to the message here (the
libations and sacrifices (v. 4), the house of the Lord (v. 4), the
festivals and feasts (v. 5)), and in v. 8 Hosea refers directly to
the rejection of his message **in the house of his God**. Since this
is most likely to refer to a major sanctuary (see the note), Wolff's
location of the saying at Samaria is improbable.

The essence of the coming punishment is that the people will
cease to enjoy the fruits of the land and will in exile no longer be
able to celebrate their festivals any more. The thought is therefore
similar to that of ch. 2 (especially vv. 11–13), with which there
are a number of parallels, but there is now an explicit reference
to exile (vv. 3 and 6), as befits the later situation after the
Syro-Ephraimite War when a new threat to the people's security
had appeared. Curiously, in view of the outcome, it is Egypt (v.
6 – see the note) which is envisaged as the primary place of exile,

as in almost every other passage of Hosea which speaks of exile at all. The exception is v. 3 here. Hosea's view of the future is shaped by the idea of the reversal of salvation-history (and in due time the reversal of the reversal), and this evidently led him to speak of Egypt in this way in his later oracles (cf. 7:16; 8:13; 11:5). An Assyrian conquest (cf. 10:6; 11:5) would not necessarily, even on a purely political estimation, have resulted in an Assyrian exile, as the policy was more to remove conquered peoples from their homelands than to gather them into Assyria itself.

The introductory challenge and its justification in the second person singular (v. 1) is followed by a passage in the third person (vv. 2–7a) in which Hosea sets out the gloomy prospect which results from apostasy and makes rejoicing so inappropriate. In v. 5 he breaks out again into direct address to the people, this time in the second person plural, as he underlines the coming cessation of the festivals. The tradition has recorded a protest against this unseemly message, no doubt to reinforce the prophet's accusation: **The prophet is a fool, the man of the spirit is mad** (v. 7b: cf. Wolff, *Das Zitat im Prophetenspruch* (BET 4), Munich, 1937, p. 20 = *GS*, p. 47). This may have been the response of a leading official at the sanctuary: at any rate it is not addressed directly to Hosea, but is formulated as a contemptuous comment about him (cf. 4:4 and the note there). Undaunted, Hosea resumed his diatribe and concluded it with the same summary formula as appears in 8:13.

Apart from some textual corruption (especially in vv. 6 and 8) and a possible gloss in v. 8 (see the note), the passage has probably come down to us in its original form. The use of two-stress lines, particularly in the dialogue at the end, is noteworthy. The view of earlier commentators that v. 9b is secondary because of its similarity to 8:13 (see Harper) no longer finds favour and the more persistent attribution of v. 4b to an editor seems (see the note) to be due to a misunderstanding of it. Rudolph has recently argued that v. 6, while Hosean, has been interpolated into this passage, because it presupposes a quite different situation in which people were already seeking security from hostilities by what they no doubt intended as a temporary emigration to Egypt. This is a possibility, and the fact that the ritual consequences of exile seem to be no longer in view adds some weight to the argument. It is not conclusive, however, as such flight to Egypt may be envisaged by the prophet only as a future event, and there is no reason why he should not have gone on to speak of consequences of the coming exile different from those which had concerned him earlier.

9:1. Hosea's opening words seem to be a direct negation of a call to rejoice such as might have opened a harvest festival in one of the sanctuaries of northern Israel (cf. Dt. 16:14; Ps. 32:11; 97:12; Jl 2:21, 23). They are grounded in an accusation which reintroduces the image of prostitution from ch. 1–4 (cf. 6:11) to describe the nation's abandonment of Yahweh their God. There is no place for rejoicing now, when the time of reckoning has come (cf. v. 7).

Exult not: MT has *'el gîl*, "to exultation", and this seems at first to gain support from the similar phrase in Job 3:22 (G. R. Driver, *JTS* 39 (1938), 158). But that passage may well be corrupt (cf. NEB) and the English translations are probably correct to follow the reading *'al tāgēl* indicated by Vss. This makes for neat parallelism, and the *t* could have been lost through haplography before *g*, to which it is quite similar in the early Hebrew script.

like the peoples: Israel's worship is branded as being on the same level as that of other nations, no doubt particularly the Canaanites: cf. D. W. Harvey, in B. W. Anderson and W. Harrelson (eds.), *Israel's Prophetic Heritage* (FS J. Muilenburg), London, 1962, pp. 116–127. The idea that Israel has imitated the religious practices of her neighbours (or may do so) is a commonplace of both exhortation and prophecy (e.g. Lev. 18:24–30; Dt. 13:6–11; Ezek. 20:1–8; 2 Kg. 17:7–12, 15), but nowhere is it introduced in as radical a way as in Hosea (cf. 6:6; 8:11–13).

a harlot's hire: Heb. *'etnān*. This is how Hosea portrays the people's view of the fruits of the land in 2:12: they are the return she gets for her promiscuity with her "lovers". In her desire for them she mistakenly turns to other gods, not realizing that it is Yahweh himself who is the giver of all (2:5, 8–9). NEB translates "idol", probably on the basis of Mic. 1:7, but an interpretation based on Hosea's own straightforward use of the imagery is preferable. Strictly speaking the Heb. has only **hire**. A recently published Ugaritic text suggests that *'etnān* may once have been a more general word for "fee, payment" (*Ugaritica V*, no.7.74, 76 = *CML*, p. 139).

upon all threshing floors: The Heb. (which is supported by Vss.) adds *dāgān*, "of grain" (cf. NEB), which seems otiose. A small change to the vocalization would permit the translation "upon all threshing floors (you have loved) grain", with "grain" being an explanation of **hire** earlier in the verse (cf. 2:12 and Rashi here). Kuhnigk treats *dāgān* as a proper name, (cf. on v. 2), Dagan (or Dagon) being the Canaanite god of grain and according to the Ugaritic texts the father of Baal (cf. *IDB*, vol. 1, 756), but this is unnecessary. The phrase need not imply that the **threshing floors** themselves were the scenes for the worship condemned by Hosea, and while episodes like those recounted in Jg. 21:16–24 and Ru. 3 may well have been common, there is no evidence that they were part of the official celebration (cf. on 4:13–14).

9:2. This and the following verses (to v. 7a) are an announcement of the judgment that is the consequence of Israel's apostasy. Failure of the crops, exile from the land and the termination of worship at the great festivals are the intertwined themes of this threat. They belong naturally together, because the festivals both presupposed and were intended to safeguard prosperity in the land which Yahweh had given. The first and third themes are also found in 2:9–13 and they form the main stock here, into which Hosea has grafted the additional theme of exile (vv. 3 and 6), which now appears as the cause of the people's inability to enjoy the fruits of the land and to perform acts of worship.

shall not feed them: The verb *rā'āh* is primarily used of a shepherd feeding his flock (cf. 4:16), so MT involves a bold metaphor. LXX seems to preserve a variant reading derived from *yada'*, "know", hence NEB: "shall know them no more" (cf. *HTOT*, p. 248). In view of the breadth of meaning of *yāda'* (cf. on 13:5) this reading could be translated "shall provide for them no more". It is hard to choose between the two readings, which differ (as far as the Heb. consonants are concerned) only in the substitution of *daleth* for *resh*, a very easy corruption when the letters are so similar. There is no justification for Kuhnigk's radical reconstruction of the line, in which the consonants of this

and the preceding word are redivided to form two divine titles
to accompany "Dagan" in v. 1 (see the comment on **upon all
threshing floors**) and "Tirosh", a god of wine, later in this verse
(pp. 112–13).

the new wine shall fail them: them implies the substitution
of *bām* for MT's *bāh* ("it"), a change that is supported by many
Heb. manuscripts and Vss. (cf. *HTOT*, p. 248, *BHS*). It is not
an easy error to explain palaeographically or from the context:
one possibility is that the scribe responsible for it was familiar
with the law in Lev. 5:22 (EVV. 6:3), where a form of the verb
translated **shall fail** is followed by *bāh*. On **the new wine** see the
comment on 4:11. As noted above, Kuhnig thinks that the Heb.
word is the name of a god here (and in 7:14, where **wine** stands
for Heb. *tîrôš*), but the use of a verb that usually has a personal
subject can be ascribed to poetic licence. A close parallel to the
expression occurs in Hab. 3:17, where there is no question of a
god being meant. The meaning is simply that they will have no
new wine to drink (cf. Jl 1:5).

9:3. the land of the LORD: This Heb. phrase is unique in
the OT, but similar phrases occur in Jos. 22:19, Isa. 14:2 and
those verses which speak of the land inhabited by the Israelites
as "the heritage of the Lord" (1 Sam. 26:19; 2 Sam. 14:16 etc.).
The idea that the land was Yahweh's is expressed in a number
of other passages (cf. *TDOT*, vol. 1, 401–402). It includes the
idea of his ownership of the land (Lev. 25:23) but probably also
those of his presence and his rule there to a greater degree than
elsewhere. On the relationship between these ideas and that of
Yahweh's presence in a temple cf. Clements, *God and Temple*,
pp. 50–55, where it is suggested that the latter symbolized
Yahweh's ownership of the whole land and confirmed his people's
possession of it. Israel's apostasy will lose them the privilege of
living in **the land of the LORD**: they face eviction.

Ephraim shall return to Egypt: Cf. 8:13 and the note
there.

they shall eat unclean food in Assyria: This is the first time
in the book that an exile to Assyria is explicitly mentioned as
the punishment for Israel's sins: the political reality behind the
numerous images used by Hosea at last emerges into the light of
day (cf. 9:6(?); 11:11). The deportation of a defeated population

was a regular part of Assyrian imperial policy: cf. B. Oded, *Mass Deportations and Deportees*. The idea that the **food** eaten in a foreign land would be **unclean** added a further dimension to the anguish of those who meticulously attended to the demands of the ritual law. It reappears in Ezek. 4:13 (a later addition to the original saying: cf. W. Zimmerli, *Ezekiel* (Hermeneia), Philadelphia, 1979, p. 171) and arises from the fact that **Assyria** belonged to other gods (cf. 1 Sam. 26:19), which affected every aspect of life there (cf. Am. 7:17). On the concept of uncleanness see the comment on **defiled** in 5:3. For Hosea himself the defilement of Israel was already a present reality (5:3; 6:10).

9:4. It is normally thought that Hosea speaks here of sacrifice ceasing altogether (cf. 3:4), but the meaning may be that sacrifice will cease to be offered to Yahweh, because it is presumed that in a foreign land Israel will have to make her offerings to the local gods. Exile will put an end to pretence and those who are devoted to other gods (v. 1) will be taken to a place where it is natural to practise their worship.

They shall not pour libations of wine: The implication must be that such offerings, which were widespread in the ancient world, were also made to Yahweh in Hosea's time. They are often mentioned in the later Priestly Code in connection with other kinds of offerings (e.g. Exod. 29:40–41; cf. Jl 1:9, 13), but this is the only firm evidence (apart from Gen. 35:14 and perhaps 2 Sam. 23:16) for their being offered to Yahweh before the exile.

they shall not please him with their sacrifices: In itself this would be a natural thing for Hosea to say (cf. 6:6 and Jer. 6:20), but linked as it is with a reference to the cessation of offerings to Yahweh it is surprising, and seems to imply that at the present time **sacrifices** do **please** Yahweh, which contradicts 6:6 and 8:11. A non-evaluative word seems to be required instead of **please** and many scholars since A. Kuenen have emended *ye'erbû*, **they shall ... please**, to *ya'arkû*, "they shall lay in order" (from *'ārak*, a word that is common in cultic contexts, e.g. Lev. 1:8). But, as G. R. Driver saw, it is possible to conjecture an appropriate meaning for *ye'erbû* on the basis of cognate words in South Arabian and Syriac (*JTS* 39 (1938), 158–59; Rowley (ed.), *Studies in Old Testament Prophecy*, p. 64), and this appears to be the basis for the rendering in NEB ("they shall not bring . . .": cf. JB).

Their bread shall be like mourners' bread ... : Their bread is not in the Heb. or the Vss. and is based on an emendation first proposed by Kuenen (cf. *BHS*). MT may be rendered: "They [i.e. the sacrifices] shall be to them like mourners' bread, which defiles all who eat of it". **mourners' bread** is the most likely rendering of Heb. *lehem 'ônîm*, a phrase which is commonly restored in Ezek. 24:17, 22 (for other possibilities see Rudolph, p. 172; *HAL*, p. 22). The food in a house where there had been a recent death clearly shared in the defilement that was believed to attach to a dead body (cf. Num. 19:11–16; Dt. 26:14; Hag. 2:13) and if eaten would transmit the defilement to others, thus rendering them unfit to participate in the worship of Yahweh. Hosea's point is that the sacrifices offered in exile (or, if **their bread** is read with RSV, all food eaten there) will defile Israel, i.e. place her outside the community of Yahweh's worshippers, just as much.

all who eat of it shall be defiled: This is probably not so much a prediction as an assertion of cultic law (cf. above). The very wording conforms to a common pattern which may have belonged originally to the language of priestly instruction (Lev. 17:14; Jer. 2:3; cf. Exod. 12:15, 19; Lev. 7:25; 19:8). It shows how close Hosea stands to priestly tradition. Compare the Mishnah tractates Ohaloth and Tohoroth (Danby, pp. 649–76, 714–32) for later developments of these practices.

for their hunger only: I.e. it will serve a purely physical purpose. The use of *nepeš* (usually "life, soul, person") for **hunger** (cf. Ps. 78:18) could arise from an original meaning "throat", as in Isa. 5:14 and Ps. 69:1 (cf. H. W. Wolff, *Anthropology of the OT*, London, 1974, pp. 11–14). The English versions assume that this and the following line refer to the exiles. On this basis commentators have found it difficult to regard the words as Hosea's and they are assigned to later editors (Wolff, Rudolph, Mays). But it is better to see these lines as a continuation of the simile and to regard **their** as referring to the **mourners**: "their bread is for their hunger only; it may not enter the house of the Lord". Cf. Dt. 26:14, where a worshipper dedicating his tithe is to state that no part of it has been eaten during mourning. Those in

mourning experienced isolation from the worship of Yahweh, and
Hosea is saying that by being taken into exile the whole people
will be similarly isolated from **the house of the LORD**. In the
light of Exod. 23:19 and 34:26 the reference may be specifically to
the offering of firstfruits, which were perhaps already in Hosea's
time taken to one of the great national sanctuaries. But it is clear
from Dt. 26:14, cited above, that the prohibition applied also to
the tithe. If, as is probable, these verses were first spoken in the
course of a harvest festival at Bethel (cf. above), the rulings to
which Hosea alludes would have been very much in the people's
minds at the time. The wording of this prohibition finds a parallel
in Dt. 23:18, which also shows that by **the house of the LORD**
Hosea here certainly means a temple, and not the whole land (cf.
on 8:1).

**9:5. the day of appointed festival ... the day of the feast
of the LORD**: Similar expressions occur in 2:11, a further indication of the close connection between that chapter and the present
passage. **the feast of the LORD** probably refers specifically
to the feast of ingathering, later Sukkoth (Tabernacles), which
apparently enjoyed a certain prominence over the other great
pilgrim-festivals (cf. Lev. 23:39; 1 Kg. 8:2; 12:32–33). For a
judicious account of it cf. de Vaux, *Ancient Israel*, pp. 495–506.
appointed festival is a more general expression for any regular
religious gathering (cf. Lev. 23:2), but Hosea may have had the
three great pilgrim-festivals (Passover/Unleavened Bread, and
Weeks/Firstfruits, in addition to Sukkoth) particularly in mind,
because it was these whose celebration would be excluded by the
coming exile and the destruction of the sanctuaries. The prophet's
pointed use of direct address (**What will you do ...** : cf. 6:4; 8:5)
is again noticeable here.

9:6. they are going to Assyria: to Assyria is based on a
conjectural emendation of the Heb. *miššōd* to *'aššûr*, first suggested
by Wellhausen. The meaning of MT is represented by JB, "from
the devastation" (cf. NEB), and this gives a satisfactory sense:
even if they escape from the devastation to come they will
never return, they will perish in Egypt. "Devastation" (*šōd*) is
a favourite word of Hosea's (cf. 7:13; 10:2, 14; 12:2). For **behold**
(Heb. *hinnēh*) as in effect equivalent to "if" see *BDB*, p. 244a (cf.
1 Sam. 9:7; 2 Sam. 18:11).

Egypt shall gather them: This could at first sound as though at least a haven in **Egypt** would be available to the refugees. But as the sequel shows (cf. **bury**), **gather** refers to the gathering up of a body for burial (Ezek. 29:5: cf. Jer. 8:2; 25:33). It is striking that the same word is used of Yahweh in 8:10, but the image is probably different there.

Memphis shall bury them: Memphis, located on the west bank of the Nile about thirteen miles south of Cairo, was one of Egypt's oldest cities and had sometimes been the capital in the Old and New Kingdom periods (cf. *IDB*, vol. 3, 346–47). Although no longer the capital in Hosea's time, it was still an important administrative and religious centre over which numerous battles were fought (cf. Kitchen, *TIP*, index). This in itself would explain why it, of all the cities of Lower Egypt, was picked out for mention here. But it is possible that then, as now, it was well known also for its vast burial-grounds (and the Pyramids nearby), in which case it would be particularly apt in this context. **bury them** is the Piel form of the verb, which is appropriate to a mass burial, but equally significant is the fact that it produces a rhyme (in addition to alliteration) with **gather them** in the preceding line (*t^eqabb^eṣēm . . . t^eqabb^erēm*: cf. on 8:7).

Nettles shall possess their precious things of silver: their precious things of silver renders a very obscure Heb. phrase, *maḥmad l^ekaspām*, in a way that involves two linguistic difficulties and produces an improbable meaning: silver would not be left to be overgrown (Rudolph). Several commentators agree that this phrase is not the object of **shall possess**: the Heb. verb includes the object suffix "them" (not represented in RSV), which may be taken to imply "their land" (NEB). The obscure phrase is rendered by NEB, "the sands of Syrtes shall wreck them", treating *maḥmad* as a name for a dangerous bay on the north coast of Africa (cf. the place Macomades mentioned by Pliny, *H.N.* 5.25) and relating *l^ekospām* (for *l^ekaspām*: cf. *HTOT*, p. 248) to a verb *kāsap*, "break", cognate with Akkadian *kasāpu* (cf. G. R. Driver, *JSS* 5 (1960), 424). This is not at all appropriate to the context. Best perhaps is the suggestion to read *maḥmādām l^ekospām*, "what they desire shall be their undoing [or 'shame']" (cf. Zeph. 2:1 for this meaning of *ksp*): "what they desire" is taken by Rudolph to mean "Egypt", but it may refer to the lands and houses (**tents**) which Israel loved so much (cf. Mic. 2:2).

in their tents: Or "dwellings" (NEB), for which Heb. *'ōhālîm* sometimes stands, especially with the connotation of "homes" (e.g. Jg. 19:9). The sense of these difficult lines must be that the houses in the cities of Israel will be left uninhabited and will become overgrown. A similar picture of the devastation of Edom occurs in Isa. 34:11–17.

9:7. The conclusion to the announcement of judgment emphasizes that its time has already arrived. **have come** (for such repetition in Hosea cf. 6:4; 7:8–9; 11:8) is in the perfect tense, in contrast to the imperfects of the preceding verses, which point more vaguely to the future. Nor is there talk here merely of parental chastisement, as in 5:2 and 10:10, but of **punishment** (cf. 1:4; 2:15; 4:9, 14; 9:9; 12:3) and the **recompense** dispensed by God according to traditional belief (Dt. 7:10; 2 Sam. 3:39).

Israel shall know it: This statement is by no means as banal as it seems: hitherto **Israel** has displayed a remarkable ability not to **know** what was happening (cf. 4:11; 7:9, 11). LXX, "Israel shall suffer evil", read *yēdᵉʿû* **shall know**, as a form of *rāʿaʿ*, "be evil", and gives no support to the suggestion that a second root *yᵃdaʿ*, meaning "be humble, humiliated", is present here (see Emerton, *JSS* 15 (1970), 152–53, against D. Winton Thomas, *JTS* 41 (1940), 43–44, and NEB). Nor is LXX likely itself to represent the original reading. JB, "Israel protests" (in the next line), like Wolff, follows the reading presupposed by LXX but connects it with a different verb *rûaʿ*, which can mean "cry out", though not usually in the sense "protest". The straightforward rendering of RSV is to be preferred.

The prophet is a fool, the man of the spirit is mad: These words are best taken, with most commentators, as words spoken by Hosea's hearers, or one of them: they express total incredulity at what **the prophet** has said about coming disaster. **fool** (*'ewîl*) is a word often used in Proverbs for a person with no comprehension of the real world, particularly one whose words are not worth listening to (cf. Prov. 10:14; 14:3).

the man of the spirit: The more common designation was "man of God" (1 Kg. 17:18), but subjection to the **spirit** of Yahweh is often mentioned in prophetic narratives (e.g. 1

Kg. 18:12). Hosea is here associated by his hearers with this
phenomenon, although both he and the other early classical
prophets seem to have deliberately avoided such language (in
Mic. 3:8 the words "with the Spirit of the Lord" are probably a
later addition: see the commentaries). **mad** is used elsewhere in a
derogatory sense of ecstatic behaviour, including that of prophets
(1 Sam. 21:16; 2 Kg. 9:11; Jer. 29:26).

because of your great iniquity . . . : After the interruption
Hosea either explains that his "raving" is the direct consequence
of the people's **iniquity** (Harper, JB) or, more probably, resumes
his message of judgment from v. 7a by restating (cf. 4:4b) the
reason for the coming catastrophe in new terms. The word **your**
has a singular reference and may denote a specific person who
had interrupted Hosea. The reference to **hatred** is amplified
in v. 8 and identifies hostility to the prophet himself as a new
reason for judgment (cf. Am. 2:12; 7:16–17). It is also possible
to render: "It is because of the greatness of your iniquity that
the hatred [sc. felt towards God's prophet] is so great" (Wolff,
Rudolph, Mays). On this view the point is that the very hostility
which Hosea experiences provides further proof that his earlier
accusation was true.

hatred: Heb. *mastēmāh*, as in v. 8: these are the only occurrences of this word in the OT. In post-biblical literature it
reappears as part of an epithet of Satan (CD 16:5, 1QM
13:11 – *DSSE*, pp. 109, 141) and even, in the book of Jubilees
(e.g. 10:8), as an alternative name (Mastema) for the Tempter.
But no such connotations are present here.

9:8. The first part of this verse is very difficult and many
different explanations and emendations of it have been proposed
(for a review see R. Dobbie, *VT* 5 (1955), 199–203). MT has
"Ephraim lies in wait [or 'is a watchman'] with my God; a/the
prophet, a fowler's snare . . ." RSV involves only slight changes
to the vowels of two words (*sōpēh* for *sōpeh*, *'am* for *'im*) and
an alteration to the punctuation. Hosea himself appears as a
watchman in 5:8 and 8:1, and later prophets use the same
term (Jer. 6:17; Ezek. 3:17; 33:7). On the other hand, it is
difficult to construe **Ephraim** as the subject, as MT requires.
The other change, from "with my God" to "the people of my
God" removes a phrase that is barely intelligible in the context

and replaces it with an apt expression which fits well with Hosea's usage (cf. 6:11; 9:17). None of the more extensive changes that have been proposed (cf. *BHS*, JB, Rudolph) is necessary, but it is possible that the words **The prophet is** (Heb. *nābî'*) are, as Wolff thinks, an explanatory gloss. The original text would have then read: "The watchman of Ephraim, the people of my God – a fowler's snare is on all his ways . . ." The prophet thus reminds his hearers of his own role as the guardian appointed by Yahweh for his **people** before contrasting this with their hostility towards him by the use of a vivid metaphor. NEB's interpretation of this verse is unusual in several ways, of which *HTOT* (p. 248) gives little hint: MT's text (though not its punctuation) is closely followed, but a distinction is presupposed between **Ephraim** and the (persecuted) "people of God", which is very unlikely.

A fowler's snare: Cf. Ps. 91:3. Earlier Hosea had used hunting imagery to characterize the behaviour of the priests and the royal house (5:1–2: cf. pp. 139–40), and it may well be they who are in mind here too, but now it is clearly God's prophet himself who is their prey.

in the house of his God: This is most naturally taken as a reference to a temple (cf. v. 4), the more so in view of the numerous indications of a festival setting for vv. 1–7a, with which the present dialogue is closely associated. Those commentators (e.g. Wolff, Rudolph, Mays) who find such a designation for the corrupt sanctuary impossible on Hosea's lips miss the point: it is clear (cf. 8:2; 9:4) that worship had not ceased to be offered to Yahweh in the sanctuaries, and so Hosea could if it suited him (as here) use **his God's** traditional claims to reinforce his accusation. Even in the place where, as a common citizen (1 Kg. 2:28), he could expect to find safety, he faces intense **hatred**.

9:9. They have deeply corrupted themselves: Or "They have gone deep into corruption". The reference is to the evil behavio ir of **Ephraim, the people of my God** (v. 8), not to their fate. Since there is no object expressed in the Heb., NEB's "They lead them [sc. the people of God – see on v. 8] deep into sin" is not likely: for the intransitive use of *šiḥēt* cf. Exod. 32:7; Dt. 9:12; 32:5. *BHS*, following Wellhausen and other older commentators, reads *šaḥ᷒tô* for *šiḥētû*, giving "They have made deep his pit". This is a small change which continues the hunting metaphor,

but it is unnecessary and unsupported by the Vss., and should
be rejected.

as in the days of Gibeah: On **Gibeah** see the note on 5:8: **the
days of Gibeah** are mentioned again in 10:9. The comparison
here must be with the well-known succession of atrocities of
which a (late?) account is given in Jg. 19–21 (unless some episode
otherwise unknown to us is meant). The fact that Saul's home was
at **Gibeah** (1 Sam. 10:26) would not account for its mention here,
but the story in Judges was clearly remembered as one of gross
evil (cf. 19:30), from which the editors of that book distanced
themselves by locating it in a dark age before the advent of
monarchic rule (cf. 19:1; 21:25). Hosea, on the other hand, finds
it all too good a paradigm of his contemporaries' behaviour.
Since the beginning of the story concerns the treatment of the
concubine of a Levite from "the hill country of Ephraim" (19:1),
it may have been particularly well known in those Levitical circles
with which Hosea has sometimes been associated (Wolff), but it
must also have been more generally known for Hosea's allusion
to be picked up.

he will remember . . .: The subject is clearly Yahweh, who
has most recently been referred to as **his God** at the end of the
previous verse. NEB's passive rendering is based on a conjectural
modification of the vowels of MT (cf. *HTOT*, p. 248), for which
there is no support in Vss. This concluding prophecy of judgment
is closely paralleled in 8:13 (see the note there), but it also echoes
the reference to **punishment** in 9:7a, where the same Heb. root
is used.

A SINFUL HISTORY BEGETS
A BARREN FUTURE

9:10–17

There is an important contrast between the section of the book of
Hosea which begins here and the one which precedes it (4:1–9:9).
The latter contains scarcely any allusions to the early history
of Israel, and those which there are have a negative character
(6:4; 8:4; 9:9). Even the references to a **return to Egypt** (8:13;
9:3) point rather to the bondage of Israel's ancestors than to

any divine act for their liberation. On the other hand, from 9:10 onwards Hosea repeatedly alludes to the traditions about the divine initiative in choosing and delivering Israel in the patriarchal age, the Exodus and conquest and the institution of the monarchy, which formed the heart of the traditional north Israelite cult theology (cf. Pss. 80–81; 1 Kg. 12:28; Gen. 28:10–22 (JE)): "Like grapes in the wilderness, I found Israel" (9:10; cf. 10:1–2, 9–15; 11:1–7; 12:2–14; 13:1–11). Only here does the emphasis on the election traditions identified by G. von Rad once again come to expression, after its initial development especially in ch. 2. Hosea's treatment of these themes is everywhere polemical, and he insists both on the divine demand which accompanied the acts of election and on the disastrous consequences for the present of Israel's ancient repudiation of her Saviour (cf. Vollmer, *Geschichtliche Rückblicke*, pp. 115–20). But he does not deny the historical cultic affirmations themselves (except, apparently, for those relating to the monarchy, and even these are in a paradoxical sense affirmed in 13:11), and it is significantly here, and on the basis (it would seem) of the historical traditions (cf. ch. 2!), that a new message of hope enters Hosea's preaching (11:8–9, 11; 14:1–8). Yet the historical traditions contribute little or nothing to the substance of this hope; just as in 2:18–25, it is a creation-based theology which is central here. For the most part this feature of Hosea's teaching (which has been said to be accompanied by a more reflective, more private character of speaking) seems to belong to the later years of his activity, though 12:2–9 is probably an example from his early years (see the introduction to 11:12–12:14).

The limits of 9:10–17 are clearly defined both by subject-matter and by literary form. It begins with a historical retrospect (like the next section, cf. 10:1–2) and is held together by the themes of Yahweh's change in attitude from love to hate towards Israel and the infertility and exile which will follow from this, and also by a series of echoes of the story of Saul in 1 Sam. Formally divine speech predominates, in contrast to both the preceding and the following sections (the next divine I is in 10:10). The absence of direct address (except in v. 10) is also a notable change from vv. 1–9. But in v. 14, and probably also in v. 13, the prophet speaks *in propria persona*, and the solemn conclusion in v. 12 also points to a break in the unit before v. 13. Some (e.g. Wolff) see the intrusive section (which according to Wolff consists only of v. 14) as the prophet's response to the preceding oracle, which expresses an initial challenge to its message of doom in the form of an intercession, but then issues in acquiescence in the divine will (pp. 166–67). This may be the intention of the text in its present form, but on closer examination vv. 13–14 prove to move in the opposite direction to vv. 11–12 and 15–16. Vv. 13–14 begin with the threat to the living "sons of Ephraim" and in consequence seek an end to childbirth, because life is no longer worth living, whereas vv. 11–12 and 15–16 treat the curse of infertility as the primary divine intention and the killing of older children as the remedy for those who, as it were, escape. It is therefore likely that vv. 13–14 are of a separate origin from the rest of the passage and were inserted into it because of their similarity of theme. There is, however, no reason to think that they are not by Hosea (cf. 10:14–15; 13:16). The remaining verses give two overlapping treatments of the same themes. Since Wellhausen it has been customary to transpose v. 16 to follow v. 11 or to place v. 16a before v. 11 and v. 16b after it (Rudolph), but the existing sequence of verses is perfectly intelligible (see Wolff, Mays, Jeremias). The two parallel sub-units may have originated on separate occasions, but in view of the otherwise unexplained pronouns (**their, them**) of v. 15 it is more likely that they are two stanzas of a single poem. It is worthy of note that whereas the first stanza relates Yahweh's hostility to Israel to a time far removed from that of Hosea, the second derives it from a place that was still (cf. 12:15) at the heart of the religious life of the northern kingdom: it is the present generation as much as their forefathers who bear the blame for the imminent catastrophe. Little can be said about the occasion of this proclamation, but the preference for third-person references to the people may indicate, as Wolff thinks, that it was delivered privately to a group of sympathizers after opposition at a major festival (at Gilgal?) had made it impossible for the prophet to continue his public ministry (cf. 9:8 and **they have not hearkened to him** in v. 17), a situation which might also explain the repeated use of language drawn from the conflicts between Samuel and Saul in an earlier period.

9:10. Like grapes in the wilderness: This and the following image express in a very sensual way the delight which Yahweh took in **Israel** when he **found** them in Egypt (12:13; 13:4). Grapes would be a particular delight to a thirsty desert traveller (cf. Num. 13:23). It is not necessarily implied that they grew there, though in oases like En-gedi (Ca. 1:14) or Jericho this was possible. Hosea does not elaborate the cause of Yahweh's delight, as Jeremiah was later to do (Jer. 2:2): his point is the subsequent change in Yahweh's attitude and *its* cause (v. 10b: cf. v. 15).

I found Israel: Israel stands here, as Wolff observes, for the whole people, whose united history in the pre-settlement period (and later: cf. 10:1, 9) is taken for granted, not the northern kingdom alone. Wolff sees here an allusion to a "finding" tradition which existed alongside the Exodus tradition and spoke of the decisive encounter between Yahweh and Israel as being in the wilderness (cf. R. Bach, *TLZ* 78 (1953), 687, and von Rad, *OT Theology*, vol. 1, p. 177n.). But the parallelism with the following line, the Masoretic punctuation and the word-order all indicate that **in the wilderness** is part of the image, not a reference to Israel's history, so that whatever is to be made of the other passages said to reflect this tradition (Dt. 32:10; Jer. 2:2; Ezek. 16:5), it plays no part here.

Like the first fruit on the fig tree: A favourite image of OT poets: cf. Isa. 28:4; Jer. 24:2; Mic. 7:1. The figs which grow on the branches from the preceding year are especially tender (Wolff). Hosea's choice of images from the world of nature seems to be a deliberate reappropriation of the themes of the fertility cult. But they are also characteristic of love-poetry (cf. Ca. passim).

in its first season: Heb. *berē'šîtāh* is literally "at its beginning", and might therefore bear this meaning (*BDB*). But it is more natural to render "as its firstfruits" (*beth essentiae*), with LXX and Symm., and it may then be regarded as a gloss on the rare word (*bikkûrāh*) used earlier in the verse (so Wolff, JB: cf. Syr.). NEB seems to take this view, as "with joy" is more likely to be an interpretative addition than an attempt to render *berē'šîtāh*, but neither *HTOT* nor the footnote indicates a departure from MT.

I saw your fathers: NEB "their fathers", following the inferior LXX reading, and again without acknowledgment of the departure from MT. If accepted it might refer to the patriarchs as opposed to the Exodus generation.

Baal-peor: This is generally the name of the Moabite deity to whom the Israelites **consecrated themselves** according to Num. 25:3–5 (cf. Dt. 4:3b, Ps. 106:28) at the end of their journey through the wilderness. The present context, however, requires that it be interpreted, as in Dt. 4:3a, as a place name which is presumably equivalent to Beth–peor or Peor (Num. 23:28; Dt. 3:29). Numerous place-names are compounded with the name Baal (cf. *BDB*, p. 128), and they must refer to settlements centred on a prominent shrine of **Baal**. The full form of the name would then have been "Beth-Baal-peor" (cf. Beth-Baal-meon in Jos. 13:47 and line 30 of the Moabite Stone: Gibson, *Textbook*, vol. 1, p. 75).

consecrated themselves: The verb is *nāzar*, which is elsewhere used of sacral abstinence and particularly of the Nazirite (Num. 6:2 etc.). There is therefore heavy irony in its present use.

to Baal: More precisely "to shame" (JB, cf. NEB), Heb. *labbōšet*, but the prophet undoubtedly means **Baal** by this disparaging term (cf. Jer. 3:24). Later scribes extended this usage to other passages, substituting *bōšet* for "Baal" (2 Sam 2:8; 11:21; Jer. 11:13). M. Fishbane, *Biblical Interpretation in Ancient Israel*, p. 71, thinks that scribal activity is responsible for the periphrasis here, but this is not necessary.

detestable: Heb. *šiqqûṣîm*. The contrast with their previous desirability is pronounced. A related word is used of that which is ritually impure (Lev. 7:21 etc.), and this word itself was frequently applied later to alien gods (e.g. 2 Kg. 23:13, 24).

like the thing which they loved: The Heb. contains no equivalent to **thing**, and "him whom they loved" is equally possible. In either case the reference is to Baal.

9:11. Ephraim's glory: glory commonly refers to the outward splendour which accompanies wealth or military power (Isa. 10:3, 16 – cf. Hos. 10:5). But in Ps. 3:4 **glory** seems to refer to Yahweh as the one who is glorified (cf. Ps. 106:20; Jer. 2:11; and the notes on Hos. 4:7), and such a reference might be seen here (cf. **when I depart** in v. 12). This interpretation provides a better basis for the consequences in v. 11b than a reference

to wealth or power: the departure of Yahweh, who is the true
giver of fertility (not Baal), naturally hinders procreation. Cf.
I Sam. 4:21–22. The use in 10:5 may be of a similar kind, but
with reference to idolatrous worship.

no birth . . . : The Heb. idiom (cf. *BDB*, p. 583) marks these
things as the consequence of what has just been said: "so that
there shall be no birth . . ." The three terms form a sequence of
increasing severity; infertility and barrenness will prevent even
conception from occurring, a fate still more severe than that
intended by Pharaoh (Exod. 1:15–22).

9:12. According to many commentators (see the introduction
to this section) v. 16 (or at least its latter half) originally stood
between vv. 11 and 12, but there is no evidence for this, and a
poet like Hosea did not need to arrange his thoughts in such a
logical order.

Even if they bring up children: The reference is presumably
to **children** already born: all hope of a continued existence for
the people will be taken away when Yahweh **departs**.

Woe to them: Cf. 7:13. The Heb. here is very emphatic,
literally "For (it is) indeed woe (which will come) to them",
and the line seems to conclude a unit.

when I depart: For the withdrawal of God's presence as the
means of his judgment cf. 5:6, 15, and also (with reference to
Saul) I Sam. 18:12; 28:15–16. The efficacy of cultic worship
was bound up with the presence of the deity in his temple (cf.
Clements, *God and Temple*, ch. 4 and 5), so that his withdrawal led
inevitably to the collapse of the cult and an end to his blessing.
The Heb. orthography is unusual but possible (cf. *GK* §6k),
but the meaning is not affected if the small change from *śûrî*
to *šûrî* is made (Sellin, *KB*, Wolff). More extensive changes to
MT have been proposed (*BH³*, Rudolph), but they are scarcely
necessary.

9:13. Ephraim's sons . . . are destined for a prey: The
interpretation of this line is very uncertain. RSV is based on
the text presupposed by LXX (cf. Wolff, Mays, JB), as MT is
unintelligible. The differences are in fact relatively slight, and
could be due to common scribal errors. NIV and Andersen and
Freedman vainly try to interpret MT, while other renderings,
including NEB's "As lion-cubs emerge only to be hunted . . .",

attempt to create an expression more closely parallel to v. 11 at the expense of more drastic emendation of the received texts. The words **as I have seen** may refer to visionary experience, if we assume that here (as in v. 14) the prophet speaks *in propria persona*. Wolff thinks that divine speech continues here (cf. v. 12) and consequently concludes that **Ephraim** is charged with exposing **his sons** to unnecessary danger, probably in capricious military expeditions. But it is more likely (see the introduction to this section) that v. 13 begins a separate unit dealing with similar themes from a slightly different perspective.

for a prey: Or "to be hunted" (cf. NEB).

Ephraim must lead forth: In the Heb. the line begins with a difficult "and", which G. R. Driver took to be a *waw* of comparison (*JTS* 39 (1938), 160: cf. NEB "so"). Perhaps this should be joined to an unexplained *h* at the end of the previous line to form *hô*, "Alas!" (cf. Am. 5:16): then translate, "Alas for Ephraim! He must lead forth . . ."

to the slaughter: Literally "to the slayer" (NIV), which ought to stand, despite the support for RSV's alternative rendering in LXX.

9:14. In the light of the doom which he foresees for the children of the Ephraimites the prophet can only pray that no more may be born or reared. Paradoxically barrenness is now a sign of God's favour (cf. Job 3:11–16; Lk. 23:29 par.).

Give them, O LORD: The language is highly ironical, for the "gift" of children was highly prized in Israel (cf. 1 Sam. 1:11; Ps. 127:3; 128:3–6; also names such as "Jonathan", meaning "Yahweh has given"). The prophet prepares for the unexpected content of his prayer in this extreme situation by the question **what wilt thou give?** (cf. Ps. 120:3 for similar rhetorical questions before a curse).

a miscarrying womb: So most modern versions, literally "a womb that makes someone childless" (cf. LXX). The Heb. root is the same as that translated **bereave** in v. 12.

9:15. This and the two following verses recapitulate the themes and forms of speech used in vv. 10–14: first Yahweh speaks of the origin of the breach between him and Ephraim and the infertility which will now result from this (vv. 15–16), and then the prophet adds his own comment, this time drawing in themes from elsewhere in the book.

in Gilgal: The fact that **Every evil of theirs** is located at **Gilgal** (see on 4:15) perhaps makes it unnecessary to decide between a reference to cultic misdemeanours (cf. 12:11 and perhaps Jg. 3:19) and one to the foundation of the monarchy under Saul (1 Sam. 11:14–15). Already under Saul **Gilgal** was the scene of sacrifices of which a prophet was critical (1 Sam. 13:8–14). It may be no accident that this very verse contains possible references both to the sanctuary (**my house**) and to the ruling elite (**their princes**). The role of **Gilgal** as Israel's first encampment west of the Jordan may also be in the prophet's mind: he may well have judged the memorial stones an **evil** (Jg. 3:19: cf. 10:1–2).

I began to hate them: The verb, which denotes Israel's rejection by Yahweh in untypically positive terms (contrast the negative formulations in 1:6, 9; 2:2, 4; and later in this verse), is used of God only here in Hosea, but compare Am. 5:21, 6:12 and Jer. 12:8. **began** is not expressed by a separate word, but by an inchoative use of the perfect (Wolff). Possibly a more normal interpretation of the perfect should be preferred here, such as "I hate" (Mays) or "I did hate" (cf. NEB).

The wickedness of their deeds: This is one of the earliest attested occurrences of this phrase (cf. Isa. 1:16), which became popular with Jeremiah (4:4; 21:12) and the Deuteronomists (e.g. Dt. 28:20).

I will drive them out of my house: It is widely held that **my house** here and elsewhere in Hosea means the land of Canaan (cf. on 8:1). In general this view is to be rejected and a reference to a temple of Yahweh preferred, as is also possible here. But both the context and the terminology used are strongly reminiscent of the law about divorce in Dt. 24:1–4, which includes the words "sends her out of his house" (cf. also Lev. 21:7, 14). Hosea may therefore be using divorce language in a metaphorical sense here, just as he uses marriage language (and possibly divorce language) in ch 2 (see G. I. Emmerson, *VT* 25 (1975), 708; *Hosea*, p. 133). In this case **my house** might mean more generally "my domain" and refer to the land as a whole, so that already here there would be a reference to exile (cf. v. 17).

I will love them no more: cf. the name of Hosea's daughter **Not pitied** and its interpretation in 1:6, although a different verb is used here (*'āhēb* instead of *riḥam*).

all their princes are rebels: There is a play on words in the Heb., *kol śārêhem sôrᵉrîm*, which recurs in Isa. 1:23. It may have been in Hosea's time a slogan of groups opposed to the ruling elites. The verse has a rounded chiastic structure: the first and last lines declare Ephraim's sin, the second and fifth Yahweh's response (using the antithetical terms **hate** and **love**), and the middle two his imminent action and its cause.

9:16. The controlling image changes back in this verse to that of a fruit tree (cf. v. 10), which is **stricken,** perhaps by disease (cf. Jon. 4:7–8; Ps. 105:33), and dead from the **root** up, so that it can **bear no fruit.** The word **stricken** is also often used of the defeat of a nation, and Hosea may have chosen it deliberately with the double meaning in view. There is a further paradoxical play on words between **Ephraim** and **fruit** (Heb. *pᵉrî*), as in 14:8, perhaps with intentional reminiscence of the popular etymology of the name (cf. Gen. 41:52). The verse repeats the thought of vv. 11 and 12 in different words, but this is not a reason for transposing it to there (see the introduction to this section).

9:17. My God will cast them off: The prophet himself summarizes what has been said in the preceding divine speech, and in doing so he reverts to the personal language used in v. 15: **cast them off** (Heb. *mā'as*) is a word used by Hosea in 4:6 of the rejection of the priesthood, but it could also be used of a rejected wife (Isa. 54:6) It occurs several times in 1 Sam. with reference to God's rejection of Saul (15:23, 26; 16:1), who had also **not hearkened** to Yahweh (cf. 1 Sam. 15:19, 22; 28:18). What had previously been seen only in the replacement of Saul by David was now to happen to the whole kingdom.

DOOM FOR KING AND HIGH PLACE

10:1–8

The main theme of this passage, with which it begins and ends, is the destruction of the **altars, pillars** and shrines (**high places**) which were the focus of contemporary religious practice (vv. 1, 2 and 8). But tightly interwoven with it is the powerlessness

and coming fall of Israel's **king** (vv. 3–4, 7). The connection
is natural, because the king was, like the cult, regarded as the
guarantor of national security and prosperity, and because the
cult, at least at the major sanctuaries, was under royal control
and designed to ensure divine protection for the king and his
court (cf. Am. 7:13; Ps. 80:17). The form of the passage indicates
that it was not a public oracle (or series of oracles) like, e.g.,
9:1–9: divine speech is not employed and the references to
Israel are all in the third person. Wolff has suggested that
this passage, like others in the later chapters of the book, was
spoken by Hosea to a small group of sympathizers or disciples.
It has been objected that we have no evidence of the existence
of such a group, but it is probably necessary to envisage one to
account for the preservation and arrangement of Hosea's oracles.
It remains possible, however, that passages like this were drafts
"written for the prophet's own later use" (Rudolph).

The common subject-matter, the inclusion between vv. 1–2
and 8, the formal discontinuity with the divine speech which
precedes and follows, and the return to "beginnings" in vv. 1
and 9 all set clear outer limits to this section. The questions
of its inner structure and unity are more contentious. Against
an older tendency to discern secondary material, especially in
vv. 3–4 (cf. Harper) and a more recent analysis of the passage
into three originally separate units (1–2, 3–4, 5–8: see Rudolph)
Wolff has maintained the unity of the passage, with accusation
predominating in vv. 1–5 and threat in vv. 6–8. There is certainly
no compelling reason to mark off any sections as later additions,
and the view that vv. 3–4 belong to a later historical period
than vv. 1–2 (as variously argued by Harper and Rudolph) is
unconvincing (see below). But an examination of the structure
of the passage makes it doubtful that it has been transmitted as it
was originally composed. From one point of view the structure is
very symmetrical, as Jeremias has pointed out: vv. 1–2 and 8 deal
with **altars** and sacred **pillars**, vv. 3–4 and 7 with the **king**, and
vv. 5–6 with the calf-image. This matches the carefully balanced
composition of v. 1b (**the more . . . the more . . . ; improved
. . . improved**) and of vv. 1–2 as a whole (**altars . . . altars;
pillars . . . pillars**), as well as the parallelism of the succeeding
themes in vv. 3–6 and 7–8 (the **king** (vv. 3–4, 7); the cult (vv.

5–6, 8)). If MT is followed at the end of v. 6 (reading "plan" for **idol** of RSV), it is true, this parallelism is marginally diminished, but it remains a striking feature. The problem is over whether vv. 3–6 and 7–8 are in their original order. In the detailed notes on v. 3 it is suggested that what the people will say and feel is not a very strong explanation for the coming devastation of the shrines; this would be more convincingly provided by v. 7, with v. 8 being a kind of reprise of vv. 1–2. The prophet's anticipation of the people's reaction to the catastrophe in vv. 3–6 would more naturally have followed the actual description of it in vv. 7–8. It is possible, therefore, that vv. 3–6 were placed in their position by a redactor. Why he would have done this can only be conjectured, but it seems most likely to have been due to a wish to associate what he (mistakenly – see the notes on vv. 3 and 4) took to be an indictment of the people for their failure to "fear the Lord" and their lack of fidelity to one another with the strictures on the cult in vv. 1–2, so as to build up a stronger account of the people's guilt before the announcement of doom in vv. 6–8.

There is only a little evidence by which to date this passage. V. 1 may refer to the period of prosperity under Jeroboam II (though a reference to a much earlier period is also possible), but this need not mean that it was spoken then: the **altars** and **pillars** no doubt remained in place. The reference to tribute in v. 6 (cf. the note) implies that Israel is already subject to Assyrian demands and so must be later than around 740, when Menahem first paid tribute to Assyria. The fact that only a single calf is mentioned in v. 5 makes it probable that the passage is later than the destruction of Dan by Tiglath-pileser III in c. 733. V. 4 probably refers to the frequent fluctuations in foreign policy in the 730s and perhaps the 720s (cf. on 7:11). Since v. 3 explicitly relates what the people *will* say it need not, indeed it cannot, be later than the capture of Hoshea by the Assyrians c. 724. Perhaps the most likely setting is around the time of Hoshea's intrigues with Egypt, which are referred to in 2 Kg. 17:4 and are apparently to be placed in the second or third year of Shalmaneser V's reign (726 or 725). Against the background of renewed optimism and self-assertion, Hosea declared again (to his disciples?) that neither their cultus nor their king and his policies would be able to save the people when the Assyrians returned, as they surely would, and that indeed both the cultus and the king were destined for destruction. Only after this would the people begin to realize how foolish they had been. The resemblance to 3:4 (and 5) is striking: there the removal of the pillars and other cult objects is connected with that of the king and presented as a form of discipline which will cause the people to return to Yahweh. This passage does not go quite so far, and is probably to be dated a little before ch. 3.

10:1. Like 9:10–17 this section begins with a positive statement about Israel's past, and here also the image of the **vine** is used. The image may be traditional: it is used in Ps. 80:8–13, a community lament from the last days of the northern kingdom and therefore contemporary with Hosea's later ministry, but there it forms the basis for a plea for divine aid. Here it refers to a time of prosperity which saw a multiplication of **altars** and sacred **pillars**, a development which Hosea apparently viewed critically (cf. 6:6; 8:11) and which was about to be brought to an end (v. 2b).

a luxuriant vine: The usual meanings of *bāqaq* ("empty, lay waste") are unsuited to describe a **vine** (unless a passive form is read with Targ. – cf. NJPS "ravaged"), but the meaning **luxuriant** finds support in an Arabic cognate and most of the Vss., and it is generally adopted here. NEB, "a rank vine", following Symm., interprets the word in a derogatory sense, but it is not the flourishing of **Israel** that is criticized, only her misuse of her prosperity (cf. 2:8). The meaning "well-watered" (cf. Aq.), proposed by Kuhnigk, p. 117, is less secure.

that yields its fruit: Heb. *pᵉrî yᵉšawweh lô*. The rendering is uncertain and rather weak. Wolff and others render "its fruit is like it" (i.e. abundant), while NEB's "ripening its fruit" is based on a comparison with Arabic *sawwa* proposed by Nyberg. The sense most apposite to the context is obtained by emending *yᵉšawweh* to *yiśgeh*, "its fruit is great" (so JB, cf. LXX).

he improved his pillars: NJPS is closer to the Heb., which has a plural subject (similarily LXX), cf. **their** in v. 2. But a change from singular to plural is unlikely in mid-sentence (cf. **his country**), and the verb should perhaps be regarded as intransitive: "his pillars improved" (cf. 1 Sam. 20:13). The word underlying **improved** is Heb. *ṭôb*, "good", which can be used of a fine appearance (cf. NEB, REB) as well as fruitfulness (cf. 2 Kg. 3:19, 25; Ec. 11:6). The sense and the word-play can be captured by rendering: "The finer his land, the finer the pillars became." The sacred **pillars** (*maṣṣēbôt*) played a part in both Canaanite and Israelite worship and archaeological evidence of them has been found at Hazor, Gezer and Arad. They were apparently tolerated in early Israel (Gen. 28:18; Exod. 24:4), but laws both in Exodus (23:24; 34:13) and in Deuteronomy (16:22) declared them to be illicit. They are thought to have represented a deity or a dead ancestor. For further discussion of their significance see C. Graesser, *BA* 35 (1972), 34–63, *IDBS*, 668–69, and V. Fritz, *Tempel und Zelt* (WMANT 47), Neukirchen, 1977, pp. 48–52.

10:2. Their heart is false: Literally "is smooth, slippery", according to the most likely interpretation of MT *ḥālaq*; cf. Jer. 17:9 for the sense. This verb and its derivatives are mainly used of "smooth", i.e. flattering, speech (cf. Ps. 55:21), but they could apparently be used of deceptiveness at a deeper level too (cf. Ezek. 12:24). The meaning is not very different if we render "divided", from a different root *ḥlq* (with JB – cf. Vss.), but this requires a change to the vowels of MT.

now they must bear their guilt: In Hosea **now** often refers to the imminent judgment of Yahweh (cf. 5:7; 8:13; also v. 3 below). For **bear their guilt** as the meaning of *'āšam* see on 5:15.

The LORD: Heb. *hû'*, "He", but the reference to Yahweh is clear and emphatic.

will break down: The verb is elsewhere a technical sacrificial term for the breaking of animals' necks (*'ārap*, from *'ōrep*, "neck"), and specifically the necks of those animals which "are not to be sacrificed in the legitimate cult" (Wolff); again Hosea's language is deliberately offensive and ironical (cf. on 9:10, 14), as he envisages the disappearance of the whole apparatus of temple worship (cf. 3:4).

10:3. A logical connection between this and the preceding verse is made by **For**, but it is strange to find a threat against the sanctuaries confirmed by a statement about what people will **say** after their king has been taken away. It is vv. 7 and 8 which really provide the rationale for the threat in v. 2, while vv. 3–6 describe what the people's reaction will be to the fall of their king and the plundering of the royal temple (Am. 7:13) at Bethel.

These latter verses, with their mocking of the disillusionment which is to come, seem to have been inserted into the oracle, which they perhaps originally followed. The reason for this is not completely clear, but it may have been due to a wish to give greater prominence to what were seen as reasons for judgment in vv. 3–4.

For now they will say: Here again, as in v. 2, **now** refers to the time of the coming catastrophe, in which the people will to a degree come to their senses and acknowledge that their trust in each successive new **king** has been misplaced. For the expression of similar hopes by the prophet that the people will be brought to a better mind by disaster cf. 2:7; 3:5; 5:15. There is no reference here to a party who disowned the initially pro-Assyrian puppet-king Hoshea while he was still on the throne (*contra* Robinson and Weiser).

We have no king: Hosea more often cites actual or imagined words of his contemporaries as a reason for judgment (2:5, 12; 4:4; 8:2; 9:7; 13:10), but here they form part of his description of the time of judgment itself (cf. v. 9), and occasionally they belong to a prophecy of salvation (2:23; 14:2–3): cf. Wolff, *Das Zitat*, pp. 49–51, 73–74 (*GS*, pp. 73–75, 94–95). This citation begins in the style of a lament, moves into confession and ends with disillusion.

for we fear not the LORD: Or "did not fear . . ." Only here does Hosea use "the fear of the Lord" as a term for faithfulness to Yahweh: elsewhere he prefers the term "knowledge" (2:20; 5:4; 6:3, 6). "The fear of the Lord" is an important theological theme of the Elohistic material in the Pentateuch, which is probably of north Israelite origin, as well as of Deuteronomy (Jeremias: cf. Wolff, *Int* 26 (1972), 158–73): see, e.g., Gen. 20:11; Dt. 6:2.

and a king, what could he do for us? Or "what was the king able to do for us?": for the modal imperfect cf. *GK* §107r.

10:4. They utter mere words: As they stand in MT these two lines constitute an accusation of the same people who speak in v. 3, and the reference is probably to a general failure to honour agreements that have been made, however solemn (cf. 4:1–2). But LXX points to a slightly different text (*dabbēr* for *dabberû*), which can best be rendered: "Words! Words! False oaths! Making alliances!" (cf. JB). If, as seems likely, this is more original, Hosea here continues to put words into the mouths of the population, as they answer their own question with a cynical assessment of what their kings have achieved (Wellhausen). The result of it all is not the intended prosperity and security but judgment, which **springs up like poisonous weeds** where better things were expected (cf. the similar language used to make a different point in Am. 6:12). The MT reading then redirects the criticism away from the kings in particular to the people as a whole: such generalizations of accusations are a common feature of the reinterpretation of prophecy.

judgment: Heb. *mišpāṭ*: for its meanings see the note on 5:1. Some see here a reference to the multiplication of "lawsuits" (NEB, NIV) or to the degeneration of the administration of "justice" or order (Wolff, NJPS). But such meanings are less likely if the verse was originally concerned with the folly of royal foreign policy (see above).

10:5. The prophet continues to look forward to the reactions of the people to a coming Assyrian invasion, which will be disastrous for the official cult-centre as well as for the royal capital: the **inhabitants** will **tremble** at the imminent loss of their precious image.

the calf of Beth-aven: On **Beth-aven** as a name for Bethel see on 4:15, and on **the calf** see on 8:5. MT in fact has a feminine plural form, *'eglôt*, "heifers", which is probably a mistake not for the ordinary word for **calf** (*'egel*) but for an abstract noun *'eglût*, "calfhood", which differs only by one vowel and may have been coined by Hosea himself to mock the image in which so much trust had previously been placed (Rudolph).

Its people shall mourn for it: A barbed reference to the fact that Israel has ceased to be Yahweh's people (1:9). NEB footnote has "the high god and his people mourn" (reading *'āl wᵉᶜ'ammô*), where "the high god" is understood as a title for Baal (see the note on 7:16).

its idolatrous priests: Heb. *kᵉmārāyw*. This word, which is widely used in other Semitic languages for "priest", is found in Heb. only as a term of opprobrium for the functionaries of cults that are regarded by the speaker as illicit (2 Kg. 23:5; Zeph. 1:4).

shall wail over it: MT reads *yāgîlû* from *gîl*, which normally means "rejoice, exult" (cf. 9:1). Such a meaning hardly fits here, so RSV and JB follow a popular emendation to *yelîlû* (cf. *BHS*). But Vss. all support MT and recent commentators have rightly sought ways of retaining it, since there is a potent word-play with **has departed** (Heb. *gālāh*). There is evidence, especially in Ps. 2:11, that *gîl* can refer to any deeply felt emotion, including fear (cf. *BDB*, and especially A. A. Macintosh, *JTS* NS 27 (1976), 1–8), so that "lament" would be a legitimate translation of MT here (so Rudolph, Mays, NEB). NEB also reads *'ālû* in the sense "howl" (cf. Arabic *'awlun*) for *'ālāyw*, **over it** (*HTOT*, p. 248: cf. Rudolph). Others retain *yāgîlû* in its normal sense of "rejoice" (Wolff, NJPS, NIV), but the resulting translations are tortuous.

10:6. Yea, the thing itself: I.e. even the precious calf-image will eventually have to go the way of previous gifts sent to the Assyrians (cf. 5:13).

to the great king: *lᵉmelek yārēb*, as in 5:13, where see the note.

of his idol: MT reads *mēʿᵃṣātô*, "of his plan", which has seemed out of place as a reference to political strategems (a related word occurs in 11:6, where RSV has "fortresses"). RSV, like JB, follows Wellhausen in reading instead *meʿᵃṣabbô*, a word used by Hosea in 4:17, 8:4, 13:2 and 14:9. Others see MT's *mēʿᵃṣātô* as an unusual form of the word for "wood" (*ʿēṣ*), with the same reference (Rudolph, NIV, Jeremias), or derive it from a word *ʿeṣāh* which has been thought to mean "disobedience" on the basis of Syriac and Arabic parallels (so NEB, following Kennicott and G. R. Driver, in *FS Nötscher* (BBB 1), p. 54). In fact "his plan" makes good sense, since the removal of the idol will finally show how ill-conceived Israel's hopes of survival through submission to Assyria were (so Wolff – cf. NJPS and REB), and the political disappointment with which vv. 3–6 began is thus alluded to again at the end of the unit.

10:7. Samaria's king shall perish: The prophet, with some boldness, now speaks directly of the downfall of the reigning **king**, as he does again at the end of the following section (v. 15; cf. 1:4). On **Samaria** see the note on 7:1. As in 8:5–6, it is possible that the name here refers to the northern kingdom as a whole, or rather that part of it which remained free from direct

Assyrian control. The Heb. for **Samaria's king** (lit. "Samaria, her king") is unparalleled (though a similar idiom exists in Akkadian), which has led many commentators to punctuate the verse differently: "Samaria shall perish, her king (shall be) like a twig [see below] on the face of the waters" (Wolff, JB), which others paraphrase with "Samaria and her king shall perish like . . ." (NEB, NIV – on the type of parallelism presupposed cf. Watson, *Classical Hebrew Poetry*, p. 157).

like a chip: The meaning of Heb. *qesep* here is uncertain, but *qᵉṣāpāh* in Jl 1:7 ("splintered") is surely related and this supports the rendering **chip** or better "twig" (cf. LXX, Syr.) rather than the "foam" of AV and NJPS (cf. Targ., Vulg., Ibn Janaḥ, and H. R. (C.) Cohen, *JANES* 2/1 (1969), 25–29 and *Biblical Hapax Legomena*, pp. 24–25). For Arabic cognates cf. J. Blau, *VT* 5 (1955), 343. In either case the image conveys the helplessness of the **king** as the irresistible doom strikes.

10:8. The high places of Aven: Heb. "and the high places . . .", probably underlining the fact that the destruction of the sanctuaries would be the consequence of the collapse of political leadership. **high places** (Heb. *bāmôt*) occurs only here in Hosea: apart from some places where it refers to a natural feature ("high ground", e.g. Mic. 1:3; 3:12) or a part of the body (Job 9:8; Dt. 33:29), this word clearly refers to a man-made place of sacrifice which was not necessarily on high ground (cf. P. H. Vaughan, *The Meaning of* "bamâ" *in the Old Testament* (SOTSMS 3), Cambridge, 1974, pp. 29–31). The precise scope of the term remains a matter of dispute: Vaughan (pp. 31–35) and M. Haran, *Temples and Temple-Service in Ancient Israel*, Oxford, 1978, pp. 18–25, argue that it means a kind of altar (cf. the LXX rendering here and in some other passages), but some passages are more compatible with the view that it referred to a complete shrine (e.g. 1 Kg. 3:2). In any event, it is clear from other passages that the worship at the **high places** is also referred to in 4:13–14 and probably in 10:1–2, and that a term which was originally neutral (1 Sam. 9:12–25) came in later editorial strata of the OT to denote a place which was by definition one of illicit religious practices (e.g. 2 Kg. 17:11). W. F. Albright's theory that they were connected with funerary practices has been refuted by Vaughan, pp. 15–20, and W. B. Barrick, *VT* 25 (1975), 565–95. See further

TDOT, vol. 2, 139–45, and Balz-Cochois, *Gomer*, passim. There can be little doubt that Hosea's polemic in passages such as this (cf. **the sin of Israel**) made an important contribution to a change in attitude towards the **high places**. The rendering **of Aven** presupposes that Heb. *'āwen* is here short for *bêt 'āwen*, the name used by Hosea for the shrine at Bethel (cf. 4:15, 10:5 and the notes). The plural **high places**, however, unless it is a mocking plural of majesty, suggests that *'āwen* should be taken in its ordinary sense of "wickedness" (NIV, JB: see the note on "evildoers" in 6:8), and the reference will then be to the multitude of shrines throughout the land (cf. v. 1, and 4:13).

Thorn and thistle shall grow up: For this picture of the abandoned **altars** cf. 9:6, though the word for **thorn** is different there. **grow up** (*ya'ᵃleh*) is a verb also used of sacrifices (cf. 1 Kg. 18:29), so its use may be ironical.

on their altars: The antecedent of **their** is **Israel**, who are also the subject of the verb in the next line. The reference to the **altars** recalls vv. 1–2 and holds the whole unit together by means of an inclusion.

and they shall say . . . : There is again some irony in the appeal to the **mountains** and **hills** for protection, as these were mentioned together before as places of sacrifice in 4:13. The sense appears to be that the people will choose to be buried alive rather than fall into the hands of the cruel invaders, of whom Hosea speaks in 10:14–15, 11:6. Alternatively, perhaps it is from Yahweh, conceived as a wild animal (cf. 5:14; 13:7–8) that they are thought to seek refuge. Only here in this unit is there any hint of the consequences for the common people of this coming catastrophe.

TWO ORACLES OF COMING WAR

10:9–15

This is a passage where the interpretation of certain words (see the detailed notes) and the sequence of thought pose exceptional difficulties, even where the general meaning of individual verses is plain enough. 10:9 clearly begins a new "historical retrospect" (cf. 9:10; 10:1) and vv. 14–15 bring the threat of judgment to a climax which is comparable to those which conclude the two preceding sections (cf. also 11:5–7). There is some continuity of theme between vv. 9–10 and 13b–15, while vv. 11–13a seem to be held together by the repeated use of agricultural metaphors. But recent commentators have generally agreed that the passage falls into three clear sub-sections, which were originally quite independent of one another or formed separate parts of a dialogue between Hosea and his audience. On this latter view they can only be related to one another by assuming that the prophet takes up real or anticipated objections to what he has said from his audience (Wolff). The first sub-section (vv. 9–10) is a typical judgment-oracle comprising accusation and announcement of judgment, and the third is of a similar type, although clear indications of divine speech are missing in this case. The middle section (vv. 11–13a) contains no explicit threat, only an indictment, but the latter is reinforced by what are seen as references to Yahweh's election of Israel (v. 11b) and his original instructions to her. On this view v. 12 is not addressed directly to Hosea's contemporaries as a call to repentance but expresses in pictorial language the demands of the covenant laid upon Israel as a "yoke" in the distant past – demands which, as v. 13a makes clear, she has failed to fulfil. In this way some coherence can, it is suggested, be given to the very varied speech-forms of the central section and, according to Wolff, the abrupt changes of subject in vv. 11 and 13a are due to the need to relate the message of judgment to the election traditions and reply to an objection raised by a representative of the royal court.

There are, however, a number of reasons for doubting this widely held interpretation, and the passage seems to require an explanation which takes much greater account of redactional activity. It should first be noted that at several points the text speaks in the past tense not only about the sin of Israel but also about her punishment: "so I have come . . ." in v. 10 (cf. LXX), "you have eaten the fruit . . ." in v. 13, and especially both parts of v. 15 (see the note). This reflects the perspective of one standing after the event, and it is at least possible that in these verses we are dealing with interpolations into an original text which spoke of the disaster as still in the future.

There are also a number of reasons why the account of the middle section (11–13a) given above is far from satisfactory.

Those who adopt it refer v. 11b to the past. But the Heb.
imperfects there are more naturally taken to point to the future.
In addition, it is doubtful whether Hosea would have used the
image of a yoke to refer to the covenant relationship, as he
elsewhere portrays it in quite different terms (cf. 2:15), while
the idea of a yoke seems to be used to describe bondage to an
alien power (11:4, possibly 11:7). In any case, it is particularly
difficult to view v. 12 as words addressed to Israel's ancestors.
The necessary words of introduction (e.g. "I said") are missing,
it is not clear why repentance (signified by breaking up the fallow
ground) should then have been enjoined, and there is no point in
the words **it is time to seek the LORD**. The two latter features fit
much better into Hosea's own times, and it is especially plausible
to associate them with the similar passage in 6:1–3, which, as
we have argued above, belongs to the situation after the fall of
Samaria, when Hosea (or his followers) may have sought to
continue his ministry among the survivors of the catastrophe.
This is also a likely setting, as we have seen, for some other parts
of the text which seem to speak about judgment as already past.
On the other hand, the passage does contain sections which look
forward to judgment and justify it in typical prophetic style by
reference to the people's sins (vv. 9, 10b, perhaps 11, 13b–14).
These must have been uttered before the fall of Samaria.

The nucleus of the passage therefore appears to consist of two
judgment-oracles. The first comprises most of vv. 9–11; if v. 10a
was present at this stage, the first verb was presumably future
in meaning (*waw* consecutive plus perfect), and the past tense
implied by LXX is due to a subsequent reorientation of the
text. Both accusation and announcement of judgment display
a developed typological reading of Jg. 19–21 which finds its
closest parallel in Hos. 2; the detailed correspondences are
set out by Wolff, p. 184, and Jeremias, pp. 133–34. In v. 11
the prophet introduces the picture of the farm animal which
he had earlier used (4:16) to portray Israel's disobedience.
Its first part contrasts Ephraim's present rebelliousness with
her original willingness to obey Yahweh: the conjunction w^e
which links this verse to v. 10 in MT (and is ignored in
modern translations) should be translated "But". The picture
is then extended to embody a repetition of the announcement of

judgment in the form of subjection to a yoke and a harder and unrewarding task.

The second judgment-oracle (vv. 13b–14) is addressed to a singular "you" who bears some position of responsibility (cf. **your people** in v. 14) and may well be the king. The redactor who added v. 15 (see below) may still have been aware of this (cf. **the king of Israel**). In this case too the accusation precedes the announcement of judgment, which is reinforced by a comparison with a well-known atrocity. The use of this *exemplum* is quite different from those in Am. 1–2, which appear among the accusations levelled against neighbouring peoples (cf. 11:8 for a similar use of an older tradition by Hosea). In this case the charge is a misplaced faith in military might. This is an unusual theme for Hosea (8:14 is a later addition; cf. the introduction to ch. 8), but one which finds a parallel in Deuteronomy (17:16) as well as in later prophecies of Isaiah (30:16; 31:1). On the general theme of misplaced trust see *TDOT*, vol. 2, 90–92.

After Samaria had fallen and her king had been deposed, the second oracle was supplemented by a redactor who used the plural "you" (vv. 13a, 15) to refer it to the whole people, to indicate that they had indeed reaped what they had sown (the thought is already in 8:7) and the prophet's words had come true. V. 10a may have been modified at the same time (cf. above) with a similar intention. A further addition was v. 12, which offered hope of restoration by employing the same language of sowing and reaping in a positive sense. This saying appears to have been known to Jeremiah (cf. Jer. 4:3). Perhaps it was only after these redactional additions had been made that vv. 9–11, which also threatened war and used an agricultural metaphor (albeit one comparing Israel to a farm animal rather than to a farmer), were prefaced to vv. 12–15. In due course **Judah** was inserted in v. 11 to extend its application to the southern kingdom, perhaps only after the fall of Jerusalem to the Babylonians (cf. on 5:5).

The occasion of the delivery of the original oracles can only be conjectured. V. 13b implies a time of military strength and confidence which might be soon after the conclusion of the alliance with Damascus c. 734, or alternatively some time during the short reign of Shalmaneser V (727–722), when Israel had Egyptian support (2 Kg. 17:4). The historical reference in v.

14 (see the note) perhaps lends slight support to the second alternative, which also fits the location of this passage after vv. 1–8.

10:9. From the days of Gibeah: This time the "original sin" of Israel is identified, as in 9:9, with the outrage committed against a Levite's concubine by the citizens of a town of Benjamin (Jg. 19–21: on the location of **Gibeah** see the note on 5:8). As then, **war** is destined to follow, and it will be **nations** (better "peoples") who are **gathered against them**, not merely the other Israelite tribes (as in Jg. 20:11). **Gibeah** was vulnerable to attack from the south (cf. 5:8), but its mention here may be an instance of "theological geography", with the whole kingdom or its capital being referred to as "a second Gibeah" (cf. Mays).

you have sinned, O Israel: LXX reads "Israel sinned", which is more consistent with the literary form of vv. 9–11.

they have continued: This is a possible meaning for *'āmᵉdû* lit. "they have stood" (cf. Ru. 2:7; Ec. 8:3), and there is no justification for inserting "in rebellion" (so NEB, adding *ûmārᵉdû* after the paraphrastic rendering of Targ.).

10:10. I will come against the wayward people: For **I will come** MT has "in my desire", i.e. "when I please" (NIV). RSV adopts an emendation based on LXX and Targ.; the emended text can also be rendered "I have come" (Wolff, Mays, NEB). The idea of a "coming" of Yahweh to help his people was known in Israel's liturgical traditions (e.g. Jg. 5:4; Ps. 80:2 (where a different Heb. verb is used) – cf. Exod. 20:24 and *TDOT*, vol. 2, 44–49), and Hos. 6:3 and 10:12 draw positively on this tradition. Here, however, as often, a familiar term is given an unexpected and doom-laden use by one of the prophets (see below on v. 15 and compare Amos' handling of traditional ideas). The words **against the wayward people** are in MT connected with v. 9, as in JB and NIV, but grammar and style are improved if they are taken with v. 10 (so also NEB).

when they are chastised: RSV follows Vss., which appear to be based on a slightly different Heb. text from MT. MT *bᵉ'osrām* gives "when they are bound" or, according to a suggestion of Nyberg adopted in NEB, "in hordes" (cf. Driver, *JTS* 39 (1938), 272–73). This latter view is based on a comparison with Arabic *bi'asrihum* and involves an unnecessary recourse to comparative philology. REB, "to chastise them", represents the acceptance of a popular emendation (cf. *BHS*) instead.

for their double iniquity: So the versions other than Targ. and most modern translations. It is not generally recognized that MT *'ōnōtām* implies not this but the interpretation given by Targ., "like the binding of the team [sc. of oxen] to its two rings [sc. of the yoke]" (cf. *'ayin* in later Heb., e.g. M. Kel. 21:2), which fits in well with the ploughing metaphors of the following verses. It is, however, an extremely odd way to introduce the metaphor, and the usual interpretation (reading *'ǎwōnōtām*) is probably correct. The **double iniquity** has been variously explained (for similar phrases cf. Isa. 47:9, 51:19, and especially Jer. 2:13). In the context it most likely refers to ancient and more recent **iniquity** (on *'āwôn* see the note on **corruption** in 7:1).

10:11. This short unit (see the introduction to this section) concludes with a further image (cf. 9:10; 10:1) expressing the contrast between **Ephraim**'s original disposition and her (sin and) coming punishment. A related comparison is made in 4:16; see also 11:7 for a possible reference to the **yoke** as a figure for subjection.

and I spared her fair neck: I.e. Yahweh did not subject her to the burden of being a draught-animal. **spared** is literally "passed by" (Heb. *'ābartî*): cf. Mic. 7:18 and Harper, p. 354. Many commentators emend this phrase, without versional support, to yield the translation "I have laid a yoke on her fair neck" (so Rudolph, Mays, NEB, JB, NIV: cf. *BHS* and *HTOT*, p. 248, for the emended Heb.), but this is unnecessary and (unless the verb is unjustifiably rendered in the future) introduces the image of the yoke too soon.

I will put Ephraim to the yoke: Heb. *hirkîb* is commonly used of making a person ride an animal, and its unique use here has been much discussed. Two recent suggestions are that the verb in fact basically means "to drive", which would fit the situation of ploughing (S. Mowinckel, *VT* 12 (1962), 285), or that it may mean "to fit together, harness" (S. P. Brock, *VT* 18 (1968), 395–97). In any case the general sense is clear and there is no place for more outlandish conjectures such as that of NJPS, "do advance plowing" (cf. Arabic *krb*).

Judah must plough: The reference to **Judah** is generally regarded as an addition designed to make Hosea's threat applicable also to the southern kingdom: either "Israel" originally stood in its place (JB) or the subject of **must plough** was "he", referring to **Ephraim** (NEB). The former suggestion is preferable, as "Israel" can function as a middle term which in different senses is parallel both to **Ephraim** (cf. v. 6) and **Jacob** (12:12). Wolff has questioned whether **Judah** need be redactional, in the light of the possible reference of **Jacob**, which Hosea only uses elsewhere in 12:2, 12, to the whole tribal league, and in 5:8–14 we have followed the common view that the references to **Judah** are original. But it remains probable that both here and in 12:2 **Judah** belongs to a secondary level of the text (cf. the careful review of both contexts by Emmerson, *Hosea*, pp. 63–65 and 83–6).

10:12. The prophet extends the agricultural metaphor into an exhortation, with two differences: Israel is now compared to a farmer rather than to his animal, and the ethical terms **righteousness** and **steadfast love** (*ḥesed*: cf. on 2:19) displace the threat of judgment conveyed in v. 11. The Heb. actually reads "sow *in* righteousness" (cf. NEB) and "reap *according to* steadfast love", and the two commands may be equivalent to a conditional promise (cf. *GK* §110i and Num. 5:19), especially if **righteousness** refers to what is expected by Yahweh of Israel and **steadfast love** is (unusually for Hosea) what she can expect of him. For the imagery of sowing and reaping cf. 8:7 and the note.

break up your fallow ground: The same image is used in Jer. 4:3, in a similar context: its most obvious meaning is that something neglected is to be attended to, something unfruitful is to be transformed by cultivation. In both prophetic contexts it is natural to see this as a picture of repentance (compare the next phrase).

for it is time to seek the LORD: NEB (cf. *BHS*) emends to *kî 'ēt* to get this meaning, which is indicated in the Peshitta and the Lucianic text of LXX (cf. *HTOT*, p. 248). But the change is unnecessary, as MT's *wᵉ'ēt* can have the same sense (cf. *GK* §158a and Ps. 60:13). That it is now high time **to seek the LORD** is evidently the underlying meaning of the preceding image. Compare 5:15 and 6:1, 3; although different Heb. words are used there, the sense is similar. This seeking is scarcely that of ordinary worship (according to 5:6 this is in vain), but refers, like the uses of *dāraš* in Am. 5:4–6, to a penitential act in a time of crisis, probably detached from the sanctuaries, to which Hosea and Amos (or their disciples) summoned the people. See Hunter, *Seek the Lord!*, pp. 71–79.

that he may come and rain salvation upon you: The language is commonly related to 6:3 and 14:5; in the latter case a penitential prayer precedes. Compare also Isa. 45:8. Yahweh's coming is in fact a return, in view of his withdrawal from his people according to 5:6 and 15. **salvation** is Heb. *ṣedeq*, a word whose meaning ranges between "(act of) righteousness" and "(act of) salvation" (see on **righteousness** in 2:21). Since a cognate word, *ṣedāqāh*, lies behind **righteousness** earlier in this verse, NEB ("just measure of rain") and NIV ("righteousness") seek to bring out the play on words and the ethical element in Yahweh's response. There is indeed an ethical element, but it is in no sense an idea of reward or merit: as 11:8 makes clear, it is Yahweh's own consistency as a God of compassion and **steadfast love** which in the end gives ground for hope, not a *do ut des* conception of religion.

The verb translated **rain** (cf. 6:3 **waters**) more commonly means "teach", and it is sometimes so understood here (cf. Hunter, p. 154 n. 2, for references, to which NJPS, "obtain a teacher of righteousness", should be added). This seems less appropriate to the context, but such an understanding of the text may have contributed to the title "Teacher of Righteousness" used by the Qumran sectaries of their founder (see CD 6:11 (*DSSE*, p. 103), and the commentaries on Jl 2:23).

10:13. The first three statements of the verse continue the agricultural metaphor and the direct address of v. 12, but in the form of statements about what has already happened (there is no manuscript support for the change to "and you shall eat the fruit of lies" proposed in *BHS* and adopted by NJPS). The third statement, and probably also the second, indicates the consequences of Israel's **iniquity** or "wickedness" (*rešaʿ*, only here in Hosea). The **lies** are most probably the duplicity shown in dealings with foreign powers (cf. 7:11; 10:4; 12:1–2), although Hosea has already condemned **lying** in a more general sense in

4:2 (*kaḥēš*, the same root as here), and 7:3 uses the same word of court intrigues.

Because you have trusted in your chariots: The **you** here (and throughout the remainder of this verse and v. 14) is singular, rather than the plural form used in vv. 12–13a. This recalls the initial address in v. 9 according to MT, and the point here may be to indict the collective policy of the nation. Another possibility is that vv. 13b–14 are addressed directly to **the king**, whose downfall is explicitly referred to in v. 15 (where the address is once again in the plural to **the house of Israel**). **chariots** follows LXX's reading, with most modern commentators and versions: it makes for an excellent parallel to **warriors**, whereas MT's "your way" (*darkᵉkā*, which is only slightly different in the Heb. consonantal text) is vague and general. The chariotry of Samaria was renowned (cf. *ANET*, p. 279, for Ahab's contribution to the anti-Assyrian coalition at Qarqar, and S. Dalley, *Iraq* 47 (1985), 31–48, for the later use of Samarian officers in the Assyrian army) and a natural source of pride. If MT is retained it should perhaps be related to an alternative use of the root *drk* for "strength", which is paralleled in Ugaritic and may occur in Prov. 31:3 (so NIV: cf. Kuhnigk, p. 89, *HAL*, p. 223).

10:14. among your people: Or "against" (Heb. *bᵉ*) **your people**. JB changes one consonant of the Heb. to read "in your towns" (cf. Wellhausen, *BHS*); Kuhnigk, p. 125, maintains that MT can mean this, with references to other instances in Heb. and Ugaritic. There is no difficulty with the usual interpretation.

as Shalman destroyed Beth-Arbel: An event of exceptional cruelty, which was well known to Hosea's hearers, is evidently referred to here: compare the allusions in Am. 1–2, which may in some cases have long preceded the prophet's own time. Neither of the proper names here is without problems. Three interpretations of **Shalman** are possible, and the choice between them affects the identification of **Beth-Arbel**, a place not mentioned elsewhere in the Bible or in contemporary texts. **Shalman** may be a short form of the Assyrian name Shalmaneser, in which case the reference might be to the campaigns of Shalmaneser III (858–824: cf. *CAH*, III/1, p. 489), or more probably to those of Shalmaneser V (727–722), the eventual conqueror of Samaria according to 2 Kg. 18:9–10. 2 Kg. 17:3 records that he "came up against" Israel early in his reign, and **Beth-Arbel** may have been destroyed at this time. Alternatively **Shalman** may represent Salamanu, the name of a king of Moab who paid tribute to Tiglath-pileser III along with Ahaz of Judah c. 735–733 (*ANET*, p. 282). In this case a Transjordanian location for **Beth-Arbel** is preferable, either at Irbid (Aharoni, *Land of the Bible*, 2nd ed., p. 431; Abel, *Géographie*, vol. II, 267) or on the Moabite-Israelite border (Wolff). But there is no evidence that Salamanu made any such raids to the north. If one of the Assyrian kings is meant it is also possible to identify **Beth-Arbel** with one of the two places named Arbela in Galilee, which are mentioned in later texts (for details see M. Avi-Yonah, *Gazetteer of Roman Palestine* (Qedem 5), Jerusalem, 1976, p. 30).

mothers ... with their children: Elsewhere this phrase refers to real mothers and their offspring, whether human (Gen. 32:12) or animal (Dt. 22:6–7), and the verb **dashed in pieces** is particularly used of the slaughter of **children** (e.g. 2 Kg. 8:12; Hos. 13:16). The reference is therefore less likely to be to "a mother-city and its dependencies" (Wolff, *KB*) – the latter are in any case usually referred to as "daughters" – than to the horrifying atrocities themselves which were soon to be repeated (cf. 13:16).

10:15. The text of this verse has been transmitted in two different forms. RSV, like JB and recent commentators (see also Emmerson, *Hosea*, pp. 131–32), follows LXX in reading it as a reference to a future judgment (**it shall be done**) upon **the house of Israel**. However, the verb at the beginning of the verse in MT is most naturally taken to refer to the past and it speaks not of **the house of Israel** but of "Bethel" (on both points the other Vss. agree). This text could be translated either "Thus has Bethel done to you . . ." or "Thus he [i.e. God] has done to you, O Bethel . . ." For the variation between "Bethel" (= "house of God") and **house of Israel** cf. the similar situation in Am. 5:6. The MT reading looks like a comment added after the event, pointing out how the city and shrine of Bethel were indeed destroyed in accordance with Hosea's threat (cf. v. 8). The LXX reading (which in fact has "I will do . . .", not **it shall be done**) appears to generalize the saying by making it apply to the whole people, while also rendering it as a future threat in closer conformity with the rest of the passage.

In the storm: MT, supported by most of the Vss., reads "at dawn", implying that **the king** quickly succumbed (cf. below) to an enemy attack. There may be deliberate irony in the expression, since it was a widespread belief that "in the morning" Yahweh would come to his people's aid (cf. Ps. 143:8 and *TDOT* vol. 2, 226–28). RSV's **In the storm** follows a once-popular but wholly conjectural emendation first suggested by Wellhausen (*bassa‛ar* for *baššaḥar*): most other versions and recent commentators rightly retain MT.

shall be utterly cut off: The verb is that which is rendered **perish** in v. 7. The form (Heb. perfect) may have a past meaning (cf. Vss.), and it is attractive to see a correlation being made here between Hosea's threat in v. 7 and the actual course of events recorded in 2 Kg. 17:4–5, according to which the recalcitrant **king** Hoshea was imprisoned by the Assyrians at the very beginning (cf. "in the morning") of their final campaign against Samaria.

DIVINE LOVE – SLIGHTED BUT NOT EXTINGUISHED

11:1–11

The last of the present series of "historical retrospects" (further examples occur in 13:1–3, 4–11: cf. also 12:2–9, 12–13) goes well beyond the others in its scope, since for the first time it incorporates the Exodus from Egypt and, even more strikingly, a confident expression of hope for renewal after the coming judgment (vv. 10–11). V. 1 is clearly a new beginning, while the end of the section is (unusually for Hosea, but cf. 2:13) marked by the oracle-formula, "says the Lord". 11:12 is more closely linked by its subject-matter to 12:1 and even to 12:2–9 than it is to what precedes it, so that the Heb. chapter division, which makes it the first verse of the next chapter, is more natural. Most of the present section is in the form of a divine speech about Israel/Ephraim, but v. 8 and part of v. 9 are directly addressed to Israel as **you**, and in v. 10 Yahweh is unusually referred to in the third person (MT also has some third-person forms in v. 3, but these are inferior readings: see the note). Vv. 1–7 exhibit a common structure, with accusation predominating in vv. 1–4 and announcement of judgment in 5–7, but the accusations are reinforced by being set against the background of divine acts of love towards Israel (vv. 1, 3a, 4), which also form the basis for the quite new element in vv. 8–11. Here divine self-questioning and reconsideration leads to an abandonment of the total extinction of Israel, but it is clear from vv. 10–11 that the punishment of exile has not been eliminated, even if it is no longer seen as permanent.

The text is in places difficult to restore and interpret with certainty (see the detailed notes), and in some cases the problems affect major issues of exegesis. Wolff has argued that the imperfect verbs in vv. 5a and 6 are not futures but (iterative) presents, embodying respectively an accusation (cf. 7:11) and an interpretation of disasters that are already under way, so that the historical review continues to v. 7 (similarly Mays). On this view there is no announcement of a decision about the future until vv. 8–11. This certainly reduces the tension between different parts of the passage, but it is scarcely possible to understand v. 5 at least in the way suggested. Rudolph seeks to ease the transition to v. 8 in a different way, by finding in v. 7 a statement about a future penitential response resulting from the catastrophe (as in 5:15 etc.), but his detailed exegesis of the verse is unsound (see the notes). On both these views see further Jeremias, in *Die Botschaft und die Boten*, pp. 226–31. Jeremias himself finds it necessary to assume that some time must have elapsed between vv. 6 and 7, to leave space for the failure to respond to Hosea's message which the latter verse presupposes. Hence he regards vv. 1–6 and 7–11 as two separate rhetorical units. While this is possible, it is not necessary, for the failure to respond may not relate specifically to the message in vv. 1–6, but to Hosea's preaching more generally: for Israel's long-standing obstinacy cf. v. 2 and also 4:16 and 5:4.

The disagreements over vv. 8–11 raise deeper issues about the nature and coherence of Hosea's preaching, and indeed about the history of classical prophecy in general. There is no doubt that these verses as they are most naturally understood involve the renunciation of some statements made elsewhere in the book (see especially 5:6; 8:5; 13:9, 14). A number of commentators have consequently argued that the words are either secondary additions or in fact capable of being interpreted in a threatening sense. Wellhausen and Nowack saw v. 8a as threatening and vv. 8b–11 as non-Hosean, while Marti extended the threatening interpretation to the whole of vv. 8–9 (cf. Robinson and the two editions of Peake's Commentary) and regarded vv. 10–11 as inauthentic. These views no longer find much of a following (except in relation to v. 10), partly for reasons discussed in the notes below and partly because it no longer seems necessary to deny that a prophet may have modified his message in the course of time (cf. von Rad, *OT Theology*, vol. 2, 129–30; Fohrer, *Studien*, p. 233). But there remain some doubts about the unity of the passage which have in part a similar basis. Thus Fohrer regards vv. 8–9 as a quite separate oracle from 1–7, although both are by Hosea (*Studien*, pp. 222–24, *Introduction to the OT*, p. 422; cf. Vollmer, *Geschichtliche Rückblicke*, pp. 60–61). This view rests in part on form-critical considerations, and it can be traced back to H. Gressmann's pioneering application of Gunkel's insights to the prophetic literature (cf. *Die älteste Geschichtsschreibung*, pp. 372–37). But it also results from the belief that there can be no direct route from the judgment-oracle of vv. 1–7 to the salvation-oracle in vv. 8ff.: according to Fohrer these passages belong respectively to the first and third phases of the development of Hosea's message. The form-critical argument is of little weight in itself, since Hosea's sayings do not as a whole conform rigidly to well-known patterns to the extent that, e.g., those of Amos do. Moreover, when the two sections of the passage are examined in detail, it appears that the latter does not contradict anything which has been said in the former, and in fact they belong so closely together that an original association between them is very likely. It is no coincidence that it is specifically this historical retrospect, which contains the strongest affirmations about Yahweh's love for Israel and several images which particularly emphasize his gracious provision (vv. 1, 3, 4; cf. the return of the designation "my people" in v. 7), which is followed by the **How can I . . . ?** of v. 8. It is precisely as Israel's apostasy is shown in the worst possible light by contrast with Yahweh's generosity to her that the question is unexpectedly raised for the prophet, whether Yahweh can after all ultimately abandon his **son**. On the other hand, it is clear that vv. 8–9 presuppose that the full force of Hosea's message of judgment remains, unabated by, for example, a call to renewal through repentance. Moreover, v. 11 (which Fohrer regards as a later addition) answers precisely to the threat in v. 5 and presupposes that it or something like it has preceded. Far from it being the case that the two sections are incompatible with each other, each requires the other if they are to make full sense. This has implications for the development of Hosea's message which are examined more fully in the Introduction.

It remains to consider the import of this passage and the occasion(s) which gave rise to it. It may first be noted that, as is more fully argued in the detailed notes, v. 10 contains a series of additions from a later date, which bring the promise of v. 11 more fully into line with other passages in the book (e.g. 3:5) or with much later conditions and expectations (see below, p. 264–65). The latest of these additions probably was not made until the 5th century B.C., when Israelites had spread much more widely through the surrounding peoples than Hosea himself had anticipated and their regathering was expected to follow on Yahweh's judgment on the Gentiles as a whole. Possibly (see the note) v. 5b is also a later addition. The original oracle is constituted by the remainder of the passage. Commentators who treat it as a unity have not generally considered precisely what modification it made to Hosea's earlier message of judgment. The issue may be stated as follows: do vv. 8–9 embody the expectation that the threat of an Assyrian invasion, with all the consequences indicated in vv. 5–6 and elsewhere in the book, would not after all be realized? Or do they speak of the continuation of Israel's relationship with Yahweh through the imminent catastrophe and as a result portray that catastrophe not in terms of final rejection (9:7) but of chastisement, a term already encountered in Hosea's preaching (cf. 10:10)? In view of the hope expressed in v. 11, which assumes the dispersion of Israel, the latter alternative must be preferred. The coming catastrophe is no longer seen as an expression of Yahweh's "fierce anger" (cf. 8:5) or an inability to reconsider (13:14) or the destruction of a people for whom he no longer has any love (13:9; 9:15), but it will still happen, as the inevitable consequence of Israel's persistent apostasy. The future tenses of vv. 5 and 6 imply that the catastrophe is still to come, i.e. that the oracle was spoken before the fall of Samaria in 722. But it cannot belong much before that date, since 10:1–8 and 9–15 appear to date from well into Hoshea's reign and neither contains such an explicit expression of hope as we find here.

11:1. When Israel was a child: Once again an oracle in this section of the book begins with a historical retrospect, in this case with specific reference to the treasured Exodus tradition. The place which this tradition held in the northern kingdom in Hosea's time can be clearly seen in Ps. 80, especially vv. 8ff., where it forms the basis of an appeal to God for help. **child** (Heb. *na'ar*) need not mean an infant, as in Ezekiel's allegory (Ezek. 16:4–6), and could refer to a boy as old as seventeen (Gen. 37:2). But v. 3 implies that, figuratively speaking, Yahweh's care for Israel began at a very early age.

I loved him: As the sequel shows, the depiction of Yahweh's love in Hosea is not restricted to sexual categories, common as these may be (cf. 2:14; 3:1). A father's love for his child is also a favoured image in the OT (Ps. 103:13), and it is especially well suited to portray the aid which Yahweh graciously gives to his people. It is commonly assumed that it is as a father that Yahweh is portrayed here, but the images used in vv. 3–4 relate to aspects of child-rearing which have traditionally been at least as much the mother's responsibility as the father's. For such a representation of Yahweh cf. Isa. 49:15 and M.-T. Wacker, *Concilium* 206 (1989), 103–111.

I called my son: The use of **called** for the deliverance from **Egypt** is unusual, and it emphasizes the role of the divine word in the Exodus tradition (cf. Exod. 3; also Hos. 12:13). Israel's election seems to be seen here not so much in terms of adoption, as in terms of the call of a prophet (cf. 1 Sam. 3:4ff.; Isa. 49:1), a theme which is developed further in Isa. 43:1, 51:2 and 54:6. The designation of Israel as **my son** also has its roots in Exodus (4:23): it is perhaps the popular counterpart to the Jerusalemite use of this image for the special relationship of the Davidic kings to Yahweh (Pss. 2:7; 89:26; 2 Sam. 7:14). Cf. 1:10, 11:10 (but see the note) and Dt. 1:31, 8:5.

11:2. The more I called them: MT, supported by Targ., Syr. and Vulg., reads "they called to them", which has been taken

to refer either to prophetic teaching (Targ., Rosenmüller) or
to those who would lure Israel away from Yahweh (Vollmer,
Geschichtliche Rückblicke, p. 57f.). It seems unlikely that Hosea
would have left room for such diverse interpretations, and RSV
is probably right to prefer the reading presupposed by LXX,
keqorᵉ̓î instead of *qarᵉ̓û*. The reference will then be to prophetic
calls for repentance (cf. 12:10), one of which survives in a cultic
context in Ps. 81:6–16. The corrupt reading could have arisen
as a result of the mistake made in the transmission of the next
phrase.

the more they went from me: Again RSV follows LXX
with good reason, against MT's "they went away from them",
which is the consequence of running two words, *mippānay*, **from
me**, and *hēm*, **they** (emphatic subject of the next line: cf. 8:4),
into one, *mippᵉnêhem*, "from them". For the meaning cf. 4:10. To
judge from 9:10 this accusation refers to idolatry practised after
the settlement in Canaan.

the Baals: Cf. on 2:13.

and burning incense: The same Heb. (Piel of *qṭr*) is translated by RSV in 4:13 by **make offerings**, and there the same
verb **sacrifice** occurs in the parallel line. JB and NEB render
qṭr here as a reference to offerings in general. The central idea
behind *qṭr* appears to be "making smoke". As a result derivatives
such as *qᵉṭōret* are used for "incense". But the verb often appears
in contexts where sacrifice in general seems to be meant (e.g. Am.
4:5), and the Piel is only occasionally used of incense in particular
(Jer. 44:23: the Hiphil is more common in this latter sense, at
least in the priestly source). JB and NEB should be followed
here. The association of *qṭr* and *zbḥ* (**sacrifice**) is common in
Kings (e.g. 1 Kg. 22:44) and was possibly derived from Hosea.

11:3. who taught Ephraim to walk: The verb has a very
unusual form (Tiphel – cf. *GK* §55h) and meaning, and both
may be characteristic of the north Israelite dialect of Heb.

I took them up in my arms: The Heb. in fact has "he took
them (in what is again a very unusual form, *qāḥām*, though cf.
Ezek. 17:5 for a similar abbreviated form of *lāqaḥ*) in his arms",
but in the middle of a passage expressed in the first person this
cannot be right, and the reading indicated by Vss. is preferred
by all modern translations. The original error may have been due

to dittography, $z^e r\hat{o}\,{}^\prime \bar{o}t\bar{a}yw\;w^e l\bar{o}\,{}^\prime$ being written for $z^e r\hat{o}\,{}^\prime \bar{o}tay\;w^e l\bar{o}\,{}^\prime$, and the verbal form may subsequently have been altered to accord with this (cf. on v. 2).

but they did not know: The expression is analogous to that in 2:8, where see the note.

that I healed them: The metaphor shifts somewhat awkwardly to that of the divine physician, but Hosea has a particular liking for this image (cf. 6:1; 7:1; 14:5 – note also 5:13). The reference is to Yahweh's repeated restoration of his people after a time of trouble, as illustrated, for example, in the saviour-stories in the book of Judges. In other words, a new point is being made: despite the fact that Yahweh had bestowed a father's (or a mother's) care and training on Israel in her early history (and this was a prominent part of her cultic traditions), she failed to recognize that her recovery from periods of political weakness was due to his help. NEB renders "that I harnessed them . . ." and couples these words with the next verse: this assumes that Heb. $r\bar{a}p\bar{a}\,{}^\prime$ could have the meaning "bind" (so G. R. Driver, *JTS* 39 (1938), 162, citing Arabic *rafā*, which is of questionable relevance). There is no justification for departing from the normal meaning here, especially in view of Hosea's predilection for the healing metaphor.

11:4. I led them with cords of compassion: Better "I drew them . . ." (or "I sought to draw them . . .", in view of the imperfect): Heb. *māšak* is used literally of an animal pulling a load (cf. Dt. 21:3; Isa. 5:18) but also metaphorically of any kind of inducement to follow (Exod. 12:21; Jg. 4:6; Job 21:33), including that of a lover (Ca. 1:4). The only **cords** which Yahweh used were those of **compassion**, literally "of man" (Heb. $^\prime\bar{a}d\bar{a}m$). No exact parallel to this use of $^\prime\bar{a}d\bar{a}m$ exists, but it is intelligible in the light of the frequent pairing of $^\prime\bar{a}d\bar{a}m$ with $b^e h\bar{e}m\bar{a}h$, "beast" (these **cords** are such as befit men, not animals) and of the parallel expression **bands of love**. It has been pointed out that both $^\prime\bar{a}d\bar{a}m$ and $^\prime ah^a b\bar{a}h$ (**love**) resemble Arabic words for "leather" (Driver, *JTS* 39 (1938), 161–62: cf. NEB mg.), and in one place $^\prime ah^a b\bar{a}h$ may actually have this meaning in Heb. (Ca. 3:10: cf. *HAL*, p. 18). But such a meaning would be quite inappropriate here, since the point is that Yahweh has treated Israel in a way unlike the use of real **cords** and **bands**, and seeks to draw her to him, albeit without success, only through his **love** for her.

and I became . . . : RSV's interpretation, which follows MT closely, presumes a continued use of imagery drawn from the world of agriculture: Yahweh's consideration for Israel is like that of a kind farmer who **eases the yoke** on the oxen's **jaws**, to give them respite, at least for a time, from their burden (so Targ., Syr., and in more modern times AV, NIV and commentators such as Harper, Rudolph and Jeremias). However, MT as it stands more naturally refers to the lifting of a yoke on to the oxen than to its removal (cf. Aq., Symm., Vulg., NJPS), and there is the added difficulty that a yoke (unlike a bridle: cf. Isa. 30:28) presses not on the **jaws** (or "cheeks", which *lᵉḥî* can also mean) but on the neck or shoulder (cf. Isa. 9:4; 10:27). The efforts made to get round this latter difficulty (G. Dalman, *Arbeit und Sitte in Palästina*, vol. 2, Gütersloh, 1932, pp. 99–100; Rudolph, p. 215, n. 14) are forced and unconvincing. It is therefore preferable to read "I became to them like those who lift a young child [*'ûl* instead of *'ōl*, 'yoke'] to their cheeks", an image drawn, like those in vv. 1 and 3 (and the rest of v. 4), from the nurture of young children (so JB, NEB, following van Hoonacker, Wolff etc.) and developed further in Dt. 1:31 and Isa. 46:3–4 (cf. Num. 11:12–14).

one who eases: MT *mᵉrîmê* is plural, "those who lift . . ." Vss. all imply a singular form, which leads most interpreters to delete a *yodh* and read *mērîm* (cf *BH³*, *BHS*). Kuhnigk (p. 133) follows M. Dahood in retaining the *yodh* as an old genitive (singular) ending: it might equally be regarded as an ending for the construct state of a singular noun (cf. *GK* §90k, and Hos. 10:11). The vocalization of MT would then be due to the misunderstanding of a rare grammatical feature.

and I bent down to them: Heb. *wᵉ'aṭ* (Hiphil of *nāṭāh*) is generally so understood here, and this would fit the image of parent and child well. But the Hiphil is more commonly used of "inclining the ear" to a prayer (e.g. 2 Kg. 19:16; Dan. 9:18), and perhaps even without *'ōzen*, "ear", this could be the meaning here (cf. *BDB*, p. 641a): "I inclined my ear to their cry." **to them** is literally "to him", as from here to the middle of v. 6 the people are referred to by (collective) singular pronouns (except for v. 5b – see below).

and fed them: MT has only "(I) fed": on **them** see the end of the next note. Both verbs in this line are iterative imperfects, like **I led them** earlier in this verse, and represent repeated actions in the past. The theme of Yahweh feeding his people has particular relevance to the wilderness period (Dt. 8:3, 16 etc.), but compare also Hos. 2:8, 15, which refer to the products of the land of Canaan.

11:5. They shall return to the land of Egypt: Cf. 8:13, 9:3 and the notes there. The transition from past blessing to future judgment, without any intervening reference to Israel's sins, is abrupt (though cf. 10:11), but probably deliberately so: thereby the change in Yahweh's attitude and Israel's status, which is adequately justified elsewhere, is shown with particular clarity, and the opposition between this verse and the Exodus allusions in v. 1 emphasizes this. Wolff and others interpret the line as an accusation to complete the common pattern, but this is not necessary and runs counter to Hosea's other uses of the "return to Egypt" theme (see further Jeremias, in *Die Botschaft und die Boten*, pp. 226–29).

MT prefaces *lō'*, "not", to this line, which can be understood (with difficulty) as an exclamation, "No!" (NJPS), or as introducing a question, "Will they not return . . . ?" (NIV). J. A. Soggin, *BiOr* 9 (1967), 42, and Kuhnigk, p. 134, see an instance of emphatic *lamed* here: "Surely they will return . . ." This is possible, but already in LXX there is evidence that *lō'* was being read as *lô*, "to him", and taken with the previous verse as the object of **fed**: hence RSV's **them** there.

. . . to return to me: There is a play on words here, the same verb, *šûb*, lying behind **return** as earlier in the verse. The need for this returning is shown in v. 2, **the more they went from me**. For Israel's failure to **return** cf. 5:4, 7:10: the latter verse is probably redactional, and there is some reason to think the same here (Jeremias, *Die Botschaft und die Boten*, p. 229), although both style and the demands of the context tie the accusation closely to the first part of the verse.

11:6. The sword shall rage against their cities: This and the following lines explicate the threat of a "return to Egypt" in terms of a violent invasion, presumably by the Assyrians, which Hosea anticipates will be the consequence of Israel's sins, especially her scheming with Egypt (cf. the note below on **fortresses**). The verbs have also been understood as iteratives referring to the present (Wolff), implying that these verses were spoken in the middle of a crisis to interpret its meaning to Hosea's disciples (cf. on 7:12). **rage**, Heb. *ḥālāh*, is better rendered "whirl" (cf. Jer. 23:19). For **cities**, Heb. *'ārāyw*, NEB has "blood-spattered altars" (cf. Mic. 5:14), assuming the existence of a Heb. cognate of Arabic *ġariyun*, "stone daubed with blood" (cf. G. R. Driver, *Canaanite Myths and Legends*, Edinburgh, 1956, p. 142 n. 26); but it is unlikely that a **sword** would be used to demolish altars, and in other respects too this theory is unsatisfactory (cf. E. W. Nicholson, *VT* 27 (1977), 113–17). REB rightly reverts to "cities".

the bars of their gates: The meaning of Heb. *baddāyw* here is not at all clear. *bad* seems to mean "bar" in Job 17:16 and it is often used for "pole" in the priestly source (e.g. Exod. 25:13). But since **consume** (Heb. *klh* Piel) commonly has a personal object, several commentators see here another word *bad*, meaning "idle talkers" (so NEB, "their prattling priests": cf. Isa. 44:25; Jer. 50:36). This word would make a good parallel to "counsels" in the next line if it were taken to refer to the politicians of the day (Wolff), since it evidently carries connotations of boasting and pride (cf. Isa. 16:6; Jer. 48:30). The emendation to *bānāyw*, "their sons" (Weiser, JB, *BHS*), has no ancient support and produces a weak sense.

in their fortresses: RSV quite unnecessarily adopts a conjectural emendation which goes back to Wellhausen. MT means "because of their schemings" (NEB; cf. NIV, NJPS), and its reading is supported by LXX, Symm., Syr. and Targ. The noun used here also occurs in Ps. 81:12 (a north Israelite psalm) and elsewhere.

11:7. My people: In line with 1:9, this expression is not often found after the early chapters of Hosea (but cf. 6:11). Its reappearance here serves to underline the pathos of Yahweh's rejection by Israel. The Heb. in fact reads "*But* my people . . .": despite the judgment that is threatened (or, on Wolff's view, already beginning), Israel is unmoved. In view of this connection Jeremias' proposal (see the introduction to the chapter) to see v. 7 as the beginning of a new sub-section is unacceptable.

are bent on turning from me: The verb tālāh/tālā' normally means "hang", and there is no close parallel in Heb. to the usage presumed by RSV here. But cognate words in Syriac and Ethiopic are sometimes used for "attachment" (cf. E. A. Speiser, *JBL* 44 (1925), 190; *BDB*, p. 1068a), and the same semantic development may have occurred in Heb. This renders unnecessary emendations such as those favoured by JB and Mays (see *BHS* for details); Rudolph's bold mitlā'îm, "strive after", has the additional disadvantage of requiring a unique meaning for the root l'h. **turning**, Heb. meṣûbāh, is derived from the same root as **return** in v. 5, but regularly denotes a **turning** away from Yahweh (cf. 14:4 ("faithlessness"); Jer. 2:19 etc.), so that there can be no question of this verse referring to penitence on Israel's part (Rudolph).

so they are appointed to the yoke, and none shall remove it: The Heb. of this line and its meaning are, in Wolff's words, "quite uncertain". A literal rendering of MT would be: "To 'al [which could mean "above"] they call him/them, together he shall not raise up." LXX presupposes a similar Heb. text, corrupted at certain points, and is of no help here. Most recent commentators have opted for one of two approaches to the problems, each of which has a long history. The difference between them centres on their treatment of 'al. RSV, following the example of Aq., Symm., Th., Vulg. and probably Targ., reads 'ōl, "a yoke", for 'al, and regards this as the object of "raise up" (cf. Harper). Others find in 'al the name or title of a pagan deity to whom Israel vainly turns in time of trouble instead of to Yahweh: either ba'al, "Baal", is read instead (JB – cf. Wolff, Mays), or 'al itself is taken to be a title for Baal, meaning "Most High" (so already in AV, following Ibn Ezra and Kimchi, and now in NEB and JB: cf. Nyberg, *Studien*, pp. 88–89, Kuhnigk, pp. 137–38, and Jeremias ad loc.). Compare the notes above on 7:16, where similar uncertainties exist. The line thus either reaffirms the political subjection already announced in vv. 5–6 or extends Yahweh's complaint about Israel's fruitless apostasy, which is its cause.

11:8. However the end of the previous verse is to be understood, it ends on a note of helplessness for Israel, to which vv. 8–9 gradually but graphically present an answer, by means of a rare glimpse into the complex motives that operate in Yahweh's character. These verses have often been described as the high point of the book of Hosea, but it is more accurate to call them its pivot or turning point, since it is in other passages, especially 2:14–23 and 14:4–8, that the consequences of this divine "change of heart" are most fully and profoundly expounded. But their significance is not at all diminished by this, the more so since a central strand in classical prophecy (seen in Jeremiah, Ezekiel, Deutero-Isaiah and Jonah) takes its theological justification ultimately from them.

How can I give you up, O Ephraim ... : These questions must be understood, as they generally are today, as an expression of Yahweh's anguish at the prospect of totally abandoning his people (v. 7), who are like a son to him (v. 1). For the exclamatory **How** used in this way cf. Gen. 39:9, Ps. 137:4. To read these lines, as once was popular, as a threat (so Wellhausen, Marti etc.: cf. Jer. 3:19 for such a use of "How") would produce a grotesque picture of Yahweh gloating over the prospect of the destruction of his people which is totally at odds with Hosea's thinking elsewhere. Such an interpretation can also only prevail if v. 8b is regarded as an interpolation or as expressing an inclination to compassion which Yahweh repudiates, and neither of these views is convincing. The underlying reason for this reading of the verse is the same as that which still leads others to deny that vv. 8–9 can be a continuation of vv. 1–7, namely the assumption that the aspects of threat and promise in them are irreconcileable. But, as we have argued above (in the introduction to this chapter), it is precisely the unusually drawn-out reflection on Yahweh's love and care for his people in the past (vv. 1, 3–4) which permits the change of intention which begins to emerge in v. 8, and, on the other side, v. 8 itself has its point of departure in nothing other than the threats which appear in vv. 5–6 (and, on one interpretation, 7).

hand you over: Heb. *māgan* was until recently thought to be related to *māgēn*, "shield", hence the curious renderings of LXX, Vulg. and AV (cf. *BDB*, p. 171). But, as Targ. and Symm. saw, the context requires the meaning **hand you over**, and it is now clear that etymologically *māgan* (also in Gen. 14:20; Prov. 4:9) is related not to *māgēn* (root *gnn*) but to words in other Semitic languages with the sense "give", such as Phoenician and Ugaritic *mgn*, and to *maggān*, "gift", in later Hebrew (*HAL*, p. 517). It is possible that Hos. 4:18 contains a derivative of this root (see the note on **shame more than their glory** there).

like Admah ... like Zeboiim: Dt. 29:22 links these two names with Sodom and Gomorrah as places which were legendary for their sin and their total devastation in early times (cf. Gen. 19:24–28). Gen. 14:2, 8 also associate them with Sodom and Gomorrah (and a fifth city named Bela or Zoar) in an alliance. Tradition placed these cities in the Jordan valley (cf. Gen. 10:19; 13:10–12), but no precise identification of them is possible, if they even existed. The much-publicized claim that their names occur in documents from Ebla of the third millenium BC has been refuted as far as **Admah** and **Zeboiim** are concerned and remains unconfirmed in the other cases (cf. R. D. Biggs, *BA* 43 (1980), 78, 82; J. F. Healey, *ExpT* 91 (1979/80), 327).

My heart recoils within me: recoils is literally "is turned" (*nehpak*), which could refer either to mental disorientation (cf. Lam. 1:20) or to a change of purpose (cf. Exod. 14:5). In the present case the latter is more probable (so NEB, NIV and NJPS: see also the next note): for **heart** (Heb. *lēb*) as the locus of purpose and will see Wolff, *Anthropology*, pp. 40–58. **within me** is literally "upon me" (*'ālay*), a strange idiom which is also found in Pss. 42:4–6, 11; 43:5.

my compassion: In its two other occurrences Heb. *niḥûmîm* is translated "comfort(ing)" by RSV (Isa. 57:18; Zech. 1:13: compare the related verb in v. 17). There is therefore no need to emend to *raḥ*a*may*, "my compassion" (Wellhausen, BHS), even if it is this noun which is used elsewhere with the verb **grows warm and tender** (Gen. 43:30; 1 Kg. 3:26). NEB's "remorse" (cf. LXX, Vulg.) is based on the fact that the related verb can mean "repent, relent" (see, e.g., Jon. 3:9, 4:2 and J. Jeremias, *Die Reue Gottes*, Neukirchen, 1975), but the lack of parallels for such a meaning of *niḥûmîm* is against this. The contradiction to 13:14 should be frankly acknowledged: the most likely explanation is that passage belongs to a different, probably earlier, stage in Hosea's ministry from the present one. The contrast is no greater than, e.g., between 9:15b on the one hand and 3:1 and 14:4 on the other.

11:9. I will not execute my fierce anger: Yahweh declares that he will not after all put into effect the **anger** which is aroused in him by Israel's idolatry (cf. 8:5). Yahweh's **fierce anger** (*ḥarôn 'ap*) is a frequent theme of the prophetic message of judgment, especially in Jeremiah (e.g. 4:8), but the only close parallel to the present statement is in Jon. 3:9: "God may . . . turn from his fierce anger, so that we perish not."

I will not again destroy Ephraim: Lit. "I will not return to destroy Ephraim." This idiom can refer to a repeated action of the same kind (e.g. Gen. 26:18) and might therefore here announce the renunciation of further punitive measures by Yahweh (say, after the Assyrian invasions of 733). But **destroy** (*šiḥēt*) is such a strong word (it is used repeatedly in Genesis of the destruction of Sodom and Gomorrah: cf. Gen. 13:10, and the note on **Admah** and **Zeboiim** in v. 8 above) that repetition seems inconceivable. The idiom may therefore have its alternative sense of "act contrary to a previous action" (cf. 2:9): Yahweh undertakes not to reverse his previous acts of blessing (cf. vv. 1–2, 4 above) by the destruction of his people (cf. NEB, NJPS). Either way this represents a withdrawal of the threat announced in 13:9 (see the note). Cf. Ezek. 20:17 for a partial parallel. Marti (followed by both editions of Peake's Commentary) proposed that both this and the previous statement should be read as questions without the usual interrogative particle *hᵃ-* (cf. 13:14a): "Shall I not . . . ? Shall I not . . . ?" The promises would then be turned, in effect, into renewed threats (cf. Robinson). A similar meaning could theoretically be obtained by reading *lō'*, "not", in each case as the emphatic *lamed* (cf. on v. 5). But this is not the most obvious reading of the Heb. and after v. 8 such an interpretation is most improbable; moreover it is not the case (as Marti claimed) that the following statements can only justify a message of judgment (see below).

I am God and not man: This may be understood to mean that Yahweh as **God** rises above the human responses of anger and vengeance, and shows mercy instead. This is certainly the sense of the similar statement in Isa. 55:6–9, and the idea that mercy is fundamental to Yahweh's being ("name") is strongly expressed in Exod. 34:6–7 and related passages (such as Jl 2:13). It is, alternatively, possible that it is the notion of divine faithfulness

which is uppermost in the prophet's mind here: it is this which is
the crucial distinction between **God** and **man** in Num. 23:19–20,
and v. 8a has already implied that there is an unbreakable bond
between Yahweh and his people (cf. also v. 7).

the Holy One in your midst: As an attribute of Yahweh
Holy (*qādôš*) often stands for what Rudolf Otto called the
mysterium tremendum et fascinans, "the mystery which inspires
fear and wonder" in human experience (cf. 1 Sam. 6:20),
and in prophecy it comes to designate his opposition to all
that is evil (cf. Am. 4:2). But in the phrase "The Holy One
of Israel", which is particularly common in Isaiah, a sense of
Yahweh's commitment to his people can often be discerned (cf.
Isa. 10:17; 40:25; Pss. 71:22; 89:19). Possibly in this phrase,
and here in Hos. 11:9, *qādôš* is practically synonymous to "God"
(cf. also 11:12 below; and further W. H. Schmidt, *The Faith of
the OT*, Oxford, 1983, pp. 152–56). Particularly in association
with the phrase **in your midst** the emphasis would be on the
relationship between Yahweh and his people: for this phrase (as
in Exod. 34:9) reaffirms the divine presence whose withdrawal
had earlier been proclaimed (5:6, 15).

and I will not come to destroy: MT has "and I will not
come *beʿîr* ['into the city'?]". This has seemed unsatisfactory
to many interpreters, including RSV, which emends *beʿîr* to a
form of the verb *bēʿēr*, "destroy", as in a frequent formula in
Deuteronomy (e.g. 13:5, "purge"; cf. also Isa. 6:13, where it is
translated "burned"). But *ʿîr* here may be not the common word
for "city" but a different word, which is translated "anguish" in
Jer. 15:8 and could be applied here to "rage", a different kind
of intense emotion (so *BDB*, Wolff, Jeremias, *HAL*, p. 777, NIV,
NJPS): cf. Syriac *ʿayārāʾ* = "hate, revenge". NEB's "with threats"
is obscure, but may be based on G. R. Driver's comparison with
Arabic *ġāra* (*JQR* 28 (1937–38), 113).

11:10. They shall go after the LORD: The change back to
the third-person reference to Israel (**They**) is awkward, but it is
exactly paralleled in 14:4 and in part prepared for by **Ephraim**
in v. 9. More difficult is the abandonment of divine speech here,
especially as it returns in v. 11. It is most likely that this verse
contains a series of interpolations designed to fill out the brief
announcement of salvation in v. 11. (see further the introduction

to this chapter). The present phrase (which NEB gratuitously omits) envisages a time when Israel will once more be obedient and loyal to Yahweh instead of following other gods (cf. 2:5, 13): the closest analogies to it are 2:7 and 3:5 (cf. also Jer. 2:2 (of the wilderness period); Dt. 13:4; 1 Sam. 12:14; 2 Kg. 23:3). A redactor wished to emphasize that the return from exile would need to be preceded by a return to single-minded devotion to Yahweh, after earlier straying and obstinacy (vv. 2 and 5b).

he will roar like a lion; yea he will roar: yea represents Heb. *kî*, understood as an emphatic particle; it may alternatively mean "when" (cf. NEB, NIV, NJPS) or "because". The idea of Yahweh roaring **like a lion** is found in the context of an eschatological judgment on the nations in Jer. 25:30 and Jl 3:16, as well as Am. 1:2, which is probably to be seen as a late editorial introduction to Amos' oracles against foreign nations. These two short lines (which could be alternative readings) therefore fix the time of the ingathering of the exiles by an allusion to Yahweh's "roaring" against the nations. The redactor(s) very likely had the passages cited above specifically in mind. Once this allusive character of the addition(s) is recognized, the oddity of Yahweh being said to **roar like a lion** at a time of his people's deliverance is removed. NEB renders the second phrase, "No, when I roar, I who am God . . .", glossing over the change to the third person in this verse and seeing the pronoun **he** (*hû'*) as a specific pointer to the divine subject (cf. 10:2).

and his sons shall come trembling from the west: On **shall come trembling** see the note on the next verse. Hosea's oracles otherwise give no hint of a scattering of exiles to the **west**: this is a theme which arises only in much later prophetic passages such as Isa. 11:11, 60:9, Jl 3:6–7 and Ob. 20. A redactor evidently felt the need to supplement the references to Egypt and Assyria in the next verse so as to bring the prophecy into conformity with the extent of the diaspora in his own day. The word **sons** perhaps refers to the distant descendants of Hosea's contemporaries who would participate in this ingathering: RSV, like other modern versions, assumes that the reference is to Israel as the **sons** of Yahweh (cf. 1:10), but Heb. *bānîm* is unspecific and could equally well mean "their sons".

11:11. they shall come trembling: Heb. *yeḥerdû*, from *ḥārad*.

a sudden movement, as in Ru. 3:8 ("was startled"), and many LXX manuscripts support such an interpretation here. Cf. also Ibn Janaḥ (as reported to me by A. A. Macintosh) and Akkadian *ḫarādu* IV = "wake, watch". Hence JB and NEB have "they will come speeding/speedily". In the present form of the text, after v. 10, it is not surprising that a reference to fear has been seen here, but it may not have been what Hosea originally intended. The comparison with **birds** and **doves** most probably refers to the speed and ease with which the exiles will return (cf. Targ.).

from Egypt . . . from the land of Assyria: Cf. 9:3 and 11:5. Here at least, as in 9:6, a real "return to Egypt" seems to be envisaged, preceding a fresh deliverance **from Egypt** (cf. v. 1).

and I will return them: Reading *waha͟šîbōtîm* for MT's *wᵉhôšabtîm*, "and I will cause them to dwell", which is followed by JB etc. RSV's rendering is supported by LXX, Targ. and Syr., and fits more easily with the following **to their homes**.

says the LORD: The "oracle formula" *nᵉ'um yhwh* occurs at the end of an oracle in Hosea only here and in 2:13 (for a different use cf. 2:16, 21, which like the present verse are oracles of salvation). In all four verses it probably serves to underline the divine authority of a particular oracle. Wolff, p. xxx, seems to think that the "oracle formula" is a conclusion rounding off the whole of chs. 4–11 and corresponding to the introduction in 4:1, but this reads too much into it.

C. CHAPTERS 12–14
Death and New Life for Guilty Israel
DECEIVERS REJECTED AND PROPHETS VINDICATED
11:12–12:14 (Heb. 12:1–15)

This section, and especially the references to the Jacob tradition in vv. 3–6 and 12, has attracted much discussion in recent years (for bibliography see Jeremias, p. 154 n. 15, S. McKenzie, *VT* 36 (1986), 311–22, and Neef, pp. 15-49). This is no doubt because such references to patriarchal tradition are rare in prophecy (for a later example cf. Jer. 31:15), and also because the passage affords a striking example of "inner-biblical exegesis", which is now a subject of widespread interest (cf. M. Fishbane, *Biblical Interpretation in Ancient Israel*, Oxford, 1985: on this passage see pp. 376-9). Much remains uncertain about its interpretation, as the detailed notes will show. A major source of difficulty is that there is often a lack of clear progress of thought from one verse to the next, although themes and even words reappear in widely separated verses. This has led to ingenious but speculative interpretations which have, on the one hand, read the passage as a highly sophisticated and allusive literary composition (R. B. Coote, *VT* 21 (1971), 389-402) or, on the other, sought to rearrange its different parts into a more logical order (Rudolph). Others have tried to explain the above-mentioned characteristics by regarding it as an early example of the genre of midrash: this is more plausible if one is thinking of the work of a redactor (Jeremias) rather than that of the prophet himself (M. Gertner, *VT* 10 (1960), 272-84). The reader does indeed become so used to subtle allusions and cross-references that it is difficult to know when (or whether) careful exegesis should stop seeing such connections.

The passage is located between two extensive sections (11:1-11 and 13:1-16) with which it has only a superficial relationship (see the notes on 11:12 and 12:9). The break before it is particularly sharp, and the view that chs. 12-14 (including 11:12) constitute an originally separate collection of Hosean oracles appears likely (so, e.g., Wolff, Jeremias: see pp. 35-36). Within 11:12-12:14

changes in the subject-matter and introductory formulae can
help to identify several originally independent sayings of Hosea.
11:12-12:1 is a saying which, like 7:8-13 and 8:7-10, categorizes
the foreign policy of the northern kingdom (on the reference
to **Judah** see below) as disloyalty to Yahweh. 12:2 is an
introductory formula which is very similar to 4:1a at the
beginning of the previous main collection of Hosea's oracles
(4:1-11:11): in this case the **indictment** is developed by a
series of allusions to the stories of the patriarch Jacob, whose
craftiness and opposition to God foreshadowed the dishonest
behaviour of his descendants, which is itself described in vv.
7-8. The announcement of judgment in v. 9 brings this second
unit to a typical conclusion. The remaining verses (10-14) do not
form a coherent sequence, and the theme of deceit disappears, to
be replaced by others: prophecy as the means of divine action
(10, 13), obscure charges against Gilead and Ephraim (11a, 14),
the doom of the Gilgal sanctuary (11b) and further allusions to
the Jacob stories (12), which probably account for the placing of
the whole group of sayings after 12:2-9. Probably four originally
separate sayings can be distinguished (vv. 10, 11, 12-13, 14: see
the detailed notes). Vv. 11 and 12-13 may have been associated
on the catchword principle (**field** in v. 11 (*śāday*); **land** in v. 12
(*śᵉdēh*)); the other sayings may have been added because they
also bear on the theme of Yahweh's vindication of his persecuted
prophets.

The following genres are represented: 11:12-12:1 is a divine
lament over Ephraim, 12:2-9 is a judgment-speech in which the
charge is elaborated by a historical retrospect, while the sayings
in vv. 10-14 comprise an announcement of judgment (10: as
usual in divine speech), two short judgment-speeches (11, 14)
and a two-part antithetical historical retrospect (12-13). In no
case is there any reason to doubt the Hosean authorship of the
original sayings, but there are signs of redactional activity in
them. 12:2-9 has been transformed into an anti-Judah oracle
by the substitution of **Judah** for "Israel" in v. 2 (cf. 5:5, 6:11a
and 8:14, where a reference to **Judah** has been added), and v.
5 is probably an insertion from the Babylonian period, which
may be designed to draw attention to the following admonition
as an appeal to the Judaean exiles to mend their ways (cf.

Dt. 30:1-6). The reference to **Judah** in 11:12 is probably also
secondary, but its setting is hard to specify. If, as seems likely,
it originally contrasted Judah's situation with Israel's (so RSV
and JB, following LXX), an origin in the period of Hezekiah
or Josiah is possible, but a post-exilic origin could not be ruled
out. At any rate, the formulation of the additional material in
this verse seems to presuppose the combination of the two main
collections of Hosea's sayings (4:1-11:11; 11:12-14:8), in view of
the dependence on 11:9.

Dating the sayings in their original form is, as always, difficult.
11:12-12:1 presuppose the vacillation between Assyria and Egypt
which seems to have begun only in the reign of Shalmaneser V,
and therefore cannot be earlier than 727. 12:2-9 contain no clear
references to contemporary events that can be dated, but the
mention of Ephraim's prosperity (v. 8) fits best in the early part
of Hosea's ministry, before the Assyrian invasions of 734-733.
The sayings in vv. 10-14 are too short to permit even a tentative
dating.

11:12. Ephraim has encompassed me with lies: The critical
tone of this verse marks it off from vv. 8-11, and the mention
of **lies** and **deceit** links it clearly with ch. 12 (cf. vv. 1, 3,
7), so that the Heb. chapter division, which makes this the
first verse of ch. 12, is to be preferred. **me** is taken by most
commentators to refer to Yahweh, who then protests because
his people **Ephraim** have surrounded him, like a hostile army,
with their acts of dishonesty. This interpretation accords well
with 12:1, which begins a catalogue of different kinds of **deceit**.
Wolff's view, that Hosea is speaking about the people's hostility
towards him in particular (**me**), recalling 9:7-8, is an interesting
possibility and leads him on to an original interpretation of the
words **but Judah . . . the Holy One**, but it should probably be
rejected.

the house of Israel: The only other authentic occurrences
of this expression in Hosea are in 1:4, 6, if we are correct in
supposing that in 5:1 and 10:15 it is redactional (cf. LXX
at 10:15) and that in 6:10 there is a scribal error. It was a
well-established term for the northern kingdom (1 Kg. 12:21),
which subsequently came to be applied, after 722, to Judah (Isa.

5:7; Mic. 3:1, 9). Probably an inclusive use to refer to the whole twelve-tribe league lies behind these narrower definitions.

but Judah is still known by God: Text and interpretation are very uncertain here and in the next line, as a comparison of different translations will show. MT here has "and/but Judah is still *rād* with God . . .", and to accord with the next line this should be a favourable statement about Judah (cf. Wolff, Mays). It is, however, difficult to justify a rendering of *rād* in the favourable sense required ("goes", "is faithful"), as the closest parallels rather have connotations of rebellion (Gen. 27:40; Jer. 2:31). RSV and JB therefore suppose that MT is corrupt here and follow instead a reading based on LXX: whereas, it is implied, Yahweh has ceased to have anything to do with the northern kingdom, **Judah is still known** (in the strong sense found in Am. 3:2) by him. Such a distinction between the two kingdoms would be unusual for Hosea himself (cf. 5:10-14), and if this line of interpretation is followed the verse (or at least its second half) should probably be attributed to a pro-Judaean redactor with an outlook similar to that expressed in Psalm 78 (cf. 1:7). The alternative is to take MT here at its face value as a statement critical of Judah (cf. NEB, "Judah is still restive under God" (after Driver, *PEQ* 79 (1947), 125); NIV, "Judah is unruly against God") and adopt a different interpretation of the next line (cf. below). **God** here is not the usual word *ʾelōhîm*, but *ʾēl*, as in v. 9.

and is faithful to the Holy One: Jerusalem prided itself on being "the faithful city", but it was a claim which Hosea's younger contemporary Isaiah vigorously challenged (Isa. 1:21-23). For **the Holy One** Heb. has *qᵉdôšîm*, lit. "the holy ones". This can be regarded as a plural of majesty referring to the one God, as in Prov. 9:10, 30:3. The word is then equivalent in meaning, though slightly different in form, to that used by Hosea in v. 9, so that (see the end of the previous note) the terminology of this verse is very close to that of that earlier divine declaration. Wolff takes the plural form here in its normal sense and sees it as referring to "the circle of Levites and prophets closely associated" with Hosea (on which see the Introduction, p. 31), to whom (he supposes) Judaeans were lending support. 2 Kg. 4:9 has a comparable use of the word "holy". Those (cf.

above) who retain MT in the previous line in its natural hostile meaning either see *qᵉdôšîm* as referring to other gods (NEB: cf. Ps. 89:5, 7 and Anderson ad loc.) or emend it to *qᵉdēšîm*, "male cult-prostitutes" (Cornill, Jeremias: cf. 4:14), or, as is possible, treat **faithful** as an attribute of **the Holy One**: "even against the faithful Holy One" (NIV: cf. *GK* §132h).

12:1. Ephraim herds the wind: Or "feeds on the wind" (cf. NEB, NIV). **the wind** here represents something empty and fruitless (cf. 8:7).

and pursues the east wind: The symbolism of **the east wind** adds a new feature, which exposes further the folly of **Ephraim**'s behaviour (cf. 7:8-9, 11): for it is the khamsin or sirocco which blows from the desert (13:15) and devastates the land by its heat and dryness (cf. Isa. 27:8; Jon. 4:8; Ezek. 17:10; also D. Baly, *Geography of the Bible*, pp. 67-70). Some think it refers especially to Assyria, which lay to the east, but it probably stands for the dangers of foreign alliances in general: today's friend may be tomorrow's foe.

they multiply falsehood and violence: The introduction of **violence** (*šōd*) into the accusation is surprising and, when taken together with metrical considerations, provides some reason for the view that this line is secondary. But *šōd* elsewhere in Hosea refers to destruction suffered rather than **violence** inflicted (cf. 7:13; 9:6; 10:14), which it can stand for in other prophetic books (e.g. Jer. 6:7; Am. 3:10). Perhaps, then, the line means "their many falsehoods will bring them great destruction", a thought which is close to that of 7:13 and apt to the present context, which is concerned with the peril as well as the disloyalty of **Ephraim**'s present policies.

they make a bargain with Assyria: bargain represents Heb. *bᵉrît*, on which see the note on **covenant** in 6:7. Here the meaning is certainly "treaty" or "alliance", as other modern versions translate the word, and the reference is probably to the vassal-status accepted by Hoshea at the time of his accession in 732.

oil is carried to Egypt: Presumably as a present to the king of Egypt in connection with negotiations such as those reported in 2 Kg. 17:4 (cf. Isa. 30:6). According to D. J. McCarthy **oil** (i.e. olive oil) played a central role in diplomacy, being used in the process of treaty-making itself, so that the phrase would imply the actual making of an alliance with Egypt (*VT* 14 (1964), 215-21 – see further *Treaty and Covenant*, 2nd ed., p. 287 n. 20).

11:12 and 12:1 can be taken together. As elsewhere, Hosea pours scorn on the rapid and vain changes in policy between loyalty to Assyria and loyalty to Egypt (cf. 7:11; 10:4), but the whole principle of seeking security from foreign powers is also viewed by him as a challenge to Yahweh's role as the nation's one true saviour (13:4), and as disloyalty just as serious as the explicit worship of other gods (cf. 8:9-10; 14:3).

12:2. The LORD has an indictment against Judah: The same Heb. word (*rîb*) is used here as in 4:1 (see the note on **controversy** there). The quasi-legal terminology need not presuppose a "covenant-lawsuit" procedure as such, though there is evidence of prophetic diatribes being delivered in a cultic setting in the northern kingdom (Ps. 81) and also in Jerusalem (Ps. 50), and Hosea's preaching could have been modelled on these. If this verse is indeed the introduction to vv. 3ff., then **Judah** must have displaced an original "Israel" here, as many commentators (but not Rudolph) have agreed (cf. NEB), because of the parallel allusions to folk-etymologies of the names **Jacob** and "Israel" in the two halves of v. 3 (see the note there). Given the original twelve-tribe connotations of both these names and Hosea's readiness to condemn **Judah** elsewhere, it was a natural enough change for a redactor to make when this oracle was being transmitted in the southern kingdom.

and will punish . . . : These two lines closely resemble the end of 4:9, but the Heb. construction is slightly different.

12:3. The following verses allude repeatedly to the stories of Jacob/Israel in Genesis 25-35, with the intention of finding the sins of the present generation already foreshadowed and in a sense fixed by those of the national patriarch. After v. 2 there can be no doubt but that the presentation of Jacob is intended to be uncomplimentary, and attempts to interpret it in a positive sense (so in recent years P. R. Ackroyd, *VT* 13 (1963), 245-59, and Neef, pp. 15-49, following the lead of older commentators such as Jerome) must be regarded as misguided. On the other hand, there is no need to suppose that Hosea represents Jacob the patriarch as a polytheist, as suggested by E. M. Good, *VT* 16

(1966), 137-51, R. B. Coote, *VT* 21 (1971), 389-402, and earlier scholars mentioned by Ackroyd, p. 256. Probably Hosea knew the Jacob-tradition in substantially the form in which it has come down to us in Genesis, though small variations can be detected (see the notes on vv. 4a and 6). The significance of this critical use of the Jacob-tradition should not be underestimated. Gen. 28 was presumably still in Hosea's time the *hieros logos* of the Bethel sanctuary and the nucleus of the promises made to Jacob there probably served, along with the Exodus tradition, as a strong basis for hope that Yahweh would continue, come what may, to stand by his people. It is characteristic of Hosea, as we have seen, to transform almost the whole of Israel's history into "disaster-history", but here he touches its very source and finds it as amenable to his message of doom as to the hopes placed in it by his contemporaries (cf. L. Eslinger, *JSOT* 18 (1980), 91-99; S. McKenzie, *VT* 36 (1986), 319).

In the womb he took his brother by the heel: The verb used here is *'aqab*, and it makes a play on the name **Jacob** (Heb. *ya'aqōb*), which looks as though it is derived from this verb. It probably does not mean **took ... by the heel** but "supplant, overreach" (cf. JB, NEB), as is clear from its use of Jacob's later deceit in robbing his twin brother Esau of his birthright and his father's blessing (Gen. 27:36). The tradition in Gen. 25:26 associated Jacob's name with a different word *'ēqeb* = "heel", and this evidently provided the basis for Hosea's new charge that Jacob was a supplanter from birth, and indeed before it. In fact the name Jacob was probably derived from neither of these words but from a homonymous root found in numerous Amorite and other personal names which meant "protect" (cf. H. B. Huffmon, *Amorite Personal Names in the Mari Texts*, Baltimore, 1965, pp. 203-204; R. de Vaux, *The Early History of Israel*, London, 1978, p. 199), but there is no evidence to show that this was known to any of Hosea's Israelite contemporaries.

in his manhood he strove with God: The allusion is to the story of Jacob's wrestling with God at Penuel in Gen. 32:22-32, and the verb **strove** (*śārāh*) occurs there in the explanation of the name "Israel" (v. 28) as "he who strives with God (*'ēl*)". **manhood** translates Heb. *'ōn*, which is something of a keyword for this chapter, as it also lies behind "wealth" in v. 8 and its sound is very close to that of *'āwen*, "iniquity", in v. 11, which also forms part of Hosea's nickname for Bethel (v. 4) in 4:15 and 10:5. LXX picked up what was probably an intended allusion to the latter word and translated *'ōn* here as if it were *'āwen*. The effect is to hint already that Jacob's struggle was not the epic encounter which tradition had handed down.

The correspondence between the portrayal of Jacob and contemporary sins denounced by Hosea should not be overlooked. He is a deceiver, like Israel in 11:12, and at odds with God, like Israel, who faces first a struggle in the divine law-court (4:1; 12:2) and then a fight to the death in open combat (13:7-8).

12:4. He strove with the angel . . .: RSV's rendering, while supported by LXX (cf. JB), conceals the fact that MT envisages a different verb here from the end of the preceding verse, namely *śārar*, "rule", which would make for a synonymous parallelism with **prevailed**, and provide a different basis for the name Israel from that alluded to in v. 3 (cf. L. Eslinger, *JSOT* 18 (1980), 93-94). The fact that Jacob **prevailed** is stated in Gen. 32:28 (cf. v. 25), but the Genesis story does not call his adversary an **angel**, nor does it speak of Jacob's weeping in this connection. Both these features also disturb the present context, for it seems to undermine Hosea's purpose to downgrade Jacob's opponent to an **angel**, and it is puzzling that after "prevailing" Jacob apparently behaves like the losing party. Various solutions to these difficulties can be proposed. NEB follows Nyberg's suggestion (*Studien*, pp. 94-95) to read *'ēl*, "God", for *'el* (**with**), and take it together with **the angel** as the subject of the line: "The divine angel stood firm and held his own . . ." The next line then describes Jacob's humiliating plea for divine help, a feature which can find some basis in Gen. 32:26. A more radical solution along these lines is to regard **the angel** as a pious gloss and translate: "But God proved himself lord and prevailed" (Wolff, Jeremias, following in essence M. Gertner, *VT* 10 (1960), 277, 281). If RSV is retained, the words **he wept . . . favour** must be seen as showing that Jacob's victory was shallow and short-lived, since he still had to adopt a submissive attitude to secure God's blessing. In this polemical context the mention of **the angel** would be understandable: Hosea plays down Jacob's victory by saying that it was only a victory over an angel, not God

himself, who remained supreme. The fact that the word used in v.
3 (and in Gen. 32:28) for **God** can also mean "a god", i.e. a lesser
heavenly being than the supreme God, provided an opening for
such a reinterpretation of the tradition.

he wept and sought his favour: Jacob must be the subject
here, with **his** referring to **the angel** (or God – cf. above). In
view of possible allusions to contemporary cultic traditions in the
context (see below on **and there God spoke**), it may be justified
(as J. R. Porter pointed out to me) to detect here an echo of a
practice of ritual weeping at Bethel, for which cf. perhaps Gen.
35:8 and Jg. 2:1-5: see also Hos. 7:14 and F. F. Hvidberg, *Weeping
and Laughter in the Old Testament*, Leiden and Copenhagen, 1962,
pp. 98-146. W. L. Holladay observed that the verbs **wept** and
sought his favour appear in the Jacob-tradition in the story of
his encounter with Esau (Gen. 33:4, 8, 10), which follows the
Penuel episode. Vv. 3-4a could then be seen as a chiasmus,
with the allusions to the Esau-stories surrounding those to the
Penuel-tradition (cf. McKenzie, who strengthens the argument
in some respects) and serving (as above) to offset the claims
made on the basis of the latter. But it seems better to relate
the weeping to the Penuel episode, as this provides a stronger
link with the divine response which follows.

he met God at Bethel: The Heb. literally reads "at Bethel he
met [lit. 'found'] him": both subject and object are unspecified, **at
Bethel** is placed emphatically at the beginning, and the verb is a
Heb. imperfect (like **spoke** in the next line) and most likely refers
to a repeated action. As NEB indicates, **God** must be the subject
here as well as in the next line (where again the Heb. contains
only pronouns): for "found" cf. 9:10. Two encounters with God
at Bethel are recounted in Genesis, one before Jacob's journey
to Aram-Naharaim (28:10-22), the other after it (35:1-15). In
view of the iterative imperfects, it may not be necessary to choose
between these alternatives: these lines may refer to a tradition
that God repeatedly **met** and **spoke with** Jacob **at Bethel**. But
there are some indications that Hosea may have had the earlier
encounter more particularly in mind (see the notes on the next
line and on v. 6), and if he did he seems to have known the
Jacob-stories in a different order from that which eventually
became fixed in Genesis.

and there God spoke . . . : The Heb. simply has "he spoke", but the address to Jacob in v. 7 requires that God be the speaker here. Gen. 35:13-15 contains three statements about God speaking with Jacob at Bethel. One of these (v. 14) is referring back to the story in ch. 28 and it seems on other grounds to be the only one of the three which belongs to the older Pentateuchal tradition; the others, which refer to God speaking with Jacob in the immediate past, belong to the priestly source, which is certainly later than Hosea (cf. Fohrer, *Introduction*, pp. 153, 179). **With him** follows the reading presupposed by LXX and Syr. ('*immô*): but MT's "with us" ('*immānû*) can be retained, implying that for Hosea Jacob embodies his descendants, and the words addressed to Jacob in v. 7 apply equally to his own generation. The **there** would indicate, perhaps, that the following exhortation expresses what Hosea believed to be the true word of Yahweh from Bethel (see also the notes on v. 6).

12:5. the LORD the God of hosts: This is the only occurrence in Hosea of a title which is much more common in Amos (e.g. 3:13). For a recent study of it, with bibliography, see J. A. Emerton, *ZAW* 94 (1982), 1-9; the possible meanings of **hosts** are set out by Ringgren, *Israelite Religion*, pp. 68-69. The verse is a variant of a formula which occurs in Deutero–Isaiah, Jeremiah and redactional additions to Amos (4:13; 5:27; cf. 5:8; 9:5-6), where it serves either to conclude a doxology or to identify the one who is speaking or acting by this majestic title. Here it lends additional solemnity to the words which follow in v. 6: it is likely, though not certain, that it is a later addition.

his name: Lit. "his memorial", *zikrô*, a common equivalent to *šēm*, the regular word for "name" (cf. Exod. 3:15; Ps. 135:13), which Hosea again uses in 14:8 (see the note on **their fragrance** there).

12:6. For the first time in this chapter direct address is used, with singular pronoun and verb forms which reappear in a further divine speech in v. 9. Hosea's version of God's words to Jacob at Bethel should be compared with that in Gen. 28:13-15 (of which Gen. 35:9-12 is the later priestly version), which probably corresponds closely to the form of the tradition known to Hosea's audience.

by the help of your God return: cf. Gen. 28:15, "I . . . will bring you back to this land", where the Hiphil form of *šûb*, **return**, is used of Jacob's eventual journey back to Canaan from Aram-Naharaim. **by the help of your God** is literally "by your God" (cf. the phrase in 1:7, "by the Lord their God"): it cannot mean, JB, NIV and NJPS notwithstanding, "to your God". The Heb. verb here is strictly an imperfect, so that the words may, like Gen. 28:15, contain a promise, "you . . . shall return".

hold fast to love and justice: Better ". . . loyalty" (Heb. *ḥesed*: cf. NEB) **and justice** (*mišpāṭ*). These words have no parallel in Gen. 28, and introduce an element of demand which is missing from all but the latest of the divine promises to the patriarchs in Genesis. On these qualities see the notes on 2:19 and 5:1. Only here and in 2:19 do they occur together in Hosea and only in these two passages, in our view, does *mišpāṭ* have the meaning **justice**, rather than "judgment" (see the notes on 5:1, 11; 10:4). While "loyalty" is a distinctive feature of Hosea's understanding of Yahweh's demands (see especially 6:6), *mišpāṭ* is more characteristic of Amos (see 5:24) and Isaiah (see 1:17). Wolff has shown that *mišpāṭ* in this sense was a special concern of the wisdom tradition (*Amos the Prophet*, pp. 59-67): and in the light of what follows it is particularly striking that the phrase "a just balance" (*mō'zᵉnê mišpāṭ*) occurs in Prov. 16:11. But *mišpāṭ* also appears in Ps. 97:2 and 99:4, passages which are now usually ascribed to the pre-exilic cult in Jerusalem. More striking still is the occurrence of "loyalty" and **justice** together in Ps. 101:1, in a text which is normally understood as a royal psalm. Bethel was the royal sanctuary of the northern kingdom (Am. 7:14): was Hosea perhaps alluding here to its own socio-ethical traditions? For the status of such traditions in the Jerusalem temple cf. E. Otto, *ZAW* 98 (1986), 161-79.

and wait continually for your God: The idea of "waiting" for God (*qwh*) is a common one in the OT, especially in the Psalms (27:14; 37:34; 40:1; 130:5) and the book of Isaiah (8:17; 40:31; 49:23; 51:5): it refers to patient, trustful endurance, usually in a time of trouble or need. The verb is not used elsewhere by Hosea to characterize Israel's proper attitude to Yahweh, but he uses the related noun *tiqwāh* in 2:15 to mean "hope". It represents well the norm from which Israel transgressed when she sought a remedy for her "sickness" in foreign alliances (cf. 5:13) or in military strength (10:13). **continually** (*tamîd*) is characteristic of the devotional language of the Psalms (16:8; 25:15 etc.), and Ps. 71:14 is particularly close in meaning to the present verse.

12:7. A trader, in whose hands are false balances ... : The prophet's polemic reverts to the contemporary situation (cf. v. 2), but the figure of the patriarch Jacob is still in view, for he too had a penchant for falsehood (cf. Gen. 27:35, where the same word *mirmāh* is used). The Heb. for **trader** here is *kᵉnaʿan*, which is so used in Ezek. 16:29, 17:4 and Zeph. 1:11, but it is none other than the ordinary word for "Canaan", so that there is the unmistakable implication that by her behaviour Israel has become indistinguishable from the hated and despised Canaanites. This linguistic development, which had taken place long before Hosea's time, was a consequence of the great involvement of the Canaanites in sea-borne trade (*POTT*, pp. 40, 43), a tradition which was continued and extended in the first millennium by the remnant of the Canaanites who retained their separate existence, the Phoenicians (*ibid.*, pp. 274-77). **false balances**, which are mentioned again in Am. 8:5, may be a general expression for dishonesty in trading: so far as we know, it was by tampering with the weights rather than the **balances** themselves that swindles were concealed (cf. Dt. 25:13-16; Am. 8:5). Such practices were deprecated also in law and maxim (Lev. 19:35-36; Prov. 20:10). See *IDB*, vol. 1, 343, for illustrations of the remains of a weighing set from Ugarit and a picture of weighing on a balance from an Egyptian tomb.

he loves to oppress: The accusation is intensified: such practices are on a par with the more blatant oppression and extortion which are condemned elsewhere by the prophets (Ezek. 22:12; Am. 4:1).

12:8. "Ah, but I am rich ...": RSV understands Ephraim's boast as an answer to the charge of dishonesty, but it is better (cf. NEB, JB) to see Heb. *'ak* (**Ah, but**) as emphatic rather than adversative: "Surely I am rich ..." Ephraim's arrogance, which leaves no place for a recognition of the divine source of his prosperity, then becomes a further aspect of his alienation from Yahweh.

but all his riches can never offset the guilt he has incurred: The sense of this line is uncertain. MT and LXX differ considerably and in neither case is the Heb. without problems. RSV, like JB and NEB, follows LXX in seeing it as a statement about Ephraim which undercuts his boastful claims in terms apt to Hosea's teaching. MT differs in having first-person instead of third-person possessive suffixes and a different vocalization of two words, which makes the line a declaration by Ephraim of his innocence: "All my gains bring me no guilt which would be sin" (Wolff, cf. NIV, NJPS, REB). The choice between these alternative readings is difficult, but MT has the advantage that it yields a better contrast with the emphatic divine self-introduction at the beginning of the next verse. Either way there is an echo between the two lines in Heb. which the English versions do not represent: ". . . I have got wealth [māṣā'tî 'ôn – cf. 'ôn (**manhood**) in v. 3] for myself, but my gains will not get me guilt [yimṣe' 'āwôn]."

12:9. I am the LORD your God from the land of Egypt: The verse begins emphatically: "*But I . . .*" (we'ānōkî). Ephraim's words are answered by a new divine utterance, which takes its basis not in the Jacob-tradition, like v. 6, but in the Exodus-tradition which, according to the admittedly polemical narrative in 1 Kg. 12:28, had also been celebrated at the Bethel sanctuary. This line reappears in 13:4 and is related to a cluster of similar self-introductory formulae (Exod. 20:1 (par. Dt. 5:6); Ps. 81:10), on which see W. Zimmerli, *I am Yahweh*, Atlanta, 1982, pp. 16-28.

. . . in tents, as in the days of the appointed feast: If this translation, which is supported by LXX, Syr. and Vulg., is correct, there must be a reference to the practice of celebrating the major **feast** of the year – that is, the feast of ingathering in the autumn – while living in **tents. tents** may here refer generally to temporary dwellings such as the "booths" (sukkôt) which later gave a new name to this festival (cf. Lev. 23:42-43, Dt. 16:13-15 and de Vaux, *Ancient Israel*, pp. 495-502). In an effort to find a further instance of the "reversal" theme (cf. on 8:13), some have seen here a reference to a festival of the wilderness period (H. J. Kraus, *Worship in Israel*, Oxford, 1966, p. 132) or have rendered mô'ēd (**appointed feast**) by "meeting" (sc. with Yahweh in the wilderness: so Robinson, Wolff, JB); while others, following Targ., read instead mē'ād, "of old" (Driver, *JTS*

39 (1938), 162, comparing *GK* §130a for the construction: so also NEB, NJPS). These suggestions seem less likely than the straightforward festival reference, which would have particular point in a context which is so concerned with the sanctuary traditions of Bethel. At any rate, the general implication is clear: the houses and cities where the Ephraimites live and have amassed their treasures are shortly to be abandoned (9:6; 11:6 – cf. 8:14). On tent-dwellers in the second and first millennia BC, see D. J. Wiseman, in *Biblical and Near Eastern Studies*, FS W. S. LaSor, ed. G. A. Tuttle, Grand Rapids, 1978, pp. 195-200. The evidence cited there relates chiefly to the Hebrew patriarchs and other pastoral semi-nomads. Thus Yahweh declares that the wealthy merchants will revert to the life-style of their forebears, such as Jacob himself. Jeremias regards this verse as a message of salvation (pp. 155-56), but there is no hint here of the possibilities which emerge in 2:14-15 and 3:3-5.

12:10. The sequence of thought in the next few verses is far from logical, although they have certain points of contact both with each other and with the main stock of the passage. They give the appearance of being originally separate fragments of Hosea's preaching or, in the case of vv. 12-13, perhaps further reflections by Hosea's disciples on the themes of his original saying.

I spoke to the prophets: RSV is probably correct in this case to ignore the w^e ("and") with which the verse begins in MT, as it serves only to link this collection of fragments secondarily with the main oracle. The verbs in this line refer to the prophets who have preceded Hosea, whom Yahweh here owns as his spokesmen (cf. 6:5), perhaps in answer to the people's tendency to ignore or make fun of them (cf. 9:7). The specific reference here is apparently to v. 9 or perhaps to vv. 4-6, which, in view of the divine speech, may have been understood as the words of a cultic prophet like the one who speaks in Psalm 81:6-16.

and through the prophets gave parables: The verb used here (*dāmāh* I) means "be like" and, in the Piel, "compare, imagine", and so here *BDB*, RSV, NEB, and NJPS give it the unique meaning "made likenesses", **gave parables:** the reference would then be to the use by **prophets** of symbolic actions and perceptions and vivid imagery alongside ordinary speech and vision reports (cf. Lindblom, *Prophecy*, pp. 137-41,

165-73; A. R. Johnson, *The Cultic Prophet in Ancient Israel*, 2nd ed., Cardiff, 1962, pp. 42-44; C. Westermann, *The Parables of Jesus in the Light of the Old Testament*, Edinburgh, 1990, pp. 25-112). R. B. Coote (*VT* 21 (1971), 397-401) saw here a specific reference to the "similitudes" in the next three verses, but only the latter part of v. 11 really has such a character. Vss. (except Targ.) support the association with *dāmāh* I, but not in exactly the sense that is now popular. A derivation from *dāmāh* II = "destroy", which Hosea uses several times (e.g. 4:5), is also possible; the fact that it is not found elsewhere in the Piel is not a serious objection and the sense obtained (cf. JB "and through the prophets I will deal out death") is close to what Hosea has said in 6:5 (so Wellhausen, Mays). There is a change in the Heb. verb-form at this point, which may indicate (cf. JB) a transition to a statement about the future: presumably the meaning would be, as in 6:5, that it is through the power-laden words of **the prophets** that Yahweh brings his judgment to pass.

12:11. Again the connection with what has preceded is not close, though **iniquity** recalls the charge of oppression in v. 7. The accusation and announcement of judgment are directed specifically against **Gilead**, i.e. the Transjordanian tribes (cf. 6:8), who apparently made particular use of the shrine at **Gilgal** by the river Jordan (see on 4:15): see N. H. Snaith, *VT* 28 (1978), 330-35 for the suggestion that this practice is reflected in Joshua 22. Emmerson, *Hosea*, pp. 139-45, translates the first part of the verse: "Though Gilead was wealthy, they have indeed become nothingness . . ." According to her, **iniquity** (*'āwen*) is a deliberate revocalization in the light of 6:8 of an original reading *'ôn* = "wealth" (which is used in v. 8; cf. v. 3), and this obscured the fact that the saying was originally about the short-lived prosperity of the rich. This then, for her, explains the point of the second half of the verse, which is that even the expensive offerings of **bulls** are powerless to prevent the coming devastation of the **altars**. Only later, in a Judaean context where centralization of the cult was an issue, was objection raised to the Gilgal sanctuary as such. An advantage of this view is that it renders unnecessary speculation about whether the **bulls** were offered to pagan deities, as already implied by Targ. and Vulg. and assumed by many modern scholars; some of the latter emend the text to read "to bull-gods" (NEB, cf. G. R. Driver, *JTS* 39 (1938), 162-63) or "to demons" (*lᵉšēdîm*: so Hitzig, Wellhausen, Harper – cf. *BHS*), assuming that haplography has occured after *baggilgāl*. But there is no real need or justification for a change to MT: if the verse is not entirely clear, this may be because it has been handed down as an isolated saying.

like stone heaps on the furrows of the field: I.e. broken down and left as piles of rubble. '*al* (**on**) is better rendered "beside" here (cf. NEB): the **stone heaps** may have been "landmarks", i.e. boundary markers, such as can still be seen today in Palestine (see the note on 5:10), or simply piles of stones cleared from the land which was to be cultivated (Weiser). Note the baneful pun between **stone heaps** (*gallim*) and **Gilgal**, a name for which Amos also coined new associations (Am. 5:5).

12:12-13. These two verses should certainly be taken together, as shown by their matching repetitive form, which is even clearer in Heb., and the use of the same Heb. verb (*šāmar*) for both **herded** in v. 12 and **was preserved** in v. 13. They comprise a couplet which succinctly exposes the contrast between Jacob/Israel's mercenary character and the honoured role which prophets have had and continue to have in Yahweh's dealings with his people.

Jacob fled ... did service: The terms, and the episodes chosen for citation (cf. Gen. 27:42-45; 29:15-30), are designed to show the ignoble side of the patriarch's life.

to the land of Aram: Aram stands for a people who occupied most of what today is Syria: here the reference is to the north-eastern extremity which was known as "Aram Naharaim" – that is, "Syrian Mesopotamia" (Gen. 24:10).

for a wife ... and for a wife: Heb. *bᵉ'iššāh*, with *beth pretii*. The repetition may refer to the two wives of Jacob, Leah and Rachel, but it also serves to underline that Jacob's humiliation was "only" for the sake of a woman, just as Israel of Hosea's day humiliated itself in the rituals of Baal worship which were designed to create fertility.

by a prophet ... by a prophet: Again the Heb. preposition in the repeated phrase is *bᵉ*, so that the parallel in form to the previous verse is extremely close. The **prophet** is Moses: the tradition about him alternates between claiming him as the first of the prophets (Num. 11:16-30; Dt. 18:15-20) and emphasizing his superiority to all others (Num. 12:6-8; Dt. 34:10-12). The inclusion of this saying is evidently intended to add further weight to the statements in v. 10 by associating the prophetic tradition with the saving event of the Exodus itself, which had also been alluded to in the original saying of Hosea (v. 9). This suggests that the opposition and rejection experienced by Hosea himself continued into the time of the redactor who put together vv. 10-14. Am. 3:7, which is from the Deuteronomistic editors, served a similar purpose but exhibits less creative interaction with prophetic and narrative tradition than is present here.

12:14. This short message of judgment against **Ephraim** does not follow closely on the contents of the two preceding verses; but it forms a forceful conclusion to vv. 2-14 as a whole and corresponds to the introductory v. 2 in its emphasis on the fittingness of the divine judgment that is to come.

his LORD: In writing **LORD** in capitals RSV implies that the Heb. has "Yahweh", but this is not the case here: the word used (only here in Hosea) is *'ādōn*, which means "master" or "husband" and could be used of an earthly king (e.g. Gen. 40:1) as well as of God, who is clearly meant here. The title emphasizes Yahweh's right to deal as he thinks fit with his "servant" Israel.

will leave his bloodguilt upon him: This particular expression is not found elsewhere. 2 Sam. 1:16 and 1 Kg. 2:32 are similar, and for Heb. *dāmîm*, "blood", as equivalent to **bloodguilt** Exod. 22:2 and Ps. 51:14 provide further parallels. The assumption here appears to be that **bloodguilt** of itself has baneful effects and Yahweh has only to **leave** it alone (this, not "bring down" (JB), is the meaning of Heb. *nāṭaš*) for judgment to follow. The idea of an order in nature which automatically brings about the evil consequences of sin is seen by some in 4:3 (see the note there). This conception may also be implicit in the following words **and will turn back**, lit. "and will cause to return" (so K. Koch, in J. L. Crenshaw (ed.), *Theodicy in the Old Testament*, London, 1983, p. 65), though they make it clear that it is not a process which is independent of Yahweh. The nature of the **provocation** remains obscure, but the terms **bloodguilt** and **reproaches** are perhaps more specific than is usually recognized.

On the one hand, while Hosea repeatedly condemns murder (1:4; 4:2; 7:7), one passage specifically links this charge with Gilead (6.8-9), mentioned above for its **iniquity** (v.11). On the other hand, **reproaches** are most likely to have been directed against Yahweh and as such recall the treatment of his prophet in 9:7-8. Given the concern of two verses in this collection of sayings with the vindication of the prophets (vv. 10 and 13), it is possible to speculate that this verse too (and v. 11?) relates specifically to this theme, so that one might see here a reference to the persecution of Hosea and other prophets of a similar mind. The whole of ch. 12 is seen by Utzschneider (*Hosea*, pp. 186-230) as a text about "prophetic conflict": this may be correct for vv. 10-14 at least.

DEATH IS UNAVOIDABLE FOR GUILTY ISRAEL

13:1-16 (Heb. 13:1-14:1)

This chapter is characterized by the recurring theme of death as the impending (and even, in v. 1, the present) fate of Ephraim/Israel, from which there is no escape because Yahweh, the only true deliverer, has turned against her. Even though possibilities of hope may seem to exist, one by one these are snuffed out according to vv. 12–16. There are three main sections (1–3, 4–8, 12–16), each of which begins with a historical retrospect establishing the guilt of Ephraim/Israel (1-2; (4)5-6; 12-13) and continues with an announcement of judgment (3; 7-8; 15-16). But while the first section is a simple example of the prophetic judgment-speech, the second and third are amplified respectively by a taunt (9-11) – which could have an independent origin – and a divine soliloquy (14), which reinforce their doleful message. Throughout the chapter there is an abundance of imagery (see vv. 3, 7-8, 13, 15), which is remarkable even for Hosea.

The original settings of the sayings are not always easy to specify. Vv. 1-3 probably make no reference to specific historical events of Hosea's time (see the note on v. 1) and could belong to almost any stage of the prophet's ministry. The only basis for an approximate dating is the fact that historical retrospects seem to typify the style of Hosea's preaching in his later years. The taunt in vv. 9-11 implies that Israel has lost the protection which she believed was afforded her by her king, and this only fits the situation c. 724, when Shalmaneser V had captured Hoshea and "bound him in prison" and was besieging Samaria (2 Kg. 17:4-6): vv. (4)5-8 may therefore be taken as Hosea's gloomy prognosis of the outcome of the siege. Vv. 12-16 seem to be a little earlier. Israel has enjoyed a period of prosperity (v. 15) and needs to be reminded that the evil of the past has not been quietly forgotten (v. 12); a final catastrophe symbolized by **the east wind** will soon come, from which Yahweh has no intention of rescuing them (v. 14). This seems to fit the time around Shalmaneser's accession in 727, when the northern kingdom enjoyed some recovery from the disasters of the late 730s, and negotiations with an Egyptian dynast were opened, which could be referred to in v. 15.

The arrangement of these oracles adopted by the collector is therefore not based on purely chronological factors. He may have wished to place vv. 12–16 at the end of the sequence so that the references to **iniquity** and **sin** in v. 12 could be explained by the more specific illustrations given in vv. 1–2 and 6. It is also possible that the *inclusio* created by the references to guilt and death in vv. 1 and 16 was deliberately sought. There is no evidence of "catchword" connections between the end of one oracle and the beginning of the next, but the common concern with death makes it easy to see why they were associated together. There is no certain case of redactional modification in these sayings. The suggestion of Jeremias that, like part of 8:6, part of v. 2 and the whole of v. 3 derive from a Judaean redactor influenced by Deutero-Isaiah lacks a solid basis. Possible later additions are v. 4, which is an unnecessary and somewhat awkward introduction to vv. 5–8 and consists of phrases paralleled elsewhere, in some cases only outside Hosea (see the detailed notes), and the final line of v. 16, which is grammatically irregular. In the former case one might recognize here the reciprocal influence of Deuteronomistic preaching on Hosea's oracles, just as this very oracle seems to have been the basis of Dt. 8:11–20 (see A. J. Poulter, *Rhetoric and Redaction in Deuteronomy 8* (Diss., Cambridge, 1989), pp. 171–83, 205–10). It is clear from the variant text of LXX in v. 4 that parenetic interest in this passage persisted even later.

13:1. When Ephraim spoke . . .: As interpreted by RSV (cf. JB, NIV), the verse begins by recalling the dominant place occupied by the tribe of **Ephraim** in early Israel (see the note on 4:17) and then speaks of its downfall due to the worship of Baal. For the contrast cf. especially 9:10. NEB ("When the Ephraimites mumbled their prayers") takes *rᵉtēt* (**men trembled**, lit. "(there was) trembling") as the object of **spoke** and sees a reference here to prayers offered to Baal, but it is doubtful whether these were "mumbled" (cf. 7:14). REB, "Ephraim was a prince and a leader", follows those who have associated *rᵉtēt* with Arabic *rattu*, "prince" (cf. Rudolph, p. 237), and reads **spoke** (*dbr*) as a word for "leader" (as in Aramaic), but this seems far-fetched. The meaning "trembling" for *rᵉtēt*, which occurs only here in the OT, is now paralleled in the Qumran Hymns (1QH 4:33; Vermes, p. 164), as well as in rabbinic Hebrew and Aramaic.

he was exalted in Israel: Heb. *nāśā'*, "lift up", is perhaps used intransitively here (cf. L. Kopf, *VT* 8 (1958), 186, and Num. 14.1, Ps. 89.10); alternatively *niśśā'*, "was lifted up", or *nāśî'*, "(was) a prince", can be read without altering the consonantal text and with support from Syr. and Targ. NEB, "God himself denounced Israel", retains the usual transitive meaning of *nāśā'* and assumes an ellipse of *qôl*, "voice" (for which cf. Driver, *JTS* 39 (1938), 163, who gives other instances); but the preceding line probably provides no basis for a divine denunciation (cf. above).

and died: Death is a recurring theme of this chapter: see vv. 7–8, 14 and, with the association with **guilt**, 16. Here Hosea speaks of it not as an imminent danger, but as something already past: but to what disaster does he refer? Many commentators think that the Assyrian invasion of 733 is meant (e.g. Wolff, Mays), but the **And now** of v. 2 seems to refer to the whole monarchy period (see below), and if so, **died** must allude to earlier events, such as the disaster at Baal-peor (9:10) and perhaps those of the Judges period (cf. Jg. 2:11–15). Clearly death does not stand for extermination here, since the people survive to **sin more and more** (v. 2): it means an end of vitality and exclusion from "Yahweh's sphere of influence" (Wolff, *Anthropology of the OT*, pp. 106–107).

13:2. And now they sin more and more: Better "And now they sin further" (Wolff): the Heb. indicates a persistence in **sin**

(and, as will appear, a new kind of sin) rather than a gradual increase.

and make for themselves molten images: To apostasy is added idolatry; to the breach of the first commandment is added the breach of the second (Exod. 20:3–6). Given the prominence of **images** in Canaanite worship, such a progression was unavoidable. **molten images** (Heb. *massēkāh*) refers in several other passages to the golden calves made by Aaron (Exod. 32:4, 8; Dt. 9:16; Neh. 9:18; Ps. 106:19) and Jeroboam I (1 Kg. 14:9; 2 Kg. 17:16), and this is appropriate here also (cf. 8:4–6). A reference to small metal plaques and statuettes (Wolff; Hahn, pp. 357–58) is less likely, since they would hardly be recipients of sacrifice (cf. below).

idols skilfully made: The Heb. for **skilfully made** is unusual (though cf. *GK* §91e), and Wolff and *BHS* propose following LXX and Vulg. and reading *keṯabnîṯ*, "according to the form of (idols)" for MT's *kiṯbûnām*. But this would imply that the **idols** were distinct from the **molten images**, when it is more likely that they are different words for the same thing. MT is to be preferred, with the recent EVV. (including NEB, despite *HTOT*, p. 249).

of their silver: If the reference is to the golden calves (cf. 8:4), **silver** must stand here as a general word for "wealth". Cf. 9:6.

all of them ... they say: Jeremias regards these words as a Judaean gloss in the spirit of Deutero-Isaiah (cf. below on v. 3).

Sacrifice to these: to these, *lāhem*, is awkwardly placed in the Heb. and is probably due to dittography (cf. the preceding *kullōh* and the following *hēm*). The following words of MT are most precisely rendered: "They say, 'Those who offer human sacrifice kiss calves'", though it is perhaps possible to translate, "They say, 'Those men who offer sacrifice . . .'" (NJPS, NIV mg: cf. *GK* §128l). LXX, which RSV follows closely, reads **sacrifice** as an imperative instead of a participial form (*zibḥû*, not *zōbeḥê*), and **men** can then be the subject of **kiss**. This reading also makes the best sense of **they say**, which is otiose otherwise. To Hosea the sacrificial ritual is as invidious as the adoration of the calf-images (for the manner of which cf. 1 Kg. 19:18).

13:3. The first two lines of this verse are almost identical to 6:4b, where the same images are applied to the speed with which

Israel's love (*ḥesed*) disappears. There is no need to suspect the text, as Weiser does: the prophet evidently favoured the images and reused them. They may even have been a formula deriving from poetic oral tradition (cf. R. C. Culley, *Oral Formulaic Language in the Biblical Psalms*, Toronto, 1967). The rapid and total demise which awaits Israel is further emphasized by the addition of two further images drawn from domestic life as distinct from the world of nature. It is theoretically possible to understand the **they** as referring to **calves** in v. 2 (so apparently Jeremias, with the result that he attributes the whole of v. 3 to Judaean redactors influenced by Deutero-Isaiah), but this is by no means necessary.

the chaff that swirls: The verb **swirls** (*sāʿar*) is more often used of wind than chaff, and a slight emendation of the vowels, supported by LXX, would produce a passive form more in line with normal usage (so Wolff, Rudolph, *BHS*, JB, NEB). But even active forms seem sometimes to be used of what the wind causes to swirl (cf. Jon. 1:11; Isa. 54:11), so MT may be retained.

like smoke from a window: smoke is a common image for what is transitory (Ps. 37:20; Isa. 51:6). Windows were often high above ground level (*BRL*, p. 80), which would assist the escape of **smoke**. The word used here (*ʾarubbāh*) is not the normal word for **window**, and may refer to an opening in the roof (cf. NEB "chimney"), like the "windows" (*ʾarubbôt*) of heaven in various OT passages (Gen. 7:11; 8:2; 2 Kg. 7:2; Mal. 3:10).

13:4 Another historical retrospect (cf. on 9:10–17), and probably a new oracle, begins here. The statements in v. 4 are all closely paralleled in other passages (see the detailed notes), and it has therefore often been thought that the whole verse is a later addition (Vollmer, *Geschichtliche Rückblicke*, pp. 68–69). LXX certainly amplified it (see below). The emphatic pronoun in v. 5 (**It was I**) and the reference to the wilderness (cf. 9:10) would constitute a perfectly acceptable beginning for the oracle. See further the introduction to this section.

I am the LORD your God from the land of Egypt: Cf. 12:9 and the note there. In the Heb. the verse begins with an "And", which provides a weak and probably secondary link with vv. 1–3 (unless the *waw* is an emphatic *waw* (cf. *GK* §154a, note; Blommerde, *Job*, p. 29), adding to the majesty of the divine

self-introduction). After **your God** LXX adds "who established
the heavens and created the earth and whose hands created all
the host of heaven, but I did not show them to you for you
to go after [i.e. serve] them. And I brought you up . . ." The
final words are also added in LXX, Syr. and Targ. in 12:10,
and 12:13 is the obvious source in each case. The rest of the
addition is loosely based on such passages as Isa. 40:26; 45:12;
48:13; Dt. 4:19; Jer. 8:2, and seems to represent an Alexandrian
Jewish warning against astrology such as can also be found, e.g.,
in Philo, *On the Creation* 45–46. See further J. H. Charlesworth in
The OT Pseudepigrapha, London, 1983, vol. 1, pp. 473–80.

**you know no God but me, and besides me there is
no saviour:** The language is reminiscent of Deutero-Isaiah,
especially Isa. 45:21. It is true that "knowledge of God" is
a characteristically Hosean expression (cf. on 2:20), but the
sense here is somewhat different, being closer to "be acquainted
with", as (negatively) often in Deuteronomic-Deuteronomistic
preaching (Dt. 11:28; 13:2 etc.; Jer. 7:9; 19:4; 44:3). Hosea
speaks of others who might "save" (*hôšîaʿ*) Israel, but in 1:7
it is probably a redactor who speaks of Yahweh doing so (see
the note), and the noun **saviour** as a divine epithet seems
otherwise to be confined to later literature. In their present
context these words are not so much a statement of doctrine
as an anticipation of the threat and the taunt in vv. 7–11 (cf. esp.
v. 10): if Israel repudiates her only **saviour**, nothing remains for
her but destruction.

13:5. It was I who knew you: Cf. Am. 3:2. LXX has
"I shepherded you", which presupposes a slightly different
Heb. text, which many regard as more original than MT
(Wolff, Rudolph, Mays, NEB, JB): it leads well into v. 6
and recalls 4:16, where the same verb is used. Even if **knew**
is correct, it probably has the sense of "care for" (cf. Ps. 1:6;
Nah. 1:7: *TDOT*, vol. 5, 468), so the difference in meaning is
not great.

in the land of drought: drought (Heb. *talʾubôt*) only occurs
here, but the meaning is indicated by an Arabic cognate (known
already to the Jewish tradition: cf. Ibn Janaḥ, Kimchi), by
the Peshitta and by the context (cf. also 2:5 and 13:15 for
Hosea's view of **the wilderness**). There is no justification for

the rendering "burning heat" (NEB, NIV – cf. Wellhausen, Marti, Nowack).

13:6. But when they had fed: From here to v. 8 Yahweh speaks about Israel (**they**) rather than directly to them. MT's *kᵉmarʿîtām* is unusual but can perhaps be defended as an Aramaizing form of the infinitive (Nyberg, Rudolph: cf. the nore on 8:10), giving a meaning equivalent to the emendation assumed by RSV.

to the full: Or "they were satisfied" (JB). The next word in the Heb. repeats the same sense, but this is not a reason to delete it (*BHS*, tentatively) or to emend it (Harper, Rudolph): the line reflects common features of poetic style (cf. Watson, pp. 208–10, 279–80). For the thought cf. 10:1, in the light of which the present verse should be taken to refer to the enjoyment of the fruits of the land of Canaan, not the manna in the wilderness. Hosea knows nothing of a rebellion against Yahweh in the wilderness (contrast, e.g., Dt. 9:7; Ezek. 20:21).

their heart was lifted up: Cf. Dt. 8:14, in a very similar passage, with three occurrences of "forget" (see below) and other verbal parallels to vv. 4–6. There is a particularly strong possibility that Hosea's invective was the basis for the Deuteronomic parenesis in this case. For a concern with the **heart** in Hosea cf. 4:11; 7:6, 11, 14; 10:2 (and v. 8 below – see the note).

they forgot me: A characteristic accusation of Hosea's (cf. 2:15; 4:6; 8:14), which was taken up in Deuteronomy (6:12; 8:11, 14, 19; 9:7) and Jeremiah (2:32; 3:21; 13:25; 18:15). Cf. the references to a lack of knowledge (e.g. 4:6; 11:3).

13:7. So I will be: The future rendering is supported by LXX. MT points to a past tense, cf. NJPS, "So I am become . . .", which can be retained alongside the following imperfects, which are most naturally construed in a future sense, though they might be iterative presents (as in NJPS) and refer to the repeated blows which Israel suffered at Yahweh's hands in the last years of Hosea's ministry.

like a lion: Cf. 5:14. For **lion** (Heb. *šaḥal*) NEB has "panther" (a synonym for **leopard**), as it does in 5:14, following LXX. But apart from these isolated renderings in LXX there is no reason to think that *šaḥal* meant this.

I will lurk: In the Heb. this comes at the end of the line, and LXX, Syr. and Vulg. read instead "(. . . by the way) to Assyria", which presupposes a different vocalization of the same consonants ('*aššūr* instead of '*āšūr*). Robinson follows these versions, assuming that the reference is to the dangers faced by those who were deported to Assyria in 733 (cf. 2 Kg. 15:29). If MT is retained (with Targ.) the verb is best explained by reference to the hostile sense of *šūr* = "watch", as in Jer. 5:26 (on which see J. A. Emerton, in *Festschrift for H. Cazelles* (AOAT 212), Neukirchen, 1981, pp. 125–33), and several instances of the derivative noun *šōrēr* in the Psalms (e.g. 5:9, "enemies" (lit. "watchers")), rather than by importing a meaning "jump, attack" from Arabic and Akkadian (Eitan, Rudolph).

13:8. I will fall upon them: Heb. *pāgaš* means "meet" (cf. Prov. 17:12, and NEB here): the attack is described in the next phrase. The (she-)**bear robbed of her cubs** was proverbial for her rage (2 Sam. 17:8; Prov. 17:12).

their breast: Lit. "that which encloses their heart" (cf. NJPS), cf. NEB "their ribs". The Heb. reference to "their heart" may be intended to recall the reference to the pride of Israel's heart in v. 6.

and there I will devour them like a lion: there (Heb. *šām*) lacks a specific antecedent (unless "the way to Assyria" is read in v. 7: see above). JB, "their flesh" emends the Heb. by adding two letters (cf. Sellin; Driver, *JTS* 39 (1938), 164), but this is pure conjecture. Wolff and Rudolph follow earlier scholars in supposing that *šām* here and elsewhere (e.g. Zeph. 1:14) could have a temporal sense, "then" (cf. Arabic *ṯ'umma*), but this is only a slight improvement and a sense like "there and then", "on the spot" (NEB) may need to be assumed. The remainder of JB's rendering, "and dogs shall eat (their flesh)", is based on LXX (cf. Syr.), which presupposes a different vocalization of Heb. from MT and is also followed by a number of commentators. For the sense obtained cf. 1 Kg. 21:23–24. But LXX's rendering is likely to be secondary (it involves the assumption of an Aramaic emphatic ending) and due either to misunderstanding or to a desire to avoid the exceptional severity of the imagery applied to Yahweh in MT.

as a wild beast would rend them: The Heb. lacks an equivalent to **as**, but RSV's rendering can be defended by reference to Ps. 58:9 (cf. 90:4: *GK* §118r) and Targ. JB, NIV and NJPS (cf. Wolff) ignore this possibility and unnecessarily introduce the idea that Israel will be devoured by real wild animals (for which see Lev. 26:22; Dt. 28:26; Jer. 5:6; Ezek. 39:4) or the nations as symbolized by them (Rudolph). NEB renders "I will rip them up" instead of **would rend them** (cf. *BHS: HTOT*, p. 250, does not note the emendation assumed), but this is also unnecessary. However, whichever interpretation is chosen, the consequence for Israel is the same: "In this oracle, as in 13:3, Hosea sees no future but total annihilation for the Israel to which he speaks" (Mays). Even Amos (5:1–2; 8:2–3) is no more severe than this.

13:9. I will destroy you: This rendering requires an unsupported change to the Heb. consonants. MT can be rendered "You are undone" (NJPS – cf. Williams, *Hebrew Syntax* §160) or, with a change to the vowels supported by Syr., "I have destroyed you" (NEB, Mays).

who can help you? RSV follows LXX and Syr., reading *mî* for MT's *kî bî*. *kî* should perhaps be retained and the line translated, "For who can . . . ?" Since Israel has repudiated her only saviour (vv. 4 and 6), she has no protection left: hope placed in the royal house is illusory (v. 10: cf. 10:3), since this too is in Yahweh's hands (v. 11). Cf. the (vain) hopes placed in a king by the later Judaean community (Lam. 4:20).

13:10. Where . . . : Vss. (as twice in v. 14) strongly support this interpretation of Heb. *ʾĕhî*. It should probably be regarded in all three places as a dialectal variant for the normal *ʾayyēh*, "where", though if it is, its development from or to the normal form remains unclear.

where are all your princes, to defend you: MT reads "in all your cities and your judges". RSV, like JB, presupposes a series of small changes (one of which is supported by LXX) which creates two closely parallel lines of poetry, and follows an approach favoured by commentators from Houtsma to Wolff. NEB, NIV and NJPS keep closer to MT, merely eliminating the "and" (*wᵉ*), but the resulting line division is not attractive. It is probably best to translate "from all your enemies, and your judges . . ." (cf. Rudolph, Mays), rendering *ʿāreykā* ("your cities") as "your enemies", from a noun *ʿār*, as probably in Ps. 139:20 and 1 Sam. 28:16 (cf. Kimchi on the former passage, *HAL*, p. 829, and

for a possible etymology the note on 11:9 above), and reading
m(n), "from", for *b*ᵉ, "in", assuming a very common confusion of
letters. On "judges" see the note on "their rulers" in 7:7, where
the same Heb. word is used as here, again in close association
with **king**(s).

of whom you said, "Give me a king and princes": The
allusion is clearly to the episode described in 1 Sam. 8, where
the people's desire for a **king** and his function as a military
leader (cf. vv. 4–5, 19–20) are both mentioned. There too, as
here, the idea is prominent that monarchic rule was neither a
blessing nor pleasing to Yahweh (vv. 7–18), but the history of this
anti-monarchic strand in Israel is difficult to fix with certainty: cf.
A. Gelston, *OTS* 19 (1974), 71–85, who perhaps underestimated
how radical Hosea's attack on monarchy was, and F. Crüsemann,
Der Widerstand gegen das Königtum (WMANT 49), Neukirchen,
1978. There was a deep-seated tradition among the northern
tribes of resistance to the claims of the Davidic dynasty in
Jerusalem (cf. 2 Sam. 20, 1 Kg. 11–12), but Hosea may have
been the first northerner to voice the idea that even monarchy in
the northern kingdom was a contravention of Yahweh's original
purpose. Cf. also Utzschneider, *Hosea*, pp. 105–28.

13:11. I have given you kings: The verb here and in the
next line is an imperfect, which most likely has an iterative sense
referring to a succession of **kings** (cf. NJPS). The point made in 1
Sam. 8 about the first king, Saul, is thus extended to other kings.
According to Wolff, this verse is a blanket repudiation of all the
kings from Saul on (cf. Jeremias), but Rudolph thinks it applies
(because of the positive hope in 1:11) only to the northern kings
from Jeroboam I onwards, and Gelston (art. cit., p. 84) relates it
to the *coups d'état* of Hosea's own time. In view of the allusions to
1 Sam. 8 and the fact that the **kings** are **given** as well as taken
away in **wrath**, it is hard to escape the conclusion that a total
rejection of the institution of monarchy is intended here. 1:11
and 3:4–5 need to be interpreted in the light of this.

**13:12. The iniquity of Ephraim is bound up . . . kept in
store**: The general idea conveyed here is clear enough – Israel's
iniquity is compared to a carefully guarded treasure (cf. the
metaphor in Dt. 32:34). There is archaeological evidence from
Megiddo and Arad of silver being **bound up** and buried for safe

keeping (cf. G. I. Davies, *OTS* 24 (1986), 45, 51 n. 68; also Mt. 25:18; Lk. 19:20), and a related verb is used in such a connection in Dt. 14:25 and 2 Kg. 5:23. Others (e.g. Mays, NEB) believe that a written record is in view, pointing to the way that these were **bound up** and sealed (cf. Isa. 8:16: R. Hestrin et al., *Inscriptions Reveal*, Jerusalem, 1973, pp. 16, 24–25). This perhaps reads more into the Heb. than is justified and the former view is preferable. W. G. E. Watson, on the basis of parallels in Akkadian incantations, has suggested that **bound up** refers to the effects of the unabsolved sin and that the word translated **kept in store** (*ṣᵉpûnāh*) has the alternative meaning "hidden, unknown to the perpetrator" (*VT* 34 (1984), 242–47). But it is unlikely that Hosea would be referring to such practices, and the proposals mentioned earlier are closer to his actual wording here.

13:13. The tragic image of a child who is ready to be born but fails to appear occurs elsewhere in the OT as a picture of extreme helplessness and futility (2 Kg. 19:3; contrast Isa. 66:9), but Hosea gives it an unusual twist by blaming the child (**he is an unwise son**). Rudolph may be correct to see an echo here of a popular response to the situation ("stupid child"), but it is one which also corresponds to Hosea's frequent berating of Israel for her senselessness (cf. 4:6, 11; 7:9, 11). As a result the opportunity for life is missed, an idea which also appears in 4:16, 5:4, 7:1 and 7:13. Thus this verse expresses the hopelessness of Israel's situation which results from her failure to recognize that her iniquity is her greatest problem. The precise occasion of the opportunity for life remains unclear because of the ambiguity of the imperfect tense of the verbs. RSV implies that it exists at the time when Hosea speaks (cf. **for now**, and see the note below), but the reference may be, as it seems to be in 7:1, 13, to repeated occasions when, through prophetic summonses (11:2) or external circumstances (2:6–7; 5:15), Israel had been called to return to Yahweh. It is also possible that a still future occasion is in mind (see below), when Israel will once again reject the opportunity of life through her senselessness.

come: Or "shall come", perhaps as the consequence of the accumulation of **iniquity** (v. 12).

for now: RSV follows a different reading from MT (*'attāh* for *'ēt*), supported by the Hexaplaric and Lucianic recensions

of LXX, Syr., Targ. and Vulg., and defended by Driver, *JTS*
39 (1938), 164. Others render "at the right time", a sense
which Rudolph rather doubtfully claims can be gained from
MT, and which may need to be obtained by emendation (cf.
BHS, Robinson).

he does not present himself: Or "he will not present
himself".

13:14. Shall I ransom them . . . : The Heb. here and in the
next line does not include the usual particle (h^a) to indicate a
question, and if taken alone these two lines could equally well
be read as declarations of God's intention to rescue Israel: "I
will ransom them . . . I will redeem them . . ." (so Vss., AV,
NIV and NJPS: likewise Weiser among recent commentators).
But neither the preceding nor the following context makes this
probable (see the note on **compassion** later in the verse). As
in the previous verse, the possibility of deliverance is mentioned
only to be denied. It will take further reflection on Yahweh's
loving care for Israel in the past (cf. vv. 4–5) to bring the
prophet to the breakthrough into hope that occurs in 11:8–9,
11. This passage should therefore be dated shortly before ch.
11. On **ransom** (*pādāh*) see the note on **redeem** in 7:13. **redeem**
here is a different verb, *gā'al*, which had important uses in family
and cultic law (cf. Ru. passim; Num. 35:12 etc.; Lev. 27:13 etc.),
but from early times was also more widely used as a synonym
for "deliver" (cf. Gen. 48:16; Ps. 72:14), especially perhaps
where some responsibility for the well-being of the victim was
felt to exist: cf. Isa. 52:9, where "comforted" is cognate with
compassion below. See further *TDOT*, vol. 2, 350–55.

O Death . . . O Sheol: Some see here evidence of a mythological way of thinking, according to which evil and particularly
death were sent by powers other than Yahweh. This possibility is
the more attractive since the discovery in the mythological texts
from Ugarit that Death (*mt*) was viewed there as a divine being
who could engage in conflict with a god such as Baal, (see the
Excursus on Baal in the Ugaritic texts, above, pp. 92–93). **Sheol**
in the OT is normally the underworld (the Greek Hades), the
place of the dead (cf. Ringgren, *Israelite Religion*, pp. 243–46),
but it is occasionally spoken of in personal terms, e.g. in Isa.
5:14, to which there is a close parallel in the Ugaritic texts (cf.

Curtis, *Ugarit*, pp. 70–72, 104–105, 110–11), and **the power** of
(lit. "hand") **of Sheol** two lines above suggests a more than
spatial meaning. But as often in poetic texts, it is difficult to
be sure to what extent real mythological beliefs underlie what
may be no more than vivid personification. In any case the
implication of the texts is that it is Yahweh himself who
summons the destructive powers to act according to his decision
(just as in Hab. 3:5 "plague" and "pestilence" form part of his
entourage).

   where ... where: See the note on **Where ...** in v. 10.

   your destruction: Heb. *qeṭeb* is used twice elsewhere of
"pestilence" (Dt. 32:24; Ps. 91:6), and this meaning fits the
parallelism here well (so JB, NJPS). RSV follows the less
specific meaning that seems to be required in Isa. 28:2. LXX
and Syr. render "sting" (so NEB), with some support from Arabic
cognates (cf. *HAL*, p. 1020), but such can also be brought forward
in support of the rendering "pestilence" (Blau, *VT* 7 (1957), 98).
In later Judaism Qeteb was the name of a demon (cf. Jastrow,
Dictionary, p. 1346), but the presence of **your** is against its being
a proper name here.

   Paul quotes these two lines in a slightly different form in 1
C. 15:55 as an expression of hope in the resurrection from the
dead, a quite different sense from what they originally meant. Cf.
C. K. Barrett, *The First Epistle to the Corinthians*, London, 1968,
pp. 382–83. But probably LXX already understood the verse in
a positive sense: cf. also Ps. 49:15.

   Compassion is hid from my eyes: The **Compassion** which
might motivate Yahweh to rescue his people is no longer available. Heb. *nōḥam* only occurs here and is cognate with *niḥûmay*,
"my compassion", in 11:8. Once again a possible source of hope
is mentioned in this verse, only for it to be snuffed out. Only in
11:8–9 and 2:14 is this harshness softened. The suggestion that
nōḥam here means "vengeance" (Ewald, Weiser, NJPS), so that
the line as a whole would have a positive sense, is based on a
rare usage of the root and is unlikely to be correct.

   13:15. The first line of this verse is very uncertain as to both
text and interpretation: **as the reed plant** (cf. BHS) assumes a
conjectural emendation of MT, which reads "among brothers";
and the Heb. underlying **may flourish** (*yaprî'*) is unusual in

two respects. A less far-reaching emendation yields "among the reeds" (NEB, NJPS, JB), which Wolff takes to be an allusion to the benefits gained from close relations with Egypt (cf. on 12:1): the word used for "reeds" is of Egyptian origin. As RSV and others interpret it, the line speaks of a period of relative prosperity, but one which will soon come to an end.

the east wind: See the note on 12:1. Rudolph (p. 241) suggests that **the wind of the LORD** may have a superlative sense, "a mighty wind". On the possible use of divine names to express the superlative see D. Winton Thomas, *VT* 3 (1953), 209–19, 18 (1968), 120–23. Here it seems less likely than the idea that the wind is sent by Yahweh to effect his purpose of destruction, though (as Winton Thomas emphasized) the two possibilities need not exclude one another.

and his fountain shall dry up: MT has "shall be ashamed" (*yēbôš*: cf. NEB), but it is much more likely that a form of *yābēs* = "be dry" originally stood here, as in LXX and 4QXII? (M. Testuz, *Semitica* 5 (1955), 37–38). In fact LXX makes **the wind of the Lord** the subject, taking the verbs as Hiphils, and is followed in this by *BHS* and JB. These effects are so similar to those produced by Mot's "swallowing" of Baal in the Ugaritic myth (cf. CTA 6.4.25–26 = *CML*, p. 78) that one may wonder whether Hosea's line of thought was not to some extent guided by a knowledge of the same story, given the invitation to Death (*mwt*) in v. 14.

it shall strip his treasury of every precious thing: At this point the nature-language is left behind and the historical reality of an enemy invasion and its consequences begins to appear (cf. v. 16). No doubt the reference is to a further Assyrian attack, and in view of this **the east wind** might refer to the general direction from which the Assyrians came as well as to the enervating effects of the sirocco. It is not essential to take **the east wind** as the grammatical subject of **shall strip**, as the verb may have an indefinite subject which would be equivalent to a passive (*GK* §144d: cf. NIV).

13:16. Samaria shall bear her guilt: Heb. *te'šam*, from *'āšam*: for the sense see the note on 5:15. Here too LXX suggests the meaning "be destroyed", which can be reached either by relating the form to Heb. *šāmēm*, "be desolate", or by positing a second verb *'āšam* with the same meaning, as in NEB. But since **Samaria** stands, in view of the next two lines, for the population rather than the city itself, the rendering **bear her guilt** is probably to be preferred.

their little ones . . . : Cf. 10:14 and the note, also 2 Kg. 8:12, 15:16, Am. 1:13 for further references to such atrocities. The final line in MT reads "its pregnant women . . ." (LXX has **their**), which arouses the suspicion that it may have been added from another, lost, oracle. The verb **ripped open** is the same as that translated **rend** in v. 8.

TWO SAYINGS ON RENEWAL
14:1–8 (Heb. 14:2–9)

In the Vss. and the early editions of MT 13:16 is joined to ch. 14, and its threats against Samaria form the immediate background to the verses which follow. But its content and form link it much more closely with ch. 13 (see the note above), and a break after it is indicated by the Masoretic "open section" and the space in the early (Qumran?) fragment published by Testuz (*Semitica* 5 (1955), 37, cf. pl. 1, fig. 2). The chapter division followed by RSV and all modern commentators is therefore preferable.

Formally ch. 14 falls into three distinct sections. V. 9 is clearly a concluding exhortation of a kind that ends several other biblical compositions, and will be dealt with separately below. The remainder of the chapter comprises a prophetic exhortation which incorporates a model prayer of penitence (vv. 1–3) and a proclamation of salvation with a didactic conclusion (vv. 4–8). The exhortation to repentance is addressed to **Israel** (v. 1), and there is no good reason to see it as anything other than a public utterance. A communal response is evidently expected, but the language used in v. 2 (see the notes) seems deliberately to exclude the idea that sacrifices should be presented, in line with the divine declaration in 6:6, and there is no reason to envisage a gathering at a traditional cult centre. The introduction to the prayer is remarkably abrupt and lacks the citation of the divine name, which is normal at the beginning of laments of all kinds (H. Gunkel, *Einleitung in die Psalmen*, Göttingen, 1933, pp. 121–22, 212–13). This section resembles 6:1–3 closely in function, but

the close identification of the prophet (or his disciples) with the
nation, indicated there by the use of the first person plural, is
lacking here.

The proclamation of salvation in vv. 4ff. employs as usual the
first person singular pronoun to refer to Yahweh, but it speaks
of Israel for the most part in the third person (singular or
plural), only turning to direct address in its final line (see the
notes on v. 8). It is in this respect comparable to passages like
Isa. 41:17–20 and 42:14–17, rather than to the "assurance of
salvation" exemplified in Isa. 43:1–7. A distinctive feature is
the incorporation in vv. 5–6 of a "portrayal of salvation", which
has formal, stylistic and substantive similarities to the genre
of blessing (e.g. Num. 24:5–9). Since the pronominal suffixes
referring to Israel in these verses are singular, whereas those in vv.
4 and 7–8 are (except for **from them** at the end of v. 4) plural, it is
possible that this section is an older piece of tradition which was
taken up unmodified by Hosea to convey the renewal of Yahweh's
ancient promise to his people. In any case, the content of these
verses is to be closely compared with the promise of renewed
fertility in 2:21–22 (cf. also 6:3). Wolff and Jeremias also draw
attention to the parallels to the imagery in these verses in ancient
Near Eastern love-poetry (especially the Song of Solomon (see
the detailed notes): the texts in *ANET*, pp. 467–69 (especially "f"
on p. 469), and M. Pope, *The Song of Songs*, pp. 54–85, should also
be compared). The reference to Yahweh's love in v. 4 and Hosea's
extensive use of the marriage image strengthen the case for such
dependence. It should be stressed, however, that other types of
poetry also make use of imagery, including the same images, and
that Hosea himself is distinguished by a remarkable richness of
similes and metaphors, many of them certainly not derived from
love-poetry. Too exclusive a dependence on this genre should
therefore not be attributed to him here.

The relation between the exhortation to repentance and the
proclamation of salvation has been the subject of considerable
discussion, and raises some important theological issues (see the
notes on v. 4). The traditional view (cf. Targ., Vulg., Rashi and
Kimchi) is that the promised salvation and blessing is conditional
upon the penitence called for in vv. 1–3, and this probably gives
a true account of the present text, except that it should be

emphasized that even on this view Yahweh's declared readiness to **heal their faithlessness** plays an important part in encouraging the people to take seriously the invitation to repentance, just as in laments generally the people derive confidence from their knowledge of the loyalty and faithfulness of Yahweh (cf. Gunkel, *Einleitung*, pp. 131, 232–36). Just such a theology seems to be implied in Jer. 3:22–23, which appears to be a more orderly presentation of the message of Hos. 14 (cf. also Dt. 30:1–10). But here it may well arise from the redactional combination of two originally quite separate units, belonging to different situations in the prophet's (or his disciples') ministry. This would help to explain the formal and theological distinctions between them. The combination of prophetic address to the people with divine speech about the people is unlikely to be original; and, while vv. 1–3 embody a cautious hope for renewal through penitence and renunciation of the false gods whose worship has brought disaster, such as is also expressed in 6:1–3(?), 10:12 and 12:6, vv. 4–8 present an unconditional divine promise of renewal which, as in 2:14–23, will extend to both inward and outward circumstances and render further association with idols utterly unthinkable. It is this latter passage which carries forward the "new word" of 11:8–9, whereas vv. 1–3 perhaps represented originally the kind of call to which, according to 11:5, 7, Israel had failed to respond. The fact that there are elements of continuity between the two sections, such as the root *šûb* in vv. 1, 2, 4 and 7, the emphatic renunciation of idolatry and the affirmation that Yahweh is Israel's true Saviour in vv. 3 and 8, is not incompatible with a separate origin for the two units if we recognize that both derive from the prophet's (or conceivably the disciples') grappling with the same central issues of the time.

The occasions of these two sections may well therefore not be the same and the question of the authenticity of each of them can be examined separately. 14:1 (**you have stumbled**) clearly presupposes a national disaster, but this could be the consequences of the Assyrian invasion c. 733 (2 Kg. 16:29; *ANET*, pp. 283–84) rather than the final catastrophe of 722. In its present position, after 13:16, the latter may be intended, but this need not be the original reference. The renunciation of the quest for Assyrian support (v. 3) recalls 5:13, which probably criticizes the policy which put Hoshea on the throne c. 732, and vv. 1–3 as a whole fit well with 5:15. Jeremias has argued that these verses cannot be from Hosea himself (cf. Marti), pointing especially to contacts with the sayings of Isaiah (esp. Isa. 2:7–8) and to the lack of any reference to Baal or the king as false objects of trust (pp. 169–72; cf. id., *Der Botschaft und die Boten*, pp. 231–33). These arguments are not compelling, particularly if the saying originated in the aftermath of the Syro-Ephraimite War (see also the notes below on v. 3).

On the other hand, vv. 4–8 presuppose the change in Hosea's message in 11:8–9, which probably occurred in the last months or even weeks before the fall of Samaria in 722. The question of their authorship is intimately connected with the authorship of 2:14–23, where similar ideas are found (see the introduction to that section). Here too Jeremias has reverted to an older critical view which ascribed these verses to later writers, although he himself emphasizes the continuity with genuine sayings of the prophet by calling them disciples of Hosea. If this is granted, it seems overbold to deny, as most other recent commentators have held, that these verses might represent the final word of the prophet himself. In any case, it is their content and their situation which matter most, not their mouthpiece.

14:1. Return, O Israel: Similar calls to **Return** are to be found in 6:1 and, in figurative language, in 10:12, as well as in 14:2. Elsewhere, however, Hosea speaks of Israel as unable (5:4) or unwilling (7:10) to **Return**. The way through this impasse is provided, at one level, by the enlightenment which disaster may be expected to bring and, at another, by the "healing" spoken of below in v. 4 (see the note there).

to the LORD your God: For the title cf. 12:9 and 13:4. The implication is that, contrary to what was said in 1:9, the covenant relationship remains in being, or is being revived (for the latter cf. 2:23).

for you have stumbled because of your iniquity: The language is taken from 5:5 (for **stumble** see also 4:5 and 14:10), but the change of tense is significant: the prophet now speaks in the aftermath of the disaster, calling for repentance rather than threatening judgment (cf. 6:1). It remains uncertain to which

catastrophe he originally referred here, that of 734–733 or that
of 722 (see the introduction to this section): the redactor who
placed the passage here presumably had 722 in mind.

14:2. Take with you words . . .: The verbs here are plural,
whereas those in v. 1 are singular: the change may reflect a greater
concern with an individual response (Rudolph, Jeremias), but
there is considerable fluctuation between the two forms in this
passage (see on vv. 4, 7 and 8) and it may not be justified
to build too much upon it. The use of **Take** with **words** is
unusual and may already (see below on **we will render**) signal
the replacement of the valueless sacrificial cult (cf. 5:6) by a
purely penitential liturgy, as "taking" is a common element in
sacrificial contexts (e.g. Exod. 29:19; Lev. 14:12).

"Take away all iniquity . . ." In the Heb. the verb unusually
stands between **all** (*kol*) and **iniquity** (*'āwôn*), but there are parallels to this in 2 Sam. 1:9 and Job 27:3, and it is possible either to
take *kol* in an adverbial sense, "wholly" (*GK* §128e), or to see here
a "broken construct chain", as apparently in 6:9 and perhaps in
8:2 (cf. D. N. Freedman, *Biblica* 53 (1972), 534–36; Kuhnigk).
NEB renders "Thou dost not endure iniquity", reading *kî lō'* for
kol (*HTOT*, p. 250), with some support from LXX, but this does
not fit the context so well. The verb (*nāśā'*) is the same as that
translated **forgive** in 1:6, so that the prayer is for the very thing
which is denied in the opening summary of Hosea's message. For
other contrasts with ch. 1 see the notes on 14:1 and 14:3.

accept that which is good: So also NJPS. The problem is to
know what is meant by **that which is good**. One might think
of the virtues praised in 6:6 (cf. 1 Sam. 15:22 and Mic. 6:8,
where the word *ṭôb* (**good**) is actually used), which Israel may
be presumed now to exhibit. This would fit in with the striving
to **know** Yahweh in the similar penitential passage in 6:3. But
an alternative translation should probably be accepted, such as
NIV's "receive us graciously" (with the small change of *ṭôb* to
ṭûb) or NEB's "accept our plea" (reading *ṭēb* and assuming the
currency of its Aramaic meaning in Heb., as is suggested also for
Ps. 39:3 and Neh. 6:19: cf. R. Gordis, *VT* 5 (1955), 89–90, and
Barr, *Comparative Philology*, pp. 16–17).

and we will render the fruit of our lips: Prayers of sup-
plication in the Psalms frequently lead into vows of a thankful

response, often in the form of a vow to praise God and (cf. v. 3) serve him faithfully (cf. Gunkel, *Einleitung*, pp. 247–50). So it is here, and **render** (*šlm*) is a word used particularly of the fulfilment of a vow (e.g. Dt. 23:21). For **the fruit of our lips** MT reads "(as?) bulls our lips", which can only with great difficulty be taken to mean "in the place of bull-offerings the words of our lips" (cf. NJPS). RSV, like JB, Wolff and Mays, follows LXX, which may presuppose only a different vocalization of the Heb., if a case of "enclitic *mem*" is accepted here (Kuhnigk, pp. 155–56: see also Blommerde, *Job*, p. 32, and Barr, *Comparative Philology*, p. 31–33). The phrase **the fruit of our lips** does not occur elsewhere in the OT (though cf. Isa. 57:18; Prov. 18:20), but it became popular later (cf. 1QH 1:28–29 = *DSSE*, p. 152, Ps. Sol. 15:3, Heb. 13:15). NEB, "we will pay our vows with cattle from our pens", surprisingly follows a more extensive emendation of MT which introduces a word translated "sheepfolds" in Ps. 68:13 (cf. Gen. 49:14; Jg. 5:16: see R. T. O'Callaghan, *VT* 4 (1954), 171), but the sense produced is entirely alien not only to Hosea's own teaching but to that of the redactors whose work is evident elsewhere in his book.

14:3. The people's response continues with the renunciation of some of the chief objects of Hosea's prophetic critique, though not in words that are slavishly borrowed from his other oracles: alliance with the super-power **Assyria** (cf. 5:14; 12:1), trust in military strength (10:13) and the worship of idols (8:8; 13:2). Jeremias (pp. 171–72) draws attention to the absence of references to Baal and the misplaced hopes in the king, both central Hosean themes, and on the other hand the closeness of the language used to certain passages in Isaiah (2:7–8; 30:16; 31:1–3; cf. Mic. 5:10–14). From this he concludes that these verses were composed by disciples of Hosea after they had fled to the southern kingdom and come into contact with the group around Isaiah. Some passages in Hosea certainly may derive from such a setting, though a still later date for them is also possible (see on 1:7 and 3:5, and perhaps 11:12), but here the case against Hosean authorship is scarcely decisive.

and we will say no more, "Our God" ... : Cf. Isa. 42:17. But the theme is one that is firmly rooted in Hosea: it is over-sceptical to regard 8:6 and 13:2 as later additions

(Jeremias). "Our gods" (NEB, NIV: cf. LXX) is also a possible rendering of the Heb. here.

In thee the orphan finds mercy: In MT the line begins with *ᵃšer*, which probably means "because" here. Since **finds mercy** (*ruḥam*) can be used of parental love (Isa. 49:15; Ps. 103:13), NEB's rendering, "For in thee the fatherless finds a father's love", captures an important dimension of the original (cf. 11:1). For Yahweh's care for **the orphan** cf. Exod. 22:22–23; Dt. 10:18; Pss. 10:14, 18; 68:5; 146:9; Prov. 23:10–11; Jer. 49:11: Isa. 9:17 is uncharacteristic. The point here can only be that Israel is like a helpless **orphan** and at last recognizes where her help can truly be found. Confidence in God's favour is often expressed in laments (cf. Gunkel, *Einleitung*, pp. 235–36). Once again the statement is deeply rooted in the language of Hosea's earlier oracles, particularly those in chs. 1–2. 2:4 is especially close, since there Yahweh says that he will not "have pity" (*riḥam*, the verb used here) on Israel's children, because they are not his. But the same verb occurs again in the symbolic name of Hosea's daughter Lo-Ruhamah (1:6) and in the verses which speak of the reversal of that designation (2:1, 23 – see also the note on **mercy** in 2:19).

14:4. I will heal their faithlessness: The change to divine speech signals the conclusion of the prophetic exhortation and the beginning of an oracle of salvation comparable to those in 2:14–23 and 11:8–9. The precise relationship between the oracle and the exhortation has been much discussed. It is possible that originally there was no relationship, but the question of the link between them envisaged by the collectors of Hosea's oracles would still arise, and Jer. 3:21–23 appears to be based on vv. 1–8 seen as a connected unit. But is the oracle the basis for the exhortation (Wolff, Jeremias), so that Yahweh's gracious word has the priority? Or is the oracle his response to the penitential prayer of the people, according to the liturgical pattern which many recent commentators have seen behind the whole passage (Rudolph)? In the latter case Ps. 81:6–16 would parallel the thought closely: it probably reflects an instance of liturgical prophecy itself. For further discussion see the introduction to this section.

In this verse the language continues to echo Hosea's earlier sayings closely, especially ch. 11. On **heal** see the note on 11:3; but the restoration now has an inward aspect, possibly paralleled in 2:19–20, but most clearly taken up in the salvation-oracles of Jer. 31:33–34 and Ezek. 36:25–27 etc. (cf. Dt. 30:6). The imagery varies, but in each case the message is that Israel's stubborn refusal to respond to Yahweh's call will be overcome by an inward change initiated by Yahweh himself. **faithlessness** is the word rendered "turning away" in 11:7 (*mᵉšûbāh*), and it is natural to translate it in a similar way here (cf. Kimchi): NJPS "affliction", with support claimed from Jer. 2:19 and 3:22, is quite without justification.

I will love them freely: The theme of Yahweh's **love** is also prominent in ch. 11 (vv. 1, 4) and, while 9:15 speaks of its withdrawal, 3:1, like this passage, declares that it will be renewed. **freely** (*nᵉdābāh*) is used of those who volunteer for war-service (Jg. 5:2, 9; Ps. 110:3) as well as offerings beyond the call of duty (e.g. Lev. 7:16), so that it may here contribute the idea of unmerited **love**. But in Ps. 68:9 it refers to the abundance of God's gifts, and the sense may be similar here: cf. JB, "I will love them with all my heart", a declaration that would prepare well for the possibly erotic imagery of the following verses (see the notes).

for my anger has turned from them: Cf. 11:9. Wolff (p. 232; cf. Marti) regards this line as a later addition because **them** is represented by a singular pronominal suffix, "him" (used in a collective sense). But the passage fluctuates several times between singular and plural forms. Possibly, as Harper (p. 413) suggested, this line gives the basis for the announcements which follow, where Israel is also referred to by singular pronouns: one might translate it, "Now that my anger . . ."

14:5. Vv. 5–7 portray the renewal of Israel, which is the result of a return of divine favour (cf. v. 5a), in a series of vivid images drawn from the natural world, which can be seen as a direct answer to the images of judgment used by Hosea, especially in 13:7–8. Some of the comparisons used here are paralleled in love-poetry, but not all; some are reminiscent of the wisdom literature, others echo earlier sayings of Hosea himself (see the detailed notes).

I will be as the dew: Here (unlike 6:4; 13:3) **dew** is an image not for transience but for refreshment and blessing (cf. Gen. 27:28; Prov. 19:12). In view of what follows, its role in the growth of vegetation must also be in mind (cf. Hag. 1:10; Baly, *Geography*, pp. 43–45).

as the lily: This comparison is paralleled only in the Song of Songs, where it is frequent (e.g. 2:1–2) and stands for beauty of both appearance and smell (5:13). The precise identity of Heb. *šôšannāh* is uncertain: it may be a term for the iris family (Wolff) or even for wild flowers in general (*IDB*, vol. 3, 133).

he shall strike root as the poplar: For **the poplar** (Heb. *libneh*) MT and Vss. have "Lebanon", as at the end of the two following verses, and this should probably be retained. The reference may be to the roots of the great trees of Lebanon (NIV, NJPS: cf. Targ.), as the Heb. can be translated "as on Lebanon" (*GK* §118t), or alternatively to the poetic idea that high mountains have deep roots (Job 28:9). Lebanon is mentioned several times in the Song of Songs (3:9; 4:8, 11, 15; 5:15; 7:4) but also occurs frequently in other types of poetry: cf. K. H. Bernhardt, *Das Alte Libanon*, Leipzig, 1976, esp. pp. 51–58.

14:6. his shoots shall spread out: This should be taken closely with the last clause of v. 5, with which it forms a single poetic line: the strong roots are the precondition for vigorous growth. The comparison of Israel to a tree is found in Ps. 80:11, where the spreading **shoots** (or "branches") appear to denote territorial expansion. Here the cedar may be meant, in view of the preceding clause: for its **shoots** cf. Ezek. 17:4. This comparison also occurs in love-poetry (Ca. 5:15).

his beauty shall be like the olive: The same image is applied to Israel in her halcyon days by Jeremiah (11:16), who uses it especially with reference to the olive's fruit. The comparison does not occur in the Song of Songs, and **beauty** (Heb. *hôd*) is not used of sexual attractiveness: it normally refers to the splendour or majesty of a king or of God himself (cf. Pss. 45:4; 96:6).

his fragrance like Lebanon: There is a close parallel in Ca. 4:11, and there is no need for the emendation to "like incense" (*lebōnāh*), based on Targ., which is still mentioned by *BHS*. The **fragrance** of **Lebanon** was due not only to the cedars but also to a multitude of other aromatic plants (Kimchi: cf. Guthe cited by Wolff ad loc.).

14:7. They shall return: The images are briefly suspended and a direct announcement of a return of the exiles intervenes (cf. 11:11). **return** (*šûb*) may be understood as an auxiliary verb, yielding the translation: "they will again (dwell)" (NIV). For the plural form of the verb, which is continued throughout this verse, compare the plural pronouns in v. 4a.

and dwell beneath my shadow: Heb. has "those dwelling in his shadow". LXX, Syr. and Targ. support the reading of a finite verb in place of the participle, but the reading **my** for "his" (which likewise involves only a small difference in the consonantal text) is conjectural and designed to maintain the first-person reference to God (cf. vv. 4–5). This is probably mistaken: the **shadow** is that of Israel portrayed as a tree (cf. vv. 5b–6), now revived to new life in its land, to which those who have been exiled are expected to return (Ward). **shadow** is an image used in love-poetry (e.g. Ca. 2:3), but also elsewhere (e.g. Ps. 80:10). There may be an allusion to the preferred shade of real trees (4:17).

they shall flourish as a garden: Heb. "they shall make grain live", but the use of the Piel of *ḥāyāh*, "make . . . live", of crops is unparalleled and improbable, and Vss. all support "they shall live", of which **they shall flourish** is a paraphrase. **as a garden** (*kaggān*: cf. Harper) is a conjectural emendation of "grain" (*dāgān*), but it is better to retain MT and render "like grain" (Kimchi, Ward, NIV: cf. *GK* §118r), in view of the parallel comparison in the following line, where another of the staple products of Canaan is mentioned (cf. 2:8–9, 22).

as the vine: For the image cf. 10:1, Ps. 80:8–16, Ca. 7:8 and Isa. 5:1ff.

their fragrance shall be like the wine of Lebanon: their fragrance (cf. AV, RV, NJPS) is a mistranslation of Heb. *zikrô*, which means "his [or 'its'] fame [lit. 'memory']" (cf. NIV, NEB). The mistake goes back to Kimchi and Ibn Ezra, who were presumably influenced by the phrase in v. 6. The singular pronominal suffix should be taken seriously (cf. "his shadow") and may refer to Israel as a continuing entity as distinct from the exiles in particular. It is also possible, though less likely, to relate the suffix to **the vine**: hence JB, "(vines) as renowned as the wine . . ." For **Lebanon** JB reads "Helbon", following Budde and Sellin: this does introduce the name of a well-known wine (Ezek. 27:18: for other references and the location of Helbon see Zimmerli, *Ezekiel*, vol. 2, p. 67), but it is an arbitrary emendation and unnecessary, for sources ancient, medieval and modern attest the excellence of Lebanon wine in general (cf. Harper, p. 414, where the reference to Pliny's *Natural History* should be to 14.74; Wunsche, pp. 594–95 (Kimchi, citing "Asaph the Physician", on whom see *JE*, vol. 11, pp. 162–63)). For **wine** as an image of sweetness see Ca. 7:10 (cf. 1:2; 4:10).

14:8. O Ephraim, what have I to do with idols? So MT, but the sense is improved and the contrast with the next line is stronger if we read with LXX, "What has Ephraim to do with idols any more?" (reading *lô* for *lî*: so JB, NEB). For **Ephraim**'s previous preoccupation with **idols** see 4:17; 8:4; 13:2.

It is I who answer and look after you: For **you** MT has "him", which should be retained. Israel was always deluded when she attributed her prosperity to Baal and not to Yahweh (2:5–8, 12; cf. 13:4–6), but now, after the judgment and restoration, it should be even clearer that Yahweh is the true provider of her needs. The theme of Yahweh's **answer** is developed more fully in 2:21–22. Wellhausen noted the similarity of sound between the two verbs used here and the names of the Canaanite goddess Anat and the sacred pole or asherah, and suggested that these names, by a bold "takeover bid", might have orignally stood in the text: "I am his Anat and his asherah." More is now known about these objects of devotion and their attraction for Israelites, and Wellhausen's suggestion has recently found fresh support (M. Weinfeld, *Studi epigrafici e linguistichi* 1 (1984), 122–23). But MT makes good sense as it is, and one may doubt whether Hosea would have indulged in such a flagrant equation of Yahweh with two Canaanite divinities (cf. 2:16–17). At most there is here a dismissive allusion to the sound of their names (cf. J. Day, *JBL* 105 (1986), 404–406). NEB, "I have spoken and I affirm it", gives the second verb a meaning based on those of Syriac and Akkadian cognates (cf. G. R. Driver, in *Studies in Old Testament Prophecy*, ed. H. H. Rowley, London, 1952, pp. 67–68), but both this and the unusual (but possible) meaning given to Heb. ʿānāh (**answer**) are artificial.

like an evergreen cypress: The precise species of tree denoted by Heb. *bᵉrôš* is disputed and some think of a pine tree (NEB, NIV) or a type of juniper (*IDB*, vol. 2, 293: cf. LXX here). For **evergreen** (Heb. *raʿᵃnān*) read "luxuriant", following D. Winton Thomas, *SVT* 16 (1967), 386–97: NEB's "that shelters you" is a misconceived paraphrase. Yahweh is here uniquely compared to the abundant life seen in the rich growth of foliage on a tree, and there may be a deliberate allusion to the mythological idea of the tree of life which was widely current in the ancient Near East (cf. Gen. 2:9; 3:22; Prov. 11:30; E. O. James, *The Tree of Life*, Numen Suppl. 11 (1966), C. Westermann, *Genesis 1–11*, London, 1984, pp. 211–14). However, this was not usually portrayed as a conifer. Day, *JBL* 105 (1986), 404–406, argues for a particular connection with the goddess Asherah, who (it seems) was represented by a stylized tree. A direct comparison with the natural species seems most likely. Comparisons with trees are found in love-poetry, as noted on vv. 5–6 above, but apparently they are not seen as sources of fertility.

from me comes your fruit: Better "It is from me that your fruit comes": the word order of the Heb. emphasizes **from me**. At this climactic point (not before: cf. above) the divine speech becomes a direct address to **Ephraim**, who has till now been referred to in the third person. For a similar change cf. 11:8–9. **your fruit** is probably meant in a wide sense which includes not only all kinds of crops but also the offspring of animals and man, of which Yahweh, the source of life, is the giver. There may be an intentional word-play between **fruit** (*pᵉrî*) and **Ephraim**, as in 9:16, but now in the positive sense already given to the name in Gen. 41:52.

CONCLUSION

14:9 (Heb. 4:10)

The final verse of the book provides a rare and revealing reflection on the meaning of the book as a whole (cf. the very different coda in Mic. 7:18–20). It uses language typical of Proverbs and other

wisdom books and encourages a generalized practical reading
of the sayings of Hosea. As in the wisdom literature, mankind
is divided into two groups, **the upright** and **transgressors**: for
this pair of terms cf. Isa. 53:11–12, 58:1–2, but the latter word,
like **stumble**, may have been chosen by a redactor because Hosea
favoured it. Similar concluding sayings are found in Ps. 107:43,
Ec. 12:13–14 and Sir. 50:28–9: they appear to derive from a
scribal setting in post-exilic times where a wide range of biblical
traditions was valued as a means of inculcating a piety which had
both legal and more speculative aspects (cf. Sir. 39:1–11 and G.
T. Sheppard, *Wisdom as a Hermeneutical Construct* (BZAW 151),
Berlin and New York, 1980, pp. 129–36). As such it betokens
continuing confidence in the value of the prophet's sayings and
bears witness to a particular way in which they may continue to
speak to later generations. It is not the only or most natural way
in which they can be heard, but it perhaps continues the line of
interpretation which had earlier led a redactor to place the call
to penitence in 14:1–3 between the sustained threat of death in
ch. 13 and the promise of new life in 14:4–8 – only now these are
alternatives, not successive manifestations of Yahweh's direction
of his people's history.

14:9. The book concludes with a didactic comment unlike
the ending of any other prophetic book. The closest parallels
are Ps. 107:42–43 and some editorial additions to the book of
Jeremiah (e.g. 2:31a; 9:12a). The verse should perhaps be seen
as embodying two distinct comments on the book as a whole,
since *kî*, rendered **for** in RSV, can be understood as an emphatic
particle ("surely": so Wolff, Sheppard, Jeremias).

Whoever is wise, let him understand: Taken this way, the
comment assumes an optimistic view of human understanding
and encourages careful study of the preceding prophetic oracles
(**these things**). But it is also possible, and perhaps truer to
the Heb. idiom, to render: "Who is so wise that he can
understand these things?" (Wolff; cf. LXX, Vulg.). In this case
the difficulty, and perhaps the impossibility, of understanding the
oracles transmitted is the point, and this might be related both
to the obscurity of many passages from a linguistic point of view,
which still troubles commentators, and to the incompatibility

of the hopes expressed in them with conditions existing in the author's time, which was probably after the exile.

whoever is discerning . . . : Or "who is so discerning that he knows them?" For an earlier use of this vocabulary in Hosea see 4:14 and the note.

for the ways of the LORD are right: Or "surely the ways . . ." (cf. above). **the ways of the LORD,** which are referred to by **them** in the following lines, must here mean the pattern of life which Yahweh requires in his people (so often, especially in conjunction with the metaphorical use of **walk,** in Deuteronomy (8:6; 10:12; 11:22, 28 etc.), but also in the Psalms (25:4; 51:15; 81:13 etc.) and elsewhere), not Yahweh's general guidance of history (Weiser, cf. Rudolph). This probably indicates that the redactor saw the function of Hosea's oracles as being guidance in right living (for this conception of prophecy cf. 2 Kg. 17:13 and perhaps Dt. 18:15ff.). A similar, practical reading of the prophets is suggested by the ("wisdom") addition in Am. 5:13 and later in Dan. 9:10 and M. Aboth 1:1. See further R. E. Clements, *Prophecy and Tradition*, Oxford, 1975, pp. 49–57, and J. Barton, *Oracles of God*, London, 1986, pp. 154–61. **right** (Heb. *yāšār*) is used, as in Ps. 19:9, 119:137 and Neh. 9:13, to affirm that Yahweh's commands are more than arbitrary divine fiats; they deserve to be obeyed because they can be seen to be **right**.

the upright: Or "the righteous" (Heb. *ṣaddiqîm*), a word found only here in Hosea, but one that is very common in Psalms and Proverbs as a general term of moral and religious approval.

but transgressors stumble in them: transgressors (*pōšᵉʿîm*) is not the normal opposite of **upright,** which is "wicked" (Heb. *rāšāʿ*), and it may have been chosen by the redactor because of the frequency of related words in Hosea (especially 7:13; 8:1), which carry with them the connotation of defiance. **stumble** is likewise a Hosean word (cf. 4:5; 5:5; 14:1). For **in them** "on them" (NJPS) may be the better rendering: **the ways of the LORD** are then themselves portrayed as an obstacle to the progress of **transgressors,** just as Yahweh himself is in Isa. 8:14–15. Alternatively the meaning could be as in Jer. 18:15.

INDEX

(in some cases only more extensive discussions are included)